Cornell University Library

KF 4764.B14

Equality under the constitution :reclaim

D1241201

337   olin

OLIN LIBRARY — CIRCULATION
DATE

WITHDRAWN FROM
CORNELL UNIVERSITY LIBRARY

EQUALITY UNDER
THE CONSTITUTION

OLIN
KF
4764
B14

EQUALITY UNDER THE CONSTITUTION

Reclaiming the Fourteenth Amendment

JUDITH A. BAER

CORNELL UNIVERSITY PRESS

Ithaca and London

Copyright © 1983 by Cornell University Press

All rights reserved. Except for brief quotations in a review, this book, or parts
thereof, must not be reproduced in any form without permission in writing
from the publisher. For information, address Cornell University Press,
124 Roberts Place, Ithaca, New York 14850.

First published 1983 by Cornell University Press.
Published in the United Kingdom by
Cornell University Press, Ltd., London.

International Standard Book Number (cloth) 0–8014–1555–1
International Standard Book Number (paper) 0–8014–9888–0
Library of Congress Catalog Card Number 83–6220
Printed in the United States of America
*Librarians: Library of Congress cataloging information appears
on the last page of the book.*

*The paper in this book is acid-free and meets the guidelines
for permanence and durability of the Committee on Production
Guidelines for Book Longevity of the Council on Library Resources.*

Contents

Preface

Americans think they believe in equality. We know that we are not equal in condition. Whatever Alexis de Tocqueville found in the 1830s, the realities of income distribution, education, and job opportunities today force us to acknowledge that we live in what is in many ways an inegalitarian society. But we cherish the ideal.

This was not always the case, though the idea of equality has always been available to us as a people. Thomas Jefferson's statement in the Declaration of Independence that "all men are created equal" has been an axiom of American political thought, but it has by no means been a "truth" that was "self-evident" to all Americans. The defenders of slavery rejected the notion, and so did some opponents of school integration in the 1950s. But today the opponents of vigorous enforcement of civil rights laws find it necessary to affirm their commitment to racial equality, while opponents of the Equal Rights Amendment, including the president of the United States, insist that they believe that men and women are equal. However often the word "but" follows these statements—and it usually does—the speakers believe their own words.

Americans do not practice what they preach. But the contradiction is not only between ideal and reality. In fact, Americans do not believe in equality at all. When I began this book, I was pretty sure of the truth of that statement; now I am convinced of it. We accept the ideal only to a limited extent. We agree that some people once thought inferior to adult white males are in fact their equals and we may oppose distinctions based on religion, race, or wealth, but in principle we accept many other kinds of hierarchical arrangements and asymmet-

7

rical relationships. We do not quarrel much with the general principle of dominance and inequality.

An example of this acceptance comes from an article by the historian Howard Zinn, published in 1965. Writing of the civil rights movement, Zinn discussed the conditions under which southern blacks ("Negroes" in 1965) lived, and the effects of racism on them. "Their entire way of life," Zinn declared, "is conditioned by . . . the fact that the women must be office cleaners rather than stenographers, that the men must be porters rather than foremen."[1] Look at that sentence. Does it not imply that it is wrong for job opportunities to be limited by race, but all right to have them limited by sex, class, and education?

Another example dates from 1967, the year in which the Selective Service System stopped giving draft deferments to graduate students. President Nathan Pusey of Harvard University made a comment about this decision which he intended to be witty, and most people who heard it agreed. "Next year," Pusey quipped, "we shall be left with the lame, the halt, the blind, and the female." The women's liberation and disability rights movements are now strong enough so that an executive who made such a remark might well be forced to resign, as Earl Butz had to resign from President Ford's cabinet when he made a racist joke. But in the 1960s—the radical, mellow 1960s—a crack like Pusey's was considered funny.

Still another example comes from Joseph Persico's biography of Nelson Rockefeller. Persico describes a staff meeting at Governor Rockefeller's estate:

> T. Norman Hurd, then state budget director and a leading authority on public finance, was explaining a passage when a towheaded child bounded into the room. Dr. Hurd stopped as Nelson swept three-year-old Mark, his youngest son, onto his knee. As Dr. Hurd started to speak again, Mark began talking. Nelson stopped to listen, not to Dr. Hurd but to Mark. Hurd stopped too, with a frozen smile. Thus we plodded on, halting whenever Mark had something to say. "Yes, that's right, Marky. That's a two. And that number is a nine. See, we're on page twenty-nine," Nelson patiently instructed his son. Everyone grinned on cue.
> I thought of how I was raising my own children. I did not like them to interrupt when I was talking to friends, and I did not enjoy having other people's howling Indians intrude on good conversation. But, little Mark went on happily having his say, while his father responded and we waited. Nelson Rockefeller was passing along an unspoken lesson ab-

---

[1] "Abolitionists, Freedom-Riders, and the Tactics of Agitation," in Martin Duberman, ed., *The Anti-Slavery Vanguard: New Essays on the Abolitionists* (Princeton: Princeton University Press, 1965), p. 448.

sorbed from his own father—"These people work for us. Never mind their age, their position, they defer to you." Thus are young princes bred.[2]

The gratuitous reference to "howling Indians" is revealing enough. But Persico's point is that young Mark is learning from his father that rich people are better than the rest of us. Persico implies that such hierarchy is unjust, and most readers would agree that it is wrong to expect the nonrich to be silent while the rich speak. But it is perfectly proper (however unrealistic) to expect children to be silent, or perhaps absent, while adults speak. "Never mind their age, their position"— these factors, not wealth, are what *should* matter. A hierarchy based on wealth is wrong, but a hierarchy based on age is legitimate. Again, the principle of inequality is accepted—it is just limited. In none of these examples can we tell which principle is the rule and which the exception.

This book reveals many examples of this kind of thinking. I do not emphasize the old problems of racism and sexism. Nor do I stress economic inequality, although much of what I say has economic implications. I am primarily concerned with new issues—though they are old problems—which have gained attention only in recent years. One of these topics is preferential treatment, a new wrinkle in the old controversies over racial and sexual equality. I deal also with the rights of children, older people, and the disabled, all of whom have been the focus of new civil rights movements. Finally, I take up the rights of homosexuals, a group long subject to public hostility, who have also begun to make public claims. And in each case, I discover that we, as a people, have not taken the principle of equality far enough, and that the language and history of our Constitution urge us to take the principle further.

"But," a reader may ask, "why the Constitution?" Even readers committed to the study of constitutional law may wonder, "Why these particular issues, and not others?" And, since every isssue I address is one on which opinions are vehement and varied, "Why your particular answers to these questions?" The first question is the easiest to answer. I emphasize the Constitution because I am fascinated by constitutional interpretation, because I believe it must be the province of social scientists, philosophers, and historians as well as lawyers and judges, and because I think we can learn much from court opinions and legislative debates about normative questions. Such scholarship is particularly important in this area because, as I argue in the book,

---

[2] *The Imperial Rockefeller* (New York: Simon & Schuster, 1982), p. 17.

constitutional equality has been and continues to be badly and dangerously misunderstood. We need to know, we do not know enough, and much of what we think we know is not true.

Then why choose these groups, and these claims? I examine them partly because they are topical, because there is just enough material on each of them to allow fresh discussion (except in the area of reverse discrimination, where the material is voluminous, but which no student of equality can ignore). I also found that these new claims are related to one another, and to earlier causes. Children's rights have much in common with the rights of the disabled, and many of the litigants who figure prominently in Chapters 7 and 8 were in trouble partly because they were black. But why these problems rather than others that are also interrelated and topical, or, for that matter, why choose claims that have been made rather than seek to discover claims that have not yet been made, but perhaps should be?

My answer to this question and my conclusions have personal roots. Scholars are often warned—at least, this particular scholar has often been warned—to remain detached and objective, to keep themselves out of their work. It is true that scholarship is a different enterprise from either advocacy or autobiography. But I am convinced that personal opinion and experience need not distort inquiry, but can inform and enrich it. *Equality under the Constitution* reflects this conviction. It is not a detached book. The analysis is as impartial and balanced as I know how to make it, but I have not tried to hide my opinions. And while I did resist the temptation to include autobiographical anecdotes, this book is not divorced from the life of the person who wrote it.

I am one of that apparently diminishing tribe that considers the term "bleeding-heart liberal" a compliment rather than an insult. Readers who disagree with me are forewarned that resort to that particular epithet will not devastate me. But my deepest political conviction is my commitment to feminism. I have never begun a sentence with "I'm not one of those women's liberationists, but . . ." I am one of them, proudly and unabashedly. My first efforts had feminist themes. This book, by contrast, concerns itself with sexual equality for only a small fraction of its length. But *Equality under the Constitution* is a feminist book. My commitment to women's rights has molded my thoughts about the subjects I address here.

Feminism has helped me to regard the traditional family with something less than reverence. This skepticism has influenced my thinking—not only what I think, but the ways in which I think—about parent-child relationships and about homosexuality. Feminism has taught me that all human beings have rights and interests distinct from the rights and interests of others, even those others who are closest to them. This knowledge has allowed me to question some common assumptions about the rights of older and younger people. All these insights have led me not only to make certain arguments, but, even earlier, to decide that these concerns are worth studying.

One of the most important lessons I have learned in and from the women's liberation movement has been to suspect *any* generalizations about the abilities and characteristics of groups of people—not only to question their validity, which is easy, but to think about the reasons why such generalizations are made and the purposes they serve. Such remarks as "Woman's place is in the home," "Twelve-year-olds aren't mature enough to decide where they want to live," and "Deaf people can't be nurses"—all of which come into this book—are general statements that are hard to verify and may well be wrong. Less obviously, such remarks are ways of assigning roles and allocating power. They keep some people *in* certain places and *out of* other places, which are thereby reserved for other people. Such statements are ways of preserving inequality. That insight led me to a central thesis of this work.

This book shows that statements about characteristics, abilities, and capacities have often been the bases for arguments either for or against equality. That information will surprise no one. But I go on to say that the idea of equality which was embodied in the Declaration and which the authors of the Civil War amendments wrote into the Constitution is *not* derived from ideas of equal capacity or merit. The Declaration does not say or imply that all men, all races, or all groups are equal in any ability. Jefferson did not believe that, and neither did most of his contemporaries or most members of the Reconstruction Congress. Indeed, Jefferson shared with many proslavery writers a belief in the innate inferiority of blacks. The proponents of equality and the defenders of slavery differed on another point entirely. To the former, "all men are created equal" meant that all are entitled to rank equally, to be treated as equals, and to enjoy equal rights. It was precisely this notion that the latter group resisted. They insisted that legal equality depended on a certain level of capacity—wisdom, virtue, or whatever—and that where that capacity was lacking, or had not been shown to exist, no right to equality existed. This was not the American theory of equality, but what I have called the antitheory. Unfortunately, it has been the antitheory, not the theory, that has most influenced judicial interpretation. Courts have tended to read the equal-protection clause as though its interpretation did indeed depend on the characteristics of persons. Far from enlarging the Fourteenth Amendment, the Supreme Court has mutilated it.

My opinions about the interpretation of constitutional rights and the role of the courts in deciding cases involving these rights are of the sort generally described as "liberal" and "activist." They correspond better to those of Hugo L. Black and William O. Douglas than to those of Learned Hand and Felix Frankfurter. But the tradition with which I associate myself has included reservations and qualifications, typified by Justice Black's frequent warnings against writing into the Constitution one's personal theories of "natural law." Troubled by the countermajoritarian aspects of the federal court system and mindful of a substantial history of illiberal judicial activism, liberals tend to give the opposing views more than mere lip or pen service.

The received wisdom of judicial restraint is well expressed by two famous quotations from dissenting opinions. The first—of course—is Justice Oliver Wendell Holmes's remark that "the Fourteenth Amendment does not enact Mr. Herbert Spencer's *Social Statics*."[3] If that is so, then neither does it enact John Rawls's *Theory of Justice* or Ronald Dworkin's *Taking Rights Seriously*. The second quotation is the second Justice John Marshall Harlan's attack on "a current mistaken view of the Constitution . . . that every major social ill in the country can find its cure in some constitutional 'principle.'"[4] These two statements, and others like them, have influenced much of what has been written about constitutional interpretation. But I have come to suspect that such trenchant phrases do more harm than good when we permit them to guide our thinking. Their effect is often to hamper thought rather than to encourage it.

It is too easy to jump from a recognition that the Constitution does not enact Spencer, Dworkin, or anyone else to the conclusion that, if any statement reads like something one of these thinkers wrote, it is not good law. And agreement that not all ills can be remedied by a good court case (anyone who believes they can be is urged to turn right away to Chapter 8 and read it carefully) says nothing about any specific case. I am not suggesting that a judge or scholar should embrace either the cosmic view of the judicial system or the notion that constitutional doctrine can be identified with certain books. But to do the opposite—deliberately to confine one's thinking by these restraints—is to constrain too much. Bending over too far backward is

[3] Lochner v. New York, 198 U.S. 45, 75 (1905).
[4] Reynolds v. Sims, 377 U.S. 533, 624 (1964).

as dangerous as leaning too far forward. I have tried to avoid either mistake.

I shall have more to say about judicial activism vs. judicial restraint later on. At any rate, the reader will soon learn that the position I take here is unambiguously activist, and the constitutional interpretation I propound is broad, not to say lavish. These are positions that are in harmony with my own values. *Equality under the Constitution* is passionate, committed scholarship. But scholarship it remains. I seek to use the scholar's tools and skills to reveal how limited our collective commitment to equality is, and how extensive it can and should be.

This book, like any enterprise, is the product of collective effort. It could not have been finished without the help I have received at every stage of the process. Initial credit goes to Gayle Binion, who invited me to present a paper at the 1976 annual meeting of the Western Political Science Association. That project generated this book. I also thank Jonathan Casper, a discussant on the panel, for being right all along.

Research and writing were facilitated by a Project '87 Fellowship at The Brookings Institution in 1980. I am grateful to Brookings, the American Historical Association, and the American Political Science Association for that opportunity. Francis Coleman Rosenberger and Philip R. Argetsinger of the Project '87 staff were especially helpful, as were Laura Walker and Susan McGrath of the Brookings Library. The State University of New York at Albany deserves thanks for approving my leave of absence.

Several colleagues in the Nelson A. Rockefeller College of Public Policy at SUNY Albany helped me to think and write better about my subject. John Gunnell, Bruce Miroff, William Roth, Raymond Seidelman, Ronald Stout, and Charles Tarlton have been shrewd critics and interlocutors. My behaviorist colleagues Roman Hedges and Lynda Watts Powell, along with G. Bingham Powell, Jr., have strengthened my faith in the possibility of cross-subfield communication. The secretarial pool of the Graduate School of Public Affairs has expertly typed drafts of, parts of drafts of, articles spun off from, and grant applications concerning this manuscript, under the director of Maxine Morman. I owe much to her and to Edith Connelly, Suzanne Hagen, Addie Napolitano, and Ann Wright. My graduate assistants, Cheryl Pryor Shenkle and Chris Robinson, did tireless legwork, eyework, and penwork in tracking down references and materials and doing every other chore I could foist upon them.

Several scholars read all or parts of early drafts of this book, and gave invaluable suggestions and criticisms. The insight and learning of Philippa Strum and G. Alan Tarr have greatly improved the final product. Walter Murphy's thorough, penetrating critique not only took my argument apart but helped me put it back together. William K. Muir, Jr., David J. Danelski, Joseph Cooper, and Leslie Friedman Goldstein gave me opportunities to try out some of my ideas on convention panels. I thank the *Western Political Quarterly* for permission to reprint parts of Chapter 8, and *Law and Policy Quarterly* for its generosity in regard to portions of Chapters 5 and 6.

JUDITH A. BAER

Albany, New York

EQUALITY UNDER
THE CONSTITUTION

[I]

Introduction

"The nation was born with the word on its tongue." Thus one historian wrote of the idea of equality in America. "The first of those 'self-evident truths' of the Declaration was that 'all men are created equal.' Back of that was the heritage of natural rights doctrine, and back of that the great body of Christian dogma and the teaching that all men are equal in the sight of God." [1] But equality has never been a given in American life. Those egalitarian doctrines have coexisted with inegalitarian ideas and practices; coexisted not only in the same country but in the same mind. Thomas Jefferson, for instance, wrote not only the Declaration of Independence, but also of his "suspicion" that "the blacks . . . are inferior to the whites in the endowments both of body and mind." [2] Law has often reflected such beliefs, the most notorious example being the institution of slavery. Battle after battle—literal and figurative—has been fought for equality under law, and equality has not always won.

The longest and bitterest fight has been the movement for racial equality. Its first stage, the drive to abolish slavery, culminated in a civil war and three amendments to the Constitution. One of these amendments, the Fourteenth, contains the one explicit constitutional guarantee of equality: that "no state shall . . . deny to any person within its jurisdiction the equal protection of the laws." Since the amendment was ratified in 1868, this clause has become a powerful

[1] C. Vann Woodward, *The Burden of Southern History* (Baton Rouge: Louisiana State University Press, 1960), p. 75.

[2] Thomas Jefferson, *Notes on Virginia*, Query XIV, in Adrienne Koch and William Peden, eds., *The Life and Selected Writings of Thomas Jefferson* (New York: Modern Library, 1944), p. 262.

guarantee of racial equality and a bulwark for ethnic and religious minorities. It has been an effective, though limited, tool in the revival of a long-moribund movement for women's rights, and to a lesser extent has served aliens and the poor.

In the 1980s, all these groups continue to make demands for equality. But the last decade has brought new developments, too. Increasingly, these demands take new and diverse forms and come from new and diverse groups. The drive for racial equality has some new twists. One is a demand by minority groups for compensatory preferential treatment, or "reverse discrimination." Four Supreme Court decisions in the last ten years have shown how difficult it is to deal with these demands according to traditional legal doctrines.[3] And groups that had not been noted for political or litigious activism have begun to perceive themselves as disadvantaged minorities and to try to use law to redress their grievances.

We have long been conscious of racial and sexual inequalities, but now attention focuses on groups distinguishable by such traits as age, disability, and sexual orientation. The old, the young, the handicapped, and homosexuals have become more and more active in their own interests. All have made some gains and suffered some losses, both legislative and judicial.

Several federal laws have been passed to secure the rights of the disabled. The election of Ronald Reagan to the presidency in 1980, however, and the Republicans' continuing majority in the Senate in 1982 have jeopardized funding to implement these laws. Homosexuals have won and lost several campaigns for state and local antidiscrimination laws. The 1978 amendment to the Age Discrimination in Employment Act raised the age of compulsory retirement in many occupations from sixty-five to seventy.

Courts, too, are being kept busy with cases initiated by these groups, with mixed results. Much of the political pressure for the laws to aid the disabled came in response to two district court decisions upholding the right of handicapped children to an education.[4] But the first Supreme Court decision construing the Rehabilitation Act of 1973 was a unanimous ruling against the claimant. A year later, the Court's refusal to review a California case upheld a ruling that the parents of a Down's syndrome child might refuse lifesaving surgery for him.[5]

[3]De Funis v. Odegaard, 416 U.S. 312 (1974); Regents of the University of California v. Bakke, 438 U.S. 265 (1978); Steelworkers v. Weber, 443 U.S. 193 (1979); Fullilove v. Klutznick, 100 S.Ct. 2758 (1980).
[4]Pennsylvania Association for Retarded Children v. Pennsylvania, 343 F. Supp. 279 (E.D. Pa. 1972); Mills v. Board of Education, 348 F. Supp. 866 (D.D.C. 1972).
[5]Southeastern Community College v. Davis, 99 S.Ct. 2361 (1979); Bothman v. Warren B, cert. den. 100 S.Ct. 1597 (1980).

Gay activists have also met with various results. Their major judicial victory has been recognition of their First Amendment rights of association, but even this gain rests on the insecure foundation of Supreme Court denials of certiorari.[6] By the same device, the Court left in force employment discrimination against homosexuals, but lower court decisions have been patternless.[7] And the courts have consistently denied to homosexuals the rights of personal privacy granted to heterosexuals.[8]

The record on age discrimination is similarly mixed. The Supreme Court has twice reversed lower courts to sustain compulsory retirement laws.[9] At the other end of the scale, it has ruled that juvenile courts must provide notice, hearing, and counsel but not jury trials, and invalidated school suspensions without a hearing but upheld corporal punishment.[10] Thus it has shown that in some circumstances it will limit the powers of school and state over children. It is reluctant to limit parents' powers, however, and the reluctance is shared by the lower courts.[11] The Down's syndrome case I just mentioned is one example. A 1979 ruling upheld the right of parents to commit their children to state mental institutions without a hearing, and two years later the Court sustained a law requiring physicians to notify the parents of a minor before performing an abortion.[12] Many of these rulings are hard to reconcile with the guarantee of equal protection.

None of these groups enjoys full equality under law. Somehow handicapped people, homosexuals, and old or even middle-aged people are not protected against employment discrimination as blacks and

[6]Gay Lib v. University of Missouri, 416 F. Supp. 1350 (W.D. Mo. 1976); reversed, 558 F. 2d 848 (8th Circ. 1977); cert. den. *sub. nom.* Ratchford v. Gay Lib. 434 U.S. 1080 (1978).

[7]Gaylord v. Tacoma School District, cert. den. 434 U.S. 879 (1977). But see McConnell v. Anderson, 451 F. 2d 193 (8th Circ. 1971); Acanfora v. Board of Education, 491 F. 2d 498 (4th Circ. 1974); Aumiller v. University of Delaware, 434 F. Supp. 273 (D. Del. 1977); Kochman v. Keansburg Board of Education, 305 A. 2d 807 (Super.Ct. N.J. 1973); Gay Law Students v. Pacific Telephone & Telegraph, 595 P. 2d 592 (Cal. Sup.Ct. 1979).

[8]Doe v. Commonwealth's Attorney, 403 F. Supp. 119 (E.D. Va. 1975), 425 U.S. 903 (1976); Enslin v. North Carolina, 214 S.E. 2d 318 (N.C. Ct. App. 1975), 425 U.S. 903 (1976); Griswold v. Connecticut, 381 U.S. 479 (1965); Roe v. Wade, 410 U.S. 113 (1973); Cotner v. Henry, 394 F. 2d 873 (6th Circ. 1968); State v. Saunders, 381 A. 2d 333 (N.J. Sup.Ct. 1977).

[9]Massachusetts Board of Retirement v. Murgia, 427 U.S. 307 (1976); Vance v. Bradley, 440 U.S. 93 (1979).

[10]Re Gault, 387 U.S. 1 (1967); McKeiver v. Pennsylvania, 403 U.S. 528 (1971); Goss v. Lopez, 419 U.S. 565 (1975); Ingraham v. Wright, 430 U.S. 651 (1977).

[11]See Matter of Hofbauer, 393 N.E. 2d 1009 (N.Y. Ct. App. 1979); In re Phillip B., 156 Cal. Rptr. 48 (Cal. Ct. App. 1975); but cf. Custody of a Minor Child (Chad Green), 379 N.E. 2d 1053, 393 N.E. 2d 836 (S.J.C. Mass. 1978, 1979).

[12]Parham v. J. R., 99 S.Ct. 2493 (1979); H. L. v. Matheson, 101 S.Ct. 1164 (1981). See also Santosky v. Kramer, 102 S.Ct. 1388 (1982).

women are. Children do not have the same protection against institutionalization as adults do.[13] But perhaps the most striking fact revealed by these cases is that a retarded child literally does not have a
right to his life. The Constitution and laws of the United States, which
gave so much protection to blacks in the 1950s and 1960s and valuable protection to women in the 1970s, have not been so beneficial to
these groups in the 1970s and 1980s. We must ask why this is so, and
what effect the decisions have had on new groups and new claims.
Exploring these questions, and others that arise from them, requires
an inquiry into the origin, scope, and implications of a major part of
the Constitution: its guarantees of equality.

Such an inquiry is an exercise in constitutional interpretation. It
seeks to determine the meaning, or part of the meaning, of a document. The scholar who attempts such a task is confronted with problems of source and method. Where does one go to look for such meaning, and how does one proceed? In the two hundred years that
Americans have engaged in constitutional interpretation, they have
developed various approaches. This book will use, and show others
using, many of these approaches.

One source of meaning is the document itself. For my purposes, the
equal-protection clause is one logical starting point. What do the words
"No state shall . . . deny to any person within its jurisdiction the equal
protection of the laws" mean? This mode is what John Hart Ely calls
"clause-bound interpretativism."[14] It is exemplified by Justice Hugo
Black's abolutist interpretation of the free-speech clause of the First
Amendment: "I read 'no law abridging' to mean '*no law abridging.*'"[15] We can envision situations in which clause-bound interpretation of the equal-protection clause would be adequate. Suppose, for
example, a state allowed crimes against certain people—blacks, say,
or homosexuals—to go unpunished. However one reads the clause,
such action violates it. But we can also see defects in this approach,
and indeed Ely and others have criticized it extensively.[16]

A second mode of interpretation ranges through the Constitution
to gather meaning from various provisions read together. Charles L.
Black, Jr., calls this approach "inference from structure and relationship."[17] One example of this structural analysis is Justice William O.

[13] See O'Connor v. Donaldson, 422 U.S. 563 (1975).

[14] *Democracy and Distrust* (Cambridge: Harvard University Press, 1980), p. 11.

[15] Smith v. California, 361 U.S. 147, 157 (1959). Emphasis in the original.

[16] See, e.g., Alexander M. Bickel, *The Least Dangerous Branch* (Indianapolis: Bobbs-
Merrill, 1962), chap. 3; Martin Shapiro, *Freedom of Speech* (Englewood Cliffs, N.J.:
Prentice-Hall, 1966), pp. 87–95.

[17] *Structure and Relationship in Constitutional Law* (Baton Rouge: Louisiana State
University Press, 1969), p. 8.

Douglas' opinion in *Griswold* v. *Connecticut,* which finds a constitutional right of privacy established by several provisions of the Bill of Rights and guarantees derived from these provisions.[18] A structural analysis that focused on equality would lead at least as far as the whole text of the amendment that contains the equal-protection clause. Since the Fourteenth Amendment was one of the three "civil war amendments," it would make sense to move backward and forward to the Thirteenth Amendment, which forbids slavery, and the Fifteenth, which guarantees racial equality in voting rights. And since the Fourteenth Amendment speaks of "privileges and immunities," "life, liberty, and property," and "due process of law," structural analysis might lead to provisions that contain these phrases and similar ideas: Article IV, Section 2, or the Bill of Rights. These examples do not purport to exhaust the possibilities, but they do suggest some promising areas of exploration.

Some methods of interpretation go outside the constitutional text. William Harris calls these "transcendent" as opposed to "immanent" modes.[19] One external source of meaning is legislative history: the debates and surrounding sources that contain evidence of what the lawmakers who enacted a rule thought they were enacting. Justice Black used this method in his dissent in *Adamson* v. *California,* where he relied on the record of the *Congressional Globe* to argue that Congress intended to make the first eight amendments of the Bill of Rights binding on the states through the due-process clause of the Fourteenth Amendment.[20] Another sort of historical argument is the familiar one that relies on the circumstances surrounding the adoption of the Civil War amendments to argue that the equal-protection clause applies only, or mainly, to classifications based on race. Justice William Rehnquist made such an argument in his 1977 dissent in *Trimble* v. *Gordon.*[21]

An inquiry into legislative history is, to a degree, an inquiry about intent. Questions of intent are among the hardest of constitutional questions, for reasons that scholars have discussed before.[22] One difficulty is that we cannot even be sure that the written record is accurate. We do not know if what appears in the *Globe* for 1866 is what was actually said on the floor; for all we know, members may have

---

[18] 381 U.S. 479, 484 (1965).
[19] "Bonding Word and Polity: The Logic of American Constitutionalism," *American Political Science Review* 76 (March 1982):34–45.
[20] 332 U.S. 46, 105–20 (1947).
[21] 430 U.S. 762, 777–86.
[22] See, e.g., Jacobus ten Broek, "Admissability and Use by the United States Supreme Court of Extrinsic Aids in Constitutional Construction," pt. 2, *California Law Review* 26 (May 1938):437–54. For a recent discussion, see Ronald Dworkin, "How to Read the Civil Rights Act," *New York Review of Books,* December 20, 1979, pp. 37–43.

edited their remarks, as they do now.[23] Even if we could trust the record, vexing problems remain. How do we find legislative intent with respect to problems the lawmakers never faced? It is futile to inquire what the authors of the Bill of Rights thought about wiretapping. It is just as useless to ask how the Thirty-ninth Congress thought about disability rights, and for one of the same reasons: their world did not include devices that are preconditions for the integration of severely handicapped people into society to the point where any question of their rights could arise.

Where technological barriers do not exist, it is still possible that a problem that agitates the twentieth century may not have appeared to need discussion in the eighteenth or nineteenth; at least in the United States, the legal rights of homosexuals are one example. Even problems that were discussed by the lawmakers may require rethinking by us. Perhaps the most famous example here is *Brown* v. *Board of Education*, the school desegregation case. The fact that *de jure* racial segregation existed when the Fourteenth Amendment was ratified did not force the Court to legitimize it in 1954. As Chief Justice Earl Warren wrote, "public education in light of its full development and its present place in American life throughout the Nation" demanded an opposite conclusion.[24] Likewise, prayers in public schools were forbidden even though the practice was common at the time of the founding, and the First Amendment guarantee of freedom of expression has been expanded far beyond what its authors envisioned.[25]

Intent is not conclusive even when the lawmakers actually did address and resolve a specific question. More than once during debates on the Civil Rights Act of 1866 and the Fourteenth Amendment, supporters assured Congress that these measures would not touch laws prohibiting interracial marriage.[26] But in 1967 the Supreme Court ruled unanimously that these laws did deny equal protection.[27] Similarly, the Thirty-ninth Congress did not include sex-based discrimination within the Fourteenth Amendment.[28] But, as we shall see, the Court has in-

[23] See Walter F. Murphy, "Constitutional Interpretation: The Art of the Historian, Magician, or Statesman?" *Yale Law Journal* 87 (July 1978): 1752–71.

[24] 347 U.S. 483, 492–93 (1954). For an opposing view, see Raoul Berger, *Government by Judiciary* (Cambridge: Harvard University Press, 1977) chaps. 7, 13.

[25] Abingdon School District v. Schempp, 374 U.S. 203 (1963), especially the separate opinion of Justice Brennan. See Leonard W. Levy, *Legacy of Suppression* (Cambridge: Belknap Press of Harvard University Press, 1960).

[26] E.g., remarks of Senator Lyman Trumbull (R-Ill.), January 18, 1866, in Alfred Avins, ed., *The Reconstruction Amendments' Debates* (Richmond: Virginia Commission on Constitutional Government, 1967), p. 108.

[27] Loving v. Virginia, 388 U.S. 1.

[28] See, e.g., remarks of Thaddeus Stevens (R-Pa.), House of Representatives, February 27, 1866, in Avins, ed., *Reconstruction Amendments' Debates*, p. 154; Luke Poland (R-Vt.), Senate, June 4, 1866, in ibid., p. 230.

terpreted this provision to apply to such cases. By now it is established doctrine that what the framers of the Reconstruction amendments, like their predecessors in 1787, did "was to lay out in the Constitution not specific rules or objectives but broad *principles*: 'privileges' and 'immunities,' 'due process of law,' and the expansive right to 'the equal protection of the laws.'"[29] So constitutional history must search not for commands but for principles. Discoverable intent cannot bind us, but it can guide us.[30]

Precedent is another extratextual source of meaning. For judges, *stare decisis* is a rule from which departures must be justified. There is, of course, no good reason why we should be bound by past judicial errors, but the point is not that precedent is binding, any more than legislative history is, but that it is an available source.

Several remaining sources can be loosely classified together. Employing what Harris calls "transcendent structuralism," jurists have relied on such notions as "certain immutable principles of justice which inhere in the very idea of a free government," "some principle of justice so rooted in the traditions and conscience of our people as to be ranked as fundamental," and "the very essence of a scheme of ordered liberty."[31] Justice Black used to label this sort of thing "natural-law due process."[32] He thought the "fundamental values" approach was a thinly disguised way for a judge to write personal views of natural justice into the Constitution. But it is by no means obvious that such a label condemns the approach. Indeed, interpreting the Constitution according to the perceived dictates of natural law was once an accepted mode. As Chapter 3 will show, abolitionists often argued that slavery was unconstitutional because it violated natural law. Much later, Edward Corwin suggested that Americans revered the Constitution precisely because they thought it embodied natural law principles.[33] This kind of argument makes scholars uncomfortable now, but it will play a prominent part in this book.

All these modes of interpretation—and possibly others—have their

---

[29] John Agresto, review of Raoul Berger, *Government by Judiciary*, in *American Political Science Review* 73 (December 1979):1143. Emphasis in the original.

[30] If intent can be a guide, why not the intent of the ratifiers—the state legislators who debated the Fourteenth Amendment—as well as Congress? The ratifying debates may indeed be a fruitful source of evidence, but the state records are even less satisfactory than the federal ones. The almost complete absence of scholarly attention to the states reflects, I think, an agreement that the labor would not justify the gain.

[31] Holden v. Hardy, 169 U.S. 366, 389 (1898); Snyder v. Massachusetts, 291 U.S. 97, 105 (1934); Palko v. Connecticut, 302 U.S., 319, 325 (1937).

[32] For instance, in his dissent in Griswold v. Connecticut, 381 U.S. 479, 507–27 (1965).

[33] *The "Higher Law" Background of American Constitutional Law* (Ithaca: Cornell University Press, 1955).

legitimate place.[34] There is no need to use one or a few to the exclusion of all other modes. I rely on textual, structural, and in particular historical interpretations. I emphasize legislative history, but I do not mean to imply that this mode is the only legitimate one, nor do I use it exclusively. One reason that I rely so much on history is that the legislative history of the Fourteenth Amendment has been badly misunderstood, and one well-known contemporary interpretation in particular is gravely wrong.[35]

I have argued that constitutional history must concern itself not with specifics but with principles. It is in this spirit that I have approached the history of the Fourteenth Amendment. I have asked whether prevailing constitutional doctrine is in fact the best and truest rendering of constitutional principles. I have become convinced that it is not, that current doctrine is too stingy an interpretation. In order to explain that statement, it is necessary to describe that doctrine briefly.

The demand for equality under law is, in essence, a demand for like treatment against a governmental desire to impose different treatment. This demand is nowhere absolute. "In the jurisprudence of equal treatment . . . argument begins with the acknowledgement that equality before the law does not require any person to be treated in the same way but only similar treatment in similar circumstances, or an absence of discriminatory treatment except for those in different circumstances."[36] But if this were all it meant, it would mean nothing except maybe for identical twins. As Justice Robert Jackson wrote, "The equal protection clause ceases to assure either equality or protection if it is avoided by any conceivable difference that can be pointed out between those bound and those left free."[37]

In effect, then, the demand for legal equality is a demand that those who are different from one another be treated alike. Paradoxically, it may also be a demand that those who are alike not be treated alike. Only rarely is discrimination totally capricious; laws do not single people out unless there are intelligible differences between those bound and those left free. And such differences do exist, for example, among the races, between the sexes, between rich and poor, between alien and citizen. A person from one of the paired classifications is not interchangeable with one from the other.

---

[34] See Harris, "Bonding Word and Polity," for an extensive discussion and typology.

[35] See Berger, *Government by Judiciary*; Lino Graglia, *Disaster by Decree* (Ithaca: Cornell University Press, 1976).

[36] Geoffrey Marshall, "Notes on the Rule of Equal Law," in J. Roland Pennock and John W. Chapman, eds., *Nomos IX: Equality* (New York: Atherton, 1967), p. 267.

[37] Railway Express Agency v. New York, 336 U.S. 106, 115 (1949).

Not only are the differences genuine, but they are also significant, at least in some respects and for some purposes. Discrimination against red-haired or blue-eyed people are favorite hypothetical examples of arbitrary discrimination, but they have few actual counterparts. However wrong it was, it was not irrational for whites to enslave blacks, or for men who monopolized certain jobs to deny them to women.

But the differences may be important for reasons other than the ease with which dominant groups can exploit them. Few people wish to base claims for equality on an assertion that differences in skin color are as trivial as differences in hair color. Nor do proponents of sexual equality rest their case on a denial of any sexual differences. This lack of any necessary connection between equality and identity becomes more evident as we move from the traditional areas to the newer demands.

If the claim for the rule of equal law does not depend on a belief that people are identical, on what grounds, then, does it rest? Geoffrey Marshall finds in equal-treatment litigation several criteria that legal classifications must meet. He summarizes them as follows: "Roughly speaking and in ascending order three standards of criticism may be distinguished, i.e. that which is intelligible, that which is relevant, and that which is just or reasonable. A distinction between two persons or classes which is intelligible or real may not be for some purposes relevant, and a distinction which is relevant to the purpose at hand may not be sufficiently relevant to be reasonable, fair, or just."[38] All distinctions I have mentioned are intelligible. Some of them may never be relevant; others may be relevant but not necessarily reasonable; others may be relevant, reasonable, or just sometimes, but not always; some, however relevant or reasonable, may never be just.

In equal-treatment litigation, we can identify several arguments that underlie these claims. Two of these arguments challenge the general principle of discrimination, going not to the legitimacy of the discrimination imposed but to the characteristic that is the basis for it. Two additional arguments are more limited in scope, attacking particular instances of discrimination based on a given variable without rejecting all discrimination similarly based.

One general argument for equality is that it is unjust to impose discriminations on all members of a class on the basis of generalizations about them, without regard to individual differences within the class. This argument insists both that those who differ—that is, the members and nonmembers of a class—must be treated alike, and, cu-

[38] "Notes," pp. 268–69.

riously enough, the very opposite: that those who are alike—that is, all the members of a class—should, in some instances, be treated differently. By this reasoning, for example, even if men, on the average, have greater muscular strength than women, laws that prohibit all women from doing heavy work are unjust because many women are in fact stronger than many men. A second general argument is that certain human characteristics are virtually never legitimate bases for legal distinctions, under any circumstances. Such an argument is frequently made about race and increasingly about sex as well.

One limited argument for equality is that there are certain fundamental human rights of which no one may justly be deprived, even a class of people generally subject to discrimination. For example, the principle that allows us to deny drivers' licenses to the severely disabled would not justify us in depriving them of the right to vote. The fourth and final argument for equality is, to use Marshall's terminology, the assertion that a difference, real as it may be, is not relevant to the particular discrimination at issue. Thus one argument advanced for sexual equality is that differences in reproductive functions have no relationship to ability to work, to earn a just wage, or to assume the responsibilities of citizenship.

If we examine constitutional text and case law on equality, we discover that these four arguments have gained varying degrees of recognition as doctrine. The first two arguments find their way into constitutional law under the rubric of "suspect classification." The equal-protection clause has been interpreted to make certain kinds of discrimination inherently suspect, and thus tenable only on demonstration of a compelling justification for them. Race, ethnic background, and religion have been ruled suspect classifications, and some judges would treat alienage and sex this way as well.[39]

The two narrower arguments for equality enter into the doctrine, too. The Constitution has been read to establish a "floor" or guaranteed minimum level of equality, consisting of certain basic rights that must be granted to all. Thus juveniles may not be deprived of certain

---

[39] On race, see Oyama v. California, 332 U.S. 631 (1948); Takahishi v. Fish and Game Commission, 334 U.S. 410 (1948); Bates v. Little Rock, 361 U.S. 516 (1958). On ethnic background, see Hernandez v. Texas, 347 U.S. 475 (1954); on religion, Sherbert v. Verner, 374 U.S. 398 (1963). On aliens, see Graham v. Richardson, 403 U.S. 365 (1971); but cf. Foley v. Conellie, 435 U.S. 291 (1978); Ambach v. Norwick, 441 U.S. 68 (1979); and Plyler v. Doe, 50 U.S.L.W. 4650 (1982). On sex, see Sail'er Inn, Inc., v. Kirby, 485 P. 2d 529 (Cal. Sup.Ct. 1971); Frontiero v. Richardson, 411 U.S. 677 (1973).

procedural rights, nor may they lose all freedom of expression.[40] Indigent people must have the right to counsel, a trial transcript, and a divorce.[41] Homosexuals have not forfeited their First Amendment freedoms.

But other decisions, including some I have mentioned, leave some doubt as to how solid the floor is. The rights just mentioned are ranked, explicitly or implicitly, as fundamental, but the right to an education and the right to file for bankruptcy are not.[42] And as we have seen, trial by jury is not among the rights granted to juveniles, and the principle that prohibits school suspensions without a hearing does not extend to corporal punishment.

The final argument for equality, what Felix Oppenheim has called the principle of relevant differences, has had an erratic constitutional career.[43] This argument forecloses the short cut of assuming that acceptance of one kind of discrimination based on any characteristic justifies any and all discrimination so grounded. That kind of short cut has been common, however, notably in sex discrimination; such blanket acceptance did not survive the "newer equal protection" of the Burger Court.[44] "Rationality scrutiny"—a close, critical analysis of the relationship between the ends and means of legislation—has built the principle of relevant differences into equal-protection litigation.

To sum up, there are basically three kinds of differential treatment that run afoul of the Fourteenth Amendment. First, a law that lacks a close enough relationship to a good enough governmental purpose is invalid. How close is close enough varies. A law that makes arbitrary or capricious distinctions will virtually always fall, whatever the basis for the distinctions; laws that make gender-based discriminations, however, will stand if they "serve important governmental objectives" and are substantially related to achievement of these objectives.[45] Second, a distinction that violates a fundamental right will fall, unless a

---

[40] Tinker v. Des Moines Community School District, 393 U.S. 403 (1969).

[41] Gideon v. Wainwright, 372 U.S. 335 (1963); Griffin v. Illinois, 351 U.S. 12 (1956); Boddie v. Connecticut, 401 U.S. 371 (1971).

[42] San Antonio Independent School District v. Rodriguez, 411 U.S. 1 (1973); U.S. v. Kras, 409 U.S. 434 (1973).

[43] "The Concept of Equality," *International Encyclopedia of the Social Sciences* (New York: Crowell Collier & Macmillan, 1968), 5:102–7.

[44] See Judith A. Baer, *The Chains of Protection* (Westport, Conn.: Greenwood Press, 1978), chaps. 2–5; Gerald Gunther, "In Search of Evolving Doctrine on a Changing Court: A Model for a Newer Equal Protection," *Harvard Law Review* 86 (November 1972):1–48.

[45] Craig v. Boren, 429 U.S. 190, 197 (1976).

compelling justification for it can be shown. Finally, certain kinds of classifications, such as those based on race, are inherently suspect and tenable only if they meet the same strict standard.[46]

What, or whom, do these categories leave out? They exclude whatever is defined out of them: interests, such as welfare benefits or an education, which are not ranked as fundamental rights; distinctions, such as those between widows and widowers in regard to property taxes, which courts regard as relevant to a legitimate end;[47] classifications, such as economic status or disability, not regarded as inherently suspect. Thus the model leaves out many of the claims with which I am concerned. A superficial answer to the question with which I began is close at hand: certain claims are not recognized because they fall outside established doctorinal categories. But we do not know yet why and how those particular categories got established, or how well they are grounded in history, or how valid they are as ways of interpreting the Constitution.

The more research one does, the more difficulties one finds with the doctrine. "Fundamental rights," for one thing, clearly mean less for homosexuals and children than for heterosexual adults. But most of the problems I have discovered centered on the concept of suspect classification.

One problem is that the fit between the concept and the constitutional language is poor. "Classification" points to the trait that is the basis for discrimination. The term invites such questions as these: Does the equal-protection clause apply to race discrimination? to sex discrimination? to the poor? But Section 1 of the Fourteenth Amendment refers not to traits, classes, or persons similarly situated, but to "any person." The clause mentions something—"the equal protection of the laws"—which no state may deny to anyone. The questions that follow most easily from this language are not What groups are included? but What is this "equal protection of the laws"?; What idea of equality is embodied here?; What are the foundations of this guarantee?; and What principles of equality does the Constitution lay down?

A second difficulty with "suspect classification" is that the cases reveal much confusion about what makes a classification suspect. There is general agreement, however correct, about what "rational" means and what "fundamental rights" are, but, as Chapter 5 shows, there are two working definitions of "suspect classification" abroad in the courts, and they differ enough so that decisions can vary according to

[46] See San Antonio Independent School District v. Rodriguez, 411 U.S. 1, 18–39, 44–53 (1973).
[47] Kahn v. Shevin, 416 U.S. 351 (1974).

which definition a judge happens to be working with. Another problem is that the concept almost literally came from nowhere; both interpretations derive from cases that had nothing to do with the Fourteenth Amendment, and both were grafted onto later cases with little critical thought. Finally, the more one studies the legislative history of the Civil War amendments, the less support one finds for the doctrine. To sum up, "suspect classification" fails four important tests for constitutional doctrine: it does not fit the constitutional language, it is not clear, it is not rooted anywhere, and it does not conform to legislative history.

So there are logical and historical problems with the doctrine. The results it permits are equally troubling. One might expect that since the concept has two definitions, almost any claim can be included, but that is not how it works. There have been errors both of overinclusion and of underinclusion. Whatever suspect classification means, there has been general agreement that the concept includes racial discrimination; taken literally, this interpretation has led several Supreme Court justices to insist that the Constitution forbids reverse as well as invidious discrimination, despite the fact that the former is designed to help those whom the latter has oppressed.[48] Beyond race, suspect classifications have been defined as *either* those that harm "discrete and insular minorities" *or* those based on such factors as race and sex, which are beyond individual control and unrelated to individual merits.[49]

What classifications are not suspect? Age is perhaps the example that comes most readily to mind, a trait considered a legitimate basis for discrimination. It is beyond individual control, but it is related at least to some abilities, and neither the old nor the young have been viewed as a disadvantaged minority. Examples abound of laws that put special restrictions on people because of their age. Attempts have been made to fit disability into the category of suspect classifications, but they have had rough going.[50] The disabled are pretty close to powerless as minorities go, but, by definition, the category bears a relation to ability. Whether sexual orientation fits any or all of the criteria of a suspect classification is a question on which no informed agreement exists, or is likely to be reached in the future.

[48] See Regents v. Bakke, 438 U.S. 265, 269–315 (Powell); Fullilove v. Klutznick, 100 S.Ct. 2758, 2798–2803 (Stewart); 2803–14 (Stevens).

[49] U.S. v. Carolene Products, 304 U.S. 144, 152, n. 4 (1938); see Frontiero v. Richardson, 411 U.S. 677, 686.

[50] In interest of G. H., 218 N.W. 2d 441 (N.D. Sup.Ct. 1974); Marcia Pearce Burgdorf and Robert L. Burgdorf, Jr., "A History of Unequal Treatment: The Qualifications of Handicapped Persons as a 'Suspect Class' under the Equal Protection Clause," *Santa Clara Lawyer* 15, no. 4 (1975):855–910.

Must we conclude, then, that the Constitution offers only minimal protection to these groups? Such resignation is hard to accept. Age discrimination is not easily reconcilable with a commitment to equality. Though a general relationship between age and ability may exist, in particular cases it often does not. It seems strange to force an older person to retire because most, or some, or many people her age could not do her job; this situation is especially disturbing because at that end of the age scale the deprivation is permanent. At the other end, the deprivations do not last forever, but the same lack of fit between age and ability may exist, and there is an even graver problem. Children are presumed to be incapable of governing themselves, and others, primarily their parents, have that task. A very old political problem thus arises: whether or not a person is capable of self-rule, there is no guarantee that others are equipped to do the ruling.

The law presumes that parents act in the child's best interests. The tenacity with which that presumption is held, sometimes in the face of overwhelming evidence to the contrary, can be astonishing; Chapter 7 recounts several examples. The statistics on child abuse call the presumption into question by themselves. The cases show that it is very easy to move from the statement "I, as a parent, am presumed to act in my child's best interests" to "I, as a parent, have a right to treat my children as I choose, however many mistakes I make." Somehow, derivative parental autonomy becomes fundamental parental rights, and this principle is pursued virtually as far as it will go.

Discrimination against the disabled is equally objectionable if we conceive of justice as demanding that every person be given opportunities to fulfill her potential, as inconsistent with the accommodation of ignorant prejudice, and as incompatible with the imposition of constraints and burdens on those who already bear burdens enough, and bear them permanently, and through no fault of their own. And, in the final category, there is no clear reason why homosexuals should be virtually the only people who can now be fired for expressing opinions and engaging in political activity, and who are denied the right of sexual privacy.

Not only are these conclusions disturbing, but, as I shall argue, they are unnecessary. All of them, somehow or other, directly or indirectly, are traceable to the domination of equal-treatment litigation by current doctrine. But, as I have indicated, I have come to reject that doctrine, as research has borne out my first reservations. No guide to constitutional interpretation demands the conclusion that the scope of the Fourteenth Amendment is limited in this way. Indeed, as a whole, history and theory invite us to interpret these guarantees more broadly and, in the largest sense, liberally.

The suspect-classification rule was an intelligent response to the particular issues raised in Fourteenth Amendment cases in a certain time period, and a device that enabled twentieth-century judges to correct the mistakes of nineteenth-century judges. The concept has been a useful one, allowing the courts, as far as they dared, to deal sensibly with some issues, such as women's rights, not fully anticipated by the amendment's authors. But it is an idea whose time has come and gone. The best way to perceive its obsolescence is to read three of the cases I shall be analyzing at length: the majority opinion in *San Antonio Independent School District* v. *Rodriguez*, the *per curiam* opinion in *Massachusetts Board of Retirement* v. *Murgia*, and Justice Lewis Powell's tortuous essay in *University of California* v. *Bakke*.[51] Examining the Fourteenth Amendment and other constitutional guarantees of rights, I have tried here to develop a constitutional theory that will enable us to recognize important new claims while remaining faithful to philosophy, history, and law.

One of the problems I have mentioned, reverse discrimination, has already stimulated some new legal philosophy.[52] Ronald Dworkin, an American scholar who succeeded H. L. A. Hart as University Professor of Jurisprudence at Oxford, has related this problem to a general legal theory of equality:

> There are two different sorts of rights [to equality which citizens] may be said to have. The first is the right to *equal treatment*, which is the right to an equal distribution of some opportunity or resource or burden. Every person, for example, has a right to an equal vote in a democracy; that is the nerve of the Supreme Court's decisions that one man must have one vote even if a different and more complex arrangement would better secure the collective welfare. The second is the right to *treatment*

---

[51] See, respectively, nn. 46, 9, and 3 above.

[52] See,e.g., Ronald Dworkin, *Taking Rights Seriously* (Cambridge: Harvard University Press, 1977); "Why Bakke Has No Case," *New York Review of Books*, November 10, 1977, pp. 11–15; "The Bakke Decision: Did It Decide Anything?" *New York Review of Books*, August 17, 1978, pp. 20–25; "How to Read the Civil Rights Act," *New York Review of Books*, December 20, 1979, pp. 37–43; John Hart Ely, "The Constitutionality of Reverse Racial Discrimination," *University of Chicago Law Review* 41 (Summer 1974):723–41; Owen M. Fiss, "Groups and the Equal Protection Clause," *Philosophy and Public Affairs* 5 (Winter 1976):107–77; Thomas Nagel, "Equal Treatment and Compensatory Discrimination," *Philosophy and Public Affairs* 2 (Summer 1973):348–63; James W. Nickel, "Preferential Policies in Hiring," *Philosophy and Public Affairs* 3 (Spring 1974):312–30; Judith Jarvis Thomson, "Preferential Hiring," *Philosophy and Public Affairs* 2 (Summer 1973):364–84.

as an equal, which is the right, not to receive the same distribution of some burden or benefit, but to be treated with the same respect or concern as anyone else. If I have two children, and one is dying from a disease that is making the other uncomfortable, I do not show equal concern if I flip a coin to decide which should have the remaining dose of a drug. This example shows that the right to treatment as an equal is fundamental, and the right to equal treatment derivative. In some circumstances the right to treatment as an equal will entail the right to equal treatment, but not, by any means, in all circumstances.[53]

This point is crucial to any discussion of reverse discrimination. I think it is also a central point in any analysis of equality. We begin, as Dworkin insists, with the premise of a fundamental right to equal respect and concern. People have a right to equal treatment whenever and only when it will ensure that equality. Thus equal respect and concern sometimes entail the same treatment, and sometimes do not.

Dworkin's statement belongs not to the realm of constitutional law but to that of jurisprudence. But the striking feature of the statement is how well it echoes what I identify in Chapters 2, 3, and 4 as the American constitutional philosophy of equality. Dworkin's *Taking Rights Seriously* comes close to a natural law position. Dworkin criticizes legal positivist jurisprudence to assert that people have legal rights against the state independent of and beyond those explicitly granted, and that among those rights is the right to treatment as an equal. I agree that the right exists, but I argue that the right is recognized in the Fourteenth Amendment. The interpretation that I defend is based not on an idea of equality conceived of in terms of similarity or difference, but on equality in terms of entitlement or endowment, a notion that all human beings have a right to equal respect and concern. To the framers of the Fourteenth Amendment, this idea was far more important than ideas about merit or ability. The right to equal respect and concern has long been an axiom of American political thought, in spite of American political practice. This is the idea with which the nation was born, and which the Reconstruction laws belatedly wove into the Constitution's fabric.

The Radical Republicans' commitment to this idea led them to enact a guarantee of rights which was generous, open-ended, and without specified limitations. It also led them to write the fifth and final section of that amendment, which stipulates, "The Congress shall have power to enforce, by appropriate legislation, the provisions of this article." So the Fourteenth Amendment is an extensive, expansive bill

---

[53] *Taking Rights Seriously,* p. 227. Emphasis in the original.

of rights equipped with enforcement powers. Those same senators and representatives got several such laws passed: for example, the Ku Klux Klan Act of 1871 and the Civil Rights Act of 1875. *Fullilove* v. *Klutznick* upheld the minority business enterprise amendment to the Public Works Employment Act of 1977 under Section 5.[54] Although the Civil Rights Act of 1964 was enacted and sustained under the commerce power, many have insisted, and I agree, that it was a legitimate exercise of this enforcement power.[55] So, I submit, was the Rehabilitation Act of 1973.

The older claims to equality have, I think, involved situations in which the fundamental right to treatment as an equal entailed the derivative right to equal treatment. In the case of blacks, this has been clear at least since 1954. One reason that sexual equality is still so far from being a reality is that too many people have believed and continue to believe the opposite with respect to women. But no American judge has ever written about women as Chief Justice Taney wrote about blacks in the *Dred Scott* case.[56] Until the 1970s judges usually wrote about women something like this:

> That woman's physical structure and the performance of maternal functions place her at a disadvantage in the struggle for existence is obvious. . . . Though limitations upon personal and contractual rights may be removed by legislation, there is that in her disposition and habits of life which will operate against a full assertion of those rights. She will still be where some legislation to protect her seems necessary to secure a real equality of rights. . . . Looking at it from the viewpoint of the effort to maintain an independent position in life, she is not upon an equality. Differentiated by these matters from the other sex, she is properly placed in a class by herself, and legislation designed for her protection may be sustained, even when like legislation is not necessary for men, and could not be sustained.[57]

This quotation is from Justice David Brewer's opinion for the Court in *Muller* v. *Oregon*, a case that used to be read for its implications for economic legislation but is now read for its implications for women's rights. The opinion has been widely criticized for its "patronizing air of concessions made to the physically inferior."[58] I have omitted some of the best, or worst, parts here, but I think the criticism is just. *Muller*

[54] See n. 3 above.
[55] Heart of Atlanta Motel, Inc., v. United States, 379 U.S. 421, and Katzenbach v. McClung, 379 U.S. 904 (1964).
[56] See pp. 70–71.
[57] Muller v. Oregon, 208 U.S. 412, 421–22 (1908).
[58] Kate Millett, *Sexual Politics* (New York: Doubleday, 1970), p. 44. See also Baer, *Chains of Protection*, chap. 2.

is no longer good law, and under some circumstances such lengthy quotation might be an exercise in obsolescence. Here, however, it tells us a good deal about the constitutional law of equality.

It is useful to suspend anger or boredom and reread that opinion thoroughly. Justice Brewer and his colleagues did not *think* they believed women were inferior to men. They thought women deserved equal respect and concern. It is precisely because women deserve treatment as equals that they must get unequal treatment. It would not be fanciful to suggest, by analogy with Dworkin, that the Court thought women were dying from a "disease," overwork, which only made men uncomfortable. Here the fundamental right to equal respect and concern does not entail that derivative right to equal treatment.

We known now, of course, that the *Muller* Court was wrong: The fundamental right does entail the derivative right, and preventing women from working more than a certain number of hours per day did give them less respect and concern. *Muller* shows that Dworkin's distinction does not solve all problems of adjudication, and may even add a few. The line of cases beginning with *Reed* v. *Reed* indicates a change in judicial attitudes which, sadly, has not occurred in the entire society.[59]

With the new claims, the formula often does not work. Dworkin discusses one type of demand: not a claim to equal treatment, but a demand for favored treatment against a counterdemand for equal treatment. Such demands have presented the courts with issues that continue to confound them. My concern is with some claims made by people who have only recently begun to make demands. The formula fails them, too, because, again, the connection between equal treatment and treatment as an equal breaks down.

The connection fails in a variety of ways. Much legal restriction of homosexuals seems to stem from a notion that they are not entitled to the same respect and concern as everyone else. We shall find in Chapter 9 that many court decisions imply this idea. The same was also true for blacks, of course, but the Civil War amendments were slowly but finally recognized as a binding rejection of such notions. These ideas retain their form with respect to homosexuals, with results that we have seen.

Age and disability appear to have less in common with race as bases for unequal treatment than homosexuality does, and more in common with sex. Social rhetoric about children, old people, and the handicapped is so benign, superficially at least, that it borders on bathos, to

[59] 404 U.S. 71 (1971).

the point where the words "very special" in print are almost certain to refer to disabled people. Generally, we do not think we believe that any of these groups are inferior to us. We do, however, and the cases will show that we do. The sweet rhetoric masks some hostile opinions. But the legal problems seem to result from confusion, first, about whether treatment as an equal entails equal treatment, and second, about what "equal treatment" would actually be.

The disabled provide a good example. Several of their claims, such as to access to public facilities and to educational opportunity, involve the expenditure of more money and attention on them than on the able-bodied. Is this equal treatment, or favored treatment? To some extent, the disabled are favored, but to *deny* those benefits would not be equal treatment either, but disfavored treatment. What do equal respect and concern demand? Might they require unequal, compensatory treatment? In the chapters on these new demands, I shall consider how we can reconnect, or connect for the first time, the fundamental right to the derivative right. To this extent, philosophy can inform and enrich law.

To understand the equal-protection clause, it is necessary to learn what "equal" meant to its authors. That question leads back to the Declaration of Independence, but even as long ago as 1776 the word had a long history, and this history demands some exploration. So Chapter 2 is a limited project in intellectual history. I describe it as limited because in no sense have I provided a comprehensive history of the idea of equality. I am concerned with the ancestry of the idea backward from the colonists, with the roots not of the concept of equality, but of their concept of equality. Thus there is more Luther and Locke than Calvin and Hobbes, no Rousseau, and, in that chapter at any rate, there are no post-Revolution thinkers. I then take up the contradiction between the idea of equality and the institution of slavery, concentrating on that contradiction as it is manifested in the thought and writings of Thomas Jefferson. The chapter ends with an examination of the ways in which the Philadelphia Convention dealt with this contradiction.

Chapter 3 continues this exploration up to the Civil War, analyzing the antislavery writing that drew on the Declaration and culminated in the Fourteenth Amendment. This chapter also discusses proslavery writings, particularly those of John C. Calhoun. His defense of slavery expounded what became an antitheory of equality, a theory that insists, in essence, that equal rights must be earned and belong only to those with a certain degree of ability. This theory is opposed to and irreconcilable with the theory of the Fourteenth Amendment; but, as we shall see, much of the case law is closer to this view than to the constitutional theory. Finally I turn to the major Supreme Court decisions on slavery to show how the legal elite dealt with these problems. Many of the opponents of slavery thought about the Constitution in ways very different from those of judges in their day or jurists in our own. Far from being careful—or professing care—not to write their own philosophies into constitutional law, that was exactly what they strove to do.

In Chapter 4 we see some of these activists using the chance they earned actually to revise the Constitution. This chapter examines the debates on the Reconstruction laws and amendments. I draw on both primary and secondary sources, of which there are many. Here I reject the conclusions of some recent scholarship, such as that of Raoul Berger and Lino Graglia, and accept, with modifications and extensions, the conclusions of some studies from the 1950s and 1960s.[60]

The Reconstruction Congress probably anticipated, though not necessarily with much optimism, that succeeding Congresses would continue to use vigorously the Section 5 enforcement powers. But we know that they did not; that commitment did not survive the Radicals themselves. By 1876 two of the leaders, Charles Sumner in the Senate and Thaddeus Stevens in the House, were dead, the Confederate states were back in the Union, and the compromise that resolved the contested presidential election ended Reconstruction. The rest of this book focuses not on Congress, but on the courts, which became the enforcers of the Fourteenth Amendment.

Chapter 5 traces the development of constitutional doctrine from the first equal-protection cases to the present, concentrating on the suspect-classification rule. I argue in this chapter that the Court has done exactly the opposite of what such critics as Berger and Graglia accuse it of doing. Instead of going too far, the Court has not gone far enough. It has given the Fourteenth Amendment a narrow, legalistic interpretation rather than the broad one the framers intended, and at times has almost acted as though the amendment's intellectual ancestor were not Jefferson but Calhoun. I examine several decisions that reveal the flaws in the prevailing doctrine, and discover some individual opinions that come closer to the letter and spirit of the Constitution.

Chapters 6 through 9 take up, in turn, each of the issues I have chosen to deal with: reverse discrimination, age, disability, and sexual orientation. I do not try to cover all the case law on these issues, but

[60] See n. 45 above and Chapter 4.

I have emphasized significant and related problems. In each instance my exploration of both the prevailing doctrine and the alternative model has reinforced my suspicion that the latter, however flawed, is the better approach. Chapter 10 is devoted to a new theory of constitutional equality, one that I think is more faithful to the historical commitment to the equal rights of all individuals.

[2]

Equality in the American Context

"Equal," that word on the newborn American tongue, has a long and complicated history. Its source is the Latin *aequus*, which in Cicero's time had several meanings: "level," "even," "impartial," "fair," and "just." *Ex aequo loco loqui*, which is translated literally as "to speak from an equal position," meant "to speak in the Senate," as opposed to *ex inferiore loco*, "in the presence of the judges," and *ex superiore loco*, "in the presence of the people." The English word's record does not begin until sometime between A.D. 1150 and 1350— that gap of over a thousand years is significant—during which time all of those meanings became known. By 1530 it also meant "like" or "identical."

Contemporary English dictionaries typically begin their definitions of "equal" with "the same" or "identical," but none stops there. The definitions go on to include such entries as "uniform in operation or effect: Equal laws" (Random House) and "fair, just: equal laws" (*Webster's Third International*). So equality has something to do with "same," with "just," with "fair," and with law. But it is not clear just what these relationships are.

We reject the notion that these concepts are mutually interchangeable. Few Americans would be comfortable if "the same" were substituted for "equal" in the Declaration of Independence. For humankind has known for a long time that all people are not created the same. Even if we forget conventional legal distinctions, such as those between slave and master or citizen and alien, the fixed, natural differences remain. These differences include, in all societies, those between male and female and between young and old. Some of the differences among human beings, unlike those just mentioned, are inescapably distinctions that imply superiority or inferiority. Some people are stronger, wiser, more virtuous, or more talented than others. Nor is there some Great Balancing Scale that ensures that these differences among people will cancel each other, so that our cumulative grade point averages, so to speak, will be the same. Some people excel in so many characteristics that it is difficult not to label them better people, and the opposite is also true. But talking this way, about superior and inferior people, makes most of us uneasy. All these fixed, if not natural, differences did not long inhibit thinkers from asserting that human beings are equal.

Philosophical Roots of American Equality

How can one reconcile a belief in equality with all these human differences? Felix Oppenheim has written, "To claim that all men are equal in some respects can only mean that the resemblances are in some way more significant that the differences."[1] Many claims for equality have rested on notions about observable similarities. Some examples are the Stoics' belief in reason; John Calvin's belief in an equal capacity for evil, which prompted his distrust of ecclesiastical hierarchy;[2] and Thomas Hobbes's insistence that human beings have an equal passion for power and a roughly equal ability to pursue it (or to pursue it roughly): "Nature hath made man so equal, in the faculties of body and mind . . . [that] when all is reckoned together, the difference between man and man is not so considerable as that one man can thereupon claim to himself any benefit to which another may not pretend as well as he."[3] But even though we are no longer so sure that people are indeed equal in any of these abilities, we have not abandoned the idea of equality.

A look at some relevant works suggests that the resemblances on which arguments for equality depend are often less *qualities* common to all than what might be called possibilities, or better, *entitlements*, whether to divine grace, individual rights, or self-government. In this way, equality becomes linked with fairness and justice, and ultimately becomes, at least, equality under law. All of this might seem to be very

---

[1] "Equality," *International Encyclopedia of the Social Sciences*, 5:102.
[2] See, e.g., Sanford A. Lakoff, *Equality in Political Philosophy* (Cambridge: Harvard University Press, 1964), chap. 2.
[3] Thomas Hobbes, *Leviathan* (1651), pt. 1, chap. 13 (New York: Library of Liberal Arts, 1958), pp. 104–5.

old stuff, and indeed it is. But, as this chapter will show, thinkers have also clung to the idea of equality as capacity, and—particularly as they begin to translate theory into practice—are reluctant to separate equality from judgments of ability. This tension appears early in American history, and it has continued to influence constitutional interpretation up to the present. It is a large part of our present doctrinal problem, but can become part of its solution.

These concepts of equality, fairness, and justice are some of the oldest themes of political philosophy, and they continue to perplex us today. One translation of the *Ethics* renders Aristotle's definition of "just" as "(a) lawful and (b) what is 'equal,' that is, fair."[4] Aristotle goes on to refine these definitions, making it clear that the terms "lawful" and "equal" are far from synonymous (though, interestingly, the terms "equal" and "fair" appear to be), but that they do connect at many points. The *Politics* continues these themes. Although Aristotle was no egalitarian philosopher, arguing as he did that human beings were neither of equal ability nor deserving of equal treatment, his writings do contain a limited notion of equality. Not only does he emphasize proportionate equality, the allotment of equal shares to equals regardless of other differences between them, but his defense of "natural slavery" stresses the nature and the needs of the slave.

> We may thus conclude that all men who differ from others as much as the body differs from the soul, or an animal from a man (and this is the case with all whose function is bodily service, and who produce their best when they supply such service)—all such are by nature slaves, and it is better for them, on the very same principle as in the other cases just mentioned [i.e., animals and females], to be ruled by a master.[5]

"For them": slavery is good primarily for slaves, coincidentally for the master, as patriarchy is good primarily for women and children, coincidentally for the family head. There appears to be an implicit assumption that the needs of women, children, and slaves have equal ranking with those of the master. It would be dangerous to conclude too much from this passage—it does, after all, liken slaves and women to animals, who presumably enjoy no equality—but this passage needs attention because defenses of slavery will be of concern in this book, and because Aristotle's defense of slavery is vastly more humane than some American arguments. Aristotle endorses inegalitarian social ar-

---

[4] *Nicomachean Ethics*, trans. J. A. K. Thompson (Baltimore: Penguin Books, 1955), bk. 5, 1129a35–37, p. 140.

[5] *Politics*, trans. Ernest Barker (New York: Oxford University Press, 1958), bk. 1, chap. 5, sec. 8, p. 13. See also bk. 3, chap. 9, secs. 1–6, pp. 116–17.

rangements, but his defense may arise from an unarticulated premise that each individual has a right to that status which is best for her or him. What is so very vulnerable about his argument is not that premise but the insistence that some people are destined by nature for subjugation.

Whatever Aristotle's premises were, he really cannot be regarded as a forerunner of egalitarian philosophy. I include him not only for his special relevance in American history but also because, on analysis, his philosophy turns out to be less antagonistic to this strain of philosophy than might be supposed. (Interestingly, Jefferson numbered him among his intellectual ancestors.)[6] The Greek and Roman Stoics were the first egalitarian philosophers. They propounded ideas about human equality, especially the capacity to reason, which were antithetical to those of Aristotle and Plato, but even the Stoics had little to say about political arrangements, and later thinkers did not view themselves as their spiritual heirs.[7]

Egalitarian notions permeate early Christian thought, but these writers were uneasy about the relationship, if any, between spiritual equality and social institutions. The New Testament speaks to this issue in "profoundly dualistic" ways.[8] The parable of the laborers in the vineyard compares the kingdom of heaven to a vintner who pays all his laborers the same wage, no matter how long they worked. When the first workers "grumbled . . . saying, 'Those last worked only one hour, and you have made them equal to us who have borne the burden of the day and the scorching heat,'" the owner replied, "Friend, I am doing you no wrong; did you not agree with me for a denarius? Take what belongs to you, and go; I choose to give to this last as I give to you." Jesus concludes, "So the last will be first, and the first last."[9] The Gospels' exhortations to the rich and powerful suggest that this parable was far from being a defense of arbitrary power on the part of owners. A premise of equal respect and concern appears to transcend any notion of proportional reward and to demand equal treatment.

But it is problematical what conclusions, if any, about equality on earth follow from this concept of divine justice. That question is not clarified by a more famous passage: Paul's statement that "there is

[6] Carl Becker, *The Declaration of Independence* (New York: Harcourt, Brace, 1922), p. 26.

[7] See Lakoff, *Equality in Political Philosophy*, chap. 2.

[8] Sanford A. Lakoff, "Christianity and Equality," in J. Roland Pennock and John W. Chapman, eds., *Nomos IX: Equality*, p. 123.

[9] Matt. 20:1–16.

neither Jew nor Greek, there is neither slave nor free, there is neither male nor female, for you are all one in Christ Jesus." [10] Only one of those three paired classifications, "slave" and "free," refers to a difference that is purely conventional. "Jew" and "Greek" might be legal classifications, but they are more likely to refer to fixed ethnic backgrounds; and, of course, "male" and "female" refer to natural, immutable characteristics. Here again it is impossible to draw any conclusions about earthly status. Paul himself, at least, saw no apparent contradiction between this assertion and his equally famous exhortation: "Wives, be subject to your husbands as to the Lord." [11] But certain elements of the Christian tradition, "the unity of all souls in Christ and the equal promise of salvation," are egalitarian in philosophy. [12]

These Greek, Roman, and Christian writings never move in any clear way from notions of human equality to ideas about society and politics. It is not until the Reformation that Christian doctrines of equality shift emphasis from heaven to earth. Martin Luther "offered a view of Christian equality that in a number of ways resembles and presages a modern liberal view." [13] Luther's advocacy of the "priesthood of all believers" derived from his belief that all people were equally capable of achieving salvation, spiritual enlightenment, and virtue. These capacities were more important for him than the differences between sacred and secular vocations stressed by the Catholic hierarchy. [14]

But neither Luther nor any other reformer went so far as to transform an argument for religious equality on earth into one for political equality. That step had to wait until the Puritan Revolution in England. The Levellers, in particular, founded their political philosophy on a belief in spiritual equality similar to Luther's. "By nature," wrote John Lilburne, "all [are] equal and alike in power, dignity, authority, and majesty, none having by nature any authority, dominion, or magisterial power one over or above another." Therefore, "neither have they, or can they exercise any, but merely by . . . mutual agreement or consent." [15] Perhaps the most eloquent statement of Leveller philosophy is contained in Colonel Rainborough's famous response to Ireton

[10] Gal. 3:28.
[11] Eph. 5:22. See also Titus 2:3–5.
[12] Lakoff, "Christianity and Equality," p. 123.
[13] Ibid., p. 128.
[14] Martin Luther, "Open Letter to the Christian Nobility of the German Nation," (1520), in *Three Treatises*, trans. Charles Jacobs (Philadelphia: Fortress Press, 1960), pp. 12–26. See also Lakoff, *Equality in Political Philosophy*, chap. 2. Another good essay on the history of equality is in Robert J. Harris, *The Quest for Equality* (Baton Rouge: Louisiana State University Press, 1960), chap. 1.
[15] "The Freemen's Freedom Vindicated," in A. S. P. Woodhouse, ed., *Puritanism and Liberty* (London: J. M. Dent, 1938), p. 317.

in the Putney debates of 1647. Opposing Ireton's recommendation of property qualifications for voting, Rainborough declared: "For really I think that the poorest he that is in England hath a life to live, as the greatest he; and therefore truly, sir, I think it is clear, that every man that is to live under a government ought first by his own consent to put himself under that Government."[16]

Once this connection between equality and government was made, the principles of the Declaration were in sight. John Locke, writing at about the time of the Restoration, provided a strong link between British and American revolutionary thought, and in the process faced squarely the tension between equality and human differences. Early in the *Second Treatise on Civil Government,* Locke appears to ground equality in human capacity for reason and ability to know natural law, but he does not maintain consistently throughout his writings that human beings are equal in these ways.[17] Indeed, when he asserts a natural, inalienable equality among individuals, he appears to acknowledge the opposite.

> By the statement "all men are by nature equal," I cannot be supposed to understand all sorts of equality. Age or virtue may give men a just precedency; excellence of parts and merit may place others above the common level; birth may subject some, and alliance or benefits others, to pay an observance to those whom nature, gratitude, or other respects may have made it due; and yet all this consists with the equality I there spoke of as being proper to the business at hand, being that *equal right that every man hath to his natural freedom*, without being subjected to the will or authority of any other men.[18]

Here Locke denies that an equal right to freedom depends on an equal endowment of any trait, such a virtue, wisdom, or merit. People vary widely in possession of such excellent attributes, but the equal natural right that Locke propounds is independent of similarities in ability or character. A person is entitled to it by virtue of being human. The law of nature confers an equality on each individual, much as the vintner did in the parable. In a sense, natural rights takes the place, in Locke's thought, that divine grace had in the Gospels. And, inevitably, this equality has compelling consequences for secular authority.

---

[16] Woodhouse, ed., *Puritanism and Liberty*, p. 53.
[17] E.g., chaps. 2.4, 6.63, (1690), ed. Russell Kirk (Chicago: Henry Regnery, 1955), pp. 3, 43. See *Conduct of Understanding* (1697); Lakoff, *Equality in Political Philosophy*, chap. 5.
[18] *Treatise*, 6.54, p. 37.

Equality as Entitlement

Locke and the Puritans provided rhetorical resources that the Americans used extensively in their fight for independence. The Declaration of Independence echoes these themes:

> We hold these truths to be self-evident: that all men are created equal, that they are endowed by their Creator with certain inalienable rights; that among these rights are life, liberty, and the pursuit of happiness; that to secure these rights, governments are instituted among men, deriving their just powers from the consent of the governed; that when any form of government becomes destructive to these ends, it is the right of the people to alter or to abolish it, laying its foundations upon such principles, and organizing its powers in such form, as to them shall be most likely to effect their safety and happiness.

Eloquent, but not original. Years later, John Adams insisted that there was no idea here "but what had been hackneyed in Congress for two years before." But that was what the Declaration was for: not to be original political philosophy, but to express "what everyone was thinking." [19] The crucial elements of the statement are derived from what has gone before. A traditional scholarly analysis—traditional, at least, since the early twentieth century—would go something like this: Human beings are equal because God has made them equal in a certain respect; that is, God has given to each of them, equally, certain specified rights. Certain conclusions about government follow from this equality. Jefferson's "rough draft" of the Declaration (apparently his second draft, which he submitted to the committee of the Continental Congress) spelled out these conclusions: "that all men are created equal and independent, that from that equal creation they derive rights, inherent and inalienable." [20] Until recently, that has been about it, as far as equality is concerned. Carl Becker's *Declaration of Independence*, published in 1922, was acknowledged to be the definitive work on the document, and it "enshrined the Lockean interpretation of its content." [21]

But in 1978 Garry Wills questioned the received Lockean natural rights interpretation. Wills emphasized Locke, too, but it was the Locke of the *Essay on Human Understanding* rather than the *Second Trea-*

---

[19] Becker, *Declaration of Independence*, p. 24.

[20] Ibid., p. 142. See also Julian P. Boyd, *The Declaration of Independence: The Evolution of the Text* (Princeton, N.J.: Princeton University Press, 1945), p. 19; Garry Wills, *Inventing America: Jefferson's Declaration of Independence* (New York: Vintage Books, 1978), Part I.

[21] Wills, *Inventing America*, p. xxiv.

tise, the Enlightenment Locke rather than the "liberal" Locke. Wills argued that Locke's greatest influence on Jefferson and his contemporaries came not through his political theory but through his epistemology and psychology. Not only did Jefferson's writings indicate this intellectual lineage, but Jefferson owed far less to Locke than to some later thinkers who had built on him, most notably three Scots, Thomas Reid, Francis Hutcheson, and David Hume. From these leaders of the English and Scottish Enlightenment, Wills argues, Jefferson gleaned two influential ideas. First was an "egalitarian epistemology": a belief in a common sense, in a faculty of simple perception, which all rational adults possess. Second was a concept of what Hutcheson called a "moral sense," Hume called "moral taste," and Jefferson himself called "a sense of right and wrong." And it was with this ability to make moral judgments that all men were equally endowed.[22]

Wills argues that the natural rights content of Jefferson's thought has been overstressed and the Enlightenment content all but ignored. "All men are created equal" means *not* simply equal in possession of natural rights but equal in moral sense; and it is this moral sense that entitles men to these rights. If Wills is correct, our common understanding of the Declaration is wrong.

Wills is certainly right to refuse to let us neglect a significant part of Jefferson's theory of equality. Jefferson's debt to the great Scottish Enlightenment philosophers is, as Wills argues, evident and profound. As we shall see, it can provide an explanation of aspects of Jefferson's thought that otherwise can only appear self-contradictory. But there is no sound justification for discarding Locke. As Wills himself notes, the *Second Treatise* was much read in the colonies by the time of the Revolution.[23] Furthermore, it is not possible to prove from the number of times a book is mentioned that one mode of thought had more influence than another, on Jefferson or any other writer.[24] What we can conclude from Wills on the one hand and Becker on the other is either that Jefferson believed in an equality of natural rights or an equality in a certain human capacity that was the basis for these rights, or both—or that he never sorted out exactly what he meant by equality. For the purposes of understanding what the word "equal" means in the Constitution, it may not make all that much difference—a puzzling statement I shall later defend.

[22] Ibid., chaps. 12–15. See Jefferson to Peter Carr, August 10, 1787, in Koch and Peden, eds., *Life and Selected Writings*, pp. 429–34.

[23] *Inventing America*, p. 170.

[24] See, e.g., reviews by Edward S. Morgan, *New York Review of Books*, August 17, 1978; Judith N. Shklar, *New Republic*, August 26 and September 2, 1978, pp. 32–34.

The Declaration is the basis for American thought about equality, and it was to shape and influence many of the arguments made long afterward in favor of constitutional change. The idea of equality has wound a long, tortuous path from its beginnings to the American colonists, but certain themes have remained constant: a notion that in some way each person counts for the same as anyone else; that each is equal before God or nature; that each is entitled to some sort of equal ranking or, as Dworkin put it, equal respect and concern. "The poorest he hath a life to live, as the greatest he"; or, in A. D. Lindsay's paraphrase, the stupidest he as the cleverest he.[25] Even Aristotle, who may appear to be keeping strange company in this group, seems to recognize that those he considers inferior have lives to live, as do masters; these lives turn out to differ greatly, but to be based on a reckoning, however wrong, of the needs and interests of the people involved. For all these writers, reflection seems to lead to a premise of a basic entitlement to equal respect and concern. For some, this premise apparently rests on a still deeper premise of equality in some human attribute—reason for the Stoics, grace for the Christians, "moral sense" for the Scots. But the premise is just that—a premise, an *a priori* assumption about human nature rather than any kind of demonstration, let alone proof, that human beings are equal in any capacity. By 1776 this idea was so much a part of American culture that such a statement could be made in a document written to express the unity of "one people."

Philosophy and Society: The Terrible Contradiction

But if, by 1776, that was how people thought, it was not how they lived. Perfect coincidence between ideals and practice is rare, but in colonial America the dissonance was jarring. Actually there was not one contradiction but at least two, one of which is obvious and the other buried in contemporary language.

I have written deliberately of "human beings," but the writers I have discussed usually refer to "men." In the eighteenth century, this word had the same two meanings it has now: the generic one, "human being," as distinguished from other forms of life, and "adult male human being," as distinguished from woman or child. When Rainborough, Locke, or Jefferson argued that men were equal, were they including women?

[25] *The Modern Democratic State* (New York: Oxford University Press, 1962).

Rainborough spoke of "he" who had a right to live, but John Lilburne had written that "every individual man and woman in the world" was descended from Adam and Eve, and thus "all were by nature equal."[26] The colonists did not speak to this question. Perhaps they did not see a question there. The very language in which they thought and wrote obscured it. (We find here, of course, a basis for a powerful argument against the generic use of "man.") And the issue was not forced on them. Feminist thought was barely alive in the 1770s.

In the colonies, only Abigail Adams was putting such thoughts on paper, and she only in her correspondence. Her famous letter to her husband, written while he was attending the Second Continental Congress, three months before the Declaration—"If particular care and attention is not paid to the Ladies we are determined to foment a rebellion"—was ahead of its time; his response—"I cannot but laugh"— was uncharacteristic of their correspondence. The first American feminist tract, Judith Sargent Murray's *On the Equality of the Sexes*, was not published until 1790.[27] The problem disturbs us, but it is futile to look to eighteenth-century American writers for much help.

The second problem was always present, a painful tension for American revolutionaries. This, of course, was the contradiction between the ideals of the Declaration and the institution of slavery. It was almost as old as the colonies themselves. The first shipment of American slaves had landed at Jamestown, Virginia, in 1619, and by 1700 slavery was firmly established in the southern colonies. Revolutionary America had known a century and a half of slavery, and the practice showed no signs of dying out. So there flourished, side by side, an egalitarian natural rights philosophy and an institution antithetical to it.

There were efforts at intellectual reconciliation. A defense of slavery based on Aristotle was not among them; given the Declaration's commitment to natural rights, it would have had some rough going. A few proslavery tracts based a defense of slavery on the notion that blacks were too inferior to enjoy rights, and sometimes went so far as to deny that blacks were fully human, ranking them somewhere between people and apes. But the striking aspect of colonial thought is that there were few proslavery writers. Usually the contradiction between natural rights philosophy and slavery was not explained away, but acknowledged

---

[26] Woodhouse, *Puritanism and Liberty*, p. 317.

[27] Alice S. Rossi, ed., *The Feminist Papers* (New York: Columbia University Press, 1973), pp. 11, 16–24.

and deplored.[28] One historian has gone so far as to suggest that "in retrospect, the pity of antislavery's failure was that in the decade after the Revolution, success against slavery itself seemed almost within reach."[29]

There was that deleted section of the "rough draft" of the Declaration, written by Jefferson and vetted by his committee of editors, proclaiming that King George III "has waged cruel war against human nature itself, violating it's [sic] most sacred rights of life and liberty, in the persons of a distant people who never offended him, captivating and carrying them into slavery in another hemisphere . . . *determined to keep open a market where MEN should be bought and sold,* he has prostituted his negative for suppressing every legislative attempt to prohibit or to restrain this execrable commerce."[30] The king's share of the blame may be doubted; in fact, Wills has suggested that for Jefferson the king's real crime was an attempt to incite insurrection and thus *free* slaves.[31] But the antislavery import of the passage is beyond question.

Jefferson's was not a lonely voice. Vocal opposition to slavery existed by the time of the Revolution—much of it, though not all, from Quakers—and these arguments often relied on natural rights philosophy. The following statements of three pamphleteers are typical. David Cooper wrote that "every individual of the human species by the law of nature comes into the world entitled to freedom at a proper age." Arthur Lee termed slavery a "violation of justice . . . i.e., to give every man his due." John Allen defended "the sacred rights and privileges of the Africans."[32]

These tracts did not stimulate a dialogue with slaveowners. Instead:

> The ideology of the Revolution was, in a very genuine sense, what white men in America were fighting for, and even the more socially conservative gentlemen throughout the new nation—and there were many—felt

---

[28] See Winthrop Jordan, *White over Black: American Attitudes toward the Negro, 1550–1812.* (Chapel Hill: University of North Carolina Press, 1968), chap. 6; Herbert J. Storing, "Slavery and the Moral Foundations of the American Republic," in Robert H. Horwitz, ed., *The Moral Foundations of the American Republic,* 2d ed. (Charlottesville: University Press of Virginia, 1979), pp. 214–33.

[29] Jordan, *White over Black,* p. 374. See also David Brion Davis, *The Problem of Slavery in Western Culture* (Ithaca: Cornell University Press, 1966), pt. 3.

[30] Becker, *Declaration of Independence,* pp. 166–67. Emphasis in the original.

[31] *Inventing America,* pp. 70–75.

[32] David Cooper, "A Mite Cast into the Treasury," 1772; Arthur Lee, "Address on Slavery," 1767; "Watchman's Alarm to Lord N——h," 1774; all in Roger Bruns, ed., *Am I Not a Man and a Brother?: The Anti-slavery Crusade of Revolutionary America, 1688–1788* (New York: Chelsea House, 1977), pp. 187, 108, 335. See also Jordan, *White over Black,* chap. 7.

that slavery must somehow, someday, be brought to an end. Especially in view of the way their grandchildren were talking after 1830, it is important to bear in mind that during the Revolutionary War, despite the virtual absence of antislavery pronouncements in the Lower South and the cautiousness of Virginians on the subject, no one in the South stood up in public to endorse Negro slavery.[33]

It is no news, of course, that social institutions do not necessarily correspond to social ideals. Economics and pragmatics get us further toward understanding the persistence of slavery than philosophy can. But the philosophy itself was not so powerful an antislavery force as it might have been. There were tensions not only between theory and practice but within the theory itself, and those tensions reflect the profound distinction between a notion of equality as capacity and one of equality as entitlement. Many colonists could see that "all men" meant Negroes, too, and that "inalienable rights of life and liberty" meant no slavery. But it was one thing to recognize that logical imperative and another to endorse it.

Perhaps no people could have been eager to admit to full citizenship a group so different from themselves. "The physiognomic distinction would not down." But the difference was not one of appearance alone. To most observers, the vast majority of Negroes seemed grossly inferior to whites in almost every observable human trait; they were "brutish, ignorant, idle, crafty, treacherous, bloody, thievish, mistrustful, and superstitious."[34]

How one interpreted that phenomenon, of course, depended on basic beliefs about human nature. In this era, these beliefs were undergoing drastic change. The Revolutionary period was a critical juncture in the eighteenth-century version of the "nature versus nurture" controversy. Environmentalism was replacing notions of inherent nature as an explanation of human differences. The antislavery version of this argument insisted that the Negroes' deficiencies were the results of the conditions in which they were kept.

For example, Levi Hart of Connecticut declared: "There is no apparent want of capacity in the Negroes in general to conduct their own affairs and provide for themselves, but what is the natural consequence of the servile state they are in and the treatment they receive." Anthony Benezet, an early Quaker opponent of slavery, wrote that in Africa the Negroes were the equals of anyone else. But the force of his observations is weakened by the fact that they are second-

---

[33] Jordan, *White over Black*, p. 304.
[34] Ibid., pp. 278, 281 (quoting Edward Long, *Jamaica*, 2:354).

hand, based on the accounts of others rather than on his own travels; most observers contradicted him.[35] A third explanation comes from Alexander Hamilton, surely a socially conservative gentleman. During the war, while he was Washington's aide-de-camp, he wrote to John Jay, president of the Continental Congress, on the subject of Negroes in combat: "I frequently hear it objected . . . that they are too stupid to make soldiers. This is so far from appearing to me a valid objection that I think their want of cultivation (*for I think their natural faculties are probably as good as ours*) joined to that habit of subordination which they acquire from a life of servitude, will make them sooner become soldiers than our white inhabitants."[36] After the Revolution, both Hamilton and Jay helped found the New York City Manumission Society.

Environmentalist theories appealed to opponents of slavery. When evidence of Negro equality was lacking, they often set out to produce some, and with marked success. Benezet, for example, opened a school, and found Negroes educable. Other activists had similar results. When talented individuals were found—the poets Phillis Wheatley and Ignatius Sancho, for example, and the scientist Benjamin Banneker— their accomplishments were seized upon as evidence of equal abilities.

The order in which these intellectual steps were taken is important. Observers did not conclude from evidence of Negro intelligence, virtue, or any other capacity that slavery violated their natural rights. Instead, they started from natural rights premises and then went looking for evidence of equality. By the century's end, there was enough evidence to provide a basis for challenging the prevailing beliefs about Negro inferiority.[37]

But for many people the dilemma was not so simply solved. This number included Thomas Jefferson himself. He was America's leading natural rights philosopher, and he opposed slavery. The deleted passage from the Declaration is proof of that. For Jefferson, human rights derived from a person's nature as a biological being, and persons included blacks. But he did own slaves throughout his adult life, and he was convinced of the Negro's innate inferiority.

Why he was, and remained, so convinced is a mystery. The environmentalist position was available to him, since many of his contempo-

---

[35] Levi Hart, "Thoughts on Abolition" (1775); Anthony Benezet, *An Account of Guinea* (1771); both in Bruns, ed., *Am I Not a Man*. See Jordan, *White over Black*, p. 282; Davis, *Problem of Slavery*, chap. 15.

[36] Hamilton to Jay, March 14, 1779, in Bruns, *Am I Not a Man*, p. 449. Emphasis supplied.

[37] See Jordan, *White over Black*, chaps. 6 and 7; Davis, *Problem of Slavery*, chap. 15.

raries took it. He himself explained differences between whites and American Indians in environmentalist terms.[38] And during his life-time, some of his conclusions were disproved. But Jefferson's belief in Negro inferiority survived, inconsistent as it was with his philosophy. All his life he held two conflicting ideas in his mind, and through his writings he made it easy for his compatriots to do the same.

Notes on Virginia, written in the early 1780s, was widely read in Jefferson's lifetime. It contains the fullest expression of his racial views. Even outside of slavery, he insisted, the black race was deficient.

> Comparing them by their faculties of memory, reason, and imagination, it appears to me, that in memory they are equal to the whites; in reason much inferior, as I think one could scarcely be found capable of tracing and comprehending the investigations of Euclid; and that in imagination they are dull, tasteless, and anomalous. . . . It will be right to make great allowances for the differences of condition, of education, of conversa-tion, of the sphere in which they move. Many millions of them have been brought to, and born in America. Most of them indeed have been con-fined to tillage, to their own society; yet many have been so situated, they might have availed themselves of the conversation of their masters; many have been brought up to the handicraft arts, and from that circum-stance have always been associated with the whites. Some have been liberally educated. . . . But never yet could I find that a black had uttered a thought above the level of plain narration; never saw even an elemen-tary trait of painting or sculpture.
> . . . I advance it, therefore, as a suspicion only, that the blacks, whether originally a distinct race, or made distinct by time and circumstances, are inferior to the whites in the endowments both of body and mind.[39]

Considering that slaves were often forbidden by law to learn to read and write, this judgment seems both harsh and premature. Further-more, by 1780 a handful of free Negroes, such as the poets Wheatley and Sancho, had shown some degree of the abilities that Jefferson de-nied they possessed. He dismissed them peremptorily. It is possible to sympathize with Jefferson a bit. Neither was a great poet, but their work was at least equal to that of some of their white contemporaries.

The quoted passages give the impression that Jefferson wanted to believe in Negro inferiority. His "suspicion" never changed much, al-though arguments for and evidence of Negro equality proliferated in the years between the *Notes* and his death. His correspondence with Benjamin Banneker is revealing, as it may have been to their contem-poraries, for it was soon published in pamphlet form. Banneker, an

[38] *Notes on Virginia*, Query VI; Koch and Peden, eds., *Life and Selected Writings*, pp. 210–13.
[39] *Notes on Virginia*, Query XIV; *Life and Selected Writings*, pp. 257–58, 262.

astronomer and surveyor who had demonstrated his understanding of Euclid, had sent Jefferson, then secretary of state, a copy of his almanac. Thanking him, Jefferson wrote, "No body wished more than I do to see such proofs as you exhibit, that nature has given to our black brethren, talent equal to those of the other colors of men, and that the appearance of a want of them is owing merely to the degraded condition of their existence."[40] But this statement implies that he needed more proof before changing his views. Jefferson could not reach a resolution of this issue.

Two modern scholars interpret him in sharply different ways. Winthrop Jordan has written that Jefferson

> could not rid himself of the suspicion that the Negro was naturally inferior. If this were indeed the case, it was axiomatic that the Creator had so created the Negro and no amount of education or freedom or any other tinkering could undo the facts of nature. Thus Jefferson suspected that the Creator might have created men unequal, and he could not say this without giving his assertion exactly the same logical force as his famous statement to the contrary. His science-theology rammed squarely into his larger faith, and the result was intellectual wreckage.[41]

Wreckage, maybe, but some wreckage—and well worth a closer examination. Even when a person's thoughts are self-contradictory, the particular contradictions they contain may be of interest. Jefferson's belief in equality did not prevent him from holding contrary beliefs about Negroes. Even though there were good reasons for abandoning these beliefs, he never did so. His belief in equality did, however, prevent him from supporting slavery.

Jefferson's philosophy did not dictate conclusions about the actual abilities of human beings, but it did dictate conclusions about their legal status. Emancipation and separation would be preferable to full citizenship in the new country, but at any rate, men created equal must be free. For the first time, entitlement did not depend on a notion of capacity and similarity.

But maybe it was not wreckage at all. Garry Wills finds no contradiction. His analysis of the *Notes* begins not at the passage just cited, but a few pages later:

> Whether further observation will or will not verify the conjecture that nature has been less bountiful to them in the endowments of the head, I

[40] Jefferson to Banneker, August 30, 1791, in *Life and Selected Writings*, p. 508.
[41] *White over Black*, p. 453. See also Daniel J. Boorstin, *The Lost World of Thomas Jefferson* (New York: Henry Holt, 1948), chap. 2 and pp. 194–98.

believe that, in those of the heart, she will be found to have done them justice. That disposition to theft with which they have been branded, must be ascribed to their situation, and not to any depravity of the moral sense. The man in whose favor no laws of property exist, probably feels himself less bound to respect those made in favor of others . . . we find among them numerous instances of the most rigid integrity, and as many as among their better instructed masters, of benevolence, gratitude, and unshaken fidelity.[42]

Winthrop Jordan agrees that for Jefferson "the 'moral sense' was as fully developed in Negroes as in whites."[43] Where he and Wills differ is about the relative weight Jefferson gave to moral and intellectual faculties. Jordan implicitly attributes to Jefferson the notion that intelligence is the preeminent human capacity. Wills insists that Jefferson, like his Scottish intellectual forebears, ranked "moral sense" as "the faculty that gives man his unique dignity, that grounds his rights, that makes him self-governing."[44] Again, if Wills is right, we must revise our thinking about Jefferson. Belief in the intellectual inferiority of blacks would be compatible with the great principles of the Declaration, for intelligence is not the primary human trait.

It cannot be said that Wills, relying heavily as he does on extrapolations from the Scots and on quotations from Jefferson's personal, and sometimes flirtatious, letters, has proved his case.[45] But Jordan does not prove his, either. Trying to resolve this question of interpretation would be less useful than examining the passage just quoted to see what can be learned from it.

The mode of reasoning here is similar to that in the discussion of Negro intelligence. What differs is that suddenly Jefferson has become an environmentalist. Unwilling to discount nature as a cause of intellectual deficiencies, he is ready to discount it in the case of observed moral deficiency, that is, theft. Indeed, Jefferson sweeps away empirical evidence of moral incapacity as vigorously as he sweeps aside similar evidence of intellectual capacity. That, as Jordan points out, appears inconsistent.[46] Indeed, whenever I use the *Notes* in classes in American political theory, some keen-eyed student makes this point, as it was made in classes I attended as a student.

The criticism is less than devastating. There is no reason to assume

---

[42] Koch and Peden, eds., *Life and Selected Writings*, pp. 260–61.
[43] *White over Black*, p. 439.
[44] *Inventing America*, p. 227.
[45] See, e.g., Jefferson to Maria Cosway, October 12, 1786, in Koch and Peden, eds., *Life and Selected Writings*, pp. 395–407; Wills, *Inventing America*, chaps. 13–15.
[46] *White over Black*, p. 439.

that intelligence and morality are the same *kinds* of capacities; one may be subject to environmental influences and the other not. But the criticism is not answered simply by the assertion that Jefferson thought virtue more important than brains. No conclusion follows from that rank ordering about the effect of personal situations. The most striking contradiction is the different treatment Jefferson gives to evidence of intelligence and evidence of virtue. Just as he seems to want to believe that Negroes are less intelligent than whites, he seems to want to believe that they are as moral. In each case, he discounts conflicting evidence.

If equality in moral sense was what mattered to Jefferson, why did he need to believe that Negroes possessed it? Like opponents of slavery who searched for evidence of Negro intelligence, Jefferson searched, although not so hard, for evidence of virtue. His assumptions seemed to dictate his findings, not his findings his conclusions. He could not show—any more than Hume or Hutcheson could—that such equality existed. He assumed it existed. Whether Jefferson's belief in equality came from his concept of moral sense or his ideas about divine intention, the crux of the Declaration, for our purposes, is, first, that the belief is derived from a preconceived assumption, and second, that this equality entails individual rights that preclude slavery. If Jordan is right and Jefferson has contradicted himself, his belief in an equality of entitlement was so strong that it was independent of his beliefs about abilities. If Wills is right and Jefferson was consistent, his belief in equal virtue was so strong that it led him to discount evidence to the contrary. The two scholars cannot both be right, but here it may not matter who is right.

The Constitution of 1787

If the new nation had indeed taken action to end slavery, a logical place to start would have been the constitutional convention in Philadelphia in 1787. The issue was raised, but just barely. We have no evidence that delegates discussed the merits of slavery until three months into the meetings. In August, as they considered a preliminary draft constitution, two delegates did attack slavery, although their optimism about the possibility of success is open to question.

Gouverneur Morris of Pennsylvania objected to the inclusion of slave populations in apportioning seats in the House of Representatives among the states. He had made this objection before, but now he made a speech. As James Madison records it. "He never would concur

in upholding slavery. It was a nefarious institution—It was the curse
of heaven on the states where it prevailed. . . . Upon what principle is
it that the slaves shall be computed in the representation? Are they
men? Then make them citizens and let them vote. Are they property?
Why then is no other property included?"[47] His motion to delete the
clause failed, with no real debate.

Two weeks later, Luther Martin of Maryland provoked a little more
reaction by recommending the prohibition of further importation,
calling slavery "inconsistent with the principles of the Revolution and
dishonorable to the American character."[48] The nature of the ensuing
discussion is striking. One anthologist called it "the most strident debate of the Convention," but Madison's notes give no impression of
stridency.[49]

Only George Mason, from Virginia of all places, agreed with Martin. His opponents did not engage him on the merits of the issue and
try to resolve the inconsistency for him. In one way or another, some
dismissed moral questions as inapposite. John Rutledge of South Carolina declared, "Religion and humanity had nothing to do with the
question. Interest alone is the governing principle with Nations—The
true question at present is whether the Southern states shall or shall
not be parties to the Union. If the Northern states consult their interest, they will not oppose the increase of slaves which will increase the
commodities of which they will become the carriers."[50]

Oliver Ellsworth of Connecticut did not find moral principles irrelevant for government in general, only for a national government in
this particular. "The morality or wisdom of slavery are considerations
belonging to the States themselves." The convention then voted to permit "the Migration or Importation of such persons as any of the States
now existing shall think proper to admit," though in the final draft
this license was extended only to 1808. In addition to this and the
three-fifths clause, the Constitution contained a provision that "any
person bound to Service or Labor" who fled across state lines should
be returned to the master.[51] It passed without recorded debate.

This record leaves the impression of a collective wish to drop the
slavery issue as quickly as possible. It was that volatile. Whether or
not the differences between North and South were reconcilable at that

[47] Max Farrand, ed., *The Records of the Federal Convention of 1787*, rev. ed. (New
Haven: Yale University Press, 1966), 2:221–22 (August 8). See also 1:588 (July 11).
[48] Ibid., 2:364–65 (August 21).
[49] Bruns, ed., *Am I Not a Man*, p. 522.
[50] Farrand, ed., *Records*, 2:364 (August 21).
[51] Ibid., pp. 364, 371, 577; see also remarks of Baldwin of Georgia and Gerry of
Massachusetts, pp. 370–72.

point, no one wanted to risk a try. The chance for abolition, if one had ever existed, was lost. The record shows, too, how easy it was becoming to disattend to the issue by defusing the responsibility for slavery. Jefferson had tried to blame the king, and been edited. Now Ellsworth insisted that the issue was for the states to decide. Morris' and Martin's angry no was met not with a deeply felt yes, but with "It's always been this way," "Government is not based on morality," and "It's up to the states to decide." But chiefly with silence.

So by 1787 slavery had provoked intense opposition and tacit support. But in order to survive, entrenched institutions do not need defenders who match their opponents in intensity. So slavery endured, but the questions were not put to rest. In the next seventy years, the abolitionist movement—the nation's first great civil rights struggle— would return again and again to the principles of the Declaration. In this conflict, a proslavery reaction developed, and the issue was joined more clearly. The courts, after preliminary skirmishes, took the proslavery side. Ultimately the theory of natural rights and the institution of slavery could not coexist. After a great civil war, the victors wrote their theory into the Constitution. The history and context of that great change are the subjects of the next chapter.

[3]

The Roots of
Equal Protection

The Civil War amendments grew out of the conflict between the ideals of the Declaration and the institution of slavery. The Fourteenth Amendment, in particular, was not born from the war alone. Many of the men who enacted it had been involved in, or sympathetic to, the abolitionist cause. Their arguments and rhetoric were continuous with prewar attacks on the constitutionality of slavery. And as the opponents of slavery gained political strength, proslavery reaction set the issues into sharp relief. The antagonistic positions were defined still more clearly by Supreme Court decisions that came down on the proslavery side and weakened the chances of compromise. Finally, out of thirty years of increasingly polarized opinion, there emerged what became the theoretical foundations of the equal-protection clause.

The Anti-Slavery Movement

The following discussion is not intended as an argument that the Civil War was fought over political philosophy. I am concerned here with the roots not of the war itself but of a particular consequence of that war, an amendment to the Constitution. This particular investigation inevitably leads into political philosophy. There exists strong agreement among constitutional historians that the Fourteenth

Amendment had its origins in the antislavery movement.[1] And as one of them wrote, "from first to last the campaign against slavery was one predicated on Lockean theories of government."[2] Theory was a potent weapon in the arguments against slavery and, ultimately, for a constitutional amendment.

Antislavery feeling continued to grow after the Constitution was ratified. By 1804, all states north of Maryland had forbidden slavery. Congress forbade further importation of slaves in 1808, as soon as it constitutionally could. In the South, local antislavery societies managed to persuade some owners to free their slaves, but not enough to make much of a difference. Many people had hoped that slavery would die out after importation was stopped, but the institution thrived in the Deep South's plantation economy.[3]

Abolition of slavery in their own states did not long satisfy the opponents. Apparently they held a view of themselves in relation to the national government that did not exactly coincide with Oliver Ellsworth's states'-rights view in 1787. At any rate, most historians date the national movement from the early 1830s.[4] Two significant events were the founding of William Lloyd Garrison's newspaper, *The Liberator*, in 1831, and the founding of the American Anti-Slavery Society in 1833. For the next thirty years, the movement's main arguments depended on the principles of the Declaration.[5]

[1] See, e.g. John P. Frank and Robert F. Munro, "The Original Understanding of 'Equal Protection of the Laws,'" *Columbia Law Review* 50 (February 1950):131–69; Howard Jay Graham, *Everyman's Constitution* (Madison: State Historical Society of Wisconsin, 1968); Alfred H. Kelly, "The Fourteenth Amendment Reconsidered: The Segregation Question," *Michigan Law Review* 54 (June 1956):1049–86; Jacobus ten Broek, *Equal under Law*, rev. ed. (London: Collier, 1965); Louis Warsoff, *Equality and the Law* (New York: Liveright, 1938).

[2] Graham, *Everyman's Constitution*, p. 302.

[3] See Mary Stoughton Locke, *Anti-Slavery in America, 1619–1808* (Gloucester, Mass.: Peter Smith, 1965), chaps. 5 and 6; Alice D. Adams, *The Neglected Period of Anti-Slavery in America, 1808–1831* (Gloucester, Mass.: Peter Smith, 1964,) chap. 1.

[4] The chronological gap here is best filled by Adams, *Neglected Period*, chaps. 22–22.

[5] Among many primary and secondary sources, these are valuable: those cited in nn. 1 and 3; Gilbert Hobbs Barnes, *The Antislavery Impulse, 1830–1844* (New York: Harcourt, Brace & World, 1933); Gilbert Hobbs Barnes and Dwight L. Dumond, eds., *Letters of Theodore Dwight Weld, Angelina Grimké Weld, and Sarah Grimké, 1822–1844* (New York: Da Capo Press, 1970), vols. 1 and 2; Martin Duberman, ed., *The Antislavery Vanguard: New Essays on the Abolitionists* (Princeton: Princeton University Press, 1965); Dwight L. Dumond, *Antislavery Origins of the Civil War in the United States* (Ann Arbor: University of Michigan Press, 1959), chap. 3; Dwight L. Dumond, ed., *Letters of James G. Birney, 1831–1857* (Gloucester, Mass.: Peter Smith, 1966), vol. 1; William Goodell, *Slavery and Antislavery* (New York, 1853); George W. F. Mellen, *An Argument on the Unconstitutionality of Slavery* (Boston: Saxton & Pierce, 1841); Russell B. Nye, *Fettered Freedoms: Civil Liberties and the Slavery Controversy, 1830–*

The rhetoric of the national movement of the 1830s, 1840s, and 1850s echoes some of the themes of the founding period. Religious arguments continued to play a significant part, and religious leaders were prominent. Indeed, in the early 1830s the antislavery case was made chiefly in terms of religious revivalism. Evangelical Protestant clergy and seminary students from schools in Ohio, and such figures as Theodore Dwight Weld, the great revivalist minister from upstate New York, joined the Quakers in their opposition.[6] Grass-roots evangelists spread through the northern states the word of "the enormity of slavery as a sin against God and man."[7]

Such appeals were persuasive enough to mobilize latent antislavery sentiment, spurring the development of the "Free Soil" movement.[8] But as the movement matured, arguments focused increasingly on the Declaration. Here again abolitionists echoed the eighteenth-century pamphleteers in emphasizing the "self-evident truths" of natural equality and inalienable rights. Another similarity was reliance on environmentalist theories of human nature, the recurrence of arguments that "the widely assumed Negro inferiority sprang not from real differences in racial or biological or psychological endowments but from sheer lack of social and educational opportunities."[9]

What was new about nineteenth-century rhetoric was that it came to invoke not only faith and principle, but constitutional law as well. By 1848, three distinct abolitionist positions had emerged with respect to slavery and the federal Constitution.[10] One was typified by Garrison's famous description of that document as "a covenant with Death and an agreement with Hell": that the Constitution was, among worse

---

1860 (East Lansing: Michigan State College Press, 1949), chap. 6; Lysander Spooner, *The Unconstitutionality of Slavery* (Boston: Bela Marsh, 1853), chap. 5; John L. Thomas, ed., *Slavery Attacked: The Abolitionist Crusade* (Englewood Cliffs, N.J.: Prentice-Hall, 1965); Joel Tiffany, *A Treatise on the Unconstitutionality of Slavery* (1859) (Miami: Mnemosyne, 1969), chap. 2. Any historian will realize that these citations, and others in this chapter, only skim the surface. The literature on the abolitionist movement is vast, rich, and contentious, and I have not attempted to cover all of it. I am concerned with tracing a particular part of that movement in its relation to the Fourteenth Amendment.

[6]See Barnes, *Antislavery Impulse*, chaps. 1–8.

[7]*Proceedings of the Ohio Anti-Slavery Convention* (New York: Putnam, 1835), pp. 10–11, quoted in Graham, *Everyman's Constitution*, p. 173.

[8]Graham, *Everyman's Constitution*; Barnes and Dumond, eds., *Weld-Grimké Letters*; Thomas, ed., *Slavery Attacked*, pt. 2.

[9]Graham, *Everyman's Constitution*, p. 172. See also T. D. Weld to Lewis Tappan, February 22, 1836, in Barnes and Dumond, eds., *Weld-Grimké Letters*, 1:263–66; David Brion Davis, *Problem of Slavery in Western Culture*.

[10]The following discussion draws mainly from Goodell, *Slavery and Antislavery*, and Aileen Kraditor, *Means and Ends in American Abolitionism* (New York: Pantheon, 1967), chap. 7.

things, a proslavery document. Other abolitionists, such as Wendell Phillips, based this conclusion on such provisions as the three-fifths compromise of Article I, Section 2, the migration or importation clause in Section 9 of that article, and the provision for extradition of fugitive slaves in Article IV, Section 2. This group argued for constitutional amendment or, in Garrison's case, for dissolution.[11]

A second theory acknowledged the import of these provisions but insisted that the Constitution was antislavery in spirit. These "coalitionalists" sought to weaken slavery by securing the passage of federal laws rather than to change the Constitution.

Now, over a hundred years since amendments decided the issue, these two interpretations of the pre–Civil War Constitution seem realistic but obsolescent. They need not detain us long. It is the third abolitionist interpretation that is the most important for understanding the Fourteenth Amendment. This was the argument that the Constitution already forbade slavery.

In the 1830s and 1840s, this doctrine was propounded mainly by Weld himself; by two early associates of his, William Goodell and Gerrit Smith; by Alvan Stewart, a lawyer from upstate New York; by James G. Birney, a former slaveholder from Alabama; and by Lysander Spooner. Spooner, in fact, once wrote that the abolitionists would gain overwhelming support in the North if they could prove that slavery was unconstitutional.[12] If this prediction was overoptimistic, the attention devoted to constitutional arguments indicates that many writers agreed with Spooner.

With skill and imagination, these activists used nearly every possible mode of constitutional interpretation. Several writers showed a flair for constitutional exegesis which would do credit to contemporary interpretivists. Stewart and Birney, for example, both interpreted the due-process clause of the Fifth Amendment to forbid slavery:

> Many other essential rights are secured in this same article, to the citizen ... but the most essential is the one which forbids "ANY PERSON BEING DEPRIVED OF HIS LIFE, LIBERTY, OR PROPERTY, WITHOUT DUE PROCESS OF LAW." ... And on this subject, it is believed no lawyer in this country or England, who is worthy of the appellation, will deny that the true and only meaning of the phrase, "due process of law", is an indictment or

[11] *Review of Lysander Spooner's Essay on the Unconstitutionality of Slavery* (1847) (New York: Arno Press and New York Times, 1969), p. 26; Henry Bowditch, *Slavery and the Constitution* (Boston, 1849), chap. 12, in Thomas, ed., *Slavery Attacked*, pp. 117–19; and in the Thomas book, see pp. 76–79, 87–93.
[12] Kraditor, *Means and Ends*, p. 195.

presentment by a grand jury . . . ; a trial by a petit jury of twelve men, and judgment pronounced on the finding of the jury by a court.[13]

Stewart was writing in 1837, four years after *Barron v. Baltimore* ruled that the Fifth Amendment was not binding on the states.[14] Since it was the states, not the federal government, that maintained slavery, it would seem difficult to argue that the due-process clause had any bearing on the issue. But these writers did not defer to precedent. They continued to insist that the Bill of Rights, with which slavery is obviously incompatible, imposed positive duties on the states.[15]

These activists were no more bound by clause or text than by precedent. They refused to read the text in isolation from what they saw at its context. They frequently invoked the Preamble, which included justice and liberty among the goals of the new nation. Even more often they derived constitutional arguments from the Declaration. Such writers as Birney, Goodell, Spooner, and Joel Tiffany insisted that the Declaration was part of the Constitution. Some abolitionists even argued that the Declaration itself had legally abolished slavery.[16]

Birney discussed the connection in a footnote to an 1847 pamphlet. The Declaration, he wrote,

> is said not to be as obligatory on us as the Constitution, if obligatory at all. That it is not, in the same way, as obligatory as the Constitution, is readily admitted . . . [but] if after achieving our independence under the Declaration, we had voluntarily established a government entirely at variance with the sentiments we had published to the world . . . our national character would have been looked on as partaking of deceit. We are bound, then, as a nation—as much as a nation can be bound to others—*by our honor*—never to ordain any thing that shall be grossly contrary to the truths which were in our mouths, when we took our seat among the congregation of nations.[17]

So America was obligated, by its statement to the world, to incorporate, or at the very least not to traduce, the ideas of the Declaration

[13] Alvan Stewart, "A Constitutional Argument on the Subject of Slavery" (1837), reprinted in ten Broek, *Equal under Law*, pp. 282–83. Emphasis in the original. See also Graham, *Everyman's Constitution*, p. 170; Dumond, ed., *Birney Letters*, vol. 1, Introduction.

[14] 32 U.S. 243 (1833).

[15] Graham, *Everyman's Constitution*; ten Broek, *Equal under Law*, pp. 77–88, 223–24.

[16] See, e.g., ten Broek, *Equal under Law*, pp. 72–73; James G. Birney, "Can Congress, under the Constitution, Abolish Slavery in the States?" (1847), in ibid., pp. 302–3; T. D. Weld, "The Power of Congress over Slavery in the District of Columbia" (1836), in ibid., p. 256; Mellen, *Argument*, chap. 3; Spooner, *Unconstitutionality of Slavery*. See Dumond, *Antislavery Origins*, pp. 76–77.

[17] "Can Congress," p. 304n. Emphasis in the original.

in any organic document. The words of the Declaration itself had imposed this obligation. Not only was the Declaration, in effect, part of the Constitution, but, *a fortiori*, so were the principles of natural law which it expressed. Men were equal, and endowed with rights, under the United States Constitution; therefore, slavery violated it.[18]

Here is Weld, in 1836, urging Congress to abolish slavery in the District of Columbia:

> Congress has unquestionable power to adopt the Common Law, as its legal system, within its exclusive jurisdiction. . . . THE COMMON LAW KNOWS NO SLAVES. . . . By adopting the common law within its exclusive jurisdiction Congress would carry out the principles of our glorious Declaration, and follow the highest precedents in our national history and jurisprudence. . . . Who needs to be told that slavery makes war upon the principles of the Declaration, and the spirit of the Constitution, and that these and the principles of the common law gravitate toward each other with irrepressible affinities, and mingle into one.[19]

Antislavery constitutional doctrine did just what most disturbs contemporary jurists: it found ideas of justice and natural law in the Constitution. And it was with this strain of constitutional theory that several framers of the Fourteenth Amendment were most familiar and most comfortable. Some powerful members of the Thirty-ninth Congress had been associated with Weld, Birney, or their followers. Ten of the fifteen members of the Joint Committee on Reconstruction, which wrote the amendment, came from abolitionist states, where they were at least exposed to these arguments. Such influential committee members as Senators Jacob Howard of Michigan, Justin Morrill of Vermont, and William Pitt Fessenden of Maine represented abolitionist strongholds. Representative Thaddeus Stevens of Pennsylvania had been "converted" to the antislavery cause by a group of Weld's protégées.[20] John Bingham of Ohio, another House appointee to the committee and the amendment's chief author, combined the due-process and natural law arguments in a speech in Congress on February 11, 1859, that well illustrates his influential ideas.

Bingham was opposing the admission of Oregon as a state. His opposition was based on the territorial constitution, which prohibited free Negroes from holding property, making contracts, or bringing suits. These provisions, he insisted, violated the federal Constitution.

---

[18] A good discussion of this argument is contained in Robert M. Cover, *Justice Accused: Antislavery and the Judicial Process* (New Haven: Yale University Press, 1975), chap. 9.

[19] "Power of Congress," pp. 255–56. Emphasis in the original.

[20] See Graham, *Everyman's Constitution*, pp. 236, 301–2, 313.

Therefore, the supremacy clause of Article VI prohibited Congress from voting Oregon into the Union, and thus implicitly sanctioning the limitation. The controversy over Oregon had little to do with slavery, but the range of Bingham's argument was wide.

> Sir, if the persons thus excluded from the right to maintain any suit in the state of Oregon were not citizens of the United States; if they were not natives born of free parents within the limits of the Republic, I should oppose this bill; because I say that a State which, in its fundamental law, denies to any person, or to a large class of persons, a hearing in her courts of justice, ought to be treated as an outlaw, unworthy [of] a place in the sisterhood of the Republic. A suit is the legal demand of one's right, and the denial of this right by the judgement of the American Congress is to be sanctioned as law! But, sir, I maintain that the persons thus excluded from the State by this section of the Oregon constitution, are citizens by birth of the several states, and therefore are citizens of the United States, and as such are entitled to all of the privileges and immunities which are the rights of life and liberty and property; and their due protection in the enjoyment thereof by law; and therefore I hold this section for their exclusion from the State and its courts, to be an infraction of that wise and essential provision of the national Constitution ... "The citizens of each state, shall be entitled to all privileges and immunities of citizens IN THE SEVERAL STATES."

Bingham went on to make some crucial distinctions. Equality was different from capacity. Equality did not entitle Negroes to the right to vote, for example:

> Nobody proposes or dreams of political equality any more than of physical or mental equality. It is as impossible for men to establish equality in these respects as it is for "The Ethiopian to change his skin." Who would say that all men are equal in stature, in weight, and in physical strength; or that all are equal in natural mental force, or in intellectual acquirements? Who, on the other hand, will be bold enough to deny that all persons are equally entitled to the enjoyment of the rights of life and liberty and property; and that no one should be deprived of life or liberty, but as punishment for crime; nor of his property, against his consent and without due compensation?

No one might have been that bold at the 1787 convention, or in 1791, when the Bill of Rights was ratified. By the time Bingham spoke, many of his listeners were prepared to make just that denial with respect to slaves, and he knew it. But he was not ready to yield the floor. He hammered his points home:

> ... I cannot, and will not, consent that the majority of any republican state may, in any way, rightfully restrict the humblest citizen of the United

States in the free exercise of any one of his natural rights; those rights common to all men, and to protect which, not to confer, all good governments are instituted; and the failure to maintain which inviolate furnishes a sufficient cause for the abrogation of such government; and, I may add, imposes a necessity for such abrogation, to the construction of the political fabric on a juster basis, with surer safeguards.

. . . The equality of all to the right to live; to the right to know; to argue and to utter, according to conscience; to work and enjoy the product of their toil, is the rock on which that Constitution rests—its sure foundation and defense. . . . The charm of that Constitution lies in the great democratic idea which it embodies, that all men, before the law, are equal in respect of those rights of person which God gives and no man or state may rightfully take away. . . . Before your constitution, sir, as it is, as I trust it ever will be, all men are sacred, whether white or black, rich or poor, wise or simple.[21]

All this is pure Locke, and, at least to pre-Wills understanding, pure Jefferson. Bingham's language echoes the Declaration at several points. His speech included a long discussion of political rights and of his distinction between equality in political rights and equality in what Jefferson called the endowments of body and mind. Bingham's analogy, referring as it does to black people, is telling, perhaps more telling than he realizes. He makes it clear that equality does not depend on capacity, but on divine endowment. People are equal because they were made that way, though there are extreme inequalities among human beings in almost every attribute.

Bingham still held these views at the end of the Civil War, and he wrote them into a draft of an amendment he conceived of as "declaratory" of what was already in the Constitution.[22] This thesis was derived from what had gone before: from the arguments of Weld, Birney, Stewart, and the others, from the notion that the Constitution embodied the Declaration and its principles.

Bingham made that speech just two years before the war began. By then this antislavery argument had been twenty years in the making. During that time, proslavery reaction had produced arguments about humankind and about government which predictably stood in clear contradiction to those I have been examining. If the abolitionists had a theory, the South produced an antitheory, and these two arguments continue to influence and to confound our thinking about equality.

---

[21] *Congressional Globe*, 35th Cong., 2d sess., pp. 984–85. Emphasis in the original.
[22] Graham, *Everyman's Constitution*, chap. 7; ten Broek, *Equal under Law*, pp. 209–11.

The Southern Antitheory

Ultimately, people did stand up to endorse slavery. And many of them argued intelligently and lucidly. Proslavery thought divides itself into two chronological phases, which may be called the moderate and the extreme.[23] In fact, it might reasonably be suggested that these were the second and third phases, and that the first, in the 1770s and 1780s, was a latent or dormant phase. If so, the three phases correspond roughly to the vigor and effectiveness of the opposition. The harder the attack, the stronger became the defense.

Up to the 1830s, most defenders of slavery stressed moderation and compromise, and focused more on discussion of various means of gradual emancipation than on a positive endorsement of slavery itself. The change in tone and content was not due solely to the new antislavery militancy. An important turning point was the debates in the Virginia legislature in the winter of 1831–32, in which several proposals, including one for expatriation, were defeated. Thomas R. Dew, a professor at the College of William and Mary, published a review of the debates which contains the last of the moderate proslavery arguments. Defending the legislature's failure to act, Dew dwelt on the prohibitive cost of deporting the ex-slaves, of shifting from slave to free labor, and of compensating former masters (all parties assumed that compensation would be necessary, whatever policy was chosen). A minor theme is the danger of inciting slave insurrection by building false hopes. Only after developing these points at some length did Dew make this revealing statement:

> It is said slavery is wrong, in the *abstract* at least, and contrary to the spirit of Christian principles. To this we answer as before, that any question must be determined by its circumstances, and if, as really is the case, we cannot get rid of slavery without producing a greater injury to both the masters and slaves, there is no rule of conscience or revealed law of God which *can* condemn us. The physician will not order the spreading cancer to be extirpated, although it will eventually cause the death of his patient, because he would thereby hasten the fatal issue.[24]

Except for that passage, Dew and the abolitionists were arguing past one another. If there is something cold-blooded about a defense

[23] See, e.g., Avery Craven, *The Coming of the Civil War* (New York: Charles Scribner's Sons, 1942), chap. 7; Dumond, *Antislavery Origins*; William Sumner Jenkins, *Pro-Slavery Thought in the Old South* (Chapel Hill: University of North Carolina Press, 1935); Eric L. McKitrick, ed., *Slavery Defended: The Views of the Old South* (Englewood Cliffs, N.J.: Prentice-Hall, 1963), p. 202.

[24] "Review of the Debate in the Virginia Legislature," in McKitrick, ed., *Slavery Defended*, p. 31. Emphasis in the original.

of oppression couched primarily in terms of profit and loss, it is not a type of argument with which twentieth-century Americans can claim to be unfamiliar. At any rate, "cancer" was not a metaphor for slavery that appealed to later southern writers. From the 1830s to the Civil War, the defenses became more aggressive. Three writers typical of this period are George Fitzhugh and Edmund Ruffin of Georgia and one of America's most eminent political thinkers, John C. Calhoun of South Carolina.

The debate over slavery ranged over every issue that had any relation to it. No legal, political, moral, biblical, social, psychological, economic, or practical argument that could advance either side was ignored, and no argument was left unanswered, although apparently neither side deigned to read the other.[25] The proslavery response to abolitionist constitutional theory belongs to the last, militant phase of the debate. A response it is, indeed; it attacks the core of that theory, its reliance on the Declaration of Independence. Thus, as the abolitionists give us a theory of equal protection, the southerners give us an antitheory.

Fitzhugh and Calhoun, in particular, squarely confronted the theory. They did not try to reconcile slavery with the Declaration—no one ever had any success with that enterprise—nor did they make a literalist argument that the Declaration was not part of the Constitution. Instead, they denied the Declaration's "self-evident" truths. Calhoun put it this way:

> It is a great and dangerous error to suppose that all people are equally entitled to liberty. It is a reward to be earned, not a blessing to be gratuitously lavished on all alike—a reward reserved for the intelligent, the patriotic, the virtuous and deserving;—and not a boon to be bestowed on a people too ignorant, degraded and vicious, to be capable either of appreciating or of enjoying it. Nor is it any disparagement to liberty, that such is, or ought to be the case. On the contrary, its greatest praise,—its proudest distinction is, that an all-wise providence has reserved it, as the noblest and highest reward for the development of our faculties, moral and intellectual. . . .
>
> These great and dangerous errors have had their origin in the prevalent opinion that all men are born free and equal;—than which nothing can be more unfounded and false. It rests upon the assumption of a fact, which is contrary to universal observation, in whatever light it may be regarded. It is, indeed, difficult to explain how an opinion so destitute of all sound reason, ever could have been so extensively entertained.[26]

[25] Dumond, *Antislavery Origins*; Clement Eaton, *Freedom of Thought in the Old South* (New York: Peter Smith, 1951).
[26] *A Disquisition on Government*, in *The Works of John C. Calhoun*, vol. I, ed. Richard K. Crallé (Columbia, S.C.: A. S. Johnston, 1851), pp. 52, 55–57.

Thus men are neither created equal nor endowed with natural rights. Any human rights have to be earned, by wisdom, virtue, loyalty, industry, or some combination of these qualities. Apparently these rights are earned not by individuals, but by racial groups; it seems to follow that all whites in America enjoy rights, and no blacks do—at least, no slaves. And apparently the degree of merit needed to earn them is that already displayed by whites, or at least by adult male whites. But the important point to be gleaned from Calhoun is that there was a clear split between those like him, who viewed equality as an earned attribute, and those like Bingham, who regarded it as a given entitlement. That strain of American political thought which emphasizes similarities and abilities appears to belong not to the framers of the Fourteenth Amendment, but to their enemies, and thus to be an antitheory to the theory.

Slavery and Rights in the Supreme Court

William Lloyd Garrison was often accused of being extreme and unrealistic in his views on the Constitution. But ultimately he was proved right, on two counts. First, the pre–Civil War Constitution did support slavery. Second, abolition could not be achieved under this Constitution through accommodation and compromise.[27] It is customary to assign much of the blame for those two developments to the Supreme Court, specifically to its decision in *Dred Scott* v. *Sandford*. That ruling, as we shall see, did indeed go to unnecessary extremes. But two earlier decisions had greater impact. The first, *Barron* v. *Baltimore*, had nothing whatever to do with slavery. But at least for the precedent-bound, it destroyed the one solid textual argument the antislavery movement had. The second case was *Prigg* v. *Pennsylvania*, decided in 1842. These decisions indicate that experienced judges, applying their education, expertise, and lawyerly outlook to the question, were likely to reach only one result, no matter how they personally felt about slavery.[28]

The one constitutional provision that appeared, on its face, absolutely to forbid slavery was the due-process clause of the Fifth Amendment. It is hard to improve on Stewart here. American slavery was a deprivation of liberty without due process of law. *Barron* v. *Baltimore*

[27] See Kraditor, *Means and Ends*, chap. 7.
[28] 60 U.S. 393 (1857); 32 U.S. 243 (1833); 41 U.S. 539. See Cover, *Justice Accused*, pp. 238–56.

concerned another part of this amendment, but its principles applied to the Bill of Rights in general. Barron, a wharf owner whose property had been rendered worthless when the city had diverted streams, claimed that his property had been taken without just compensation. But Chief Justice John Marshall, speaking as usual for a unanimous Court, declared that the Bill of Rights was binding on Congress alone, not on states or localities. The First Amendment did seem to demand that conclusion ("Congress shall make no law . . ."), but the rest of the Bill of Rights, including the Fifth Amendment, was worded in the passive voice, so that it was not clear whose powers they restricted. Marshall, however, insisted that when the Constitution meant to restrict the states, it said so clearly, as in Article I, Section 10: "No state shall . . . pass any Bill of Attainder, ex post facto Law, or Law impairing the Obligation of Contracts." Otherwise, prohibitions referred only to the federal government, however they were phrased, as in Article I, Section 9: "No Bill of Attainder or ex post facto Law shall be passed."[29] Whatever the merits of this mode of construction (which would, incidentally, leave the states free to deny writs of habeas corpus), it also applied to the due-process clause. If the states were not bound by that clause, no challenge to slavery could be made on those grounds.

Nine years later, in *Prigg*, the Court ruled unanimously in favor of a slave owner. Seven of the nine justices wrote opinions. Some did go to extremes—and the extremes boded ill for future years—but extremists and moderates all voted the same way.

Margaret Morgan, owned by Margaret Ashmore of Maryland, had escaped to Pennsylvania. Edward Prigg, Ashmore's lawyer, got a warrant from a Pennsylvania magistrate, captured Morgan, and took her before the same magistrate, who refused to order her extradition. (As will become clear, this apparently irrational judicial behavior was justifiable.) Prigg then returned the slave, by force, to her owner. He was tried and convicted under a Pennsylvania law forbidding the kidnapping of Negroes for the purpose of forcing them into slavery in another state. Prigg challenged the law on two grounds: first, that it violated the service-or-labor clause; and second, that Congress had preempted the field by a 1793 law that established procedures for the extradition of fugitive slaves, and under which the hapless magistrate had issued his original warrant.

The attorney general of Pennsylvania made a statement that startles the twentieth-century reader. He declared that the case "was one of amity, of concord, on the part of Pennsylvania and Maryland, which

[29] 32 U.S. 243, 247.

were the real and substantial parties. They came into that Court to try a great question of constitutional law." So *Prigg*, like *Dred Scott*, was a test case, and the lawyer had no qualms about telling the Court so. That in itself would be a red flag to modern justices, but the Court's opinion referred to it quite calmly.[30]

The lawyers for Pennsylvania did not make arguments like those of Weld, Birney, and Bingham. Instead, they concentrated on interpretations of the service-or-labor clause and questions of state and federal power. Justice Joseph Story, as spokesman for the Court, rejected both sets of arguments, even though he himself was opposed to slavery.[31] He was unimpressed by Pennsylvania's notion that the constitutional provision was only a statement that masters had the right to seize their fugitive slaves. The words "shall be delivered up on Claim of the Party to whom such Service or Labor may be due" implied duties for third parties: "Now, we think it exceedingly difficult, if not impracticable, to read the language and not to find, that it contemplated some further remedial redress than that which might be made by the owner himself."[32]

It is hard to reject this piece of textual interpretation. No justice did object to it. Story's contention that the 1793 act had deprived the states of any power to regulate the disposition of fugitive slaves, however, did bother Chief Justice Roger B. Taney and Justice Peter Daniel, but only because it would have precluded the states from assisting in the capture of fugitives.[33] (It is not clear how this conclusion follows, as the magistrate's first order appears to have been rendering just such assistance.)

This ruling "in historical importance far outweighed the Dred Scott decision of 1857, because it invalidated all efforts of the Northern states to protect the civil rights and the liberties of an important class of persons under their jurisdiction."[34] All the Court needed for its ruling was the service-or-labor clause, and its interpretation was fairly straightforward. What was more interesting—and even more troubling—was the way three justices—Story, Taney, and Smith Thompson—wrote about slaveholders' rights. Story insisted that the clause "contains a positive and unqualified recognition of the right of the owner in the slave, unaffected by any state law or legislation whatsoever." That, he said, was its historic purpose. Given the trepidation

[30] 41 U.S. 539, 589, 608.
[31] Cover, *Justice Accused*, pp. 238–43.
[32] 41 U.S. 539, 613–15.
[33] Ibid., pp. 626–30 and 650–53.
[34] Dumond, *Antislavery Origins*, p. 64.

with which the framers had approached this issue, this conclusion seemed dubious, but the justices liked it. Only John McLean seemed wary: ["That the Constitution was adopted in a spirit of compromise, is a matter of history . . . the Constitution, as it is, cannot be said to have embodied in all its parts, the particular views of any great section of the Union." Taney insisted that the clause imposed on the states the positive duty—not, as in the 1793 law, the option—to enforce this right. For Thompson, the clause "affirms, in the most unequivocal manner, the right of the master to the service of his slave, . . . [and] prohibits the states from discharging the slave from such service by any law or regulation therein." [35]

This was precisely the kind of generous construction the Marshall Court had refused to give Fifth Amendment rights, also worded in the passive voice and also vulnerable to frustration by the states. Marshall might also have pointed out that if the clause had been intended as a guarantee of right, it not only was phrased in a peculiar way but was in an odd place. Surely it belonged in Article I, Section 10. If it was an affirmation of rights, it was hardly unequivocal. And it was all beside the point anyway, since the language of the service-or-labor clause effectively killed the Pennsylvania law. There was no need to refer to rights. All that was necessary was a narrowly worded opinion, but, just as Marshall had often done, Story chose to write a broad, sweeping one. Slave owners' property rights thus got the kind of ringing affirmation that the First Amendment needed eighty more years to get. In its decision in *Prigg*, the Court made clear where its constitutional sympathies lay.[36]

The *Dred Scott* decision does not require lengthy analysis here. Like *Barron* and *Prigg*, it is dead now, and much has been written about it. I quote from it because, in the light of the foregoing discussion, Chief Justice Taney's views emerge not only as prejudiced but, as a matter of interpretation, simply wrong.

Dred Scott represented a victory for the extremists in *Prigg*. In voiding the Missouri Compromise and declaring that a Negro was not a citizen within the meaning of the Constitution, the Court echoed the antitheory as propounded by Calhoun.

> It is difficult at this day to realize the state of public opinion in relation to that unfortunate race, which prevailed in the civilized and enlightened portions of the world at the time of the Declaration of Independence,

[35] 41 U.S. 539, 613, 659–60, 626–30, 634.
[36] *Prigg* did, however, rule that states need not enforce the Fugitive Slave Act (ibid., pp. 618–25).

and when the Constitution of the United States was framed and adopted. But the public history of every European nation displays it in a manner too plain to be mistaken.

They had for more than a century before been regarded as beings of an inferior order, and altogether unfit to associate with the white race, either in social or political relations; and so far inferior, that they had no rights which the white man was bound to respect; and that the negro might justly and lawfully be reduced to slavery for his benefit. He was bought and sold, and treated as an ordinary article of merchandise and traffic, whenever a profit could be made by it. This opinion was at that time fixed and universal in the civilized portion of the white race. It was regarded as an axiom in morals as well as in politics, which no one thought of disputing, or supposed to be open to dispute; and men in every grade and position in society daily and habitually acted upon it in their private pursuits, as well as in matters of public concern, without doubting for a moment the correctness of this opinion.[37]

This passage is offered not as an expression of Taney's own opinion, but as a statement of the framers' views. Indeed, it hints that opinion had become rather more enlightened. As a history of ideas, it is particularly vulnerable. "Fixed and universal" gives it away. For the opinions that Taney so labeled had not been held by Jay or Hamilton or Gouverneur Morris, or even by Jefferson. Many people had thought of disputing them; indeed, no one was eager to express them. Taney may have given an accurate statement of the views of one section of the country in 1857, but to attribute those views to the entire "civilized world" in 1776 and 1787 is to read history backward.[38] It is instructive to compare this passage with Dew's defense of slavery—or, for that matter, Aristotle's. By 1857 opinion on both sides of the issue had crystallized, and the Court—first inevitably, then enthusiastically—had come down on the side of slavery.

The main intellectual difference between the opponents and the supporters of slavery was a difference in political philosophy. The antislavery theory of equality, derived from the Declaration and its belief that all were equally entitled to rights, was countered by a southern antitheory, which rejected the principles of the Declaration and insisted that equal status had to be earned. The main difference between the opponents of slavery and the pre–Civil War Court, however, pertained not to philosophy but to modes of constitutional interpretation. Even justices who opposed slavery went about their task of ad-

[37] 60 U.S. 393, 407.

[38] See Herbert J. Storing, "Slavery and the Moral Foundations of the American Republic," in Robert H. Horwitz, ed., *The Moral Foundations of the American Republic* (Charlottesville: University Press of Virginia, 1979), pp. 216–17. On *Dred Scott*, see Don E. Fehrenbacher, *The Dred Scott Case* (New York: Oxford University Press, 1978).

judication in ways that dictated proslavery results. Single-clause interpretation and *stare decisis* had become the dominant modes. Perhaps that is unfortunate; perhaps, had the justices approached the Constitution as Stewart, Birney, Weld, and Bingham did, slavery might have ended without war. But the justices' methods led to conclusions that favored masters over slaves. Antislavery jurists paid no great deference to precedent, nor did they confine themselves to clause-bound exegesis. These men favored structural and transcendent modes of interpretation, which allowed the conclusion that the Constitution forbade slavery.

If compromise under the Constitution had ever been possible, after *Dred Scott* it was so no longer. But this eventuality was due not only to *Dred Scott*, but to what had gone before. The Constitution, as written and as interpreted, endorsed slavery. Thus it came down on the side of antitheory. Both civil war and constitutional amendment proved necessary for change. When the constitutional change came, the Congress that enacted it recurred to the arguments of antislavery, and made an unambiguous choice for theory in preference to antitheory.

[4]

Equality and the
Reconstruction Congress

Anyone who approaches the legislative history of the Fourteenth Amendment in order to glean new interpretations must do so with unease. The warnings I mentioned in Chapter 1 still apply; it is impossible to state with much assurance what any measure "intended." Scholars can trace the amendment to antislavery jurisprudence, identify abolitionists among the framers, and find the phrase "equal protection" in antislavery argument, but it is no more possible to *prove* that the Fourteenth Amendment enacted the Declaration of Independence than it is to validate either Carl Becker's or Garry Wills's interpretation of the Declaration itself. Showing that people said certain things or were in certain places at certain times, or that they read certain books or had certain associates, is not conclusive proof of any line of intellectual influence. Identifying Thaddeus Stevens, for example, among the second generation of Theodore Weld's disciples does not prove that he thought exactly as Weld, Birney, or anyone else did. Certainly he had a different task. This kind of information does, however, tell us what kinds of forces may have influenced the framers' thought, and permits qualified inferences about the roots of their ideas. If the authors of the amendment had been the lawyers who argued *Prigg* and *Dred Scott* before the Court, the amendment would have a different history.

Not only do we not know quite how members of the Joint Committee of Fifteen on Reconstruction, such as Bingham and Stevens in the House or William Pitt Fessenden and Jacob Howard in the Senate, connected their ideas to their amendment, but we know still less about what the quieter members of Congress who voted for it and the state

73

legislators who ratified it thought they were enacting. The legislative history makes it clear that even the articulate members of Congress did not mean the same thing by those provisions. That is one reason why it is so hard to determine whether a given practice was or was not meant to be forbidden. It is important to remember that legislators are often less interested in interpreting a bill than in either passing or defeating it. Their remarks tend to be positive or negative arguments, not authoritative glosses. Legislative debates are not Socratic dialogues; good points go unanswered, and arguments get made imperfectly. The debates on the Fourteenth Amendment in particular are frustrating not only because of these factors but because Section 1 got relatively little attention; Sections 2 and 3, pertaining to representation, suffrage, and the treatment of former Confederates, provoked far more debate.[1]

Another reason for caution in this task has to do with the secondary sources on the Fourteenth Amendment. This is a topic on which much excellent work has already been done.[2] The justification for yet an-

---

[1] See, e.g., Robert J. Harris, *The Quest for Equality* (Baton Rouge: Louisiana State University Press, 1960), p. 35.

[2] The primary source here is the legislative debates. They have been compiled in Alfred Avins, ed., *The Reconstruction Amendments' Debates* (hereafter, Avins). Benjamin B. Kendrick, *Journal of the Joint Committee of Fifteen on Reconstruction* (1914) (New York: Negro Universities Press, 1969), reproduces the journal and gives a history of the deliberations. Two classic general histories are Horace F. Flack, *The Adoption of the Fourteenth Amendment* (Baltimore: Johns Hopkins Press, 1908), and Joseph B. James, *The Framing of the Fourteenth Amendment* (Urbana: University of Illinois Press, 1951). A major interpretive work is William Winslow Crosskey, *Politics and the Constitution* (Chicago: University of Chicago Press, 1951), vol. 2. The two studies that I consider definitive are Graham, *Everyman's Constitution*, and ten Broek, *Equal under Law*. A divergent view is provided by Berger, *Government by Judiciary*. Cover, *Justice Accused*, also appears to disagree, but his argument applies more to the antislavery movement itself than to the effect of certain segments of it on Reconstruction.

Much of the Fourteenth Amendment scholarship consists of responses to and anticipation of particular Supreme Court opinions. The best of that work related to the Brown decision is Alexander M. Bickel, "The Original Understanding and the Segregation Decision," *Harvard Law Review* 69 (November 1955):1–65; Charles L. Black, Jr., "The Lawfulness of the Segregation Decisions," *Yale Law Journal* 69 (January 1960):421–30; John P. Frank and Robert F. Munro, "The Original Understanding of 'Equal Protection of the Laws,'" *Columbia Law Review* 50 (February 1950):131–69; Alfred H. Kelly, "The Fourteenth Amendment Reconsidered: The Segregation Decision," *Michigan Law Review* 54 (June 1956):1049–86. Articles in response to two other specific opinions, respectively Justice Black's dissent in Adamson v. California and Justice Harlan's dissent in Reynolds v. Sims, are Charles Fairman, "Does the Fourteenth Amendment Incorporate the Bill of Rights?" *Stanford Law Review* 2 (December 1949):5–139, and William Van Alstyne, "The Fourteenth Amendment, the 'Right' to Vote, and the Thirty-ninth Congress," *Supreme Court Review*, 1965, pp. 33–86. See also Alfred Avins, "The 'Equal' Protection of the Laws: The Original Understanding," *New York Law Forum* 12 (Fall 1966):385–429, and "Social Equality and the Fourteenth Amendment: The Original Understanding," *Houston Law Review* 7 (Spring 1967):640–56.

other try is that most of this scholarship predates the developments that concern us here. That which is recent is often simply wrong.[3] But because so much work has been done, my exploration of the subject will be limited to questions that bear on the new developments.

The equal-protection clause cannot be read in isolation from the rest of the Fourteenth Amendment. As the debates suggest, "the three clauses of Section 1 are mostly but not entirely duplicatory. . . . [They] refer to the protection or abridgement of natural rights."[4] The amendment, in its turn, can usefully be studied only in the wider context of Reconstruction laws. "Viewed as a unit," Richard Kluger has written, "the decade of legislation beginning with the adoption of the Thirteenth Amendment in 1865 and culminating in passage of the Civil Rights Act of 1875, may reasonably be said to have closed the gap between the promise of the Declaration and the tactful tacit racism of the Constitution."[5]

These acts and amendments were all linked. In particular, to begin with, "the one point on which historians of the Fourteenth Amendment agree, and, indeed, which the evidence places beyond cavil, is that [it] was designed to place the constitutionality of the Freedmen's Bureau and civil rights bills, particularly the latter, beyond doubt. . . . The doubt related to the capacity of the Thirteenth Amendment to sustain this far-reaching legislative program."[6] The Thirteenth Amendment, passed by Congress in January 1865 and ratified in December, had abolished slavery. Congress had established the Freedmen's Bureau in March of that year with broad powers as the temporary guardian of former slaves.

On January 5, 1866, Senator Lyman Trumbull of Illinois introduced amendments to this law and a new civil rights bill. The original version of this bill provided that "there shall be no discrimination in civil rights or immunities among the inhabitants of any state or territory of the United States on account of race, color, or previous condition of slavery."[7] The Senate did pass this version, but later the broad "no discrimination" language was dropped, partly because some legislators felt it exceeded the Thirteenth Amendment's grant of power and

[3] Most notoriously, Berger, *Government by Judiciary*, and Graglia, *Disaster by Decree*.

[4] Ten Broek, *Equal under Law*, p. 239. See also Harris, *Quest for Equality*, pp. 35–36.

[5] *Simple Justice* (New York: Alfred A. Knopf, 1975), p. 627.

[6] Ten Broek, *Equal under Law*, p. 201.

[7] *Congressional Globe*, January 12, 1866, Senate, p. 211 (hereafter *Globe*); Avins, p. 104.

partly because John Bingham and others apparently thought the Fourteenth Amendment would fill the gap.[8]

As passed, both the civil rights and amended Freedmen's Bureau bills contained identical lists of guaranteed rights. Section 1 of the Civil Rights Bill provided "that all persons born in the United States and not subject to any foreign power, excluding Indians not taxed, are hereby declared to be citizens of the United States; and such citizens, of every race and color, without regard to any previous condition of slavery or involuntary servitude, except as punishment for crime whereof the party shall have been duly convicted, shall have the same right, in every State and Territory of the United States, to make and enforce contracts, to sue, be parties, and give evidence, to inherit, purchase, sell, hold, and convey real and personal property, to full and equal benefit of all laws and proceedings for the security of person and property, as is enjoyed by white citizens."[9] Each bill met, but survived, a stronger threat than judicial review: a veto by President Andrew Johnson. While the Fourteenth Amendment was in preparation, the vetoes had not yet been overridden.

The scope of the Fourteenth Amendment is of course not identical to or limited by these two laws.[10] It is closely related to them; to the Thirteenth Amendment; and, since the suffrage question would come up during the debates, to the Fifteenth Amendment. It is also connected to the Ku Klux Klan Act of 1871, Charles Sumner's ill-fated civil rights bill of 1874, and the weakened version of that bill which became the 1875 act; the debates on these bills include extensive discussions of the meaning of the amendment they were designed to enforce. Therefore, my analysis will draw not simply on the Fourteenth Amendment's legislative history, but on the whole body of Reconstruction debates.

Some chronology will be helpful at this point.[11] A joint congressional committee was appointed in December 1865, primarily at the insistence of the famous Radical Republican from Pennsylvania, Thaddeus Stevens. This step was a victory for Stevens over the president, whose Reconstruction plans were more moderate, or at least less aggressive. Stevens and John Bingham of Ohio were the most promi-

---

[8] Kluger, *Simple Justice*, pp. 628–30.

[9] 14 Stat. 27, chap. 31 (April 9, 1866); cf. 14 Stat. 176–77, sec. 14, chap. 200 (July 16, 1866).

[10] See, e.g., Kluger, *Simple Justice*, pp. 626–34.

[11] This chronology follows Kendrick, *Journal*, pt. 2, and ten Broek, *Equal under law*, pp. 204–7.

nent congressmen on the committee. In the Senate, Jacob Howard of Michigan shared many of their views, but Fessenden of Maine, the committee's chairman, who may have assumed this task to keep Sumner off the committee, exerted a powerful moderating influence.[12] The "real moderating force," however, was probably "that anything more extreme than the Fourteenth Amendment as it is would not be sustained by the people."[13] The committee accomplished two tasks: it held hearings on the condition of freed slaves in the South, and it wrote the Fourteenth Amendment.

The effective authors of Section 1 were Bingham, Stevens, Sumner, and Trumbull. The equal-protection language was derived in part from Sumner's argument as counsel for the plaintiff in *Roberts* v. *Boston*, an early school segregation case. There Sumner derived from the Massachusetts Constitution, the French Constitution of 1793, and various classical and Enlightenment writers the notion that "according to the spirit of American institutions, all men, without distinction of color or race, are equal before the law."[14] In the Thirty-eighth Congress, Sumner had drafted a constitutional amendment declaring that "all persons are equal before the law, so that no person can hold another as a slave," but this language was not incorporated into the Thirteenth Amendment.[15]

Bingham drew on both Sumner's ideas and Trumbull's laws in drafting Section 2. The phrase "equal protection," however, was his own. It first appears in a speech before the House in 1857: "It must be apparent that the absolute equality of all, and the equal protection of each, are principles of our Constitution."[16] He included the phrase in each of his drafts of the amendment, with one exception. His first, on December 6, 1865, read: "Congress shall have power to pass all necessary and proper laws to secure to all persons in every state of the Union equal protection in their rights, life, liberty, and property." This wording was considered along with an alternative draft by Stevens: "All national and state laws shall operate impartially and equally on all persons without regard to race or color."[17]

---

[12] See David Donald, *Charles Sumner and the Rights of Man* (New York: Alfred A. Knopf, 1970), chap. 6; James, *Framing of the Fourteenth Amendment*, chap. 3.

[13] Kendrick, *Journal*, p. 135. See also remarks of Thaddeus Stevens, *Globe*, May 8, 1866, H., p. 2459; Avins, p. 212.

[14] 5 Cushing (59 Mass.) 198, 201 (1849).

[15] Ibid. See Frank and Munro, "Original Understanding," pp. 136–37; Kelly, "Fourteenth Amendment Reconsidered," p. 1057.

[16] Donald, *Charles Sumner*, p. 149.

[17] Ten Broek, *Equal under Law*, p. 205.

Stevens' draft appears on its face, and was intended, to include Negro suffrage.[18] Bingham was willing to support this idea, but not everyone on the committee was. A subcommittee draft of January 20, 1866, combined the crucial elements of both versions: "Congress shall have the power to make all laws necessary and proper to secure to all citizens of the United States, in every State, the same political rights and privileges; and to all persons in every State equal protection in the enjoyment of life, liberty, and property."[19]

A week later there occurred a change for which no historian has found an explanation. Bingham, for the subcommittee, reported this version: "Congress shall have the power to make all laws which shall be necessary and proper to secure to all persons in every State full protection in the enjoyment of life, liberty, and property, and to all citizens in the United States in any State the same immunities and also equal political rights and privileges."[20] The most significant difference is the substitution of "full" for "equal." This draft lasted only a week. Some scholars have suggested that "equal" and "full" are synonymous here.[21] That reading is not without difficulties; as Raoul Berger has pointed out, if several people get half a glass of something, everybody gets an equal serving but nobody gets a full serving.[22] If everyone gets a full glass, however, all get an equal serving; full protection for all is equal protection even though the converse is not necessarily true. Bingham may well have used the two adjectives interchangeably.

The January 27 draft was rejected by the full committee. On February 3, a fourth Bingham draft was voted out. This version gave Congress "the power to make all laws necessary and proper to secure to the citizens of each State all privileges and immunities of citizens in the several States, and to all persons in the several states *equal* protection in the rights of life, liberty, and property."[23] Later that month, this draft was introduced by Fessenden in the Senate and by Bingham in the House.[24]

Before the senators got to it, they were claimed by other business: the presidential vetoes, first of the Freedmen's Bureau Bill on February 19 and then of the Civil Rights Bill on March 27. The House had some objections to the committee bill. On February 27 and 28, several mod-

---

[18] See James, *Framing of the Fourteenth Amendment*, p. 81.
[19] Kendrick, *Journal*, p. 51; ten Broek, *Equal under Law*, p. 205.
[20] Kendrick, *Journal*, p. 56; ten Broek, *Equal under Law*, p. 205.
[21] See, e.g., ten Broek, *Equal under Law*, pp. 222, 237.
[22] *Government by Judiciary*, p. 177. See also Bickel, "Original Understanding," p. 33.
[23] Kendrick, *Journal*, p. 61; ten Broek, *Equal under Law*, p. 205. Emphasis supplied.
[24] *Globe*, February 13, 1866, S., p. 806, and February 26, 1866, H., pp. 1033–54; Avins, pp., 147, 150–51.

erate Republicans worried that the amendment would give Congress too much power. Giles Hotchkiss of New York recommended that it be redrafted as a limitation on state powers, making, perhaps disingenuously, an argument that appealed to the Radicals: ". . . your legislation upon the subject would depend upon the political majority of Congress. . . . But now, when we have the power in the Government, the power in this Congress, and the power in the States to make the Constitution what we desire it to be, I want to secure those rights against accidents, against the accidental majority of Congress." [25] The House voted to postpone decision. "The Amendment was left to brew for six weeks." [26]

Stevens had not given up on suffrage. He took advantage of the postponement; in April he sent the committee a draft prepared by Robert Dale Owen, which restated the ban on racial discrimination and provided for suffrage by 1876.[27] Bingham offered a friendly amendment: "nor shall any State deny to any person within its jurisdiction the equal protection of the laws nor take private property for public use without just compensation." [28] This draft was defeated.

Bingham then introduced this version, which was reported out by the committee on April 30: "Section 1. No State shall make or enforce any law which shall abridge the privileges or immunities of citizens of the United States; nor shall any State deprive any person of life, liberty, or property, without due process of law; nor deny to any person within its jurisdiction the equal protection of the laws." [29] This version passed, with a sentence clarifying state and national citizenship inserted at the beginning. Section 5 effectively put in most of what Hotchkiss had gotten out: "Congress shall have the power to enforce, by appropriate legislation, the provisions of this article." This version was passed by the Senate on June 8 and by the House on June 13. Just over two years later, on July 27, 1868, the amendment was ratified.

What questions can be asked of this voluminous material that will help us deal with the claims of the 1980s? Three questions, I think, are crucial. First, what emerge as the *foundations* of the guarantee of equality? Put another way, why did Congress want to ensure equal protection? Second, what *people*, or *groups*, did the guarantee include, and whom did it exclude, and why? Third, can anything new

[25] *Globe*, February 28, 1866, H., p. 1095; Avins, p. 160
[26] Kluger, *Simple Justice*, p. 630.
[27] See Fawn M. Brodie, *Thaddeus Stevens: Scourge of the South* (New York: W. W. Norton, 1959), chap. 21.
[28] Kendrick, *Journal*, pp. 83–85; ten Broek, *Equal under Law*, p. 206.
[29] Kendrick, *Journal*, p. 87; ten Broek, *Equal under Law*, p. 206.

be learned about what *rights* or *interests* the amendment did or did not protect? This third question is another version of a large question that has dominated much twentieth-century scholarship: what might be called the desegregation or *Brown* I question, or, still earlier, the incorporation or *Adamson* v. *California* question.[30] (I exclude, as tangential to this study, a fourth significant problem: the "state action" or *Shelley* v. *Kraemer* question.)[31]

Reconstruction Jurisprudence

The first question is the largest and most complex of the three. If the original Stevens draft had been the one approved by Congress and the states, we would know what kinds of state action were forbidden: any that were based on race or color. The Bingham version is not so specific. Therefore, to find out who and what were included, we need to know something about the principles behind the amendment.

The present doctrine implies that the equal-protection clause was meant to forbid two kinds of legal classifications. First, those that are arbitrary and irrational are precluded. Second, those that are "suspect" are presumed to be invalid; that is, either those based on permanent characteristics that the individual cannot control and that have little connection with individual abilities, or those directed against disadvantaged minorities, or both. If this interpretation were accurate, we might expect to find statements in the debates to that effect. But in fact there are very few such statements. We find several instances of arguments of another sort entirely.

The best interpretation of the Fourteenth Amendment grew around and out of *Brown* I. Dating from the 1950s and 1960s, this interpretation was the work primarily of Jacobus ten Broek, Howard Jay Graham, and Alfred H. Kelly, a group that nicely joins law, political science, and history.[32] These scholars maintained that the Reconstruction amendments were intended to write into the Constitution the principles of equality and natural rights contained in the Declaration.

---

[30] 332 U.S. 46 (1947).

[31] 334 U.S. 1 (1948).

[32] Ten Broek, who died in 1968, had both a law degree and a doctorate in political science; he was professor of political science at the University of California at Berkeley. Graham, now retired, was librarian of the Los Angeles County Law Library. Kelly, who died in 1976, was professor of history, Wayne State University. Respectively, their major works are *Equal under Law*; *Everyman's Constitution*, especially chaps. 1, 2, 4, 5, 7, and 14; and "Fourteenth Amendment Reconsidered."

The clause on equal protection of the laws had almost exclusively a substantive content. . . . Protection of men in their fundamental or natural rights was the basic idea of the clause; equality was a modifying condition. The clause was a confirmatory reference to the affirmative duty of government to protect men in their natural rights. This established its absolute and substantive character, though the use of the word "equal" would seem to give the clause a comparative form. Equal denial of protection, that is, no protection at all, is accordingly a denial of equal protection. The requirement of equal protection of the laws cannot be met unless the protection of the laws to men in their natural rights was the sole purpose in the creation of government. This being so, the phrase "No State shall . . . deny" becomes a simple command: "Each state shall supply," and the whole clause is thus understood to mean: "Each State shall supply the protection of the laws to men in their natural rights, and the protection shall always be equal to all men." It was because the protection of the laws was denied to some men that the word "equal" was used. The word "full" would have done as well.[33]

These conclusions might, under some circumstances, be suspect, since two of these writers, Graham and Kelly, were involved in preparing the historical brief for the plaintiffs in *Brown*. But none of their published work partakes of "law-office history," and the argument made goes far beyond what was required to overturn segregation. My own examination of the primary sources convinces me that ten Broek, Graham, and Kelly were right; and this conclusion has profound implications for the problems I deal with.

Even those who did not reach such sweeping conclusions—Alexander M. Bickel, for example, who as Justice Frankfurter's law clerk researched a long memorandum for him on this issue—found the amendment's language flexible enough to bear such an interpretation. "May it not be that the Moderates and the Radicals reached a compromise permitting them to go to the country with language which they could, where necessary, defend against damaging alarms raised by the opposition, but which at the same time was sufficiently elastic to permit reasonable future advances?"[34] Raoul Berger's study, published in 1977, rejects the natural rights thesis, but its argument is confused and ultimately wrong. Berger has two theses, which he does not clearly distinguish. Through much of his book he seems to argue that the scope of the Fourteenth Amendment is limited to those rights that its authors explicitly included and those practices they explicitly forbade. Therefore, Berger insists, since no one argued in 1866 that

---

[33] Ten Broek, *Equal under Law*, p. 237.
[34] "Original Understanding," p. 61. See also Bickel, *Least Dangerous Branch*, pp. 98–110; Kluger, *Simple Justice*, pp. 631–32.

de jure segregation was prohibited, it is constitutional. This is a basic misunderstanding of the nature of constitutional interpretation.[35]

But lurking behind this argument is a more subtle one, which deserves more attention. Berger insists that Congress intended to enact not the principles of the Declaration, but a specified set of rights derived from Blackstone, from *Corfield* v. *Coryell*, an 1823 case construing the privileges-and-immunities clause of Article IV, section 2, and from the Civil Rights Act of 1866.[36] Probably because Berger does not separate his two arguments, this one is never fully explored. But it, too, is fallacious.

His dismissal of the natural rights argument depends primarily on his assessment of the characters of its proponents: Bingham was a "muddled thinker," Sumner was widely regarded as a fool, and Stevens was roundly hated; the really influential framers were such moderates as Trumbull.[37] It is true that, to put it mildly, the Radicals had their detractors—none of what Berger says is new to anyone acquainted with this history—and that the moderates' votes were necessary to pass the amendment. But it is also true that Bingham and Stevens got the amendment written; that Bingham was in Sumner's intellectual debt; that Bingham and Jacob Howard were the provision's floor leaders; and that the debates are shot through with the sort of language Berger discounts.[38] The argument is intriguing, but it is not supportable.

"Slavery is so odious a concept," Graham wrote,

> that we are apt to forget that essentially it was a system of race discrimination and a denial of the protection of law. Slavery rested on and sanctioned prejudice; it made race and color the sole basis for accord or denial of human rights. Human chattelization was the worst aspect of it, but the racial criterion affected every phase of life and human contact. The institution stigmatized even those who had been emancipated from it. This was the fundamental problem faced by the framers of the Fourteenth Amendment. Slavery had ended, but the roots and forms of prejudice and discrimination lay untouched.[39]

[35] *Government by Judiciary*, chaps. 9, 13. See Agresto, review of Berger, *Government by Judiciary*, in *American Political Science Review* 73 (December 1979):1143.

[36] 6 Fed. Cas. 546 (Circ.Ct. E.D. Pa.); *Government by Judiciary*, chaps. 1–3, 6, 8, 10, 11.

[37] *Government by Judiciary*, pp. 145, 244, chap. 13.

[38] For only a few examples see the speeches of Stevens and Bingham in *Globe*, May 8 and 10, 1866, H., pp. 2452, 2459–60, and of Jacob Howard of Michigan, ibid., May 23, 1866, S., pp. 2764–65; Avins, pp. 212–13, 217–22.

[39] *Everyman's Constitution*, pp. 304–5.

The debates provide some support for Graham's statement, but for most speakers, what made the discrimination so odious was not that it based classification on race as opposed to some other characteristic, but that it deprived *any* persons of their rights. Only once, and then briefly, did a speaker articulate anything like the "permanent characteristics" version of suspect classification with respect to race. In 1868, Sumner, defending Negro suffrage, said:

> Age, education, residence, property, all these are subject to change; but the Ethiopian cannot change his skin. On this last distinctive circumstance I take my stand. *An insurmountable condition is not a qualification but a disfranchisement.* Admit that a state may determine the 'qualifications' of electors, it cannot, under this authority, arbitrarily exclude a whole race.
>
> Try this question by examples. Suppose South Carolina, where the blacks are numerous, should undertake to exclude the whites from the polls, on account of "color"; would you hesitate to arrest this injustice? . . . Suppose another State should gravely declare, that *all with black eyes* should be excluded from the polls; and still another should gravely declare that *all with black hair* should be excluded from the polls, I am sure that you would find it difficult to restrain the mingled derision and indignation which such a pretension must excite. But this fable pictures your conduct.[40]

But Sumner's congressional colleagues did not stress the immutability and alleged arbitrariness of racial classifications. Presumably they agreed with Sumner on the first point. But one of the most striking features of the debates is the lack of agreement on the second point. Indeed, if *any* consensus existed in this regard, it was that Negroes were inferior to whites. Berger is irrefutable on this point: "The North was shot through with Negrophobia . . . [and] the Republicans, except for a minority of extremists [sic], were swayed by the racism that gripped their constituents."[41] But Berger errs in concluding that this racism proves that the Republicans did not intend to enact a broad guarantee of equality. He has fallen into the trap of assuming that arguments for equality must rest on beliefs about merit; and, as we shall see, that was not how the Reconstructionists thought.

The record often juxtaposes the abolitionists' theory to Calhoun's antitheory. More than once Democrats expounded on the inherent in-

---

[40] *Globe*, June 10, 1868, S., p. 3026, Avins, p. 331. Emphasis in the original.

[41] *Government by Judiciary*, p. 10. Even Sumner shared these feelings. In 1834 he visited Maryland and saw slaves for the first time in his life. He wrote his family, "My worst preconception of their appearance and ignorance did not fall as low as their actual stupidity" (Donald, *Charles Sumner and the Coming of the Civil War* (New York: Alfred A. Knopf, 1960), p. 29).

feriority of Negroes. One of the clearest such statements comes from Representative Benjamin Boyer of Pennsylvania, in a debate over voting rights in the District of Columbia:

> If the peculiarities I have mentioned [color, odor, skull volume, face] are the outward badges of a race by nature inferior in mental caliber, and lacking that vim, pluck, and poise of character which give force and direction to human enterprise . . . then the Negroes are not the equals of white Americans, and are not entitled by any right, natural or acquired, to participate in the Government of this country. They are but superficial thinkers who imagine that the organic differences of the races can be obliterated by the education of the schools. The qualities of races are perpetuated by descent.[42]

The Republicans could have answered these arguments in several ways. Two modes of response to charges of racial inferiority had been popular since the previous century: the argument from gifted individual Negroes and the environmentalist defense.[43] The former argument does not appear in the debates, and the latter does so infrequently. It was made, interestingly, in response to Boyer by a fellow Pennsylvanian, Glenni Scofield.[44] The most frequent counterargument, however, emphasized inherent rights, independent of capacity.

Bingham's speech on the admission of Oregon, from which I quoted in Chapter 3, is an example of this kind of argument. Just a year later, an exchange between Senator Jefferson Davis of Mississippi, later president of the Confederacy, and Henry Wilson of Massachusetts, later vice-president under Grant, illustrates the underlying argument and counterargument. The Senate was considering an appropriation for public schools in the District of Columbia, whose population, then as now, was predominantly black. The interchange proceeded like this:

> DAVIS: . . . the inequality of the white and black races—stamped from the beginning, marked in degree and prophecy—[is] the will of God. . . .
> WILSON: I believe in the equality of rights of all mankind. I do not believe in the equality of the African race with the white race, mentally or physically, and I do not think morally. I do not believe in the equality of the Indian race with us, but upon the questions simply of equality of rights I believe in the equality of all men of every race, blood, and kindred.
> DAVIS: When the Senator says "equality of rights of all men," does he mean political and social rights—political and social equality?
> WILSON: I believe that every human being has the right to his life and

[42] *Globe*, January 10, 1866, H., pp. 177–78; Avins, p. 101.
[43] See Chapter 2, pp. 49–50.
[44] *Globe*, January 10, 1866, H., pp. 178–81; Avins, p. 102. See also the remarks of John B. Henderson of Missouri, *Globe*, March 19, 1864, S., p. 1465; Avins, pp. 66–67.

to his liberty, and to act in this world so as to secure his own happiness. I believe, in a word, in the Declaration of Independence; but I do not, as I have said, believe in the mental or physical equality of some of the races, as against this white race of ours.

DAVIS: Then the Senator believes, and he does not believe. . . . He believes in the Declaration of Independence, and intimates that he means by that all men are equal; but he immediately announces that there is a difference between the two races.

WILSON: Well Mr. President, I believe there are a great many men in the world of the white race inferior to the Senator from Mississippi, and I suppose there are quite a number superior to him; but I believe that he and the inferior man and the superior have equal natural rights.[45]

As explanation of the Fourteenth Amendment, this argument might seem premature, except for the fact that later debates echo it, and Wilson used the same rhetoric in support of Reconstruction laws. On January 22, 1866, the Freedmen's Bureau Bill produced this exchange between him and Edgar Cowan, a conservative Republican from Pennsylvania.

WILSON: We demand that by irreversible guarantees no portion of the population of the country shall be degraded or have a stain put upon them. . . .

COWAN: The honorable Senator from Massachusetts says that all men in this country must be equal. What does he mean by equal? Does he mean that all men in this country are to be six feet high, and that they shall all weigh two hundred pounds, and that they shall all have fair hair and red cheeks? Is that the meaning of equality? Is it that they all shall be equally rich and equally jovial, equally humorous and equally happy? What does it mean?

WILSON: . . . Why are these questions put? Does he not know precisely and exactly what we mean? Does he not know that we mean that the poorest man, be he black or be he white, that treads the soil of this Continent, is as much entitled to the protection of the law as the richest and proudest man in the land?

The Senator knows what we believe. He knows that we had advocated the rights of the black man because the black man was the most oppressed type of toiling man in this country.[46]

Throughout the debates, the Republicans argued from the notion that human beings were entitled to rights, regardless of their particular abilities. Notwithstanding Calhoun, and certain Democrats who followed him into Congress, equal rights did not have to be earned; they belonged to each individual, and government must secure and

[45] *Globe*, April 12, 1860, S., pp. 1682–86; Avins, pp. 24–28.
[46] *Globe*, S., pp. 339–44; Avins, pp. 109–10.

protect them. This assumption is illustrated by comments made in support of the various bills and amendments. Trumbull, for example, said that the purpose of his civil rights bill was to afford "protection to all persons in their *constitutional rights of equality before the law* without regard to race or color." [47] The Senator echoed this theme in his response to the president's veto message.

Johnson had written, ". . . a perfect equality of the white and black races is attempted to be fixed by federal law in every state." Trumbull rejected this interpretation:

> The bill neither confers nor abridges the rights of any one, but simply declares that in civil rights there shall be an equality among all classes of citizens, and that all alike shall be subject to the same punishment. Each state, so that it does not abridge the great fundamental rights belonging, under the Constitution, to all citizens, may grant or withhold such civil rights as it pleases; all that is required is that, in this respect, its laws shall be impartial. [48]

The Fourteenth Amendment itself was defended as a necessary protection of these fundamental rights. In the House, John Farnsworth of Illinois asked, "How can [a person] have and enjoy equal rights of 'life, liberty and the pursuit of happiness' without 'equal protection of the laws'?" [49] This argument bridges the gap between defenses of equal protection as an idea and as a constitutional guarantee. One reason it has been necessary to skip around so much in this analysis is that even those who agreed that the principles of the Declaration should be enacted into law had different notions about which provision was the appropriate vehicle for the purpose. The Fourteenth Amendment, as we have seen, was in part a response to those who feared that neither the original Constitution nor the Thirteenth Amendment gave Congress the power to grant equal rights, and who—realistically, as events proved—doubted the security of Trumbull's two bills. The foundations of the amendment thus had a pragmatic as well as a normative component, as Farnsworth's statement illustrates.

Investigations into the conditions of freedmen in the South added fuel to the arguments in favor of a constitutional amendment. The report of General Carl Schurz on the condition of the South in December 1865 and the Joint Committee's own hearing in the spring of 1866, for instance, revealed widespread brutality toward the former slaves and the use of "black codes" to go as far as possible toward reinsti-

---

[47] *Globe*, January 12, 1866, S., p. 211; Avins, p. 104. Emphasis supplied.
[48] *Globe*, March 27 and April 4, 1866, S., pp. 1680, 1760; Avins, pp. 194, 200.
[49] *Globe*, May 10, 1866, H., p. 2539; Avins, p. 217.

tuting slavery in fact.[50] Schurz, parodying Taney in *Dred Scott*, wrote: "The habit is so inveterate with a great many persons as to render, on the least provocation, the impulse to whip a negro almost irresistible. It will continue to be so until the southern people have learned, so as never to forget it, that a black man has rights which a white man is bound to respect."[51]

In June 1866, during the Senate debate on the amendment, John Henderson of Missouri argued for Negro suffrage in this way:

> Nearly five million people, strong, vigorous, and innured to labor, are in your midst, partially without civil, wholly without political rights. What will you do with them? You have three alternatives before you, and only three. You must kill them, colonize them or ultimately give them a part of your political power. For this last alternative the country is not pre-pared. With the two former humanity and common sense will success-fully struggle.[52]

Not only was equality a necessary condition for securing inherent rights, but it was essential in order to grant the Negroes any freedom at all. The Reconstruction package was enacted not because its fram-ers believed race was unrelated to ability, or because it was beyond the individual's power to change. Rather, the guarantees were the re-sult of the framers' commitment to the conclusion that equal protec-tion was necessary to secure those rights. The framers had little con-cern with race as an abstract category. Instead, they were trying to secure the rights of members of one oppressed race.

Equal Protection Beyond Race

Unlike the two laws the Thirty-ninth Congress passed at about the same time, the Fourteenth Amendment was not written in racial terms. It grants privileges and immunities to all citizens, and due process and equal protection to "any person." That was not the reason Bingham's language was substituted for Stevens', but once the Bingham version

---

[50] Senate Executive Document no. 2, 39th Cong., 1st sess.; Avins, pp. 87–93; See Senate Report no. 112, June 8, 1866; Brodie, *Thaddeus Stevens*, pp. 240–46; *Globe*, June 4, 7, 8, 1866, S., pp. 2938–64, 2989–92, 3010–42, app. pp. 217–23, 238–40; Avins, pp. 229–37 (Senate debate on the Fourteenth Amendment). For evidence that the problem persisted, see *Globe*, March 10, 1868, H.R. no. 21, on admission of Ala-bama and no. 30, on Bureau of Freedmen; Avins, pp. 279–83.

[51] Senate Executive Document no. 2, 39th Cong., 1st sess., p. 20; Avins, p. 89.

[52] *Globe*, June 8, 1866, S., p. 3035; Avins, p. 236.

was accepted, there was some agreement that the amendment did speak to problems other than racism.

Sometimes the language used was sweeping, even lavish. The words of Ohio's Representative William Lawrence about the Civil Rights Bill apply as well to the amendment written to secure it: "The bill, in that broad and comprehensive philanthropy which regards all men in their civil rights as equal before the law, is not made for any class or creed, or race or color, but . . . will, if it become a law, protect every citizen, including the millions of people of foreign birth who will flock to our shores to become citizens and to find here a land of liberty and law." [53]

Introducing the Fourteenth Amendment in the Senate, Howard, substituting for an ailing Fessenden, insisted that it "abolishes all class legislation in the States and does away with the injustice of subjecting one caste of persons to a code not applicable to another." He did not define "class" or "caste," and his illustration does not help here because it is racial: "It prohibits the hanging of a black man for a crime for which the white man is not to be hanged. It protects the black man in his fundamental rights as a citizen with the same shield which it throws over the white man." [54]

Some retrospective interpretations are as comprehensive as that of a Kentucky Democrat who, opposing the Fifteenth Amendment, declared that its predecessor "gives protection to . . . Negroes as well as Indians, Gypsies, Chinese, and all the Mongolian races born in the United States, men and women, young and old." In debating what became the Civil Rights Act of 1875, Senator Oliver Morton, a Union Republican from Indiana, declared that the Fourteenth Amendment "forbids all discriminations of every character against any class of persons being citizens of the United States." [55]

Every discrimination? Against *any* class? What about restrictions on voting rights, or on the contractual rights of children and married women? Well, no: those broad statements were qualified. Morton himself immediately was challenged on single-sex schools, and backed down. "This Amendment," he replied, "was intended to destroy caste, to put all races upon an equality. There is the point." [56]

[53] *Globe*, April 7, 1866, H., p. 1833; Avins, p. 206.

[54] *Globe*, May 23, 1866, S., p. 2766; Avins, p. 220.

[55] *Globe*, January 28, 1869, H., p. 691 (remarks of James B. Beck); ibid., May 21, 1874, S., app. p. 358; Avins, pp. 343, 683. Morton had consistently held to this position. As governor of Indiana during that State's ratification debates, he declared that the due-process clause was "intended to throw the equal protection of law around every person . . . not only as to life and liberty, but also as to property" (James, *Framing of the Fourteenth Amendment*, p. 159).

[56] *Globe*, S., app. p. 359; Avins, p. 683.

So how far did the amendment reach? Did its authors intend Section 1 to protect anyone other than blacks, and if so, whom? Did they intend to exclude any kinds of discrimination from the scope of the amendment, and if so, toward whom were those exclusions directed? Finally, did they have grounds for distinguishing between the groups covered and those not covered?

The answer to the first question is yes: there emerges from the debates a general agreement that the provision gave Chinese and Japanese immigrants the same protection it gave to blacks. The answer to the second question is also yes; there emerges some agreement that it did not cover women or children. The answer to the third question is yes, distinctions were made; but either they are explicitly written into the constitutional text and limited to specified claims or they do not withstand analysis.

Most of the time, supporters spoke in the familiar terms of black versus white. Howard's statement is typical. Thaddeus Stevens put it this way: "Whatever law punishes a white man for a crime shall punish the black man precisely in the same way and to the same degree. Whatever law protects the white man shall afford 'equal' protection to the black man. Whatever means of redress is afforded to one shall be afforded to all." [57]

But the country had another developing racial issue that was not ignored. Opponents kept bringing it up: did the amendment protect Orientals? A few speakers denied that it did, but their arguments are their own best refutations. Representative William Higby of California, for example, declared that the Chinese were excluded because they were pagans and foreigners, whereas the Negroes were Christians and natives.[58] That these were minority views is shown by the fact that in 1870 Congress used its enforcement power to secure to West Coast Chinese the rights to sue, give evidence, and make contracts.[59] Nevada's Senator William Stewart remarked, "Now while I am opposed to Asiatics being brought here, and will join in any reasonable legislation to prevent anybody from bringing them, yet we have got a treaty that allows them to come to this country," He continued:

For twenty years every obligation of humanity, of justice, and of common decency toward those people has been violated. . . . While they are

[57] *Globe*, May 8, 1866, H., p. 2459; Avins, p. 212.
[58] See, e.g., the remarks of Rep. William Niblack (D-Ind.), *Globe*, February 27, 1866, H., p. 1056; Avins, p. 152. See also the remarks of Senators Oliver Morton and Frederick Frelinghuysen, February 9, 1869, S., p. 1039; Avins, p. 382; and Representative James Johnson of California, May 23, 1870, H., p. 3878; Avins, p. 461.
[59] *Globe*, 41st Cong., 2nd sess., *passim*; Avins, p. 437.

here, I say it is our duty to protect them. . . . It is as solemn a duty as can be devolved upon this Congress to see that those people are protected, to see that they have equal protection of the laws, notwithstanding that they are aliens. . . . Justice and humanity and common decency require it.[60]

So the amendment protected the rights of other racial groups in addition to blacks. But what about women? The American feminist movement was almost twenty years old by that time, and it made its presence felt in the deliberations. The language of Section 1, on its face, was broad enough to protect women as well as racial minorities. Opponents of the amendment frequently pointed this out. But several of the supporters insisted that it did not apply to women. In these arguments, they tried to find distinctions between race-based legislation and sex-based legislation which would justify this interpretation. However hard they tried, they failed. Their arguments fall of their own weight—and not just with the hindsight provided by modern feminism. Even in their own time and on their own terms, most of the distinctions are specious.

During the February debates in the House, Robert Hale of New York, one of the Republicans who opposed the "necessary and proper" draft, challenged Bingham and Stevens on this point. Would the amendment strike down the legal disabilities imposed on married women? No, replied Stevens; not as long as all married women and all unmarried women were treated alike, "where all of the same class are dealt with in the same way, then there is no pretense of inequality." This admission was fatal, and Hale saw it right away: ". . . then by parity of reasoning it would be sufficient if you extend to one negro the same rights you do to another, but not those you extend to a white man."[61] Stevens did not respond to this logic, and neither did anyone else.

Other efforts to distinguish between race and sex discrimination were made in discussions of voting rights. Typical antifeminist rhetoric does appear here, but it is not dwelt on. Howard's introductory speech to the Senate on May 23 defended Section 2, which provided that "whenever, in any State, the elective franchise shall be denied to any portion of its *male* citizens *not less than twenty-one years of age*," the basis of representation in the House would be proportionally reduced. He quoted from James Madison's writings a statement in favor

[60] *Globe*, May 20, 1870, S., p. 3658; Avins, p. 449.
[61] *Globe*, February 27, 1866, H., pp. 1063–64; Avins, pp. 153–54. See also Fairman, "Does the Fourteenth Amendment," pp. 29–30.

of universal suffrage. Reverdy Johnson of Maryland, a leading opponent, asked whether this meant "females, as well as males." Howard replied:

> I believe Mr. Madison was old enough and wise enough to take it for granted there was such a thing as the law of nature which has a certain influence even in political affairs, and that by that law women and children are not regarded as the equals of men. Mr. Madison would not have quibbled about the question of women's voting or of an infant's voting. He lays down a broad democratic principle, that those who are to be bound by the laws ought to have a voice in making them; and everywhere mature manhood is the representative type of the human race.[62]

The defect of this argument, of course, is that it gives no basis for preferring the "law of nature" that regards only women and children as inferior to the version already encountered which also classifies blacks as inferior. The "representative" component of the argument, however, is repeated and expanded by others. The comments of Senator Luke Poland of Vermont on June 5 are typical. He himself was not hostile to women's suffrage: "We all know that many females are far better qualified to vote intelligently and wisely than many men who are allowed to vote; and the same is true of many males under twenty-one. . . . The theory is that the fathers, husbands, brothers, and sons to whom the right of suffrage is given will in its exercise be as watchful of the rights and interest of their wives, sisters, and children who do not vote as of their own." This theme was echoed in later discussions. Women are protected by their male relatives, and in any case are treated like human beings, but "the Negro is the object of that unaccountable prejudice against race which has its origin in the greed and selfishness of a fallen world."[63] Therefore Negro suffrage, or rather male Negro suffrage, was a necessity.

The notion that men will protect the interests of their relatives is analogous to Alexander Hamilton's statement in *Federalist 35* that workers do not need a vote because their employers will safeguard their interests, and just as false. But we do not need to engage in the questionable tactic of using a twentieth-century insight to reject a nineteenth-century argument. It is necessary to say only this: Neither

[62] *Globe*, May 23, 1866. S., pp. 2766–67; Avins, pp. 220–21. Emphasis supplied.

[63] *Globe*, June 5 and 8, 1866, S., pp. 2961, 3035; Avins, pp. 230, 236 (remarks of Senator John Henderson). See also remarks of Rep. John Broomall, March 18, 1868, H., pp. 1956–62, and of Senator Wilson, December 11, 1866, and Senator Stewart, January 28, 1869, S., pp. 64, 668; Avins, pp. 299–302, 252, 339.

children nor women are at all times assured of male relatives to protect them.[64]

Most important, discussions of voting can have only limited application to an interpretation of Section 1. Voting was covered not in
Section 1, but in Section 2 and in the Fifteenth Amendment. Both
provisions stated explicitly who was to be included. Section 2 deprived states of representation only if they disfranchised adult male
citizens. Minors, females, and aliens were omitted. The Fifteenth
Amendment forbade the states to deny suffrage on the basis of three
listed attributes: race, color, or previous servitude. Sex and age are
omitted. Two later amendments, of course, deal with these attributes.

When Congress meant to limit the scope of guaranteed rights, it
said so, enumerating the rights involved and the proscribed bases for
discrimination. Section 1 of the Fourteenth Amendment contains no
such limitations, and the text provides no basis for reading any into
it. Indeed, if anything, the wording of the Civil War amendments tends
to provide support for the inclusion of women and children in Section 1.

The debates suggest otherwise, but they do not disprove that statement. Often the framers spoke in broad terms that seem to encourage
interpretations that go beyond racial equality. When we look to the
record for guidance about which such interpretations are valid and
which are not, however, we find only confusion. The debates do not
answer this question, perhaps because it was not a crucial one to the
lawmakers. But it became crucial very soon afterward, and has remained so.

Part of the problem inheres in Senator Howard's term "class legislation," paraphrased by Stevens and others. The debates never define
this term. The examples given to illustrate it are always racial. Whenever members are pressed to reason by analogy to other traits, such as
sex and age, their reasoning collapses. Apparently "class" is a class
that includes but is not limited to "race"; the debates provide no guidance as to what other subclasses are included. The hypothetical policies mentioned by Howard and Stevens as species of "class legislation" are not much help. They speak of punishment; the law must not
punish a member of one race more harshly than one of another. As
we shall see later, this principle does not prohibit all racial discrimination. But differences in punishment are forbidden, and it may be
useful to speculate about what this prohibition may mean.

Why would it be illegal to discriminate on the basis of race with

---

[64] Avins makes this point in his introduction to the debates (p. xv).

respect to punishment? Well, we punish people for crimes; that is, for specific acts of wrongdoing for which they are responsible. Race can neither increase nor diminish a person's responsibility for a particular crime. The point is not that the person cannot help being black; rather, it is that blackness has no relation to the degree of guilt. What seems to be at issue here is classifying people according to some trait that has nothing to do with the issue at hand. We classify, of course, when we execute some murderers and not others; we establish a class of murderers put to death and murderers permitted to go on living. If we make this choice according to the particular depravity of the crime, for instance, we establish a class of depraved murderers, who are executed, and nondepraved murderers, who stay alive. This classification is legitimate (leaving aside the question of the acceptability of capital punishment) because it is related to the crime itself, and because it is based on individual responsibility and behavior. A racial classification presumes *a priori* that the "person" belongs to a group that is treated differently.

Another example of class legislation is given by Senator Timothy Howe of Wisconsin: a law taxing Negroes specifically for Negro education, in addition to a general tax for education.[65] This is not precisely a punishment, but it is an imposition of an extra burden. Of course, even in the days before income taxes, differential tax burdens were imposed. On what basis? Well, property owners pay extra taxes, for example. Again there is a relationship between burden and behavior. And the classification is subsequent, not prior, to an individual determination.

This argument begins to sound somewhat like a tentative version of one concept of suspect classification. But it is of limited usefulness because it is only what classification might mean, not necessarily what it did mean. And it implies what the members of Congress disavowed: that sex-based discriminations were likewise class legislation. We are going to have to look further for the meaning of Section 1.

Do these statements forbid, and were they meant to forbid, *all* race or class discriminations, or just those imposed on blacks? The term "class legislation" sounds neutral, but it is not clear that Howard intended it that way. All the examples he gives refer to inferior treatment of blacks. Perhaps it did not occur to the leaders in the floor fights that there might be such a thing as legislation against whites as a class. In the light of their historical experience, failure to entertain such a possibility is understandable. It is not clear whether "class legislation"

---

[65] *Globe*, June 5, 1866, S. app. pp. 217–19; Avins, p. 231.

refers to all discriminations based on a given characteristic, or only to discriminations against a class that has been oppressed.

All this discussion reveals a difficult problem in constitutional interpretation. For once, the debates contain a statement of what a clause was meant to do—include blacks and Orientals—and what it was not meant to do—include women. If intent were the only guide to meaning, this definition would negate a whole line of decisions that have ruled that the equal-protection clause does restrict, though it does not forbid, discrimination based on sex. These decisions—through no lack of intellectual honesty, but for reasons that will become clear in Chapter 5—contain no references to the legislative history. If the Court had examined this history, it might have discovered what I have found: a specific distinction that contradicts the broad principles on which it is supposedly based. This would not have been the first time such a contradiction was found between general and specific recommendations. The same thing happened, of course, in the school desegregation cases. The result there was a judicial retreat from legislative history. This retreat continued in the sexual equality cases of the 1970s. But, as I shall argue, the Court need not have retreated. Both sets of decisions were compatible with, and help enforce, the principles of Reconstruction. Both text and history suggest that what Bickel said about two other issues may also apply to the rights of women and children: "It is not true that the Framers intended the Fourteenth Amendment to outlaw segregation or to make applicable to the states all restriction on government that may be evolved under the Bill of Rights; but they did not foreclose such policies and may indeed have invited them." [66]

The Scope of the Fourteenth Amendment

The last two sections have dealt with the "why" and "who" of Section 1, but the final question, the "what," remains and perplexes. Just what rights and interests did the Fourteenth Amendment—not only the equal-protection clause but the privileges-and-immunities and due-process clauses as well—secure against the states? Some of the remarks I have quoted imply that it includes a right to be free from racial discrimination. Howard's remarks about hanging do not suggest that the amendment forbids capital punishment; they do, however, indicate that it forbids inequalities with respect to specific interests.

[66] *Least Dangerous Branch*, p. 103.

The Civil Rights Bill, too, grants to all citizens in several interests "the same right" as a white citizen.

Does it follow, then, that all racial discrimination is proscribed? Apparently not; this intention is disavowed whenever the debates reach the touchiest of all racial issues, the question of miscegenation. In response to a question from Reverdy Johnson, Trumbull and Fessenden declared that the Civil Rights Bill would not invalidate antimiscegenation laws. "Where," asked Fessenden, "is the discrimination against color in the law to which the Senator refers? A black man has the same right [i.e., none] to make a contract of marriage with a white woman that a white man has with a black woman." Trumbull made a similar statement about the Freedmen's Bureau Bill, and his argument is significant. These laws were constitutional, he declared, because "are not both races treated alike? . . . If the negro is denied the right to marry a white person, the white person is equally denied the right to marry the negro. I see no discrimination against either in this aspect that does not apply to both. Make the penalty the same on all classes of people for the same offense, and then no one can complain." [67]

So there is nothing wrong with distinctions based on race, so long as they do not treat one race as inferior to another. And it would seem that whatever applied to intermarriage would also apply to public accommodations and education. Only a specific kind of racial discrimination, that which treats one race unequally, is forbidden. The crucial question becomes whether Trumbull was right about what those laws did. In Chapter 5 I shall argue that *Brown* I embodies a fully justified conclusion that he was wrong, and that supposedly neutral discriminations are forbidden by the Fourteenth Amendment. But that was not how the Thirty-ninth Congress saw things, and that fact will have to be dealt with.

The House debates on the two bills produced another explanation for the exclusion of intermarriage from the scope of the Fourteenth Amendment. Samuel Moulton of Illinois insisted that

> the right to marry is not strictly a right at all, because it rests in contract alone between the individuals, and no other person has a right to contract it. It is not a right in any legal or technical sense at all. No one man has any right to marry any woman he pleases. If there was a law making that a civil right, it might be termed a civil right in the sense in which it is used here. But there being no law in any State to that effect, I insist that marriage is not a civil right, as contemplated by the provisions of this bill. [68]

[67] *Globe*, January 30 and 19, 1866, S., pp. 505, 322; Avins, pp. 128, 108.
[68] *Globe*, February 3, 1866, H., pp. 632–33; Avins, p. 141.

Efforts to use Congress' Section 5 enforcement powers stimulated still more debate on the scope of the amendment, and revealed large disagreements among those of its framers who were still in office. In December 1871 an amnesty bill removing the disqualification of former Confederates from officeholding under Section 3 was introduced at President Grant's request. Sumner then proposed an amendment to this bill which would have ended racial discrimination in jury selection, public accommodations, and public schools.[69] He had introduced versions of this civil rights bill before, but it had always been buried in the Judiciary Committee. Now Congress could not get rid of it so easily.

Sumner insisted that separate education deprived blacks of their Fourteenth Amendment rights. This was "no question of taste; it is no question of society, . . . it is simply a question of equal rights." In the same speech he invoked "the binding character of the Declaration of Independence in its annuciation of fundamental principles." Why was separation a denial of equal rights? In a second speech after the Christmas recess, quoting extensively from letters he had received, he argued that separate accommodations were in fact inferior ones; the insult, inconvenience, and discomfort endured by black citizens constituted inferior treatment. As for schools, "the indignity offered to the colored child is worse than any compulsory exposure . . . he is trained under the ban of inequality. . . . He is pinched and dwarfed while the stigma of color is stamped upon him."[70] Therefore, the bill was a valid exercise of the enforcement power.

Sumner met strong, sustained, and ultimately successful opposition, much of it from Trumbull. The Illinois senator had spoken of the need to remove "incidents of slavery" and "badges of servitude," but he did not agree that separate accommodations and schools were such badges. He argued that the bill was not within Congress' power. He said of education, public accommodations, and jury service just what Moulton had said of marriage. They were not civil rights, and thus were not guaranteed by the Fourteenth Amendment. Trumbull's version of civil rights was much narrower than some we shall examine. "I understand by the term 'civil rights', rights appertaining to the individual as a free, independent citizen; and what are they? The right to go and come; the right to enforce contracts; the right to convey his property; the right to buy property—those general rights that belong to man-

---

[69] *Globe*, December 20, 1871, S., pp. 240–45; Avins, pp. 575–78.

[70] *Globe*, December 20, 1871, and January 15, 1872, S., pp. 243, 250, 384; Avins, pp. 576, 579, 581. See also January 15 and 17, S., pp. 381–86, 429–34; Avins, pp. 579–85.

kind everywhere." The real purpose of Sumner's bill, "that has been misnamed a civil rights bill," was to grant not legal equality but "social rights"; it was a "social equality" bill.[71]

So two of the leading figures of the Thirty-ninth Congress had a fundamental difference of opinion about what the amendment they had enacted meant. But what did Trumbull mean by "social equality"? Arthur Boreman of West Virginia expanded on this theme: "... here it is proposed to require that ... all shall be allowed to associate together in the same schools." Francis Blair, a Missouri Democrat, had invoked "those laws which are too high to be perverted by Radical legislation, those laws which separate the races and give to each one its appropriate place on the continent."[72] So social equality had to do with mingling together, not with rights.

Sumner had enough supporters to continue the debate for four months, until, on May 14, the Senate deleted the school and jury clauses from the rider. The House took no action on it at all, though its debate also stressed the distinction between legal and social equality.[73] The amendment died, but the amnesty bill was passed.

Sumner reintroduced his original bill when the Forty-third Congress convened in December 1873, but he died in March 1874, while the bill was still in committee. In the elections that fall, the Republicans lost control of the House and lost significant strength in the Senate. Sumner was dead; Bingham, who had failed to be renominated for his seat, did not return; and when the bill came up again, it never had much of a chance. What became the Civil Rights Act of 1875 provided only that all be entitled to "full and equal enjoyment" of public facilities, with no enforcement powers.

The fact that Congress considered and rejected a bill requiring desegregation does not, of course, prove that it thought desegregation went beyond the scope of the Fourteenth Amendment. Clearly, however, some members did hold that opinion. Legislative interpretations of the amendment varied. Although Trumbull did not make the point clear in 1866, he apparently thought it did no more than enact his two bills. Berger's interpretation may indeed fit him. Sumner, however, used language similar to that of Howard, Bingham, and Stevens back in 1866. He invoked the Declaration to argue that some forms of segregation denied equal protection. Within five years after ratification, therefore, two conflicting constitutional theories had developed.

[71] *Globe*, January 19, 1866, and May 8, 13, and 14, 1872, S., pp. 319, 3189–91, 3361, 3421; Avins, pp. 108, 641–42, 652.
[72] *Globe*, May 14, and 9, S., pp. 3422, 3253; Avins, pp. 652, 644.
[73] *Globe*, May 21 and 29, H., app. pp. 597–99; Avins, pp. 656–57.

What rights *were* included? One was the right not to be branded, stigmatized, subjected to inferior treatment, relegated to a status inferior to that of other citizens; not, *at least*, on the basis of race. There is, however, some confusion as to what constitutes that kind of treatment. What else? Berger argued that the only rights protected were those listed in the Civil Rights Bill and some, but by no means all, of those in *Corfield* v. *Coryell*, which had been an obscure case before the Reconstruction Congress got onto it. In that case, Justice Bushrod Washington, riding circuit, had discussed the privileges-and-immunities clause of Article IV, section 2:

> What these fundamental rights are, it would perhaps be more tedious than difficult to enumerate. They may, however, be comprehended under the following general heads: Protection by the government, the enjoyment of life and liberty, with the right to acquire and possess property of every kind, and to pursue and obtain happiness and safety, subject, nevertheless, to such restraints as the government may justly prescribe for the general good of the whole. The right of a citizen of any one state to pass through, or to reside in any other state . . . ; to claim the benefits of the writ of habeas corpus; to institute and maintain actions of any kind in the courts of the state; to take, hold and dispose of property . . . may be mentioned as some of the particular privileges and immunities of citizens, which are clearly embraced by the general description of privileges intended to be fundamental. . . .[74]

As we have seen, Berger's scholarship is defective, and the rights listed seem far broader than he admits, but his conclusion that the listed rights are included in the Fourteenth Amendment is disputed by no one. Others have wanted to go much further. Prominent among them is Justice Hugo Black, who argued throughout most of his thirty-four years on the Court that the amendment had "incorporated" the Bill of Rights; that is, that it made all of the first eight amendments binding on the states. Black's first exposition of this theory, in a dissent in *Adamson* v. *California* in 1947, stimulated some scholarly reaction, much of it negative. Charles Fairman wrote, "In his contention that Section I was intended to impose amendments I to VIII upon the states, the record of history is overwhelmingly against him." But William Winslow Crosskey, writing in the 1950s, and Alfred H. Kelly, writing in the 1960s, found more to criticize in Fairman's article than in Black's opinion.[75]

[74] 6 Fed. Cas. 546, 551–52 (1823).
[75] Fairman, "Does the Fourteenth Amendment," p. 139; Crosskey, "Charles Fairman, 'Legislative History,' and the Constitutional Limitation on State Authority," *University of Chicago Law Review* 22 (Autumn 1954):1–143; Kelly, "Clio and the Court: An Illicit Love Affair," *Supreme Court Review* 1965:119–58. See also Stanley Morrison, "Does the Fourteenth Amendment Incorporate the Bill of Rights? The Judicial Interpretation," *Stanford Law Review* 2 (December 1949):140–73.

Who is right? The frustrating answer has to be: Neither Black nor Fairman. Certainly Justice Black, though he cited accurately, cited selectively. Two major speeches, however, explicitly support his thesis. Howard's introductory speech of May 23, 1866, quoted the same language from *Corfield*, which I have quoted, and continued:

> Such is the character of the privileges and immunities spoken of in [IV.2]. . . . To these privileges and immunities, whatever they may be—for they are not and cannot be fully defined in their entire extent and precise nature—to these should be added the personal rights guaranteed and secured by the first eight Amendments of the Constitution. . . .
>
> Now, sir, there is no power given in the Constitution to enforce and to carry out any of these guarantees. They are not powers granted by the Constitution to Congress, and of course do not come within the sweeping clause of the Constitution authorizing Congress to pass all laws necessary and proper for carrying out the foregoing or granted powers, but they stand simply as a bill of rights . . . while at the same time the states are not restrained from violating the principles embraced in them except by their own local constitutions. . . . The great object of the first section of this amendment is, therefore, to restrain the power of the States, and compel them at all times to respect these great fundamental guarantees.[76]

Black also quotes Bingham, Howard's counterpart in the House and the author of the amendment, at length. Only once, however, did Bingham say explicitly what Howard said. Inconveniently though not fatally for Black's argument, Bingham did not say it until 1871, during a debate on the Ku Klux Klan Act.[77] When asked why he had changed the language of Section 1 from the "necessary and proper" draft of February 3 to its final form, he replied:

> I had read—and that is what induced me to attempt to impose by constitutional limitations upon the powers of the States—the great decision of Marshall in Barron v. the Mayor and City of Baltimore. . . .
>
> In reexamining that case of Barron, Mr. Speaker, . . . I noted and apprehended as I never did before, certain words in that opinion of Marshall. Referring to the first eight articles of amendment to the Constitution of the United States, the Chief Justice said, "Had the framers of those amendments intended them to be limitations on the powers of the State governments they would have imitated the framers of the Constitution, and have expressed that intention."
>
> Acting upon this suggestion, I did imitate the framers of the original Constitution. . . . I prepared the provision of the first section of the fourteenth amendment. . . . [He recited it.] Permit me to say that the privileges and immunities of citizens of the United States . . . are chiefly de-

---

[76] Globe, S., p. 2765; Avins, p. 219. Cf. Adamson v. California, 332 U.S. 46, 105–7 (1947) (Black dissenting).

[77] See Fairman, "Does the Fourteenth Amendment," pp. 135–37.

fined in the first eight amendments to the Constitution of the United States. [He recited them.]
. . . These eight articles I have shown never were limitations upon the power of the states, *until made so by the fourteenth amendment.*[78]

Fairman dismisses this argument as hindsight, but his dismissal is too peremptory. Much of his own "overwhelming evidence" consists of speeches by Bingham and Stevens during the debates of 1866. What these speeches suggest is not what Fairman apparently meant to argue, that Black went too far, but that he did not go far enough. This is not surprising, for the direction in which the passages led is one in which he would have been loath to go. Black's incorporation doctrine, like his absolutist interpretation of the Bill of Rights, was intended to restrain judges, to keep them from writing their own views of justice into the Constitution. The problem is that that is exactly what such people as Bingham and Stevens were trying to do with their views. Again and again they argued that the Fourteenth Amendment protected not primarily the first 'eight amendments, but natural rights; and as the 1859 speech indicates, natural rights had a lavish scope.

Bingham restated this argument in the last major House speech before the vote:

> There was a want hitherto, and there remains a want now, in the Constitution of our country, which the proposed amendment will supply. What is that? It is the power of the people, the whole people of the United States, to do that by congressional enactment which hitherto they have not had the power to do . . . ; that is, to protect by national law the privileges and immunities of all the citizens of the Republic and the inborn rights of every person within its jurisdiction.[79]

The Radicals were indefinite about just what rights were protected, and it appears that they were not eager to run the risk of excluding much. For Kelly, the evidence against Black was chiefly

> the general aura of vagueness that surrounded the passage of the Fourteenth Amendment in the two Houses. The debate was conducted almost entirely in terms of grand symbolism—that of the Declaration of Independence in particular—and remarkably little in terms of the specific legal implications of the new amendment. There was an obvious political reason for this: the Radical Republicans were trying to reassure the mod-

---

[78] *Globe*, March 31, 1871, H., app. pp. 83–86; Avins, pp. 509–12. Emphasis supplied. Cf. Adamson v. California, 332 U.S. 46, 111–20 (1947) (Black dissenting).
[79] *Globe*, May 10, 1866, H., p. 2542; Avins, p. 217.

erates of their party without discounting too far the potential force of the amendment they were proposing.[80]

Fairman, like Berger, regarded the amendment's principal framers as muddled thinkers. A tone of disdain pervades his article.[81] And indeed, we have caught Bingham and Stevens in one error, the effort to distinguish between disabilities of Negroes and those of married women. But it was their amendment. With help from Sumner and Trumbull, they wrote it; with help from Howard, they got it passed. Their views have to be given great weight. We cannot dismiss them simply because their arguments were not always discriminating or their thoughts precise. Discrimination and precision may not be the most necessary attributes for authors of a bill of rights, especially a bill that includes and allocates the power to enforce those rights.

The debates can befuddle contemporary readers. We have been warned repeatedly not to write our own theories of natural law into the Constitution. But the authors of the Reconstruction amendments intended either to enact their natural law theories into the Constitution or to make clear beyond doubt that the Constitution already contained those theories. Howard Jay Graham has written sensibly about this confusion:

> Sharp appreciation of the pitfalls inherent in the meaning of "constitutionality," "unconstitutionality," "law," and "amendment" comes most naturally to those who have had the benefits of well-established tradition in these fields. This appreciation was what the Civil War generation lacked, and it lacked it because judicial control still was largely hypothetical, because the Constitution had not been amended since 1804, because law as a whole was much simpler, and because the natural rights—social compact theory still dominated nearly everyone's thinking.[82]

Comparison of almost any of Bingham's speeches with the *Barron* or *Prigg* opinions will illustrate this point. It was not that the Radicals were muddled thinkers. They were just not legalistic thinkers, though some of them were lawyers, yet they refused to leave law and the Constitution to lawyers and judges. This was *appropriate* thinking, for there was another obvious political reason to be vague. The amendment not only gave interpretive powers to the courts, but, more important, gave legislative powers to Congress. The Radicals may not have been much concerned with preventing Congress from removing

[80] "Clio and the Court," p. 134.
[81] See Crosskey, "Charles Fairman," p. 11.
[82] *Everyman's Constitution*, p. 323.

the disabilities of married women and legalizing intermarriage. Legislative powers are broad powers, and thus they were conceived.

But the debates on Sumner's doomed civil rights bill reveal that not everyone conceived the powers or the rights granted so broadly as the Radicals did. Trumbull's interpretation was narrower, and it was his amendment, too. Without the votes of the moderates, the bill could not have been passed. Their version of it demands attention. But there is no reason to prefer Trumbull's interpretation, as Berger does, either because Trumbull thought more like a twentieth-century lawyer than the Radicals did or because he had fewer enemies than they.

Clearly, all the ambiguities and complexities inherent in studying legislative intent are present in force in the particular case of the Fourteenth Amendment. As Earl Warren said, the evidence is inconclusive.[83] No statements about its meaning can be absolute and categorical.

Conclusion

Finally, after this long investigation, what *can* be said about that meaning? Confusion and contradiction abound, but some general conclusions are possible. The members of Congress who were most prominent in enacting the Fourteenth Amendment evinced a belief in something very similar to what Ronald Dworkin has called a right to "treatment as an equal": a right to equal respect and concern, derived more or less directly from the Declaration of Independence, which depended on the individual's very status as a human being. It was this right that prevented inferior treatment, not some notion that the freed slaves were equal to whites in ability and thus deserved equal status. This equality seemed to belong to all human beings, but what it entailed in terms of treatment, for blacks or for anyone else, was not made clear.

Not only did the Fourteenth Amendment establish this right, but it also guaranteed some specific individual rights. There was little agreement on what rights, out of an infinite possible list of interests, were included and what were not, but it is clear that the list was incomplete, though not infinite. Some interests were included and some excluded. And since the amendment contained a guarantee of equality, those rights that were included were for all persons equally. This is about as

[83] Brown v. Board of Education, 347 U.S. 483, 489 (1954).

exact a set of conclusions as it is possible to draw. Therefore, it is easy to understand, even to share, Fairman's and Berger's irritation.

The "natural law" component of the debates is especially troubling. If the Radicals could argue that their ideas of natural law belong in the Constitution, so can others. In the nineteenth century, opposing views of natural law abounded, as they do today.[84] The debates themselves contain some conflicting views. The reader will recall that Senator Blair implied in 1874 that natural law required racial segregation. Arguing from natural law principles opens up the possibility that others may do so, too, with untoward results. Although there is probably no such thing as one's *personal*, in the sense of idiosyncratic, view of natural law—any such views are picked up from the larger society—it is always difficult to show that the principles one accepts are more natural than someone else's principles.

Another problem is that, since giving these guarantees any force soon became, for all practical purposes, the task of the courts, this open-ended legislative history gives vast discretion to judges. This latitude may be disquieting to those who are wary of countermajoritarian bodies. The conclusion that the Radicals put their version of natural law into the Constitution does not give any judge the power to do the same with his or her own theory. Nor is it likely that the Fourteenth Amendment was meant to give the courts power to do everything Congress could do under Section 5. But while no one wants *courts* to amend the Constitution, neither do we want them to nullify amendments that have been passed.

I have maintained that, as valuable as legislative history is in guiding constitutional interpretation, past intent cannot dictate present decisions. It would surely be difficult to derive many commands from the Fourteenth Amendment's history, since the guarantees found there are so broad and general that they could be used to support almost anything. But one great value of this history is that the debates suggest other sources of meaning. Since members of Congress often spoke of natural law, natural rights, and fundamental rights, interpreters are encouraged to think about what these concepts meant to this Congress, and to try to discover what concepts of natural law and rights were familiar to them. Chapters 2 and 3 indicated that such discovery is not difficult. Since much of the debate links the Fourteenth Amendment to the Bill of Rights, we are encouraged to look to these guarantees. Both extratextual and structural modes of interpretation seem appropriate. But as Chapter 5 will show, the Supreme Court has pre-

[84] See Ely, *Democracy and Distrust*, chap. 3.

ferred clause and precedent, choices that have produced consistent results.

So what emerges from congressional debates is, first, a notion of equality based on natural entitlement to rights, derived from the Declaration; second, a concern with protecting certain rights, including but not limited to life, liberty, and property; and third, an intention to grant people equality under law in order to give them protection from those who would oppress and even kill them. As Chapter 5 will show, what emerges from just over a century of adjudication is far less. If current doctrine is to stand, it must rest on foundations other than legislative history. It is time, now, to turn to court decisions to see how that doctrine developed, and what those foundations might be.

[5]

From Equal Protection
to Suspect Classification

The promises of Reconstruction were not kept. Perhaps it should not surprise us that the congressional commitment to equality did not endure; at any rate, it lasted barely ten years, if that long. The last major law that passed, badly weakened from its original version, was the Civil Rights Act of 1875; and a year later it was all over. The compromise that gave Rutherford Hayes the presidency withdrew federal troops from the South and returned power to white southern Democrats. After that, slowly and inexorably, the whites reestablished their dominance and returned the blacks to subjection, though not to slavery.[1]

The Supreme Court cannot be assigned primary responsibility for this regression. But its interpretations of the Fourteenth Amendment contravened Radical Republican principles as badly as Congress and the states did. The lavish grant of liberty and equality was narrowed into a guarantee of a few rights that were not, in fact, protected; the group that benefited most from the Fourteenth Amendment in its first fifty years consisted of large corporations.[2] As late as 1935, one historian noted that

> the Supreme Court in construing the "equal protection of the laws" provision of the Fourteenth Amendment has conformed to a degree to the pro-slavery theory of a classified equality instead of to the anti-slavery theory of this essential right of every individual to equality with every

---

[1] See Kluger, *Simple Justice*, pp. 61–62; C. Vann Woodward, *The Strange Career of Jim Crow*, 2d rev. ed. (New York: Oxford University Press, 1966).

[2] The major case here is, of course, Lochner v. New York, 198 U.S. 45 (1905).

individual under the law. The Supreme Court permits the classification of persons within a State for the purpose of legislation whenever a substantial basis for legislation can be found, but the Court, of course, has never accepted the Southern idea that race is such a substantial basis.[3]

In a way, though, it had; *Plessy* v. *Ferguson* can be read as a statement of the appropriateness of certain racial classifications for achieving legislative ends, and *Plessy* was still good law in 1935.[4] Most readers would now dismiss the quoted statement as no longer true. They would be wrong. In essence, the passage still accurately describes the way in which Fourteenth Amendment cases are decided. There are some new wrinkles since 1935, but the emphasis is still on classification and discrimination rather than on the essential right of equality.

One increasingly popular school of thought maintains that if the Court initially narrowed the Fourteenth Amendment, since 1954 it has enlarged it beyond recognition.[5] I argue here that this is not true; that judicial interpretation remains stingy and niggling; and that, in particular, the doctrine of suspect classification has been superimposed on the amendment at considerable cost to individual rights. Yet it cannot be said that the Court has acted with malevolence, or even with bias. It has just acted like a group of lawyers.

The rules as developed over the years were refined in an orderly fashion, from precedent to precedent; they have traceable roots; and, initially at least, they made sense. The trouble is that they start out having little to do with the Fourteenth Amendment, and end up having less and less to do with it. A comparison of these cases with the legislative history brings home the truth of the statement of Graham's which I quoted near the end of Chapter 4. The Reconstruction Congress did not think about constitutional law in the same way that postreconstruction lawyers and judges do. It was judges, alas, that had the task of giving meaning to the Fourteenth Amendment, and the meaning they have given it has changed it drastically.

The first two Fourteenth Amendment cases heard by the Court well illustrate the flexibilities of the text. Despite the fact that the freed slaves had been Congress' paramount concern, neither case had anything to do with them. The *Slaughter-House Cases* of 1873 were brought by New Orleans butchers threatened by a state-conferred monopoly, while *Bradwell* v. *Illinois*, decided the same day, involved a woman

---

[3] William Sumner Jenkins, *Pro-Slavery Thought in the Old South* (Chapel Hill: University of North Carolina Press, 1935), p. 199n.
[4] 163 U.S. 537 (1896).
[5] See Berger, *Government by Judiciary*; Graglia, *Disaster by Decree.*

who had been denied a license to practice law.[6] Feminists have given *Bradwell* some notoriety, but our concern here has to be with *Slaughter-House*, which had greater influence on doctrinal development. The butchers, like Myra Bradwell, lost their case, but they lost primarily because of what the Court then saw as the amendment's racial preoccupations.

Justice Samuel F. Miller identified the "pervading purpose" of the Civil War amendments: "The freedom of the slave race, the security and firm establishment of that freedom, and the protection of the newly made freeman and citizen from the oppressions of those who had formerly exercised unlimited dominion over him." Although this preoccupation did not mean that *only* blacks were covered by the amendments—the Thirteenth, for example, forbade slavery for anyone—the "main purpose" of each clause of Section 1 of the Fourteenth Amendment was to benefit the former slaves. Miller's interpretation of the equal-protection clause was more definite: "In the light of the history of these amendments, and the pervading purpose of them . . . it is not difficult to give a meaning to this clause. The existence of laws in the States where the newly emancipated negroes resided, *which discriminated with gross injustice and hardship against them as a class*, was the evil to be remedied by this clause." Then, in what is surely one of the worst prophecies in Supreme Court history, Miller declared, "We doubt very much whether any action of a State not directed by way of discrimination against the negroes as a class, or on account of their race, will ever be held to come within the purview of this provision."[7] The Court's first pronouncement on this clause has a familiar ring to those versed in the equal-protection litigation of the last thirty years. The themes of unjust discrimination, of classification, and of special hostility to discriminations directed against one particular racial minority appear.

Breaking the Promise

Although the Court soon rethought its position about the scope of equal protection, the themes of *Slaughter-House* continued to direct its thinking on race. The next two major cases, *Strauder* v. *West Virginia* and *Ex parte Virginia*, arrived in 1880.[8] Both decisions struck

[6] 16 Wall. 36 (1873); 16 Wall. 130.
[7] 16 Wall. 36, 71–73, 81. Emphasis supplied.
[8] 100 U.S. 303; 100 U.S. 339.

down laws that excluded blacks from jury service, although it will be remembered that Congress had refused to pass legislation to that effect. In *Strauder*, Justice William Strong elaborated on the meaning of the Fourteenth Amendment:

> What is this but declaring that the law in the States shall be the same for the black as for the white; that all persons, whether colored or white, shall stand equal before the laws of the States; and, in regard to the colored race, for whose protection the amendment was primarily designed, that no discrimination shall be made against them by law because of their color?
>
> ... The very fact that colored people are singled out and expressly denied by a statute all right to participate in the administration of the law, as jurors, because of their color ... is practically a brand upon them, affixed by the law, an assertion of their inferiority, and a stimulant to that race prejudice which is an impediment to securing to individuals of the race that equal justice which the law aims to secure to all others.[9]

This opinion echoes—not, so far as we know, intentionally—statements made by Howard, Trumbull, and Stevens during the debates, as well as Senator Wilson's remarks about stigmatization. On examination, it intrigues because of the distinctions it makes. The law must be the same for blacks and whites; both races must be equal before the law; and there must be no discrimination *against blacks* because of their color. The first two clauses of that sentence might seem to make the third a tautology—for both races to stand equal might demand no discrimination against either—but apparently the Court did not see the matter in that light. The opinion does go on to speak not only of discrimination against blacks in particular, but of race discrimination in general. If a future black majority excluded whites from jury service, or if all Celtic Irishmen were excluded, this discrimination, too, would be unconstitutional.[10] Thus the equal-protection clause forbids special restrictions of a subordinate group by a dominant one, but it is not clear whether it forbids all racial discrimination. Hindsight should not make too much of distinctions that may be more important to us now than they were to the Supreme Court one hundred years ago. But it is interesting to note that briefs in reverse discrimination cases in the 1970s cite *Strauder* as authority against such programs—cutting off the first sentence I quoted at the second semicolon.[11]

[9] 100 U.S. 303, 307–8.
[10] Ibid., p. 308.
[11] See Ann Fagan Ginger, ed., *De Funis v. Odegaard and the University of Washington: The University Admissions Case* (Dobbs Ferry, N.Y.: Oceana, 1975), "Petitioners' Opening Brief," 1:323.

Six years after *Strauder*, the Court invalidated a law that, as applied, discriminated against Orientals. *Yick Wo* v. *Hopkins* declared that the due-process and equal-protection clauses "are universal in their application, to all persons within the territorial jurisdiction, without regard to any differences of race, of color, or of nationality."[12] *Slaughter-House*, *Strauder*, and *Yick Wo* settled this much: whatever else the Fourteenth Amendment did or did not do, it forbade invidious discrimination on the basis of race. This remains good law. But two cases decided in 1883 had limited this doctrine. The *Civil Rights Cases* restricted the scope of the amendment to discriminations imposed by state authority.[13] The Court insisted that the amendment did not reach the acts of private individuals, and invalidated two sections of the 1875 law. This principle, too, remains dogma, although the courts now have a somewhat broader notion of what constitutes "state action."

Pace v. *Alabama* dealt with a racial discrimination that did not single out one particular group. At issue was a law forbidding marriage or sexual intercourse beteen whites and Negroes. The Court found no violation of the equal-protection clause. Justice Stephen J. Field insisted that this law was no more discriminatory than Alabama's general prohibition of fornication and adultery:

> The two sections of the code are entirely consistent. The one prescribes generally a punishment for an offence committed between persons of different sexes; the other prescribes a punishment for an offence which can only be committed where the two sexes are of different races. There is in neither section any discrimination against either race. Section 4184 equally includes the offence when the persons of the two sexes are both white and when they are both black. Section 4189 applies the same punishment to both offenders, the white and the black. . . . The punishment of each offending person, white or black, is the same.[14]

That, of course, was what Trumbull and Fessenden had said. Anti-miscegenation laws were compatible with the equal-protection clause as long as they applied to both races. The Fourteenth Amendment prevented the states from treating one race as inferior to the other, but it allowed the states to separate the races from each other. It was an easy step from *Pace* to *Plessy*. There, thirteen years later, the Court upheld *de jure* segregation in railroad cars. Justice Henry Brown wrote: "A statute which implies merely a legal distinction between the white

[12] 118 U.S. 356, 369 (1886).
[13] 109 U.S. 3 (1883).
[14] 106 U.S. 583, 585.

and colored races . . . has no tendency to destroy the legal equality of the two races." Brown went on to elaborate, if not expatiate on, this point:

> The object of the amendment was undoubtedly to enforce the absolute equality of the two races before the law, but in the nature of things it could not have been intended to abolish distinctions based upon color, or to enforce social, as distinguished from political equality, or a commingling of the two races upon terms unsatisfactory to either. Laws permitting, and even requiring, their separation in places where they are liable to be brought into contact do not necessarily imply the inferiority of either race to the other, and have been generally, if not universally, recognized as within the competency of the state legislatures.

Brown then addressed himself to Plessy's failure to recognize this distinction:

> We consider the underlying fallacy of the plaintiff's argument to consist in the assumption that the enforced separation of the two races stamps the colored race with a badge of inferiority. If this be so, it is not by reason of anything found in the act, but solely because the colored race chooses to put that construction upon it. . . . The argument also assumes that social prejudices may be overcome by legislation. . . . We cannot accept this proposition. If the two races are to meet upon terms of social equality, it must be as the result of natural affinities. . . .[15]

Again, as in *Pace*, separate may be equal; both races are treated the same. It is the exposition of this argument that later got the Court into trouble. The two races are equal, but only because of the law and only before the law. This equality depends exclusively on a constitutional amendment. Furthermore, the equality that the law can establish is an artificial construct, and its scope is limited.

Legal or political equality is distinguished here from social equality, just as it was in the debates on Sumner's civil rights bill. The meaning of that term is no clearer for the Court than it was for Congress. Does "social equality" mean that the races are intrinsically equal, identical, or equivalent in worth, or does it mean that each race *thinks* the other is its equal? Whatever the concept means, it differs from legal equality in at least two ways. First, apparently only social equals flock together. For members of different races to share a railroad car is an indication of social equality, but for both races to share the jury box is an indication of legal equality. Second, social equality cannot be established by legislation.

[15] 163 U.S. 537, 543, 544, 551–52.

Plessy has been labeled "a compound of bad logic, bad history, bad sociology, and bad constitutional law." [16] Besides, the opinion contradicts itself. It denies that *de jure* segregation implies inferiority, but insists that integration would imply equality. (Every year the students in my civil liberties class take great pleasure in pointing out this contradiction.) Upholding Louisiana's power to classify Plessy, seven-eighths white, as Negro, the opinion includes this passage:

> It is claimed by the plaintiff in error that, in any mixed community, the reputation of belonging to the dominant race, in this case the white race, is *property*, in the same sense that right of action, or of inheritance, is property. . . . We are unable to see how this statute deprives him of, or in any way affects his right to, such property. If he be a white man and assigned to a colored coach, he may have his action for damages against the company for being deprived of his so-called property. Upon the other hand, if he be a colored man and be so assigned, he has been deprived of no property, since he is not lawfully entitled to the reputation of being a white man. [17]

So the races are equal before the law, but a white person may sue if mislabeled. The absurdity of the "separate but equal" rule is shown by the way its defense becomes mired in contradictions. Justice John Marshall Harlan, in his famous dissent, and a unanimous Court, in *Brown* v. *Board of Education*, make plain what by now needs no further explanation: that segregation imposed on a subject race by a dominant one does indeed constitute inferior treatment. [18]

Plessy v. *Ferguson* is an anachronism now, but one that is crucial for our understanding of constitutional equality. It has the same incredulous tone that pervades the privileges-and-immunities portions of *Slaughter-House*; surely the authors of the Fourteenth Amendment could not have intended to change the world quite this much. The Court did not entertain the possibility that drastic fundamental change was just what the authors had intended. Most criticisms of *Plessy* have emphasized its dubious distinction between legal and social equality. But it made another distinction, which has continued to influence our thinking: between discrimination against a particular race, to which the Fourteenth Amendment applied, and discrimination imposed evenhandedly on all races, which the amendment did not reach. This distinction could not bear critical analysis, but it prevailed as law,

[16] Harris, *Quest for Equality*, p. 101.
[17] 163 U.S. 537, 549.
[18] Indeed, it is likely that any form of segregation implies inferiority. I am indebted to a student in my 1979 civil liberties class for pointing this out; he used as an illustration the separation of the sexes in Orthodox Jewish synagogues.

though increasingly shaky law, until 1954.[19] And because it prevailed, the United States remained a society of racism under law, almost as if the Civil War amendments had never been passed.

The Roots of Suspect Classification

Nearly fifty years elapsed before the Court again found it necessary to theorize about racial equality. When it did, it helped to bring about the destruction of its old doctrine. The new rule came from a peculiar source, two decisions that, first, had nothing to do with the Fourteenth Amendment, and second, were as racist and repressive as *Pace* and *Plessy*: the first two Japanese relocation cases, *Hirabayashi* v. *United States* and *Korematsu* v. *United States*.

In *Hirabayashi*, Chief Justice Harlan Stone stressed the fact that the Constitution contains no equal-protection guarantee binding on the national government.[20] This interpretation was a correct literal reading, but the situation seems to have called for some structural analysis. The Court was considering an executive order that restricted individual rights on the basis of race. What *better* place in the Constitution could the judges have looked to for guidance than the Civil War amendments? Ignoring these provisions was too easy a way out in the Japanese cases. And it is disturbing that doctrines developed in cases that disavowed any equal-protection underpinnings would later be used to interpret the equal-protection clause. Such extrapolation could only weaken the guarantee.

In *Korematsu*, Justice Black announced a rule that he then failed to apply. "It should be noted, to begin with, that all legal restrictions which curtail the civil rights of a single racial group are immediately suspect. That is not to say that all such restrictions are unconstitutional. It is to say that courts must subject them to the most rigid scrutiny." Black appeared to regard this principle as axiomatic. He did not cite a single precedent to support it.[21] Lack of precedent hardly

[19] See Missouri ex rel. Gaines v. Canada, 305 U.S. 337 (1938); Sipuel v. Board of Regents, 332 U.S. 631 (1948); Sweatt v. Painter, 334 U.S. 629 (1950); McLaurin v. Oklahoma State Regents, 334 U.S. 637 (1950).

[20] 320 U.S. 81, 100 (1943).

[21] 323 U.S. 214, 216 (1944). Justice Black might have cited Skinner v. Oklahoma, at least as dictum. There Justice William O. Douglas wrote for the Court, "When the law lays an unequal hand on those who have committed intrinsically the same quality of offense and sterilizes one and not the other, it has made *as invidious a discrimination as if it had selected a particular race or nationality for oppressive treatment*" (316 U.S. 535, 541 [1942]; emphasis supplied). Perhaps, though, Black preferred not to cite this case, since *Skinner* invalidated the law at issue while *Korematsu* upheld the executive order.

mattered in *Korematsu*, since Executive Order 9066 was upheld. But *Korematsu* provided the base on which later equal-protection litigation has built. Those three sentences, which may have been intended only as dicta to sweeten a bitter pill, have been cited as precedent in subsequent landmark Fourteenth Amendment cases, which in their turn have become binding precedents. Ironically, it is this racist decision that introduced the suspect-classification rule.

But maybe not ironically. For the protection given to racial groups not only was absent from *Korematsu*, but is qualified in general. The rule does not forbid all discrimination directed against a racial group. It leaves a loophole for those discriminations that are judged necessary. Thus it has nowhere near the import of Harlan's dissent in *Plessy*: "I deny that any legislative body may have regard to the race of citizens when the civil rights of those citizens are involved." [22] Still, "rigid scrutiny" is a tougher standard than the old rational-basis test, and it would have dictated Harlan's preferred result. And *Korematsu*, on paper at least, does state that the Constitution protects the civil rights of all races, not just blacks.

As dogma, *Korematsu* is suspended in constitutional space; it is supported by no specific parts of the Constitution. But later decisions grafted Black's opening sentence onto the equal-protection clause, and some of those cases found arguments to support it. They also extended the *Korematsu* ruling in three significant respects. The rule announced there was limited, first, to *racial* discriminations; second, to discriminations *against* a racial group (thus following *Strauder*, *Yick Wo*, and *Plessy*); and third, to discriminations that curtailed the *civil rights* of a racial group. But subsequent cases negate the distinction between invidious and neutral discriminations, blur the distinction between civil rights and less vital interests, and give "suspect classification" a meaning that goes well beyond race discrimination. Still more important, these decisions have in effect put suspect classification and strict scrutiny into the Constitution itself. [23]

The End of Separate but Equal

The Court's famous opinion in the first *Brown* v. *Board of Education* case, whose elegant phrases hardly need repetition, owes no ob-

[22] 163 U.S. 537, 554–55 (1896).
[23] See Walter F. Murphy, "Civil Liberties and the Japanese American Cases: A Study in the Uses of *Stare Decisis*," *Western Political Quarterly* 11 (March 1958):3–13.

vious debt to *Korematsu*. Its emphasis was not on the suspectness of race discrimination but on the effects of a particular example of it, *de jure* school desegregation, on a particular group, black children. But some of the briefs in *Brown* and its companions did rely on the Japanese relocation cases to argue that all racial discrimination was odious and suspect.[24] *Bolling v. Sharpe*, the District of Columbia case that effectively incorporated the Fourteenth Amendment in the Bill of Rights before the reverse process had taken hold, announced, "Classifications based solely upon race must be scrutinized with particular care, since they are contrary to our traditions and thus constitutionally suspect."[25] For the first time, the court ruled that equal protection applied to the federal government.

Chapters 2 and 3 called into question the notion that racial classification is contrary to American traditions, but presumably Chief Justice Earl Warren was referring to traditions dating from 1863. The crucial point here, however, is that *Brown* and *Bolling*, two cases often read as one, in fact make two different arguments. In *Brown*, separate schools are "inherently unequal" because a racial classification that on its face applies equally to any group affected by it is in fact inseparable from the social context that produced it and reinforces the assumed inferiority of the subject group.[26] This ruling takes the *Strauder* argument a step further: segregation, like jury exclusion, is a badge of inferiority. *Bolling* echoes both *Korematsu* and Harlan's declaration that "our Constitution is color-blind, and neither knows nor tolerates classes among citizens."[27] This argument insists that something about race—it is not clear what—makes it so invidious a basis for distinguishing among people that it may be used only in extraordinary circumstances.

In these decisions, of course, each argument dictated the same results, but each arrived at those results by different means. The *Brown* argument is actually more subtle and complex than that of *Bolling*; it requires careful thought about just how a facially neutral discrimination can harm one particular group, and how we know that one race is dominant and another subject. *Bolling* provides an easier way to invalidate segregation; all one needs to do is to apply the general rule

---

[24] 347 U.S. 483 (1954). See Philip B. Kurland and Gerhard Casper, eds., *Brown v. Board of Education*, vol. 49 of *Landmark Briefs and Arguments of the Supreme Court of the United States* (Arlington, Va.: University Publications of America, 1975), "Brief for Appellants, 1952 Term," pp. 32–34; "Brief for American Veterans Committee, Amicus Curiae." pp. 248–49, 256. See also Kluger, *Simple Justice*, p. 21.

[25] 347 U.S. 497, 499 (1954).

[26] 347 U.S. 483, 495.

[27] 163 U.S. 537, 559 (1896).

that all racial discrimination is suspect to any specific instance of racial classification. The problem is that this argument not only gets to the same destination, but goes much further. The *Brown* argument applies only to racial discrimination that is linked to inferior treatment, while the *Bolling* argument rejects any racial discrimination, whatever its purpose or effect.

As each argument was fatal to *Plessy* v. *Ferguson*, each would have disposed of *Pace* v. *Alabama*. But antimiscegenation laws survived *de jure* segregation by ten years.[28] In 1964, *McLaughlin* v. *Florida* struck down a law forbidding interracial cohabitation.[29] After that, the result three years later in *Loving* v. *Virginia*, involving a law against intermarriage, was a foregone conclusion. Certainly these laws were premised on the assumed inferiority of blacks as much as segregation was. But the Court did not stress this point. Instead, it echoed *Korematsu* and *Bolling* to conclude, in 1967, that "At the very least, the Equal Protection Clause demands that racial classifications . . . be subject to the 'most rigid scrutiny' and, if they are ever to be upheld, they must be shown to be necessary to the accomplishment of some permissible state objective, independent of the racial discrimination *which it was the object of the Fourteenth Amendment to eliminate*."[30]

But was that the object of the Fourteenth Amendment? In 1953 *Brown* had confronted the Court with a problem that worried it enough to call for rebriefing and reargument. *De jure* school segregation had existed when the amendment was passed, and, as Chapter 4 showed, the legislative history suggests no intention to change the practice.[31] Although asking two opposing parties to a suit to do historical research may seem to be a dubious approach to scholarship, the *Brown* Court dealt with this problem in a legitimate way. It decided that the inherent difficulties in determining legislative intent, the conflicting arguments in the debates, and the changes in public education since the 1860s rendered the history "at best . . . inconclusive."[32]

The historical problem in the intermarriage cases was more serious. Chapter 4 showed that, more than once, members of Congress denied any intention to legalize intermarriage, and for just the reasons given in *Pace*: such laws had an equal impact on both races. But in *McLaughlin*, the Court, speaking through Justice Byron White, referred to "the historical fact that the central purpose of the Fourteenth

[28] The Court did deny review in Naim v. Naim, 350 U.S. 891, 985 (1954).
[29] 379 U.S. 184.
[30] Loving v. Virginia, 388 U.S. 1, 11. Emphasis supplied.
[31] See also Bickel, "Original Understanding."
[32] 347 U.S. 483, 489.

Amendment was to eliminate racial discrimination emanating from official sources in the States." In *Loving*, Warren did discuss Trumbull's statement but discounted it by quoting the "inconclusive" language from *Brown*. But Warren also stated that the amendment's "clear and central purpose . . . was to eliminate all official state sources of invidious racial discrimination."[33] The problem is that the framers did not consider this sort of discrimination "invidious."

As Chapter 1 pointed out, these cases represented neither the first nor the last time that the Court invalidated a practice that the framers or amenders of the Constitution had tolerated. The school prayer decisions are one example. But those rulings were legitimate because, in the light of modern reality, those specific policies violated general principles grounded in the Constitution. The problem with *McLaughlin* and *Loving* is that they laid down a general principle that the Court read into Fourteenth Amendment history, and that does not belong there. The debates not only affirm the states' power to forbid intermarriage, but they do so in words that refute the contention that the goal was to eliminate all legislation based on race. As far as intermarriage itself was concerned, the Court discussed the historical evidence and gave reasons for discounting it. But it offered no reasons—and indeed, it would be hard to find good ones—for its conclusion about the general principle.[34]

It took twenty-three years and six cases to establish the constitutional dogma that racial classifications, *all* racial classifications, are inherently suspect and sustainable only on strict scrutiny. There were serious historical problems with this doctrine. And in another ten years it would bear strange fruit, as a rule that began as an ineffective safeguard against depriving a disadvantaged group of its civil rights became an effective barrier against laws intended to remove those disadvantages. Again and again, in the reverse discrimination cases, briefs for Marco De Funis, Allan Bakke, and their *amici* urged on the Court the neutral import of *Brown, Bolling, McLaughlin*, and *Loving*.[35] And

[33] 379 U.S. 184, 191–92 (1964); 388 U.S. 1, 9, 10 (1967).
[34] This discussion is adapted from my article "Reverse Discrimination: The Dangers of Hardened Categories," *Law and Policy Quarterly* 4 (January 1982):71–94.
[35] On *De Funis*, see Ginger, ed., *De Funis v. Odegaard*: "Petitioners' Opening Brief," 1:323–25; "Amicus Curiae Briefs of American Jewish Congress," 1:347–48; "Advocate Society et al.," 1:424–25; "American Jewish Rights Council," 1:456; "Anti-Defamation League of B'nai Brith," 1:489–91; "Amicus Curiae Briefs of AFL-CIO," 2:523; "National Association of Manufacturers," 2:540. On Bakke, see Alfred A. Slocum, ed., *Allan Bakke v. Regents of the University of California* (Dobbs Ferry, N.Y.: Oceana, 1978): "Brief for Respondent in Opposition to Petition for Writ of Certiorari," 2:231; "Brief for Respondent," 5:51–54; "Amicus Curiae Briefs of Queens Jewish Community

in *Bakke*, a majority of the California Supreme Court and at least one justice of the United States Supreme Court accepted this argument as good law. "Racial and ethnic distinctions *of any sort* are inherently suspect and thus call for the most exacting judicial examination." [36]

But if *Loving* and *McLaughlin* had been written more nearly like *Brown*—if they had emphasized the link between antimiscegenation laws and racism, and shown that these laws did indeed brand blacks as inferiors—it would have been hard for any judge to write as Lewis Powell did in *Bakke*. If the Court had overturned these laws not because they were instances of racial discrimination but because they stigmatized blacks, just as segregation did, the cases would not have been very persuasive precedents against reverse discrimination. That fact by itself, of course, does not make the Court's choice of emphasis wrong. It does, however, reveal why the difference between the *Brown* and *Bolling* arguments is important, and it does invite speculation about why that particular choice was made.

It is impossible to know just why the justices chose as they did, since nothing in the record of either *McLaughlin* or *Loving* indicates that they realized they were making a choice. But there are several reasons why the suspect classification rule is attractive as a means of disposing of these cases. First, it is a neutral principle; it does not single out anyone, or any race, for special treatment. Thus it appears to provide equal treatment for all. Second, the notion that there is something wrong with race as a way of classifying people has a certain immediate appeal. The Court did not go into this matter in the segregation and marriage cases, but it has done so since, in rulings I shall be examining. To discriminate because of race is to discriminate because of a characteristic a person did not choose and cannot change; because of something one is, not something one did; and because of something unrelated—or at least not related in any predictable or measurable way—to any individual merit or ability. Such discrimination does indeed seem contrary to at least some American traditions, as Warren wrote in *Bolling*. Of course, that idea is not really what the framers

---

Council et al.," 5:78–79; "American Federation of Teachers," 5:136; "Order Sons of Italy" [sic], 5:180–82; "Young Americans for Freedom," 5:211–14; "Anti-Defamation League," 5:255–58; "Pacific Legal Foundation," 5:273–77; "American Jewish Committee et al.," 5:334–37; "Fraternal Order of Police et al.," 5:410–11; "U.S. Chamber of Commerce," 5:498–504. Ironically, and interestingly, the AFT, the American Jewish Congress, and the CIO (before its merger with the AFL) had all filed amicus briefs in *Brown* in support of the plaintiffs. The ADL had joined a similar brief prepared by the American Civil Liberties Union. See Kurland and Casper, eds., *Brown v. Board of Education, passim.*

[36] 438 U.S. 265, 291 (1978) (Powell). Emphasis supplied. See also Bakke v. Regents of the University of California, 553 P. 2d 1152 (1976).

of the Fourteenth Amendment, except possibly Sumner, were concerned about, but it does have the ring of good sense.

The third and I think the paramount reason for preferring the "suspect classification" argument to the "inherently unequal" one is that, as I have suggested, the former is simpler and easier. This is especially true in the miscegenation cases. In *Brown*, after all, the Court had been deluged with evidence of the adverse psychological effects of segregation on black children. In its much-criticized reliance on these studies, it was only doing what it had repeatedly been urged to do. In *McLaughlin* and *Loving*, the link between law and racism was far weaker. Forbidding people to bed or to marry one another solely on the basis of race is unlikely to generate feelings of inferiority as powerfully as separate schooling begun at age five. Certainly there were no "doll studies" to this effect—and at any rate, by 1964 the Court had learned just what even its admirers thought of that kind of evidence. Declaring that all racial discrimination was suspect eliminated any need to show that antimiscegenation laws were premised on racial inequality and thus provided an easier way to the conclusion that was reached.

I argue in Chapter 6 that what seemed difficult was nevertheless possible. Such an argument could have been made, and it would have been more faithful to the spirit of the Fourteenth Amendment. But by 1967 the doctrine that "race is a suspect classification" was well established. So was the principle that the Fourteenth Amendment applied to discrimination that was not racial at all. It was not surprising, therefore, that the suspect-classification rule appeared in nonracial cases. The Court was then forced to determine what classifications were suspect and which were not. In so doing, it developed criteria for judgment; unfortunately, the criteria were diffuse and contradictory.

Suspect Classification beyond Race

The Warren Court developed what has been called a "two-tier" theory of equal protection. The Burger Court has added an intermediate level and changed the rules somewhat, but has not abandoned the approach. Now, as has been true since the 1950s, equal-protection litigation emphasizes the type of classification involved and the importance of the interest threatened. Classifications that are unobjectionable and interests that are not fundamental belong on the bottom tier, where the Warren Court gave them minimal scrutiny and the Burger Court applies a tougher, but not hostile, standard of review called "rationality scrutiny";[37] some reasonable relationship must be shown between the statute and a legitimate governmental purpose. Classifications by sex occupy the middle tier, so far by themselves: they "must serve important governmental objectives and must be substantially related to achievement of these objectives." On the highest tier, the rules get really tough; laws require "strict scrutiny" and must be "necessary . . . to the accomplishment of [the state's] purpose or to the safeguarding of its interest." On this tier belong laws that threaten fundamental rights and classifications that are inherently suspect.[38]

My concern, for now, is with the "classification" component. However, the cases show that, whatever most of the justices think, the classification involved and the interest threatened cannot be dealt with in isolation from each other. We know already that race is one of the suspect classifications. Beyond that principle is confusion. The cases do not clarify the meaning of the term. They have told us that some classifications are suspect and some are not; what they do not do is tell us why. Or, rather, they offer two alternative explanations that compound the confusion.

Two sitting Supreme Court justices, in two landmark cases of the 1970s, tried to order the decisions into a general theory of suspect classification. In *Frontiero* v. *Richardson*, Justice William J. Brennan argued, unsuccessfully, in favor of assigning sex to the category of suspect classifications. He compared sex to other classes the Court had ruled suspect: race, citing *Brown*, and alienage, citing *Graham* v. *Richardson*, a case I shall discuss later. Why was sex like these classifications and unlike others? Because, wrote Brennan, "it is an immutable characteristic determined solely by the accident of birth. . . . What differentiates sex from such nonsuspect statuses as intelligence and physical disability, and aligns it to the recognized suspect criteria, is that it frequently bears no relation to ability to perform or contribute to society."[39]

This reasoning sounds sensible, but it demands some reflection. The emphasis on ability does not echo the congressional debates of 1866, or Bingham's speech of February 1859, or the Declaration. It sounds more like Calhoun's statement that liberty "is a reward to be earned . . . reserved for the intelligent, the patriotic, the virtuous, and the deserving"—reserved, at least, for those who meet the standard set by white males. Equal liberty is not a right granted by virtue of one's

---

[37] See Gunther, "In Search of Evolving Doctrine," p. 20.
[38] Craig v. Boren, 429 U.S. 190, 197 (1976); Regents v. Bakke, 438 U.S. 265, 305 (Powell). See San Antonio Independent School District v. Rodriguez, 411 U.S. 1 (1973).
[39] 411 U.S. 677, 686 (1973).

humanity, but one contingent on ability to perform or contribute. This notion is more in tune with proslavery thought than with the thought that shaped the Fourteenth Amendment. It conforms not to the theory but to the antitheory.

There are practical as well as theoretical difficulties with the *Frontiero* formulation. Nothing like that passage appears in the cases Brennan cites, and in fact, one of them says something quite different. In overturning an Arizona law denying welfare benefits to aliens, *Graham* v. *Richardson* said, "Aliens as a class are a prime example of a 'discrete and insular' minority for whom such heightened judicial solicitude is appropriate." [40]

"Discrete and insular minority": a concept very different from those stressed in *Frontiero*, and not mentioned there. The phrase has as strange a history as "suspect classification" does. It comes from Justice (later Chief Justice) Stone's famous footnote in *United States* v. *Carolene Products*, where he included prejudice against such groups among the special conditions that might call for "a more searching judicial inquiry" than usual.[41] This case had no more to do with the Fourteenth Amendment than *Korematsu* did, but it is echoed in the other major interpretive exercise of 1973, Justice Powell's opinion for the Court in *San Antonio* v. *Rodriguez*. Sustaining Texas' school-financing system, Powell declared that the "large, diverse and amorphous" class of people living in poorer school districts who were disadvantaged by the law lacked "the traditional indicia of suspectness—the class is not saddled with such disabilities, or subjected to such a history of purposeful unequal treatment, or relegated to such a position of political powerlessness, as to command extraordinary protection from the majoritarian political process." [42]

The *Rodriguez* majority opinion and the *Frontiero* plurality opinion thus contain two very different formulations of the suspect-classification doctrine. And they contradict each other. Both versions cannot be correct, since they do not both describe all classifications listed as suspect. Alienage is a status that can be changed, so it does not satisfy the *Frontiero* test, but it is labeled suspect in *Graham* because, rightly or wrongly, aliens were considered a disadvantaged minority. Arguably the handicapped do constitute such a minority, but the desperate efforts mentioned in Chapter 1 to fit them into the *Frontiero* rule are doomed. It is no wonder that even the Court is confused about what the "indicia of suspectness" are, since its own opinions establish con-

---

[40] 403 U.S. 365, 372 (1971).
[41] 304 U.S. 144, 152–53, n. 4 (1938).
[42] 411 U.S. 1, 28.

tradictory criteria. And it is not surprising that they have done so, since "suspect classification" is an idea without roots in the Constitution or its history, or even in a decision that really had to deal with its implications, and therefore can be read to mean anything or nothing.

The Exclusion of Women

The major premise of Brennan's opinion in *Frontiero* was a general theory of suspect classification. Its minor premise, of course, was that a specific kind of classification, sex, should be among those ranked as suspect. Since only three other justices agreed with Brennan, that premise failed to become law. But the facts that the Court struck down the particular discrimination challenged in *Frontiero* and that suspect classification was even mentioned themselves marked a significant change.

Traditionally, sex classifications got minimal scrutiny and were virtually always upheld. *Muller* v. *Oregon*, which I quoted in Chapter 1, declared that "woman . . . is properly placed in a class by herself," [43] and so matters stood until 1971. Within five years that situation changed, partly, one assumes, in response to the feminist movement and partly because of the new, tougher lower-tier scrutiny described by Gerald Gunther. [44] And though the Court has not gone so far as to declare sex a suspect classification, it did create a special rule for such cases.

Reed v. *Reed* began the process. At issue here was an Idaho law that gave an automatic preference to men over equally qualified women in the appointment of estate administrators. The Court's unanimous opinion announced that "to give a mandatory preference to members of either sex over members of the other, merely to accomplish the elimination of hearings on the merits, is to make the very kind of arbitrary legislative choice forbidden by the Equal Protection Clause." [45] Sex still belongs on the lower tier, but this law is so silly that it fails to survive scrutiny.

Frontiero, two years later, ended the unanimity and revealed divisions on this issue which still exist within the Court. Although eight justices agreed that male and female military personnel were entitled

[43] 208 U.S. 412, 423 (1908).
[44] "In Search of Evolving Doctrine." I have examined this development in "Sexual Equality and the Burger Court," *Western Political Quarterly* 31 (December 1978):470–91.
[45] 404 U.S. 71, 76 (1971).

to equal dependency benefits, the majority could not agree on a test for sex discrimination. Brennan, Douglas, White, and Thurgood Marshall argued for suspect classification and strict scrutiny. Potter Stewart, in an opinion one sentence long, cited *Reed.* Powell, joined by Burger and Harry Blackmun, refused to call sex a suspect classification because he thought that to do so would effectively enact the Equal Rights Amendment and thus preempt a decision then before the state legislatures. William Rehnquist, the only dissenter, did not view the classification as one based solely on sex. Thus no one directly challenged Brennan's minor premise.

How valid was that argument? Sex is a suspect classification, said Brennan, for two reasons. First, it is an immutable characteristic, and second, it has little relationship to ability. These conclusions are incontrovertible, but all they prove is that sex fits Brennan's theory. They do not prove that this theory is the better of the two; worse, they do not prove that suspect classification in any form is good doctrine. So the opinion begs not one but two important questions.

Parts of the Brennan opinion indicate some awareness of the alternative theory of *Rodriguez.* This approach demands a change in focus from the classification to the group injured by it; in other words, from sex to women. Brennan implies that this class does indeed have some of those "traditional indicia of suspectness." He mentions the "long and unfortunate history of sex discrimination" whereby "our statute books gradually became laden with gross, stereotyped distinctions between the sexes, and, indeed, throughout much of the nineteenth century the position of women in our society was, in many respects, comparable to that of the blacks under the pre-Civil War slave codes." Even well into this century, "it can hardly be doubted that . . . women still face pervasive, although at times more subtle, discrimination."[46]

The comparison between blacks and women has been known to arouse opposition. In *Bakke*, it was attacked by Justice Powell. He rejected the comparison, and since he is the author of the *Rodriguez* test, his views need attention. "The perception of racial classifications as inherently odious," Powell wrote, "stems from a lengthy and tragic history that gender-based classifications do not share."[47] In the context of *Bakke* this statement is bewildering, since it appears to dictate the conclusion that for a university to reserve a number of places in medical school for women, who now comprise about half the medical student population in this country, is acceptable when such provision for blacks is not. In general, the argument itself is plain wrong.

[46] 411 U.S. 677, 684–86 (1973).
[47] 438 U.S. 265, 303 (1978).

The merest acquaintance with the relevant history reveals that sex-based classifications have been used to consign women to inferior status. Several popular books on the subject, any of which has ample supportive evidence for that statement, have appeared in the last fifteen years.[48] It is true that sex discrimination has not always been recognized as invidious; indeed, it is hard to think of any traditional sex discrimination that has not at some time been defended as beneficial to women. But we need only reexamine these policies and these defenses to see how misguided they are and how oppressive they have been.

The varieties of sex discrimination are too numerous to list, let alone discuss, here. But it is easy to think of many policies that, applied to any adults other than women, are quickly recognizable as invidious. Denial of the vote, restrictions on jury service, and limitations of work opportunities come to mind. There is little, if any, evidence that these restrictions have ever been benefits.

If such policies are odious when imposed on men, how could they be acceptable for women? The writers of the old landmark decisions would probably have agreed with Powell's view that tragedy and odium are absent. The old cases seem to reflect not a belief in female inferiority, but a magnanimous recognition of special needs. The opinions are filled with such phrases as these: our old friend "woman's physical structure and the performance of maternal functions," "men must provide the first line of defense while women keep the home fires burning," and "woman is still regarded as the center of home and family life."[49] That last phrase is a quotation from a 1961 decision upholding restrictions on women's jury eligibility. The reader should compare it with *Strauder*.

By now, quoting these rationales is, or at least should be, enough to show that, far from being benign, these laws are part of a pattern of oppression. Ideas about female traits are generalizations as imperfect, and stereotypes as oppressive, as old notions about blacks. And whatever lawmakers *thought* they were doing, legislation on the basis of woman's traditional role in the family amounts to a role assignment by the dominant members of society for their own convenience, and that sounds suspiciously like slavery.[50] If slavery for blacks was odious,

---

[48] Just two examples are Karen De Crow, *Sexist Justice* (New York: Random House, 1974), and Leo Kanowitz, *Women and the Law: The Unfinished Revolution* (Albuquerque: University of New Mexico Press, 1969).

[49] Muller v. Oregon, 208 U.S. 412, 421 (1908); U.S. v. St. Clair, 291 Fed. Supp. 122, 124–25 (S.D.N.Y. 1968); Hoyt v. Florida, 368 U.S. 57, 64 (1961).

[50] See Baer, *Chains of Protection*, chaps. 6 and 7.

so is pseudo-slavery for women. If the denial of full citizenship to Orientals and Hispanics has been tragic, so was its denial to women.

To the extent that Powell's distinction between race and sex discrimination rests on "tragedy and odium," then, it collapses. History provides far more support for Brennan's conclusion that both race and sex distinctions have "too often . . . been inexcusably utilized to stereotype or stigmatize politically powerless segments of society."[51] The greatest difference between sex and race discrimination has been in the rhetoric surrounding them.

Whichever theory one uses, therefore, sex discrimination, or discrimination against women, is suspect. But this discussion well illustrates the irreconcilability of the two definitions. Brennan's argument in *Fronterio* implies that, since *women* have been subject to disabilities, *sex* must be a suspect classification—whether a particular law injures women or benefits them. And that conclusion does not follow from that premise.[52] The problem that haunts the reverse discrimination cases in Chapter 6 hits with full force here, too.

But the Court has not resolved any of these difficulties. The next important case after *Frontiero*, the case that has become the binding precedent, struck a compromise. In *Craig* v. *Boren*, Brennan, writing for a majority of seven, dropped suspect classification, at least for the time being. "To withstand constitutional challenge," he wrote, ". . . classifications by gender must serve important governmental objectives and must be substantially related to achievements of these objectives." The law at issue, an Oklahoma statute allowing women to buy 3.2 percent beer but no other alcoholic beverage at eighteen while men had to wait until twenty-one, fell because the statistical evidence that young men did more drunken driving than young women was not in itself closely enough related to the state's admittedly important goal of traffic safety. "While such a disparity is not trivial in a statistical sense, it hardly can form the basis for employment of a gender line as a classifying device. Certainly, if maleness is to serve as a proxy for drinking and driving, a correlation of 2% must be considered an unduly tenuous 'fit.'"[53]

The *Craig* test was applied in two important 1981 decisions. In both cases, however, the Court split badly on the results. In *Michael M.* v. *Superior Court of Sonoma County*, five justices voted to uphold a California law that provided that only males could be guilty of "statutory rape" of females, not the other way around. Both Rehnquist and

[51] Regents v. Bakke, 438 U.S. 265, 360 (1978).
[52] See Baer, "Sexual Equality," p. 478.
[53] 429 U.S. 190, 197, 199 (1976).

Blackmun felt that the law was substantially related to the important objective of discouraging teenage pregnancy, which obviously can be inflicted only by males on females. Brennan, dissenting, found "outmoded sexual stereotypes" in the law and insisted that it was too ineffective a means of discouraging teenage pregnancy to meet the "substantial relation to important objective" test.[54] Clearly, whatever qualities this test has, it does not dictate consistent results.

In *Rostker* v. *Goldberg*, the Court upheld Congress' power to require men, but not women, to register for possible conscription. Justice Rehnquist's majority opinion cited both *Craig* and *Michael M.*, concluding that "the exemption of women from registration is not only sufficiently but closely related to Congress' purpose in authorizing registration. The fact that Congress and the Executive have decided that women should not serve in combat fully justifies Congress in not authorizing their registration, since the purpose of registration is to develop a pool of potential combat troops."[55] The dissents, by Justices White and Marshall, disagreed primarily with Rehnquist's linkage of registration and combat. No opinion challenged the exclusion of women from combat or reached the issue of sexual equality. This decision will have great practical impact, but it is not a major contribution to doctrine.

So gender discrimination is in a class by itself, on a level between the two tiers, with its own rules. The standard is so slippery that it is hard to criticize, but it is equally hard to endorse. Certainly it has no support in the legislative history. The debates are confusing on this point, relying as they do on distinctions that do not stand up, but nowhere do they invite the inference that sexual distinctions were to be put midway between racial classifications and innocuous ones. History provides very limited support for either the conclusion that discriminations against women are as odious as those against blacks or the conclusion that they are permissible, and none for the intermediate conclusion. Still, these decisions are no more unfaithful to legislative history than *Brown* or *Loving* is. *Craig* v. *Boren* is so obviously a political compromise on a controversial issue that it is tempting just to leave it at that. At any rate, the only alternative we have so far is to rank some gender discriminations as suspect—and the objection to

---

[54] 101 S.Ct. 1200.

[55] 101 S.Ct. 2646, 2658. The temptation to express a personal opinion on this case is powerful. I think the case could have been dealt with nicely by what might be termed extrastructural analysis; i.e, considering both what is in the Constitution and what was *not* put in. In other words: No ERA, no draft.

that conclusion is that the suspect-classification doctrine is itself unacceptable.

Gender has not been the only category excluded from the upper tier. But gender was excluded even though it fits *both* definitions of suspect classification. The next cases include claims that fit neither definition, and one, at least, whose result appears to depend on which particular definition the judges are using. And they suggest, if any further evidence is needed, that there is something very wrong with equal-protection doctrine.

Education, Retirement, and Reverse Discrimination

However confused the rule or rules are, judges continue to use them. Some of the cases that have ruled that certain classifications are not suspect are directly pertinent here. *Rodriguez* is among them. It was a messy case; Justice Powell is quite correct in his conclusion that it was hard to identify either an exact group of people who were being deprived or a specific right of which they were being deprived.

First, although his conclusion that "people living in low-yield school districts" could not be identified with "the poor," who do bear some of the "traditional indicia," was supported mainly by a study from Connecticut, not Texas, no such identification was demonstrated in Texas, either. And as Stewart pointed out, the relevant suspect classification was "actual or functional indigency, [not] comparative poverty vis-a-vis comparative affluence." Second, whether or not education can be ranked as a fundamental right—and Powell insisted it cannot be—the children were not deprived of it; they just had less money spent on their education than did children in wealthier districts. No perfect correlation existed between expenditure and quality of education. Therefore, what Justice Marshall's dissent called "the Court's rigidified approach to equal protection analysis" seemed to demand the result the Court reached.[56]

But the dissenting argument is powerful. Marshall pointed out that the residents of the poorest districts were in fact paying proportionately *higher* taxes for a cheaper education; that there was evidence that the quality of the schooling was inferior; and that those affected were, after all, children, who did not choose where they lived. Another salient fact was that the affected district's population was 90 percent Mexican-American and 6 percent black. Marshall stressed the impor-

[56] 411 U.S. 1, 23, 61n, 29–39, 98 (1973).

tance of education and the fact that the Court had recognized as "fundamental" other rights not specified in the Constitution.[57] Taken together, those factors add up to an unequal share in an important benefit for minority children, thus militating against the legitimacy of the financing scheme.

But the rule does not permit us to take all these factors together. It demands that we weigh separately the interests involved and the classification invoked. Since the case did not fit into the categories of fundamental right and suspect classification, the law was upheld.

Marshall not only criticized this ruling, but attempted to develop an alternative doctrine for equal-protection cases. He recommended "an approach in which concentration is placed upon the character of the classification in question, the relative importance to individuals in the class discriminated against of the governmental benefits that they do not receive, and the interests in support of the classification."[58] As a test, this approach has its defects, for it does not tell us how to weigh these considerations and what standards to judge them by. Nor has Marshall done so since, although he continues to use this approach. In his dissent in *Harris* v. *McRae*, the case that upheld the Hyde Amendment, restricting federal funding for abortions, he suggested that his use of this doctrine in that context was "not dissimilar" to the *Craig* test.[59] But that observation does not help much, since it does not tell us whether that context is different from that of *Rodriguez* or any other, and if so, why. Marshall does not have a mature alternative rule for equal-protection cases, but this approach will provide a guideline by which to test these decisions.

The next set of cases provides more evidence of defects in the prevailing rule and the superiority of Marshall's developing doctrine. *Massachusetts Board of Retirement* v. *Murgia* upheld a law that forced uniformed state police officers to retire at fifty. Quoting from *Rodriguez*, the *per curiam* opinion handled the issue thus:

> While the treatment of the aged in this Nation has not been wholly free of discrimination, such persons, unlike, say, those who have been discriminated against on the basis of race or national origin, have not experienced a "history of purposeful unequal treatment" or been subjected to unique disabilities on the basis of stereotyped characteristics not truly indicative of their abilities. The class subject to the . . . statute consists of uniformed state police officers over the age of 50. It cannot be said to

[57] Ibid., pp. 80–81, 85–87, 109, 12, 99–103.
[58] Ibid., p. 99. See also Dandridge v. Williams, 397 U.S. 470, 521 (Marshall dissenting).
[59] 100 S.Ct. 2671, 2709, n. 6 (1980).

discriminate only against the elderly. Rather, it draws the line at a certain age in middle life. But even old age does not define a "discrete and insular" group, in need of "extraordinary protection from the majoritarian political process." Instead, it marks a stage that each of us will reach if we live out our normal life span. Even if the statute could be said to impose a penalty upon a class defined as the aged, it would not impose a distinction sufficiently akin to those classifications that we have found suspect to call for strict judicial scrutiny.[60]

Apparently the classification is not suspect because the class singled out is so large. The result seems to be that the larger the group restricted, the greater the chances the law will pass muster. That reasoning is dubious enough, but the opinion has an even worse flaw. If people who share a given trait do not constitute a powerless minority, I can think of no more effective way of turning them into one than by taking their jobs away.[61] By analogy, Jews are not a powerless minority in this country, but we would be suspicious if immigration officials started stamping "Jew" across their passports—and we should be. Laws can, after all, separate and isolate groups.

Three years after *Murgia*, in 1979, *Vance* v. *Bradley* sustained a federal law requiring Foreign Service employees to retire at sixty. The employees avoided both the suspect-group and the fundamental-right arguments, alleging that the law did not even satisfy the rational-basis test. The Court disagreed, citing both *Murgia* and *Rodriguez* as precedents. Its argument for the law's rationality did not limit itself to the generalizations about age and ability which had persuaded it in 1976.[62] There was more:

> The appellants submit that one of their legitimate and substantial goals is to recruit and train and to assure the professional competence, as well as the mental and physical reliability, of the corps of public servants who hold positions critical to our foreign relations, who more often than not serve overseas, frequently under difficult and demanding conditions, and who must be ready for such assignments at any time. . . . The appellants also submit that compulsory retirement at age 60 furthers this end in two principal ways: first, as an integral part of the personnel policies of the Service designed to create predictable promotion opportunities and thus spur morale and stimulate superior performance in the ranks; secondly, by removing from the Service those who are sufficiently old that they may be less equipped or less ready than younger persons to face the

[60] 427 U.S. 307, 313–14 (1976).
[61] Justice Marshall touches on this problem in his dissent (ibid., pp. 323–24).
[62] 440 U.S. 93, 96–98, 103–5, 111–12. See Massachusetts Board of Retirement v. Murgia, 427 U.S. 307, 317–18.

rigors of overseas duty in the Foreign Service. The District Court rejected each of these latter submissions and in our view erred in each instance.[63]

Whose promotion? Whose morale? Not, obviously, those of the re-tirees, but of those whose rise will be accelerated by their seniors' retirement. That rationale comes close to an absolute preference for the interests of one group of people over those of another group. What it implies, bluntly, is that the sixty-year-olds just do not count. They do not enjoy a right to equal respect and concern. How such a ranking is compatible with constitutional equality defies understanding. But such is the result of the rigidified approach that assigns age discrimi-nation to the lower tier.

A third group of cases that collide with the approach are those in-volving reverse discrimination. These cases illustrate the inconsisten-cies of the rule, for here it is of crucial importance which formulation of suspect classification is employed. The two alternatives dictate op-posite results. Powell solved that problem in *Bakke* by insisting that race was a suspect classification, not because of anything that might be said about it, but because it just was; this was a given, just as Black had said in *Korematsu*.

> Petitioner argues that the Court below erred in applying strict scrutiny to the special admissions program because white males, such as respon-dent, are not a "discrete and insular minority" requiring extraordinary protection from the majoritarian political process. This rationale, how-ever, has never been invoked in our decisions as a prerequisite to sub-jecting racial or ethnic classifications to strict scrutiny. Nor has this Court held that discreteness and insularity constitute necessary preconditions to a holding that a particular classification is invidious. These character-istics may be relevant in deciding whether or not to add new types of classifications to the list of "suspect" categories or whether a particular classification survives close examination. Racial and ethnic classifica-tions, however, are subject to stringent examination without regard to these additional characteristics.[64]

Race, then, is a suspect classification whether such a law helps or harms disadvantaged minorities. But *Graham, Rodriguez,* and *Mur-gia* are three of the cases Powell cites, and if they did not hold that discreteness and insularity were conditions of suspectness, they came pretty close. Between 1973 and 1978, then, the confusion became worse.

The Court has not adopted Powell's view, but several justices do see the matter this way. The passage I just quoted suggests that Powell

[63] 440 U.S. 93, 97–98.
[64] 438 U.S. 265, 290–91.

himself did, in 1978 at least, but some concessions he made and his vote in a later case suggest that his views may be changing. Stewart and Rehnquist go even further. In a 1980 decision, Stewart quoted Harlan's "color-blind" language in *Plessy* and Rehnquist joined the opinion. Stevens has insisted on a unilateral strict-scrutiny standard for all race discrimination.[65]

Two of the three decisions on the merits the Court has made so far in this area have sustained policies of reverse discrimination, so the Court cannot be accused of rigid adherence to the old doctrine. But the fact that at least three, and possibly four, justices do try to fit the new cases into the old category may bode ill.[66]

Conclusion

The suspect-classification doctrine, as it now precariously exists, was an intelligible response to a particular set of issues, and provided a way out of a bind into which the Court had reasoned itself over the years. But it has no roots; it distorts history; it has disquieting echoes of antitheory; it has developed in two contradictory directions; and, applied to several contemporary issues, it permits absurd results. I have not yet found any rule with which to replace the doctrine. The next four chapters provide further tests of the prevailing doctrine, and allow us to consider alternative approaches, as I explore the issues discussed in Chapter 1. Of the issues discussed, only reverse discrimination, the subject of Chapter 6, fits into the framework of traditional doctrine. Age seems to fit, too, as long as one sticks to maximum age limits, but in cases involving minors, the equal-protection doctrines do not appear, and the cases are not handled within the model. This lack of fit is even more evident when we examine cases involving disability and sexual orientation. At first glance, they may not seem to belong in this discussion at all, for they are not classified or decided as equal-protection cases. But, I shall argue, that fact in itself is indicative of still more defects in the doctrine. For these very rules hide the fact that these cases are very much concerned with equality, and by their omissions allow decisions that brand and stigmatize, relegate people to inferior status, and deprive them of any semblance of equal rights. These results confound the general principles of the Fourteenth Amendment.

[65] Ibid., pp. 319–20; Fullilove v. Klutznick, 100 S.Ct. 2758, 2798–2814 (1980).
[66] This discussion is adapted from Baer, "Reverse Discrimination."

[6]

When Equal Is Not the Same

"Reverse discrimination," "affirmative action," "preferential hiring," "preferential admissions"—all of these phrases somehow belong to the 1970s. They predated that decade—"affirmative action," for example, appears in the Civil Rights Act of 1964—but it was then that the terms came into everyday use, as the policies they describe became matters of public concern. The terms are not always interchangeable. "Reverse discrimination" bears a negative connotation that has not yet attached to "affirmative action," which may be one reason why the latter phrase is more common in academic settings. But all of these policies have one thing in common: they favor members of groups that have previously been the objects of prejudice and invidious discrimination. The factor that differentiates these groups from the "majority" is usually race or ethnicity, and, less often, sex.

There is no strong societal agreement that such compensatory discrimination is ever justified. Even people who generally support it dispute such matters as what agencies may impose it, under what circumstances, and by what means, just as they dispute whether or not particular groups qualify for such treatment. But there is threshold agreement about what the terms mean and just whom we are discussing. That such agreement exists is a revealing fact about American society. Speaking of "reverse" discrimination can be meaningful only when "direct" discrimination has existed, only because "American society is currently a racially conscious society; this is the inevitable and evident consequence of a history of slavery, repression, and prejudice."[1]

---

[1] Ronald Dworkin, "Why Bakke Has No Case," *New York Review of Books*, November 10, 1977, pp. 11.

Four Cases in Search of a Rule

I have stated that no consensus exists about the legitimacy of these policies, which I shall lump together here as "reverse discrimination." Nor is there agreement about their constitutionality. The Supreme Court is still struggling toward a resolution of these problems. There are some "boundary" cases. A series of federal court decisions have established that racial discrimination is permissible when it is designed to rectify deliberate and documented past discrimination, for instance in public education or employment.[2] One decision where the Supreme Court unanimously overturned a policy of reverse discrimination was *McDonald* v. *Sante Fe Transportation Company*, where an employer had discharged two white workers for misappropriating cargo but retained a black worker who had committed the same offense.[3] So we know that one kind of reverse discrimination is permitted and may even be required, that which redresses past racial discrimination, while another kind is forbidden, namely, different punishments for the same act. But the major cases have fallen within these boundaries.

The first two cases, *De Funis* v. *Odegaard* and *University of California Regents* v. *Bakke*, had several features in common.[4] Each involved admission to a graduate program in a state university, *De Funis* to law school and *Bakke* to medical school. The University of Washington's law school had established a scheme whereby all applicants were ranked according to a predicted first-year average (PFYA) on the basis of their grades and test scores. In 1971, the year Marco de Funis first applied to the law school, applicants whose PFYA fell below 74.5 points (out of a possible 100) were summarily rejected, unless they were black, Chicano, American Indian, or Filipino. Applicants from these four groups got a special review that gave less weight to the average. As a result, some minority applicants with scores below this cutoff point were admitted.

De Funis, whose score was 76.23, was rejected. He sued, alleging a violation of the equal-protection clause. The state trial court ruled in his favor and ordered his admission, so that he did enter the law school in September 1971. The University appealed and won in the state's highest court. De Funis then took his case to the Supreme Court. Because he had been admitted, and was in his last quarter by the time

---

[2] See, e.g., Swann v. Charlotte-Mecklenburg Board of Education, 402 U.S. 1 (1971); Franks v. Bowman Transportation Co., 424 U.S. 747 (1976); Albemarle Paper Co. v. Moody, 422 U.S. 405 (1975); Carter v. Gallagher, 452 F. 2nd 315 (8th Circ. 1972).
[3] 427 U.S. 273 (1976).
[4] 416 U.S. 312 (1974); 438 U.S. 265 (1978).

the Court heard oral argument (he ranked, incidentally, about the middle of his class),[5] the Court dismissed the case as moot.

That action effectively postponed for four years a decision on the merits. Meanwhile, Allan Bakke, a thirty-three-year-old white engineer who had been rejected by several medical schools despite excellent grades, test scores, and recommendations, brought suit against the University of California. The medical school at Davis had reserved sixteen of the one hundred places in its entering class for blacks, American Indians, Chicanos, and Asian-Americans. This policy was not only reverse discrimination, but, to use a word that bore even worse connotations, a quota. The year Bakke was rejected, minority students who ranked below him were admitted. Bakke challenged his exclusion under both the equal-protection clause and Title VI of the Civil Rights Act of 1964, which forbids racial discrimination in any program receiving federal funds.

He won his case, by a vote of 5 to 4. Of the majority, four justices— Burger, Stewart, Rehnquist, and Stevens—based their votes on Title VI, while Justice Powell insisted that both this law and the equal-protection clause forbade a racial classification of this nature. Powell argued, however, that while reserving a specific number of seats for minority applicants was illegal, the university could take race into account in a less specific way. White, Blackmun, Brennan, and Marshall joined him on this point. They dissented from the ruling against the Davis scheme, arguing that neither the Fourteenth Amendment nor Title VI forbade it.[6] Obviously, the issue had not yet been resolved. *Bakke* did not even indicate how the Court would have decided *De Funis* on the merits.

Steelworkers v. Weber, decided a year later, in 1979, was brought not under the Constitution but under Title VII of the 1964 law.[7] This section forbade employers and labor unions to "discriminate . . . because of . . . race." The Kaiser Aluminum Corporation and the United Steelworkers of America had agreed on an affirmative action plan that reserved half of the openings in craft-training programs for blacks. Brian Weber, a white production worker in Kaiser's Gramercy, Louisiana, plant, was excluded from such a program in favor of black workers with less seniority.

The Court ruled, 5 to 2, that Title VII did permit such plans. (Since private, not government, action was involved, the equal-protection

---

[5] Ginger, ed., *De Funis v. Odegaard*, "Transcript of Oral Argument," p. 1334.

[6] 438 U.S. 265, 408–21 (Stevens), 281–315, 320 (Powell), 324–79 (Brennan), 387–402 (Marshall), 402–8 (Blackmun).

[7] 443 U.S. 193 (1979).

clause was not controlling.) Justice Brennan's opinion for the majority, and Justice Rehnquist's dissent for himself and Chief Justice Burger, presented two conflicting interpretations of legislative history.[8] Stewart, who had voted against the Davis admissions plan, voted to sustain this one, without opinion in both cases. Powell, who had attacked quotas in *Bakke*, did not participate in *Weber*; not did Justice Stevens.

A year later, *Fullilove* v. *Klutznick* sustained another quota.[9] The Court ruled that a federal public works program that reserved 10 percent of spending for minority-owned businesses was within Congress' enforcement powers under Section 5 of the Fourteenth Amendment. Burger, writing for a plurality of three, relied heavily on congressional findings of past discrimination. Powell joined this opinion, but wrote a concurrence distinguishing *Fullilove* from *Bakke* on just this basis. Brennan, Blackmun, and Marshall restated their views on the general acceptability of reverse discrimination. Stewart—who appeared to be moving away from reverse discrimination as steadily as Powell was moving toward it—wrote a dissent that strongly rejected all racial discrimination, invidious or benign. Stevens and Rehnquist also dissented.

Here, at some risk, is the prevailing doctrine on reverse discrimination. The Fourteenth Amendment gives Congress the power to enact reverse discrimination plans, including quotas, at least when prior disadvantage and direct discrimination exist. For at least one justice, the same amendment forbids state agencies to establish quotas, but permits them to consider race in some nebulous way. Title VII of the Civil Rights Act of 1964, whose language forbids employment discrimination based on race, does in fact allow employers and unions to discriminate in favor of blacks, even by setting quotas. But Title VI, whose language prohibits racial discrimination in programs receiving federal money, does prevent such programs from setting racial quotas. Out of all this legislative and judicial language emerges only one firm *constitutional* rule: Congress may establish reverse discrimination programs when evidence of prior discrimination and disadvantage exists. Whether any other government-imposed reverse discrimination is acceptable, and under what circumstances, is unclear.

I am concerned here with the constitutionality of these policies, not with their wisdom or their desirability. Therefore, I confine myself to arguments that have some bearing on constitutional issues. I am asking whether reverse discrimination is compatible with the right to equal

---

[8] Ibid., pp. 197–209 (Brennan), 219–55 (Rehnquist).
[9] 100 S.Ct. 2758 (1980).

respect and concern, and whether it can satisfy the rigors of constitutional reasoning.

Qualifications, Merit, and "the Right to Be Judged as an Individual"

There are several common arguments against such policies, which I discuss in what I think can be shown to be ascending order of importance. One objection is that reverse discrimination rewards the less qualified while depriving the more qualified. Allan Bakke's case produced many versions of this argument. As a constitutional principle, however, the point is weak.

There exists at present no constitutional right to be judged according to one's "qualifications." But is there a basis for recognizing such a right? It could be argued that the fundamental right to equal respect and concern entails the derivative right to be rewarded according to merit. I agree that there are certain narrowly defined situations, such as that in *McDonald*, in which such a right exists. But, in general, no such relationship between treatment as an equal and merit holds.

Why not? Well, *why*? Are we comfortable with the idea that merit should be the only, or the principal, basis for the distribution of benefits? What about need, for instance? Besides, what does "merit" mean? One reason that it is difficult to accept such a claim is that some of the terms used have confused and arbitrary meanings. What does it mean to say that a person merits, deserves, or has earned the privilege of going to medical school or being hired? Do any standards exist, other than those chosen by the decision makers?

The term "qualifications" has similar difficulties; there is an absence of agreement as to what qualifications are.[10] To the extent that agreement exists about qualifications for medical school, for example—grade point average, score on the Medical College Admission Test, and recommendations—this agreement is the product of arbitrary decisions to weigh these factors heavily, decisions made long ago without much thought and accepted ever since. It would be bold and foolhardy to interpret the Constitution as enacting such fragile constructs.

A related argument that may appear to have more substance is that an applicant should be judged "as an individual" and not as a member

[10] See, e.g., Regents v. Bakke, 438 U.S. 265, 305–15 (Powell), 403–4 (Blackmun); Joel Dreyfuss and Charles Lawrence III, *The Bakke Case: The Politics of Inequality* (New York: Harcourt Brace Jovanovich, 1979), chap. 6.

of a group.[11] This has become a popular argument, but on analysis it turns out to have defects. Kenneth Karst and Harold Horowitz have pointed out that "any equal protection claim turns out to be a claim made as a member of a group. Indeed, any claim based on a rule of law is a demand to be treated in the same manner as all other persons similarly situated. A claim to be treated on the basis of one's 'individual attributes' either is a disguised claim to be treated as a member of a group possessed of one or more specific attributes or it is unintelligible." Dworkin has suggested that any judgment must rely on generalizations about groups. For example, establishing a GPA cutoff point, as the University of Washington did, treats both those above and those below as members of a group who share that attribute.[12]

Any standard, by definition, classifies those judged by it. It is wrong to suggest that I am treated "as an individual" if I am judged on the basis of my teaching evaluations or the number of my publications, but "as a member of a group" if I am judged by race or sex. In fact, what a demand to be treated as an individual often means is simply a demand to be treated as the privileged group has been treated; within that group, judgments may or may not have been made on merit or qualifications, however defined.

This argument is often confused with the "qualifications" argument. Grades and test scores are described as "individual" attributes because they are earned by an individual; they are acquired characteristics, as opposed to ascribed and permanent characteristics, such as race and sex. Earned attributes do have a relationship to individual *merit* that race and sex do not have, but it is hard to see how they are more related to *individuality*. A grade point average belongs to an individual; we say, "She pulled a 4.0 last semester." But we also say, "She's black." Race and sex belong to individuals, too.

The fact that these arguments, with their defects, are frequently made—and with vehemence, particularly in conversation—indicates that this issue has touched some very sensitive nerves. But the objections to reverse discrimination do not rely only on such arguments as these. The crucial point has often been that it is *race* that is the basis for choice. And such a policy bears a heavy burden of justification. It faces a ready-made, and powerful, counterargument.

[11] This argument is discussed in Nathan Glazer, *Affirmative Discrimination* (New York: Basic Books, 1975), chap. 6.

[12] Karst and Horowitz, "Affirmative Action and Equal Protection," *Virginia Law Review* 60 (October 1974):955–74, 961; Dworkin, "Why Bakke Has No Case," p. 14. See also Owen M. Fiss, "Groups and the Equal Protection Clause," *Philosophy and Public Affairs* 5 (Winter 1976):107–77; Paul Brest, "In Defense of the Antidiscrimination Principle," *Harvard Law Review* 90 (November 1976):1–54.

Race Discrimination: Principle or Interest?

The lesson of the great decisions of the Supreme Court and the lesson of contemporary history have been the same for at least a generation: discrimination on the basis of race is illegal, immoral, unconstitutional, inherently wrong, and destructive of democratic society. Now this is to be unlearned and we are told that this is not a matter of fundamental principle, but only a matter of whose ox is gored. Those for whom racial equality was demanded are to be more equal than others. Having found support in the Constitution for equality, they now claim support for inequality under the same Constitution.

The foregoing paragraph is a passage from Alexander M. Bickel's last and posthumously published book, *The Morality of Consent.*[13] It has been cited in at least three Supreme Court opinions.[14] With characteristic clarity and eloquence, Professor Bickel has made a powerful case against reverse discrimination. The argument is a strong one, for it accuses the proponents of hypocrisy and of self-serving deviation from the "neutral principles" sought in constitutional adjudication. That racial or sexual or ethnic discrimination is wrong constitutes what Herbert Wechsler would call "grounds of adequate neutrality and generality . . . transcending the immediate result that is achieved" in any given case.[15] That racial or sexual or ethnic discrimination is wrong when it favors certain groups but right when it favors other groups appears to be the very opposite of such a principle.

But this appearance is deceptive. However appealing Bickel's statement is, it is wrong. First, the great decisions of the 1950s and 1960s did not depend on the principle that race discrimination is unconstitutional, although some of them did articulate it. Second, the last sentence of the last paragraph does *not* articulate the principle on which reverse discrimination depends. The distinction between invidious and benign discrimination—or, to phrase it differently, between traditional and reverse discrimination—is not simply a matter of whose ox is being gored. The argument for any given program may be made that way, but that, after all, is how political demands are made. The distinction is a principled one, transcending any immediate result.

The charge of partiality is not the only substantial argument against reverse discrimination. In Chapter 5 I suggested that using race, sex, or ethnicity as a way of assigning burdens or benefits seems unfair on

---

[13] (New Haven: Yale University Press, 1975), pp. 132–33.

[14] Regents v. Bakke, 438 U.S. 265, 295, n. 35 (Powell); Fullilove v. Klutznick, 100 S.Ct. 2758, 2799, n. 5 (Stewart dissenting), 2810–11, n. 21 (Stevens dissenting).

[15] "Toward Neutral Principles of Constitutional Law," *Harvard Law Review* 73 (November 1959):30–34.

its face, because of the involuntary, immutable, and irrelevant nature of these traits, whatever race or sex a person happens to be. This is one reason the neutral suspect-classification rule of *McLaughlin, Loving*, and *Frontiero* has been so popular—and, I think, underlies Bickel's conclusion about the "lesson of contemporary history."

So the task I have set myself is to argue both that reverse discrimination is principled, and that law may deprive some people, but not others, because of race or sex. This argument confronts certain obstacles, but I think Chapter 4 indicates that the Fourteenth Amendment's legislative history is not paramount among them. In the two miscegenation cases of the 1960s, the Court found in that provision an intent to condemn all racial discrimination, but, in fact, speakers in Congress defended that very kind of law with an argument that contradicts that conclusion. Furthermore, the debates reveal overriding concern with the status of *one* racial group. Indeed, one scholar has suggested that the principles of the Civil War Amendments were not neutral at all; that the goal was to ensure full equality *for blacks*; and, implicitly at least, there was nothing wrong with that goal.[16] That interpretation, of course, would demand the results reached in *McLaughlin* and *Loving* as well as in the school segregation cases, but the neutral ban on discrimination does not emerge from the history. The historical evidence is permissive, neither condemning reverse discrimination nor demanding it. Resolution of the issue will have to depend on some other basis.

What is it about race that makes it seem an unfair basis for discrimination? I have devoted some space to this line of argument, but we can put it into sharper focus by considering the viewpoint of the persons affected by such policies. Someone in the position of Marco De Funis, Allan Bakke, or Brian Weber has been denied training that would greatly improve his prospects. Although it would be incorrect to state that this person has been denied benefits because of his race, it is true that his chances have been reduced because of his race. Being white hurt him. And he is no more responsible for being white than others are for being black, Hispanic, or American Indian. Nor does his race have any relationship to his ability to succeed in a training program or a professional school. It is possible to argue that race may have some relationship to a person's value as a doctor or lawyer, if one accepts certain arguments for reverse discrimination, but after all, success in medical or law school is a necessary precondition to becoming

---

[16] Louis H. Pollak, "Racial Discrimination and Judicial Integrity: A Reply to Professor Wechsler," *University of Pennsylvania Law Review* 108 (November 1959):1–34.

a doctor or lawyer. So the case for this applicant has a strong emotional and rational appeal.

But it contains some dissonances. Being white was a disadvantage to De Funis, Bakke, and Weber in one limited instance, but it is hardly a disadvantage in general. On the contrary, any white person alive in this country today has reaped unearned rewards because of race, and a white person's claim to immunity to racially based deprivations must be judged with that fact in mind. Of course, a person cannot help being white, but who would regret it?

That point leads to the paramount difference between invidious and benign discrimination. Other writers, such as Dworkin and Richard Wasserstrom, have made this argument before, but it needs to be developed here. Dworkin insists that the rejected white applicant has no right here "because in his case race is not distinguished by the special character of public insult. On the contrary, the program presupposes that his race is still widely if wrongly thought to be superior to others." Wasserstrom put it this way: "In our culture to be nonwhite—and especially to be black—is to be treated and seen to be as members of a group that is different from and inferior to the group of standard, fully developed persons, the adult white males." Therefore, "it is wrong to think that contemporary affirmative action programs are racist or sexist in the centrally important sense in which many past and present features of our society have been racist or sexist." [17]

The distinction between discrimination against blacks and discrimination against whites is that the former is part of a system that stigmatizes the group and treats its members as inferiors, and the latter is not. This character of public insult is what denies the right to treatment as an equal, and it provides a principle for decision that satisfies the requirements of neutrality. It does no violence to the purposes of the Fourteenth Amendment. And it could have provided a principled basis for the decisions of the 1950s and 1960s which instead articulated the notion that any and all racial discrimination was unconstitutional.

Standards and Subjectives

But the argument cannot stop here. To be a guide to interpretation, a rule must be intelligible and contain objective, reliable criteria for

[17] Dworkin, "Why Bakke Has No Case," p. 14; Wasserstrom, "Racism, Sexism, and Preferential Treatment: An Approach to the Topics," *UCLA Law Review* 24 (February 1977):586.

decision making. In his *Bakke* opinion, Justice Powell criticized the efforts of Justice Brennan and of Judge Mathew Tobriner of the California Supreme Court to develop such a rule as the one toward which I have been working. Brennan distinguished between "racial classifications that stigmatize—because they are drawn on the presumption that one race is inferior to another or because they put the weight of the government behind racial hatred and separatism"—and policies "designed to enable [members of disadvantaged groups] to surmount the obstacles imposed by racial discrimination." Tobriner emphasized the familiar notion of "discrete and insular minorities" who might get special solicitude from government.[18]

It was not the policies these distinctions permit that apparently most troubled Justice Powell. It was rather that he found the concepts of "stigma" and "minority" essentially without meaning. He dealt with "stigma" in a footnote, dismissing it as having "no clearly defined constitutional meaning" and "reflect[ing] a subjective judgment that is standardless." He paid more attention to the differences between "majority" and "minority." These concepts

> necessarily reflect temporary arrangements and political judgments. . . . The white "majority" itself is composed of various minority groups, most of which can lay claim to a history of prior discrimination at the hands of the state and private individuals. Not all of these groups can receive preferential treatment and corresponding judicial tolerance of distinctions drawn in terms of race and nationality, for then the only "majority" left would be a new minority of white Anglo-Saxon Protestants. There is *no principled basis* for deciding which groups would merit heightened judicial solicitude and which would not.[19]

Is Powell right in concluding that no intelligible distinction between advantaged and disadvantaged groups is possible? That "stigma" has no clear constitutional meaning is true, but not particularly significant; neither, after all, did such concepts as "suspect classification" and "clear and present danger" when they first appeared. The way they acquired meaning was through use in a series of cases, and there is nothing to prevent "stigma" from getting similar use. Still, Powell has done us a favor by reminding us that before the concept can be used as a basis for decisions, it is necessary to think about what the term means and about how to recognize the reality that the term describes. This necessity poses a problem, but it is exactly the opposite

[18] 438 U.S. 265, 357–58; 328; Bakke v. Regents of University of California, 553 P. 2d 1152, 1183 (Cal. Sup.Ct. 1976).
[19] 438 U.S. 265, 294, n. 34, 295–96. Emphasis supplied.

of the one that disturbs Powell: there are not too few standards for judgment, but too many.

"Stigma" has a dictionary definition: "a brand . . . a mark of infamy or disgrace . . . any mark or label designed to indicate deviation from some norm or standard." This language recalls that of *Strauder*—"practically a *brand* upon them"—and a phrase from the *Civil Rights Cases*—"*badges* of slavery."[20] "Stigma" is also the title of a well-known book whose sociologist author defines the term as "an attribute which is deeply discrediting."[21] We know which races this definition applies to; more important, there exist indicators of what we know.

If a stigma is a mark or brand, what constitutes a stigma? One of the best discussions of this issue comes from Richard Wasserstrom:

> We know, for instance, that it is wrong, clearly racist, to have racially segregated bathrooms. . . . How is this to be accounted for? The answer . . . can be discovered through a consideration of the role that this practice played in that system of racial segregation we had in the United States—from, in other words, an examination of the social realities. For racially segregated bathrooms were an important part of that system. And that system had an ideology. . . . A significant factor of that ideology was that blacks were not only less than fully developed humans; they were also dirty and impure. They were the sort of persons who could and would contaminate white persons if they came into certain kinds of contact with them. . . . This ideology was intimately related to a set of institutional arrangements and power relationships in which whites were politically, economically, and socially dominant. The ideology supported the institutional arrangements, and the institutional arrangements reinforced the ideology. The net effect was that racially segregated bathrooms were both a part of the institutional mechanism of oppression and an instantiation of this ideology of racial taint. The point of maintaining racially segregated bathrooms was not in any simple or direct sense to keep both whites and blacks from using each other's bathrooms; it was to make sure that blacks would not contaminate bathrooms used by whites.[22]

In a defense of the *Brown* decision, Charles L. Black, Jr., described segregation as "a picture of one in-group enjoying full normal communal life and one out-group that is barred from this life and forced into a life of its own."[23] Black pointed out that in the town of Leeville, for example, the white high school was always Leeville High, while

---

[20] 100 U.S. 303, 307–8 (1880); 109 U.S. 3, 20 (1883). Emphasis supplied. See Jones v. Alfred H. Mayer Corp., 392 U.S. 409, 439, 440 (1968).

[21] Erving Goffman, *Stigma* (Englewood Cliffs, N.J.: Prentice-Hall, 1963), p. 3.

[22] "Racism," p. 592.

[23] "Lawfulness of the Segregation Decisions," p. 425.

the black school bore some other name. *Hernandez* v. *Texas*, a case decided just two weeks before *Brown*, gave still more guidelines, and suggested that there can be more than one out-group within a community. This decision, which reaffirmed the principle that the equal-protection clause protected ethnic groups other than blacks, mentioned segregation of public facilities, the extent of participation of a group in community life, and community attitudes as indicators of disadvantage.[24] It is easy to think of similar indicators, such as income, occupational distribution, and representation in public office.

Feminist literature provides another fruitful source of indicators of stigma and disadvantage. Black's dichotomy of in-group and out-group recalls Simone de Beauvoir's statement that "humanity is male and man defines women not in herself but as relative to him. . . . He is the Subject, he is the Absolute—she is the Other."[25] Black's high school illustration sounds rather like the "Mr. and Mrs. John Jones" convention. Scholarly comparisons of race and sex discrimination have directed attention to shared features that may be more subtle. Helen Mayer Hacker's famed article in which she identified high visibility, ascribed attitudes, rationalizations of status, and attitudes of accommodation as characteristics of both blacks and women is one example.[26]

"Stigma," then, does provide a potentially usable and useful standard. If anything, the concept does too much rather than too little. But what about "minority"? There is something disturbing about relying too heavily on this concept; Judge Tobriner, in particular, did not seem to realize that a minority can oppress a majority. But that was not Justice Powell's objection. His two arguments support one another. Had he been more receptive to the concept of stigma, he might have seen ways to distinguish between those groups that qualify for reverse discrimination and those that do not. But even without that help, his argument about the difficulties of distinguishing between minority and majority does not apply to racial groups. They are easy to identify. A final objection to Powell's argument is that nothing in the Constitution prevents the government from deciding to establish reverse discrimination for some disadvantaged groups but not for others. To permit reverse discrimination does not require that it be ex-

[24] 347 U.S. 475, 479–81 (1954).

[25] *The Second Sex*, trans. and ed. H. M. Parshley (New York: Alfred A. Knopf, 1949), p. xvi.

[26] "Women as a Minority Group," *Social Forces* 30 (October 1951):60. See also, of course, Gunnar Myrdal, *An American Dilemma* (New York: Harper & Row, 1944), vol. 2, app. 5.

tended to all groups that may qualify for it. If anyone were arguing that the Constitution required reverse discrimination, Powell's objection would be a forceful one, but the operative verb is not "require" but "permit." Reverse discrimination is not a right.

To speak of stigmatization and public insult—or, if one prefers, of discreteness and insularity—can therefore provide manageable standards for adjudication. The objective criteria are there. The distinction between in-group and out-group, between empowered and disempowered, need not become bogged down in conceptual difficulties.

But a third question remains. Even if we can distinguish among *groups*, can we distinguish between invidious and benign *policies*? This question is particularly troubling and inescapable for the specialist in sex discrimination, who knows all too well that laws intended to be benign can in fact be harmful. Is it not possible that, as even Justice Brennan warned, "programs designed ostensibly to ameliorate the effects of past racial discrimination . . . may . . . reinforce the views of those who believe that members of racial minorities are inherently incapable of succeeding on their own"?[27] This question echoes a common argument against reverse discrimination, which suggests that it is in fact stigmatizing because it carries a presumption that its beneficiaries have been rewarded on some basis other than their competence.[28]

But for minorities the choice is not between favored treatment and succeeding on one's own; it is often between favored treatment and exclusion. Besides, it is difficult to see how getting a job will create a permanent presumption of inferiority, since, after all, one still has a chance to prove oneself. It is of course true that compensations can become concessions—this is not a trivial problem—but the last decade of sex discrimination cases shows that, although the Court has sometimes had trouble making those distinctions, they can be made.

These cases indicate that reverse discrimination not only can be based on stigmatizing stereotypes, but may have, singly or in combination, any of three effects. First, it may actually compensate for prejudice and oppression. Second, it may harm rather than help the group it reaches. Or third, it may do virtually nothing. Brennan's distinction between laws that stigmatize and laws that compensate is too either-orish, for there is the third possibility. This group of decisions shows that the old stereotypes are still alive, and contains examples of all three possible effects.

[27] Regents v. Bakke, 438 U.S. 265, 360.
[28] See, e.g., Thomas Sowell, *Affirmative Action Reconsidered* (Washington, D.C.: American Enterprise Institute, 1975), pp. 39–40.

When the sex discrimination cases are grouped logially rather than chronologically, definite patterns emerge. Two social security cases, *Weinberger* v. *Wiesenfeld* in 1975 and *Califano* v. *Goldfarb* in 1977, invalidated supposed benefits that in fact were burdens.[29] Each involved discriminations between widows and widowers. Stephen Wiesenfeld, whose wife died in childbirth, sued to challenge a rule that entitled only widows with minor children to benefits based on a dead spouse's earnings. Leon Goldfarb, a retired man whose wife had worked for many years before her death, was denied benefits under a regulation that restricted them to widowers whose wives had provided at least half their support.

Both regulations appeared to be, and were defended as, discrimination in favor of dependent widows. They contained "a presumption that wives are usually dependent" and would be objectionable for that reason alone.[30] But there was a graver problem, which the Court saw. The law, it declared in *Wiesenfeld*,

> clearly operates . . . to deprive women of protection for their families which men receive as a result of their employment. Indeed . . . in this case social security taxes were deducted from Paula's salary during the years in which she worked. Thus, she not only failed to receive for her family the same protection which a similarly situated male worker would have received, but she also was deprived of a portion of her own earnings in order to contribute to the fund out of which benefits would be paid to others.[31]

The same was true of Hannah Goldfarb. So these laws, like the old labor laws and possibly the draft exemption, turn out to be invidious—as well as stereotyping and patronizing. The lesson of *Wiesenfeld* and *Goldfarb* is that each case demands, first of all, a determination whether the discrimination involved is benign or invidious.

Three cases involve laws that belong in the "discard" category. The first, *Kahn* v. *Shevin*, upheld Florida's $500 property tax exemption for widows, a provision that reduced an individual tax bill by about $15. If the length of the opinion, just over three pages, is any guide, the majority found the case a simple one. Citing government statistics on median earnings of male and female workers, the Court found the law "reasonably designed to further the state policy of cushioning the financial impact of spousal loss upon the sex for which that loss im-

[29] 420 U.S. 636; 430 U.S. 199.
[30] 430 U.S. 199, 217.
[31] 420 U.S. 636, 645.

poses a disproportionately heavy burden."[32] There are several problems with this reasoning,[33] but two in particular are relevant here. First, it seems unlikely that this law, which was enacted in 1885, had any such purpose; it is far more likely that it rested on generalizations about female dependence with which the judges who ruled on earlier laws were at home. Second, a $15 credit does not confer much of a benefit.

The next case was *Schlesinger* v. *Ballard*. Here the Court sustained a Navy regulation whose effect was to allow women officers four more years of service before mandatory discharge for want of promotion than male officers got (a provision that was dropped soon after this decision). The Court majority thought this rule, too, was a compensation. Justice Stewart suggested that women officers might need more time than men to pile up comparable records, since they were excluded from combat and most sea duty. The dissenters' response to this argument was devastating. Justice Brennan showed that the regulation was part of a scheme that, far from compensating women officers, severely restricted their opportunities, and pointed out that male and female line officers do not compete for promotion.[34] The benefits conferred on women by this law were as illusory as those in Florida's tax exemption.

Nearly two years passed between *Ballard* and the next similar decision, *Craig* v. *Boren*, the 3.2 percent beer case. No one ever claimed a compensatory purpose for this discrimination; it is reverse discrimination, however, since it does benefit the previously disadvantaged group. The Court found "an unduly tenuous 'fit'" between the state's interest in traffic safety and an association so limited and arbitrary as that between young manhood and drunk driving.[35] The importance of *Craig* lies in the constitutional rule it pronounced on sex discrimination, which I discussed in Chapter 5. This rule reappears in Brennan's *Bakke* opinion as demanding "an important and articulated purpose" for reverse discrimination, whether racial or sexual.[36] My own analysis of this group of cases convinces me that, at least as far as it goes, Brennan's conclusion is correct.

A test for reverse discrimination must distinguish between legitimate and illegitimate policies and among compensation, concession,

[32] 416 U.S. 351, 355 (1974); see Ruth Bader Ginsberg, "Gender and the Supreme Court," *Supreme Court Review*, 1975, pp. 1, 4.
[33] Baer, "Sexual Equality," p. 480.
[34] 419 U.S. 498, 508–9, 511–17 (1975).
[35] 429 U.S. 190, 202 (1976).
[36] 438 U.S. 265, 361.

and trivia. Like most rules, this one works best in the situation in which it originated: a case such as *Craig*, where only the most dubious relation existed between the law at issue and any objective. *Kahn* and *Ballard* are similar cases, and in each the rule would dictate the opposite result. The *Craig* rule was actually applied in two important reverse sex discrimination cases. These are more difficult cases than any of the preceding ones; the laws not only granted tangible benefits, but had a clear connection to serious governmental purposes. These cases show that, while the *Craig* rule is not self-applying, the inevitable problems can be solved. The rule does permit the crucial distinctions.

A 1979 case, *Orr v. Orr*, overturned Alabama's sex-specific alimony law. Its roots in sexist stereotypes—"the state's preference for an allocation of family responsibilities in which the wife plays a dependent role"[37]—are obvious, but the relationship of these roots to the law itself is not altogether clear. At this point we need to consider both the importance of the law's end and the relationship between ends and means.

To require an "important" purpose is a more stringent rule than to demand a "legitimate" one, but for an end to be important it must at least be legitimate. The alimony law appears on its face to be designed to protect needy ex-wives. Indeed, the Alabama court insisted that the law was enacted for "the *wife* of a broken marriage who needs financial assistance."[38] This end is inseparable from an assumption of female dependence and financial inadequacy. This notion arises from and reinforces society's pattern of sexual stigmatization by which sex becomes a proxy for inferiority. Such legislation, as Brennan cogently argued in *Bakke* and *Frontiero*, is inherently illegitimate. This point becomes clearer if we imagine a law that provided some similar kind of benefit, upon individual qualification, only to blacks. Although blacks are indeed more likely than whites to be poor, the assumption that only blacks, and any black, may be incapable of self-support is patently racist.

Suppose, however, that Alabama's purpose was not to protect *wives* (despite what the state's own court said), but to protect spouses, and that, to paraphrase *Goldfarb*, the state coupled with this aim a presumption of wifely dependence. Justice Brennan apparently thought this was the true situation: "a legislative purpose to provide help for needy spouses, using sex as a proxy for need." If so, the ends are sex-

---

[37] 99 S.Ct. 1102, 1111 (1979) (Brennan).

[38] Orr v. Orr, 351 So. 2d, 905 (Ct. Civ. App. Ala. 1978); cited, 99 S.Ct. 1102, 1112. Emphasis supplied.

neutral—and concededly valid—but the means are sex-specific. The same sexist presumptions may exist as before, but at this point the usual secondary justification for these laws, administrative convenience, has to be considered. Even this interpretation has not exhausted the possibilites. Alternatively, the law might compensate "women for past discrimination during marriage, which assertedly has left them unprepared to fend for themselves in the working world following divorce."[39] This is a sex-specific end, but, despite patronizing undertones, it too closely resembles benign discrimination to be casually dismissed as a sexist one.

The Court found it unnecessary to resolve either of these issues. The opinion found no valid reason for using sex as a proxy for either need or disadvantage. Since an individual hearing was always required before a judge could award alimony, such wives could be helped even with a sex-neutral policy, with little additional burden on the state. Thus even the problem of administrative convenience is illusory.

In an academic context, the compensation argument deserves more consideration than the Court gave it. A good analogy here is *Ballard*. Preference for women in regard to military tenure turned out to be part of a pattern of negative discrimination rather than true compensation. (If a third analogy is forgivable, it was rather as if universities gave female junior faculty members extra probationary time while simultaneously imposing heavier teaching loads on them or a ceiling on their publications.) Some of the "discrimination during marriage" of which Justice Brennan spoke consists of legally imposed or ratified restrictions on wives, such as domiciliary dependence and domestic duties. The law of marriage and divorce is notoriously sexist and traditional; it is highly unlikely that alimony was ever designed as a form of compensation.

Even though *Orr v. Orr* itself did not demand resolution of some of these problems, future cases probably will, and this discussion shows the usefulness of the *Craig* rule. It does suggest, however, an amendment that may be necessary: not only must a law meet the test of substantial relation to important purpose, but the purpose must be one that cannot be fulfilled by sex-neutral or race-neutral means. Thus the alimony law, like Florida's tax exemption, would fall because its legitimate ends can be achieved by neutrally written laws.

Of the relevant cases, only *Califano v. Webster* remains. This is the only case that involves true benign discrimination. *Webster* involved a rule whereby old-age insurance benefits depend on a worker's average

[39] 99 S.Ct. 1102, 1112.

monthly wage earned during the years (reduced by five) during which wages were highest. Until 1972, when the scheme was equalized, a woman worker could exclude three more lower earning years from her average than a man could. In a *per curiam* opinion in 1977, the Court applied the three-month-old *Craig* rule to sustain the defunct provision. Far from being a product of obsolete generalizations about ability or dependence, the scheme "operated directly to compensate women for past economic disadvantage." [40]

The provision was not designed to alleviate poverty, using sex as a proxy for poverty. Its purpose was rather to rectify a certain kind of economic disadvantage: sex discrimination in earnings. Sex was not a proxy for anything. Ample evidence exists of the disparity between men's and women's earnings; this disparity transcends class, race, occupation, education, and all other relevant factors. Virtually all women (whether deliberately or not) have been underpaid because they are women. The importance of the law's purpose is demonstrable, and by its nature that purpose can be achieved only by sex-specific means. The only way to compensate for sex discrimination is to provide benefits on the same basis.

Webster supplies a good analogy to *Bakke*. Race has limited educational opportunities as surely as gender has restricted earnings. These disadvantages have persisted for a long time; even if proof is lacking that they have been imposed willfully, they have been imposed. Each policy helped make up for the past inequalities, and afforded real, not illusory, benefits to the groups involved. If the social security provision is constitutional, there is every good reason why preferential admissions should be.

These cases have vindicated the fears Justice Brennan expressed in *Bakke*. Too ready acceptance of reverse discrimination would be dangerous. Even recent laws can reinforce negative stereotypes, hurt rather than help, be part of a system of rules that is in fact invidious, or be so trivial as to verge on banality. Reverse racial discrimination may present fewer opportunities than sex discrimination for this type of legislation, given prevailing climates of opinion, but if we treat race and sex discrimination with equal seriousness, we must develop rules that avoid these dangers as far as possible.

Consistently with the history and spirit of the Fourteenth Amendment, we can generalize from race and sex to other attributes. To consign people to an inferior position in society, to disempower them, to insult and stigmatize them is to deny them the right to treatment as

[40] 430 U.S. 313, 318 (1977).

equals. But to discriminate against a member of a favored group in order to bring disfavored groups to full equality does not relegate the person to what has been the status of racial minorities or even of women, and therefore does not violate that fundamental right. Invidious racial and sexual discriminations should, as Brennan noted in *Bakke*, be "invalid without more"[41]—not suspect, *invalid*. That concept would remove the disgrace of *Hirabayashi* and *Korematsu* and prevent any similar decisions in the future. But benign racial and sexual discriminations are recognizable as such, and do not stigmatize, and should be permitted.

Nagging Questions

But when, and under what circumstances, should reverse discrimination be permitted? Brennan, borrowing from *Craig* v. *Boren*, has suggested a test here: that "an important and articulated purpose . . . must be shown."[42] Do we want to accept *any* such discrimination that satisfies this test? Certainly such a case as *McDonald* is worrisome, though the result is welcome. That a black person should go unpunished for misconduct that gets white workers fired is inexcusable. But it is helpful to think about *why* this situation is so disturbing. In such a case, several workers have committed an act for which each is responsible; all exercised individual choice, and all were guilty of wrongdoing. This is not, therefore, a typical case of race discrimination. It is not unlike Senator Howard's example of the black man who is hanged for a crime for which a white man is not hanged. Individual responsibility, which is exactly what is absent from most cases of race discrimination, was present, and was discounted.

In *McDonald*, two workers were punished and a third was not. That decision, in itself, is not necessarily wrong. When several people commit the same offense, they are often punished differently. Various reasons may be offered, including such factors as exculpatory circumstances and prior records. But all these factors relate to individual responsibility, motive, or intent. Punishment for wrongdoing is a distinct kind of policy; rather like course grading, it depends on individual responsibility in ways that other decisions do not. The nexus between wrongdoing and punishment is tighter than that between test scores and medical school. Punishment depends on a person's behav-

---

[41] 438 U.S. 265, 358.
[42] Ibid., p. 361. See 429 U.S. 190 (1976).

ior in a specific situation, governed by specific rules known to both the punished and the punisher. It is a special case.

There are other situations in which reverse discrimination would be disturbing. A thread that runs through discussions of this issue is the fear expressed by Justice Brennan in *Bakke* that these programs may reinforce racist notions. We have seen some examples of allegedly preferential treatment for women which reinforce sexist notions, and it is possible to imagine racial analogies. Suppose, for example, that a law provided some sort of financial benefit, upon individual qualification, only to blacks. It is true, of course, that blacks are more likely than whites to be poor. But an assumption that only blacks can be, and any black may be, incapable of self-support is clearly racist. It harms both those included in and those excluded from the benefits. This policy may sound fanciful as an example of race discrimination, but if we think of sex discrimination, it recalls *Orr* v. *Orr*. Such policies, whether designed for women or for racial minorities, are objectionable because they use sex or race as a proxy for a factor such as need, which is not only poorly related to these attributes, but related to them in a patronizing and insulting way.

Such a law differs from classic reverse discrimination in yet another important respect. It excludes individuals *entirely* from a benefit on the basis of race or sex. The deprivation is absolute. It is as if a professional school reserved all of its places for minorities, not just sixteen out of a hundred, as Davis did. Suppose, just to make the hypothetical case more interesting, that this school is not one of several within a large urban area but one that is relatively isolated, as UC Davis is. Since not everyone is free to move in order to go to medical school, such a policy could effectively prevent some people from attending at all. This is too severe a deprivation to be based on race or sex alone. (Howard, Meharry, and the Women's Medical College of Pennsylvania would not be vulnerable to this objection, since in their prime they were not only limited to blacks or women but were in effect the only institutions open to them on an equal basis. None of them is now so limited.) The character and severity of the deprivation have to be considered.

In at least three situations, then, reverse discrimination would not be acceptable. Only the second, the "black alimony" case, can reasonably be said to involve any sort of stigmatization, to imply defects in those ostensibly favored. The other two cases could survive the *Craig* test of important and articulated purpose. But the harm they inflict on the majority is too great. Total exclusion has something in common with *McDonald*. To punish differentially, or to bar people from education, training, or employment, does worse damage than to reduce their chances to compete for limited resources.

The two-tier equal-protection model does recognize similar distinctions of degree, but its rigid dichotomy between ordinary interests and "fundamental rights" will not help solve the problem. Getting into medical school is not a fundamental right, nor is escaping punishment when others escape it (although, if *McDonald* had involved criminal prosecution, that possibility could not easily be dismissed). This discussion recalls Justice Marshall's dissent in *Rodriguez*, where he rejected the two-tier model in favor of concentration on "the character of the classification in question, the *relative importance* to individuals in the class discriminated against of the governmental benefits that they do not receive, and the asserted state interests in support of the classification."[43] Some hierarchy of interests and claims has to be built into equal-protection litigation.

Conclusion

There are principled bases for distinguishing between malign and benign discrimination; between the advantaged and disadvantaged; between acceptable and unacceptable deprivations. We need not be hypocrites in order to defend reverse discrimination. Such a defense can rest on distinctions stronger than my ox versus your ox. What constitutional arguments in favor of reverse discrimination force us to do is not to reject all principle but to reexamine the landmark cases of the last thirty years. The principle that some of them articulated—that all racial discrimination is illegitimate—is not compatible with reverse discrimination. But this chapter and the last have shown that that principle was not necessary for those results.

The reverse discrimination cases, like the rulings examined in Chapter 5, show how the Supreme Court has constricted the Constitution's guarantee of equality. The decisions focus not on the foundations of this guarantee but on the traits that are the bases for classification. A broad guarantee of equality is read as a proscription of race discrimination. This construction is both less and more than what the constitutional language and history imply. As we have seen, Section 1 of the Fourteenth Amendment is not phrased in terms of race. There is no powerful reason to conclude that its scope is limited to race discrimi-

[43] 411 U.S. 1, 99 (1973). Emphasis supplied.

nation. Nor is there any powerful reason to read the Constitution as forbidding *all* racial discrimination, whomever it helped.

Supposedly "neutral" discriminations are indeed premised on notions of inferiority. But discriminations in favor of those groups that have been stigmatized, oppressed, and insulted are designed to bring these groups to full equality. Therefore, they are in accord with the Constitution, and there is no persuasive legal argument against them. They may not always be necessary; specific plans, certainly, may be unwise; and they may not achieve their purpose. It is possible, as times and attitudes get harder, that we shall see fewer and fewer of them. But these considerations are not reasons to declare such discriminations unconstitutional, and thus to frustrate efforts to fulfill the promise of the Fourteenth Amendment.

The next three chapters represent a change in focus. Now I shall be concerned not with race and sex but with age, disability, and sexual orientation. The *issue* of age discrimination may be recent, but the *fact* is very old, and legal frameworks exist for dealing with it. In the last two areas the problems go beyond questions of discrimination. The handicapped and homosexuals are the targets of discrimination, but that is not all they are subjected to. Not only will I get further and further away from traditional legal categories, but my scope will widen beyond equal protection and the Fourteenth Amendment.

I shall still be concerned with cases, but in none of the next three chapters do I attempt a comprehensive overview of the relevant case law. Nor will I confine myself to cases. Because these are new demands, some of the people who will figure prominently in the next chapters come from *60 Minutes* and the *New York Times* rather than *United States Reports* and the *Federal Reporter*. But here again I shall be concerned with what these issues can teach us about equality under the Constitution.

[7]

The Question of Age

Discriminations based on age have been among the least controversial of legal distinctions. Where a line should be drawn—at eighteen or twenty-one for voting, at sixty-five or seventy for retirement—has often been a hot issue, but the notion that a line should be drawn somewhere has rarely been troublesome. Most of us have accepted the idea that young citizens may be forced to do things adults need not do, such as go to school, or forbidden to do things adults may do, such as drinking or driving. Similarly, there is little protest when older people are forced to take drivers' tests more frequently than others. In 1980 many Americans were uncomfortable with the prospect of a seventy-year-old president, as, twenty years before, they were uneasy about one in his early forties. We have seen nothing arbitrary or unreasonable about such distinctions, but have tended to view them as recognitions of significant differences in human abilities. That, of course, is just how legal distinctions based on sex were once regarded, and that opinion has changed. One purpose of this chapter is to ask whether similar changes are needed in our thinking about age.

In many respects, age differs from all other traits on which legal classifications are based. Although, like race and sex, it is beyond individual control, it does change. What is fixed is the rate of that change. Another feature of age discrimination is that any line drawn is to some extent arbitrary and artificial, even if the states of life it demarcates are real. There are evident differences, for example, between infancy and childhood, adolescence and young adulthood, middle age and old age, but there is no exact age at which one stage ends and another begins. Eighteen is the voting age because we have to put it somewhere, not because there is any magical difference between seventeen and eighteen. A final difference between age and most bases for discrimination is that it is not easy to substitute for the neutral term a group that is the usual target, as "blacks" can be exchanged with "race discrimination" or "women" for "sex discrimination." Age-based distinctions usually reach either the young or the old, but they can single out people who are not classifiable as either. For example, fifty is not commonly regarded as the beginning of old age, but that was where the line was drawn in *Murgia.*

Because of this imprecision, the law of age discrimination may seem to be too vast and unwieldy a subject for one chapter. After all, youth and age are antonyms, not synonyms. On the face of it, there seems to be more difference than similarity between, say, laws that make minors subject to parental control and laws that oblige people over seventy to take drivers' tests more often than others do.

But suppose we compare, instead, compulsory schooling to compulsory retirement. What do they have in common? Both policies set aside a place where the young or old do or do not belong, and do they not both imply that young and old should be segregated from the mainstream of society? Do such policies reflect equal respect and concern for the people excluded? Certainly we do not send people under sixteen to school for the same *reasons* that we force people to retire at fifty, or sixty-five, or seventy. But anyone who wishes to argue, as I do, that compulsory schooling is constitutional and compulsory retirement unconstitutional must deal with the similarities as well as the differences.

Paternalism, Patriotism, and Patriarchy

Chapter 5 discussed the two major retirement cases, *Murgia* and *Bradley.* There I criticized *Bradley*, in particular, for the assumption that the interests of the retirees could be sacrificed to those of the younger Foreign Service officers. I was less concerned there with attitudes toward the aging than with the results of applying the rigid equal-protection model. Now I shall take up the specific problem, and begin by suggesting that the treatment of the aging has much in common with the treatment of the young.

At first glance, it does not seem that way. In general, with the exception of a few specific laws, older people have the legal status of all adult citizens. Children have a special, restricted status that pervades every aspect of their lives. Legally, a minor child is an "infant." The word comes from the Latin *infans*, which literally means "not having the facility of speech"; it refers, overinclusively, to children under the age of seven. The common English meaning of the word is "baby" or "young child," but the law, again overinclusively, so labels all minors of whatever age.

Infants are presumed to be incompetent. Absent contrary evidence, their parents are presumed to act in their best interests. Similar assumptions are made about schools, where attendance is compulsory. Whether or not children themselves are ever consulted about their interests depends on the particular laws of particular states; there is no requirement that they must be. The cases I shall examine reflect both the assumption expressed by the word "infant," that minors are incompetent, and the derivative assumption that the adults closest to minors act in their best interests. That the cases in question reflect these assumptions is odd, for they contain much evidence against both of them.

In a case that actually enlarged the rights of juveniles, the Supreme Court described the general situation like this: "A child, unlike an adult, has a right 'not to liberty but to custody.' He can be made to attorn to his parents, to go to school, etc. If his parents default in effectively performing their custodial functions—that is, if the child is 'delinquent'—the state may intervene. In doing so, it does not deprive the child of any rights, for he has none." [1] No rights, but many duties. Children "are expected to be good. . . . Perhaps the most important and least appreciated norm governing the lives of young people is that they are in every aspect of their presence, demeanor, and appearance *accountable*. Unlike adults, who can hold each other to account only on the basis of special entitlements and only to a limited extent, young people must answer fully to their parents." [2] And when parents do not hold their children to account, the school and the state step in, in force.

The case of Walter Polovchak illustrates this situation. Early in 1980, when Walter was twelve, his family emigrated from the Soviet Union and settled in Chicago's Ukranian community. That summer, the parents decided to return home. Walter wanted to stay, and ran away to relatives in the community. The Immigration and Naturalization Service granted him asylum, and a federal judge ruled that his parents could not take him back to the Ukraine. The parents took their case

[1] Re Gault, 387 U.S. 1, 17 (1967).
[2] Egon Bittner, "Policing Juveniles: The Social Context of Common Practice," in Margaret K. Rosenheim, ed., *Pursuing Justice for the Child* (Chicago: University of Chicago Press, 1976), pp. 73–74. Emphasis in the original.

to the Illinois courts. In December 1981 a state appeals court awarded custody of Walter to his parents, but neither state nor federal authorities made any effort to return him. The parents have since returned to the Ukraine, and the case goes on—as Walter approaches adulthood.[3]

Not surprisingly, the case has had widespread publicity. After all, it presents a conflict between two cherished American ideals: patriotism and family life. Typically, it has been the familial knee that has jerked. Opinion has tended to side with the parents. So do the American Civil Liberties Union, which took their case; the *New York Times*; and the well-known liberal columnist Ellen Goodman, who has criticized court decisions upholding parents' rights to institutionalize their children. She wrote:

> If it happened to an American family, it would be an outrage. . . . The fact is that we have given much more weight to this Ukranian boy's testimony than to any American boy of the same age.
> . . . Is he, like so many of his age, testing the limits, tasting his first tidbits of rebellion? Or can he be mature enough to choose political freedom above family?
> . . . Our laws assume [except in rare instances] that the parent is the best judge of the state of mind, the needs and the future, of the child. Whether we approve or not, we do not interfere unless they have been proven unfit.[4]

Walter, of course, is in no sense independent. Without his extended family, he would have no real choices. No more than the society Walter left does this one permit a twelve-year-old to be autonomous. Walter's choices—and they have not been his, but the courts'—are between being subject to his parents in the Ukraine and being subject to a guardian in the United States. Walter could not earn a living wage; even if he could, or if he had an independent income, he would not be allowed to control the money; and his ability to earn is limited by the fact that he must go to school. Without an income, Walter could not buy necessities.

Twelve-year-olds can do many of the things for which adults are

[3] "Boy Seeks Asylum, Defying Russian-Born Parents," *Washington Post*, July 21, 1980, p. A9. See also *New York Times*, February 20, 1981, p. 8; June 4, 1981, II, p. 14; August 4, 1981, p. 8; August 6, 1981, p. 10; August 13, 1981, p. 13; August 29, 1981, p. 8; October 22, 1981, p. 19; November 26, 1981, p. 16; December 31, 1981, pp. 1, B6; February 16, 1982, p. 12.

[4] "The Parent Is the Best Judge," *Washington Post*, August 9, 1980, p. A19. But see "Checks on Parental Power," in Goodman, *At Large* (New York: Summit Books, 1981), pp. 170–71.

paid. They can also keep themselves alive; they can buy and prepare food, clothe themselves, and get housing. But they are not allowed to earn a living wage, and therefore to get what they need. Moreover, most of the skills that children must have in order to become autonomous adults, such as reading and writing, are not taught them until long after they are capable of learning them. A twelve-year-old's dependence is as much the result of social practices as it is of personal limitations.

Is a child Walter's age "mature enough" to be independent? It is not clear why this should be the first question; why not begin instead by asking about the consequences to the child of the decision? Often what adults mean by children's "maturity" is obedience, tractability, and agreement with them. Walter, of course, has passed that test, since he agrees with most of us about where he would rather live. Sarcasm aside, Walter did give some reasons for his choice, and at first glance they cast doubt on his maturity. He spoke of his fondness for American ice cream, bicycles, "lots of food," and the fact that "you can buy many things here." [5] But what can we expect? Would it have been more mature of him to speak in clichés about American democracy? After all, children neither vote nor hold office; and, as aliens, neither could Walter's parents. Ice cream and bicycles reflect the limited range of choices available to a child, and the limited resources he commands. Expert opinions differ as to what children can do, and how mature they are, at what age, but when society denies children the power to do many of these things, the ability is beside the point.

However limited Walter's choices, his attempts to make them have disturbed many Americans. Our faith in the family, our belief that Mother and Father know best, are so great that parents get support even when few of us would agree with their decisions. The courts, too, may yet side with the parents. Few people seem to remember that only eight years before Walter Polovchak ran away from home, a similar case in Chicago, involving an even younger child, was decided in favor of the parents, and the result was tragic. Six-year-old Johnny Lindquist did not want to live with his parents, either. He had been placed in a foster home after his parents declared they could not support him. When they wanted him back, Johnny told a caseworker that he was afraid of his father and wanted to stay with his foster parents. But he was returned home; his father beat him; and in September 1972, after weeks in a coma, he died.

Of course, it would be unfair to compare the Polovchaks with the

[5] Goodman, "Parent Is the Best Judge."

Lindquists. What the two cases share is not a truth about parents, but a truth about opinion and a truth about children. *Time* wrote of the Lindquist case: "As a result, an Illinois Senate Committee has been holding hearings on whether to change child-care laws to resemble those of California, where due weight is given to the child's own wishes about custody if he 'is of sufficient age and capacity to reason.' "[6] John Holt commented on this article:

> . . . had such a law been on the books, I doubt that it would have made the slightest difference in the case of Johnny Lindquist or others like him. In the United States today what official body, what group of professional helpers and protectors of children, would agree that a six-year-old was "of sufficient age and capacity to reason"? And yet that is exactly the point of the story, and a point that *Time* magazine wholly missed. In this matter *it was Johnny who was right.* His judgment was more accurate and his reasoning better than that of the state and its adult experts. *He knew.* They did not. Will we listen any more attentively to the next six-year-old who tells us that he knows what he wants and needs? It's not likely.[7]

The lesson of the Lindquist case (and the reason I bring it up) is that a child can be right. Even a six-year-old can know what is best for him, and can make wise choices. The emotional reaction a case like Johnny Lindquist's provokes may have limited its usefulness as a lesson. The Polovchak case, generating less passion, should stimulate more thought. But so far it has been a one-sided contest between patriotism and patriarchy, with the latter far ahead.

Is it appropriate, though, to compare the Polovchak case with *Murgia* and *Bradley*? What do these cases have in common? One similarity is that both parental control and compulsory retirement depend on *generalizations* about the capacities of certain age groups. State police officers must retire at fifty because society assumes that certain physical abilities decline with age, and that therefore a person over fifty is less likely than a younger person to have acute vision and fast reflexes. Likewise, parents have control over their children because society assumes that certain mental abilities increase with age, and that therefore a twelve-year-old is less able than an adult to make wise decisions. Each of these assumptions and generalizations is correct, to an appreciable extent; both are far more accurate than common generalizations about race or sex. The relationships between trait and abil-

---

[6] "Children's Rights: The Latest Crusade," *Time*, December 25, 1972, p. 41.

[7] *Escape from Childhood* (New York: Ballantine Books, 1975), pp. 174–75. Emphasis in the original.

ity are stronger in age discrimination cases than in those cases. Thus, although it is partly a matter of degree, age discrimination probably would not fall under the *Frontiero* definition of suspect classification.

But that is a probability, not a certainty, and the outcome may well depend on what age and what restriction. It is disquieting to compare *Murgia* with *Frontiero* and *Craig*. Brennan found sex-based distinctions suspect because, like race, sex is an involuntary, immutable characteristic. Age is mutable, but it, too, is "determined solely by the accident of birth." Brennan also discussed the lack of relationship between sex and ability, and the "gross, stereotyped distinctions" on which laws have often depended.[8] Although the Court has refused to rank sex as a suspect classification, some of *Frontiero* survives as dogma. Later decisions have established that sex discrimination cannot be based on stereotyped assumptions.[9] *Rostker* v. *Goldberg* weakens this principle only to the extent that the assumptions that have led Congress to exclude women from combat are used to justify their immunity to the draft. It remains to be seen how great a departure this ruling will be.

Murgia insisted that the retirement law is not based on such stereotyped assumptions, that there is good evidence that physical abilities decline with age.[10] But even though these generalizations are supportable, they are not universally true. Some fifty-year-olds have perfect vision, just as some children have good judgment—or, at least, better judgment than adults around them. Nevertheless, the generalizations are universally *applied*; they include everyone within the group, with no exceptions.

When the Court declared in *Murgia* that the state police officers were not "subjected to unique disabilities on the basis of stereotyped characteristics not truly indicative of their abilities," it was dead wrong.[11] That was exactly what had happened. The fact that the assumptions might be more accurate than some that have been made about blacks or women does not make them any less stereotyped. The fit between age and decline is no better than that between young manhood and drunken driving in *Craig*, and yet it was sufficient. Men, women, and racial minorities may not be restricted on the basis of gross stereotyped assumptions, but the old(er) and the young(er) may be.

Not only are the generalizations imperfect, but the abilities in question are imperfectly related to the facts of the particular cases. By and large, it is true that good vision and fast reflexes are useful for a police

---

[8] Frontiero v. Richardson, 411 U.S. 677, 686, 685 (1973).
[9] See Stanton v. Stanton, 421 U.S. 7 (1975); Craig v. Boren, 429 U.S. 190 (1976).
[10] 427 U.S. 307, 313–14 (1976).
[11] Ibid., p. 313.

officer; to slip back into legal jargon, they are reasonably related to police work. But not all police tasks require them.[12] Nor do all choices require "maturity" or "wisdom." Most choices are among few and limited things.

This discussion has suggested that certain typical age-based discriminations could survive standard equal-protection scrutiny. They are neither arbitrary nor suspect classifications. But Chapter 5 showed that another working definition of "suspect classification" exists, that is, classifications used to harm a distinct, isolated minority. *Murgia* insisted that classifications affecting those over fifty did not have this effect, and what was said there is equally true of youth. It is a stage of life we all go through; and though the young, too, must contend with prejudice and stereotype, to call them an oppressed or despised group strikes us as odd.

But this analysis, applied to youth, is no more satisfactory than it was in *Murgia* and *Bradley*. Age and youth are not typically thought of as brands, or deeply discrediting attributes in Goffman's sense, but it is easy to think of features that are similar to the stigma of blackness or femaleness. Both the old and the young partake of forced segregation, high visibility, lack of money and power, and, possibly, attitudes of accommodation (consider, for example, the "cute" behavior many children exhibit). Some of the worst stigmas do not seem to have equivalents here—for example, there is no ready counterpart to "nigger" or "broad" for children ("kid" does not make it, though "brat" might)—but the question seems to be one of degree. And the *Murgia* problem still exists: the fact that a general classification does not brand, isolate, or disempower does not foreclose the possibility that particular policies based on the classification can do so. In that sense, many such laws may put the weight of the government behind oppression.

I suggested that one way to create a disadvantaged group is to deprive its members of their jobs. When new jobs are not ready and waiting for retirees and pensions are often a joke, those who no longer work may virtually no longer eat. The deprivation is not of a "fundamental right" in the traditional sense, but it can be devastating. So are the potential effects of Walter Polovchak's being forced back home.

Bradley seems even more destructive than *Murgia*. I quoted at length from Justice White's opinion for the Court, in which he stressed the younger diplomats' morale at the expense of the older officers' jobs. I

[12] For an analysis of a similar issue that touches on some of these problems, see "Height Standards in Police Employment and the Question of Sex Discrimination: The Availability of Two Defenses for a Neutral Employment Policy Found Discriminatory under Title VII, " *Southern California Law Review* 47 (February 1974):585–640.

questioned the assumption that the interests of one group could get absolute priority over those of the other. Something similar has happened in the Polovchak case. Comment on it has tended to emphasize the interests not of the child but of the parents. To some extent, of course, such comment is appropriate; the parents do matter. There have been suggestions, such as Goodman's, that the parents must be presumed to act in Walter's best interests. This assumption echoes *Time's* discussion—apropos, incredibly enough, of the Lindquist case—of "the psychic benefits of parental authority." [13] But the decision to return Walter to his parents could hardly have been based only on his presumed interests. All too often it is assumed that parental authority is supreme; parental choice beyond question; parental priority absolute. With youth, as with age in the *Bradley* decision, law, doctrine, and opinion contain some disturbing assumptions about who really matters in this society and who does not.

Standard equal-protection doctrine deals summarily with maximum age rules, relegating them to the lower tier of classifications. The young fare even worse than the old with this doctrine; in cases involving children, equal-protection questions go all but unasked. The only such issue raised in the Polovchak case—Goodman hints at it in her column—is whether Ukranian parents get equal rights with American parents. In the decisions I shall examine, no judge seriously questions the government's power to treat children differently from adults. Children enjoy constitutional rights only to a very limited extent; they may be summarily punished and even injured; and demands may be made on children—for example, that they show respect or avoid bad company—that no adult outside a prison need tolerate.

Current doctrine thus buries questions of equality. But if one conceives of the constitutional guarantees as I have suggested—as broad provisions of equal respect and individual rights, transcending questions of capacity or competence—these issues do not bury easily. For the cases show that neither senior nor junior citizens enjoy these rights. They do not receive anything close to treatment as equals. They are not entitled to equality.

Before I examine cases on children, an introductory word is in order. The media have informed us selectively on these issues, distorting our perceptions. We hear of children who assault teachers, not teachers who assault children; teenagers who "pop" pills, not students forced to take them; juveniles who more or less get away with murder, not those incarcerated for years for behavior that adults get away with.

---

[13] "Children's Rights," p. 42.

These distortions may reflect an ambivalence toward children, if not outright dislike. For readers unfamiliar with court decisions, much of the information here may be new and troubling.

The Boundaries of Parental Control

> If the universality of the childhood experience (all of us were children once) could guarantee empathy from adult lawmakers despite the absence of children from legislative assemblies, there would be no occasion to regard children as an isolated and unrepresented minority, in need of special protection, but if adults instead look with contempt at a stage they have "outgrown" and will never re-enter, then every privilege withheld by legislators or administrators from the young must become a source of suspicion.[14]

The courts have come to question, though not to discard, any general presumption of adult benevolence they may have held with respect to officials. But parents are a different story. The judges never seriously question parental benevolence. Courts presume that parents are loving and wise. This notion expresses the ideal of family life, in which we have been taught to believe. But perhaps we do not need it taught to us. Since we all had parents, we have a stake in believing in the ideal; since many are parents, they have a double stake in a flattering vision of themselves.

But we do not really know how close the ideal comes to the reality of family life. The next four cases present much evidence of disjunction, but judges tend to discount these facts as "exceptions" to the rule. There are good reasons to challenge this dismissal. Certainly parents are instructed to love their children, and often do. The parent-child relationship may indeed be one of love, but it is inevitably one of power: not only because of the law, but because of parents' greater physical prowess and power of the family purse. For the feminist who has entertained the idea that the family may oppress women, it is only a small logical step to entertain, though not necessarily to embrace, the idea that it may also oppress children. But for many people, including judges, this is a foreign and frightening thought.

It was not until 1979 that the Supreme Court decided a case involving an overt conflict between parent and child. But parents are active participants in most cases involving children, usually on their chil-

---

[14] Laurence H. Tribe, "Childhood, Suspect Classifications, and Conclusive Presumptions: Three Limited Riddles," *Law and Contemporary Problems* 39 (special issue on children and the law, Summer 1975):9.

dren's side. Some adult has to pay the lawyer's bill, and usually that person is the child's parent. Even when no fee is involved, some lawyers are reluctant to represent juveniles without parental approval. An example is the case of Paul Guilbert, a seventeen-year-old homosexual. In 1979 he sought to attend his high school junior prom in Cumberland, Rhode Island, with a male date. When the principal refused his request, the school committee denied Guilbert a hearing because his father opposed him. The Providence chapter of the ACLU refused to take the case for the same reason. The next year, however, Guilbert attended the senior prom with the same date. Aaron Fricke was eighteen and legally an adult, so he could bring suit on his own. A federal district judge ruled in his favor. School officials considered canceling the prom, but let it go on as scheduled. There were no incidents.[15]

Usually cases involving children are brought by the parent, acting as the child's "next friend."[16] As a result, the typical case carries an assumption that the interests of parent and child are identical. But, as two landmark cases show, there may be reason to wonder.

In *Wisconsin* v. *Yoder*, only Justice Douglas did wonder. He joined his eight colleagues in ruling that Old Order Amish parents could remove their children from school after the eighth grade, as their religion required, when the children agreed; but he dissented alone when there was no record of the child's wishes. Douglas cited data that showed that an appreciable number of Amish children do eventually leave their community; would they not need further schooling?[17] Education is enabling; it equips people to make decisions about their lives, and stopping it at an early age limits individual freedom—which, of course, is just what the Amish parents want. However healthy, virtuous, and law-abiding the Amish way of life is, it is also constricting, and there is evidence of severe problems behind the facade of "idyllic agrarianism."[18] No one disputes an adult's right to choose such a life, but may parents effectively foreclose all other choices for their child? On the other hand, if parents do not limit the child's alternatives, will the child ever again be able to make that particular choice? The fact that ever larger numbers of young adults choose to live under strict religious discipline suggests an affirmative answer to the second question.

---

[15] *New York Times*, April 11, 1979, p. 17; April 13, p. 10; April 16, III, p. 12; April 22, p. 29; May 21, 1980, II, p. 4; May 29, II, p. 8; May 31, p. 26. But see Buckholz v. Leveille, 194 N.W. 2d 427 (Mich. C. App., 1971), where a high school student was allowed to bring suit over his parents' objections.

[16] I.e., the closest legally competent person; however, an adult other than a parent may bring an action as a child's next friend.

[17] 406 U.S. 205, 245, n. 2 (1972).

[18] State v. Yoder, 182 N.W. 2d 539, 549–50 (Heffernan dissenting).

In *Yoder*, such questions are visible but not readily answerable. In an equally famous case, *Tinker* v. *Des Moines Community School District*, they were not even visible.[19] When three students were suspended for wearing black armbands to protest the Vietnam war, their parents went to court and won. No one saw any possible conflict. But Robert Burt, writing several years later, questioned whose First Amendment rights the decision actually protected: the children's or the parents'. A good question: many of us can recall adolescent embarrassment at our parents' political beliefs. Burt does not think this parent-child conflict was appropriately presented to the Court in either *Tinker* or *Yoder*; he argues that both were rightly decided.[20] But the general question will not go away.

Parham v. *J. R.* presented it squarely.[21] At issue was the commitment of minors to state mental institutions on the request of their parents or guardians. The institutions' authorities had to approve the commitment, but no formal hearing was required either before or after admission. A three-judge district court in Georgia had enjoined this practice, ruling that giving parents "unbridled discretion" violated due process. The judge repeatedly compared this case with *Gault*, in which the Supreme Court had held that the requirements of notice, hearing, and counsel apply to juvenile court proceedings. He pointed out that, in fact, Georgia's juvenile code had more safeguards than this law, that institutionalization could be as harmful as imprisonment, and that "there are no true 'voluntary' child admissions."[22] Judge Wilbur Owens also relied on another apposite case, *O'Connor* v. *Donaldson*.[23] There the Supreme Court had unanimously ruled that to confine a nondangerous patient against his will violated due process. Kenneth Donaldson had been committed—by his parents, note, but after a court hearing—in 1957, and, despite repeated efforts to secure his release, was held, with no further hearing, until 1974.

Explaining his reliance on these two cases, Judge Owens quoted a doctor's description of a "typical" decision to commit: "The parent may come in saying, 'I can't handle it any more; do something.' And they say at the hospital . . . , 'I think hospitalization is indicated.' The

[19] 393 U.S. 503 (1969).

[20] "Developing Constitutional Rights of, in, and for Children," *Law and Contemporary Problems* 39 (Summer 1975): 122–32.

[21] 99 S.Ct. 2493. See also the companion case, Secretary of Public Welfare v. Institutionalized Juveniles, 99 S.Ct. 2523.

[22] J. L. [*sic*] v. Parham, 412 F. Supp. 112, 121 (M.D. Ga. 1976), citing the Report of the Georgia Study Commission on Mental Health Services for Children and Youth, 1973.

[23] 422 U.S. 563 (1975).

parent would agree and that would be it." The judge concluded: "To unnecessarily confine a child in a mental hospital and thereby cause him to possibly suffer severe emotional and psychic harm, to demean himself, and to magnify social ostracism, is to deprive him of a child's freedom just as much as if not more so than a child is deprived of his freedom by being civilly committed as a juvenile delinquent."[24]

The Supreme Court reversed. All that due process required, declared Chief Justice Burger, was "some kind of inquiry . . . by a neutral fact finder . . . [which] . . . must also include an interview with the child." The decision maker must "have the authority to refuse to admit any child" and "the child's continuing need for commitment" must "be reviewed periodically by a similarly independent procedure."[25] The psychiatrists and administrators provided such a review.

One might question whether an employee of mental institution is in fact "neutral." The choice to work in such an institution presumably implies approval of that mode of treatment.[26] But the most striking features of Burger's opinion were its endorsement of both the therapeutic model of mental institutions and the traditional model of the family.

> The state through its voluntary commitment procedures does not "label" the child: it provides a diagnosis and treatment that medical specialists conclude the child requires. In terms of public reaction, the child who exhibits abnormal behavior may be seriously injured by an erroneous decision not to commit. Appellees overlook a significant source of the public reaction to the mentally ill, *for what is truly "stigmatizing" is the symptomatology of a mental or emotional illness.*

All this would be news to Kenneth Donaldson, who was incarcerated for seventeen years with little treatment or symptomatology—not to mention Senator Thomas Eagleton, forced to withdraw in 1972 as the Democratic vice-presidential candidate because he had been in a mental hospital. Hospitalization is not inevitably therapeutic, and, worse, it can be stigmatizing—even for U.S. senators. It is impossible to determine whether Eagleton's electroshock treatments helped him; what is certain is that they branded him.

Burger's ideas about family relationships were not quite so sanguine, but they, too, had a benevolent image of authority.

[24] 412 F. Supp. 112, 134, 136–37.
[25] Parham v. J. R., 99 S.Ct. 2493, 2506.
[26] There is evidence that psychiatrists tend to err on the side of commitment. See "The Supreme Court, 1978 Term," *Harvard Law Review* 93 (November 1979):95–96. The Georgia Commission found that over half the children committed did not require institutionalization.

Our jurisprudence historically has reflected Western Civilization concepts of the family as a unit with broad parental control over minor children. Our cases have consistently followed that course; our constitutional system long ago rejected any notion that the child is "the mere creature of the State" and, on the contrary, asserted that parents generally "have the right, coupled with the high duty, to recognize and prepare [their children] for additional obligations." Surely, this includes a "high duty" to recognize symptoms of illness and to seek and follow medical advice. The law's concept of the family rests on a presumption that parents possess what a child lacks in maturity, experience, and capacity for judgment required for making life's difficult decisions. More important, historically it has recognized that natural bonds of affection lead parents to act in the best interests of their children.

. . . that some parents "may at times be acting against the best interests of their children" . . . creates a basis for caution, but is hardly a reason to discard wholesale those pages of human experience that teach that parents generally do act in the child's best interests. The statist notion that governmental power should supersede parental authority in *all* cases because *some* parents abuse and neglect children is repugnant to American tradition.[27]

Whether or not parents "generally" act in their child's best interests is a question incapable of resolution. Burger has accurately stated what has been assumed, not shown. One reason that parents are assumed to act this way must be that we can frequently observe them doing things that are obviously good for their children. But when a parent does something that appears harmful, should we assume that the parent is acting in the child's interests? Do we assume so when we see a child being hit hard? Even if the parent insisted that the blows were for the child's own good, should we believe this explanation?

Civil commitment is not so clearly harmful as those actions that, inflicted by anyone but parents or school officials on anyone but children, would constitute assault. But the lower court records suggest that hospitalization can hurt children, that the commitment of children for their own good does not *make* it for their own good. Motive does not determine effect, and even if it did, the typical precommitment conversation is not reassuring about motive. Nor is *Parham*'s companion case from Pennsylvania. There the district court judge reviewed the records of the twelve children involved. Three had exhibited violent or self-destructive behavior, but two were admitted because they were "hyperactive," one because of a history (but no convictions) of "stealing and destroying property," and another for

[27] 99 S.Ct. 2493, 2503–4. Emphasis added. The interior quotes are, respectively, from Pierce v. Society of Sisters, 268 U.S. 510, 535 (1925); and Bartley v. Kremens, 402 F. Supp. 1039, 1047–48 (E.D. Pa. 1975). Emphasis in the original.

"making weird noises, refusing to do work, and talking back to teachers."[28] (These descriptions also call into question the "neutral factfinders'" powers of discrimination.) Generalities to the effect that parents act in their children's best interests should not govern cases in which such evidence exists to the contrary.

Also beside the point is any "statist notion" of governmental supremacy. Burger has cited two cases, *Pierce v. Society of Sisters* and *Meyer v. Nebraska*, which upheld the parents' rights against the state in order to uphold the parents' rights against their children.[29] Here the state does not choose between involvement and noninvolvement; what it is asked to do is to admit a child into one of its institutions. Whatever happens, state power is involved. Burger's rhetoric might be appropriate if a state committed a child without parental approval, but not when the state's choice is between using its power to admit a child and using its power to refuse. Surely the state has no duty to commit a child on a parent's request.

And it is not clear just how strong the justices' commitment to parental authority is. In another article, Robert Burt examines *Parham* in relation to several other cases. He points out that Burger, Powell, and Rehnquist voted against parents who protested their children's suspension from school or the imposition of corporal punishment, while supporting parental consent for abortion and concurring in *Parham* and *Yoder*.[30] Burt infers that for these justices "a specific authoritarian style of parenthood, rather than the status of a parent itself, warrants constitutional deference."[31]

Chief Justice Burger wrote not only of parents, but of children too, in traditional terms. "Most children, even in adolescence, simply are not able to make sound judgments concerning many decisions, including their need for medical care or treatment. Parents can and must make these judgments."[32] The Lindquist case, easy as it is to dismiss as an "exception," casts some doubt on that general principle. My

---

[28] Institutionalized Juveniles v. Secretary of Public Welfare, 459 F. Supp. 30, 36–38 (E.D. Pa. 1978).

[29] 268 U.S. 510; 262 U.S. 390 (1923).

[30] Goss v. Lopez, 419 U.S. 565 (1975); Ingraham v. Wright, 430 U.S. 651 (1977); Planned Parenthood of Central Missouri v. Danforth, 428 U.S. 52 (1976).

[31] "The Constitution of the Family," *Supreme Court Review*, 1979, p. 340.

[32] Parham v. J. R., 99 S.Ct. 2493, 2504–5. What is true of commitment is, apparently, partially true of abortion. H. L. v. Matheson, 101 S.Ct. 1164 (1981), upheld a Utah law requiring parental notification, but not consent, before a minor's abortion. Burger, again writing for the Court, expounds the same generalities about minors' general incompetence and parents' benevolent omniscience as in *Parham*. Since the *Parham* ruling is more to the point, involving actual coercion rather than consultation, I have retained it as my major example of decision making in this area.

discussion of the Polovchak case shows that many of the disabilities of children are not caused by their immature minds but are imposed from outside. As psychologist Richard Farson puts it, "We cannot assess the potentialities of children because we have never organized society to elicit them. We have probably done just the opposite."[33]

And an old problem, one that Jefferson saw, remains. Whether or not people are competent to rule themselves, can anyone else rule them? That was the crucial problem in the next three cases. It is unlikely that any of these children were competent to make the decisions that had to be made. The trouble was that neither were their parents.

It is an established rule that parents have the duty to provide children with necessary medical care.[34] When parents refuse to provide such care—for religious reasons, for example—the state will intervene. But what happens when parents reject medical advice in regard to treatment of children with life-threatening illnesses? That was the issue in the next two cases. Although the rulings differed, the results were the same: the parents prevailed and the children died.

In August 1977, twenty-month-old Chad Green was diagnosed as having acute lymphocytic leukemia. His doctors in Omaha, Nebraska, prescribed conventional chemotherapy, with which, according to their testimony, his chances of survival were slightly better than 50 percent. Chad was in remission within a month. The family moved back to his father's hometown, Scituate, Massachusetts, so Chad could be treated at the Massachusetts General Hospital. The chemotherapy and the remission continued, but in November the Greens stopped giving Chad medication without telling the doctors. They began a program that "included dietary manipulation and prayer" as well as vitamins and Laetrile. Chad soon had a relapse. The parents admitted they had stopped the chemotherapy, but refused to start it again.

> . . . according to the mother's testimony, the decision to terminate chemotherapy was not based on the parents' view that another medically effective form of treatment could be found. Rather, it reflected the parent's deep concern over the child's discomfort in the chemotherapy program, and their pessimism concerning the child's chances for cure. . . . The mother stated, "We would love for Chad to have a full and long life. But it is more important to us that his life be full instead of long, if that [is] the way [it has] to be."[35]

[33] "The Children's Rights Movement," in LaMar T. Empey, ed., *The Future of Childhood and Juvenile Justice* (Charlottesville: University Press of Virginia, 1979), p. 43.

[34] 59 Am. Jur. 2d, Parent and Child, sec. 15 (1962).

[35] Custody of a Minor Child, 379 N.E. 2d 1053, 1064 (S.J.C. Mass., 1978).

The hospital got a temporary restraining order, resumed the treatment, and got Chad back into remission. Even after his relapse, he had about a 50 percent chance of full recovery. When the Supreme Judicial Court upheld the order, the Greens left the state and petitioned for review. The court ordered them to return Chad, but they did not.[36] Chad died in Omaha in 1979.

The court emphasized the fact that there was no medical testimony in favor of the Greens' therapy, and that the hospital's uncontradicted medical testimony stated that chemotherapy would give Chad a good chance for a normal life.[37] (Good, yes; but, after all, a 50 percent chance of survival is also a 50 percent chance of death.) In the first case, the judge suggested that so young a child was unable to understand why he was being subjected to the effects of the chemotherapy, and could not be allowed to make such a decision himself. But Chad never expressed an opinion, and at any rate, the side effects were limited to constipation and stomach cramps, which were relieved with medication.[38]

Although no one who saw the Greens on television can question their sincerity or their ultimate grief, their actions are hard to accept. As the second decision said, "It is with sadness that we review the entire history of this case. . . . The judgment of the parents has been consistently poor, from the child's standpoint, and his well-being seriously threatened as a result." [39]

Joseph Hofbauer's parents won in the New York Court of Appeals, though not before they had left its jurisdiction. The facts were not identical to those of the Green case. Joey had Hodgkin's disease, not leukemia. The evidence in favor of nutritional therapy was better, but so were the boy's chances of survival with chemotherapy. (The fact that Joey was seven rather than one made no difference, ever). The Hofbauers were clear and explicit about their reasons for preferring Laetrile. They wanted to avoid the nauseous effects of traditional drugs, which Joey's father graphically described on national television. The parents appeared more optimistic about the future than the Greens had been. The court saw the matter this way:

> It surely cannot be disputed that every parent has a fundamental right to rear its child. While this right is not absolute inasmuch as the State, as

---

[36] Custody of Minor Child, 393 N.E. 2d 836 (1979).

[37] 379 N.E. 2d 1053, 1056, 1065; 393 N.E. 2d 836, 841–46.

[38] 379 N.E. 2d 1053, 1066, 1064. The parents alleged there were psychological side effects as well, but they were never shown.

[39] 393 N.E. 2d 836, 846.

parens patriae, may intervene to ensure that a child's health or welfare is not being seriously jeopardized by a parent's fault or omission, great deference must be accorded a parent's choice as to the mode of medical treatment to be undertaken. . . .

. . . Ultimately . . . the most significant factor in determining whether a child is being deprived of adequate medical care, and, thus, a neglected child within the meaning of the statute, is whether the parents have provided an acceptable mode of treatment for their child. . . . This inquiry cannot be posed in terms of whether the parent has made a "right" or a "wrong" decision. . . . Rather, in our view, the court's inquiry should be whether the parents, once having sought accredited medical assistance and having been made aware of the seriousness of their child's affliction and the possibility of cure if a certain mode of treatment is undertaken, have provided for their child a treatment which is recommended by their physician and which has not been totally rejected by all responsible medical authority.[40]

Since the Hofbauers had found several doctors who prescribed Laetrile, and they and others had testified that Joey's illness was under control, the court denied the state's petition to have Joey declared a neglected child. But the opinion gives a one-sided presentation. State physicians who had examined Joey testified that his disease was progressing.[41] There was no discussion of his chances of recovery with conventional treatment, which were fairly good. Nor was there a report of any victim of Hodgkin's recovering with Laetrile. It is easy to criticize the decision now, when we know that Joey died, but even without this hindsight, the court seems to be stretching to defend, or at least accept, the parents' judgment. Like Chief Justice Burger in *Parham*, the judges recite traditional generalizations about parents and children. And the word "fundamental" is used to describe a parent's rights, as if they stood on their own, separate from the child himself.

That was also true in a case brought to the Supreme Court a year after *Parham*. The Court denied review, although the case was literally a matter of life and death. The story of Phillip Becker has been at least as widely publicized as those of Chad Green, Joey Hofbauer, and Walter Polovchak; *60 Minutes* has devoted a segment to him. Phillip, now fourteen, has Down's syndrome, and has lived in a California residential facility since his birth. He has a heart defect common in Down's victims. His doctors wanted to perform corrective surgery, but his parents refused permission. The state courts upheld the parents, and the justices' action leaves the ruling in effect. In 1981, however, a state

---

[40] Matter of Hofbauer, 393 N.E. 2d 1009, 1013–14 (1979). This case was decided before the second Green case, not afterward.

[41] Ibid., p. 1012.

superior court judge awarded custody of Phillip to a couple who had done volunteer work at the home where he lived and who want the surgery performed.[42] I shall discuss this case at greater length in Chapter 8, but a comment of the trial judge is appropriate here. He stated, "The principle of parental autonomy is fundamental."[43] But surely it is not. Parental rights, as even Chief Justice Burger declares in *Parham*, are *derivative*, from the presumed incompetence of the juveniles and the parental dedication to the child's interests.[44] To rank them as fundamental is a serious distortion.

There is, of course, an important difference between *Parham* and *Phillip B.* and the Green and Hofbauer cases. Because media coverage was so extensive, there is ample evidence of these parents' good intentions. They acted and felt as Burger assumes most parents act and feel. But however good their intentions, the end results were the same as in the Lindquist case. Their decisions may have forfeited, and probably shortened, their children's lives. Their actions did at least as much damage as those of exasperated or even malevolent parents who commit their children. After Joey's death, his father called him "a pioneer whose purpose was to establish the right of parents to make these decisions for their children and to keep Governor Carey and his faceless bureaucrats out of the family."[45] But was this child a pioneer, or a sacrifice?

This group of cases has some disturbing implications. They show that, as far as parental control is concerned, there is little difference betwen a toddler like Chad Green and a twelve-year-old like Walter Polovchak. A child Walter's age can read, and may form opinions about medicine; after all, cancer and its treatment are becoming staple fare in mass-circulation magazines. If a stricken twelve-year-old preferred chemotherapy to Laetrile, *Hofbauer* could be used as precedent—and in New York State would have to be so used—for ruling against her.

Chad Green's case points up another worrisome aspect of these situations: that the children involved were not necessarily better off with decisions against their parents. The Greens left Massachusetts, and were able to get away with defying a court order even with wide publicity. Parents in future cases will probably have similar success, especially since they are now likely to leave before the decision, as the

[42] In re Phillip B. (and Bothman v. Warren B.), App., 156 Cal. Rptr. 48 (Ct. App., 1st D., 1979); Bothman v. Warren B., cert. den., 100 S.Ct. 1597 (1980); "Parents Bar Surgery and Lose Son's Custody," *New York Times*, August 9, 1981, p. 21.

[43] Quoted on *60 Minutes*, CBS-TV, January 1981.

[44] 99 S.Ct. 2493, 2504–5 (1979).

[45] Walter H. Waggoner, "Boy, 10, in Laetrile Case Dies," *New York Times*, July 18, 1980, IV, p. 5.

Hofbauers did. In fact, there was no one to intervene between Chad and his parents, to provide the care a young child needs, so Chad was as helpless as Walter Polovchak would be without his relatives.

Similarly, a child whose parents fail in their commitment efforts is almost certainly better off than one whose parents succeed, but being in the custody of angry, resentful parents is itself at best an unhealthy situation. Courts may be able to prevent some parental errors and abuses, but they cannot make the children autonomous. The children's freedom is limited by incapacity, whether real or superimposed. Nevertheless, it is possible that some parents would not flee after a court order; that some children would find other adults to take responsibility for them; that some parents would seek help outside an institution. The decisions, which emphasize parents' rights and children's incompetence as if it were impossible to transpose the possessive modifiers, foreclose these possibilities. Where society works hard to keep minors dependent, courts cannot free them; but we might hope that when they get through cracks in the system to gain some independence, courts will not frustrate them.

If the courts' idealized view of parents were correct, it would not matter too much how competent or incompetent children are. Wise, benevolent parental despots could reinforce their children's competence and protect them from their incompetence. If parents were such angels in the form of kings and queens, these decisions would not endanger children's rights to equality. But would such parents be likely to put their unwilling children in institutions? The best evidence against the Burger-Goodman view of the family is that any of these cases arose at all. Even if the fallible parent is an exception, it is, after all, exceptional cases that get to court. Repeated affirmations of parental power ensure that children do not get equal protection.

The Law of the School

Every parent and child in the United States is subject to compulsory education laws. All states, territories, and the District of Columbia require children within a fixed, and wide, age range to attend school, and parents to see that they do. Parents have wide discretion over their children's schooling. They are free to choose among public, private, and parochial schools, and have some control over the curriculum.[46]

[46] Pierce v. Society of Sisters, 268 U.S. 510 (1925); Meyer v. Nebraska, 262 U.S. 390 (1923).

But except when their religious freedom is involved, as in *Yoder*, parents must get their children to school.

Going to school may be the only thing the state makes all of us do. It has affected far more people than the draft did. Like the draft, compulsory schooling has become controversial, though not to the same degree.[47] But despite the strong arguments of some opponents, I am dubious about the wisdom of abandoning it. If six-year-olds were free to make choices about where to spend their time, the case for abolition might be stronger, but I think I have said enough about the ways in which children are disempowered to show that they are not free. If school were not compulsory, parents could find all sorts of reasons, bad, selfish, ignorant, or misguided, for keeping their children out. If school were only prison or conscription, we might turn a blind eye to such parents, but school is more than coercion. It teaches skills, and if these skills do not quite liberate, they do empower. There probably should be some alternatives to traditional schooling, but some compulsory education seems necessary in a society that does not ensure that we learn these skills on our own. Of course, to the extent that schools *fail* to teach, the case for compulsory attendance is weakened. Where there is no education, "compulsory school attendance functions as a bill of attainder against a particular age group."[48] Even when schools do their job, it seems logical that the fact of compulsion demands more lenience, not more stringency, from the officials who do the compelling.

If schools are not "bad places for kids," they are places where bad things can happen to them.[49] They often do not learn the skills they are there to learn, while they pick up misleading information, misinformation, and muddled thinking habits.[50] Students may learn "lessons in Practical Slavery," automatic obedience, racism, and sexism. They may be given drugs to cure their "hyperactivity"; whatever the overall merit of this treatment, it is misused and overused.[51] As *Tinker*

---

[47] See, e.g., Richard Farson, *Birthrights* (New York: Macmillan, 1974), chap. 7; Edgar Z. Friedenberg, *The Dignity of Youth and Other Atavisms* (Boston: Beacon Press, 1965); John Holt, *The Underachieving School* (New York: Pittman, 1969); Ivan Illich, *Deschooling Society* (New York: Harper & Row, 1971).

[48] Friedenberg, *Dignity of Youth*, p. 90.

[49] Holt, *Underachieving School*, pp. 15–34.

[50] See, e.g., Neil Postman, *Teaching as a Conserving Activity* (New York: Delacorte, 1979); Neil Postman and Charles Weingartner, *Teaching as a Subversive Activity* (New York: Delta Books: 1969); Charles E. Silberman, *Crisis in the Classroom* (New York: E. Silberman, *Crisis in the Classroom* (New York: Vintage Books, 1970).

[51] Holt, *Underachieving School*, p. 19. See, e.g., Friedenberg, *Dignity of Youth; Coming of Age in America* (New York: Random House, 1965); or *The Vanishing Adolescent* (Boston: Beacon Press, 1959); James Herndon, *The Way It Spozed to Be* (New York:

173

showed, schools have deprived children of so unobtrusive a mode of expression as wearing an armband. Although the Supreme Court invalidated this action, and other decisions have protected such activities as distributing "underground" publications and wearing "freedom buttons," the school may respond to "commotion and confusion" by banning the buttons. Black students may be subjected to such public insult as hearing "Dixie" played at a pep rally. Students may be punished in a variety of ways: sent outside the classroom, ridiculed, kept after school, suspended, and beaten.[52] School does provide a counterforce to parental authority, but it also subjects the child to yet another power.

Even without the footnotes, the reader has probably recognized several court decisions in the above list. I have already mentioned one of them; it is hard to discuss parental authority without getting into schools, just as it is hard to discuss the rights of children, handicapped people, and homosexuals without overlapping. Here, at least, everything is related to everything else.

Tinker has been recognized as a landmark case in students' rights. It does extend the protection of the First Amendment to the classroom, and that is important. The majority opinion declared: "It can hardly be argued that either students or teachers shed their constitutional rights to freedom of speech or expression at the schoolhouse gate." The Court had no difficulty in concluding that wearing an armband was a "symbolic act" within the free-speech clause. But there was equal emphasis on the school authorities' power not just to preserve safety but to keep to business as usual. The appropriate test for deciding whether an act was protected by the First Amendment was whether "the students' activities would materially and substantially disrupt the work and discipline of the school." Here there was no disruption, only "worry."[53]

So far, so good. But what is so bad about disruption? Recall the words of Justice Douglas in *Terminiello* v. *Chicago*: "A function of free speech under our system of government is to invite dispute. It may

Simon & Schuster, 1968); Herbert Kohl, *36 Children* (New York: New American Library, 1967); Jonathan Kozol, *Death at an Early Age* (Boston: Houghton Mifflin, 1967); Barbara Grizzutti Harison, *Unlearning the Lie: Sexism in School* (New York: Liveright, 1973); Letty Cottin Pogrebin, *Growing up Free* (New York: McGraw-Hill, 1980), chap. 23; Judith Stacey et al., eds., *And Jill Came Tumbling After: Sexism in American Education* (New York: Dell, 1974); Diane Divoky and Peter Schrag, *The Myth of the Hyperactive Child* (New York: Pantheon, 1975).

[52] Vail v. Board of Education, 354 F. Supp. 592 (D.N.H. 1973); Burnside v. Byars, 363 F. 2d 744 (5th Circ. 1966); Blackwell v. Issaquena County Board of Education, 363 F. 2d 749 (5th Circ. 1966); Tate v. Board of Education, 453 F. 2d 975 (8th Circ. 1972); Goss v. Lopez, 419 U.S. 565 (1975); Ingraham v. Wright, 430 U.S. 651 (1977).

[53] 393 U.S. 503, 506, 513, 510 (1969).

indeed best serve its high purposes when it induces a condition of unrest, creates dissatisfaction with conditions as they are, or even stirs people to anger." [54] *Tinker* implies that the school's interest in discipline overrides these interests, but may not exactly the opposite be true? Is it not especially important to have such expression in the schools, where children have to be, and where they are supposed to learn to be citizens? [55]

Freedom of speech is not all that children lose in school. An old joke in the public law field describes the difference between procedural and substantive due process as that between how you get screwed and whether you get screwed. The same distinction appears in the public law of the school. The First Amendment cases belong in the "whether" category, but there are plenty of "how" cases, too. School discipline has been a recurring issue. In 1975, in *Goss v. Lopez*, the Supreme Court upheld an Ohio ruling that the due-process clause of the Fourteenth Amendment extended to suspensions and expulsions. [56]

This case was the result of a class action challenging suspension in two senior high schools and one junior high in Columbus during a period of student unrest centering on Black History Week. This unrest had been manifested in several demonstrations, during which some property was destroyed and a police officer was attacked. Nine students had been suspended, without hearings, for up to ten days. Two students had testified that they were given no opportunity to tell their side of the story; a third said that she could not get into class at all because of the disruption.

State law required the school to notify the students' parents within twenty-four hours of any suspension or expulsion, and to give parents the reason for such action. The principal at one high school sent letters to the parents, scheduling a conference among parents, student, and officials at a date and time set by the principal. The parents, however, could not get into the school at the scheduled time because the demonstrations were still going on. A student at the other high school was suspended after she tried to get excused from classes, telling the principal that her mother had told her to come home if there were any disturbances. The letter to her parents said that she "showed a lack of respect for the principal." [57]

[54] 337 U.S. 1, 4 (1949).
[55] This is especially true in Blackwell v. Issaquena County Board of Education (upholding a school's right to ban "freedom buttons") and Tate v. Board of Education (denying the right of black students not to be publicly insulted by the playing of "Dixie" at a school function).
[56] 419 U.S. 565; Lopez v. Williams, 373 F. Supp. 1279 (S.D. Ohio 1973).
[57] 373 F. Supp. 1284–88; 419 U.S. 565, 568–71.

This narrative conveys some of the flavor of school life: the authoritarianism, the arbitrary orders, and the omnipresent double bind. But for the courts, that was not the point. What violated the due-process clause was the denial of notice and hearing. "We hold only that, in being given an opportunity to explain his version of the facts at this discussion, the student first be told what he is accused of doing and what the basis of the accusation is."[58] The hearing could be informal and immediate. If some physical danger prevented such action, notice and rudimentary hearing must follow as soon as possible. Counsel was not required, nor was the right to call or confront witnesses, but the Supreme Court left open the question of whether these rights should be required for longer suspensions or expulsions.

Lopez was a 5-to-4 decision. For the majority, Justice White emphasized the harmful effects of suspensions. Not only were ten days of classes lost, but the charges could damage the student's relationships with faculty and other students, and later, employment opportunities. "It is apparent," White wrote, "that the claimed right of the state to determine unilaterally and without process whether that misconduct has occurred immediately collides with the requirements of the Constitution."[59]

Lopez is an important protection for students, but it leaves untouched the substantive component of school discipline. "Lack of respect," something for which no adult could be punished by the state, may still be an offense. Furthermore, the closeness of the vote suggests a need to look at minority opinions—at least, it does in retrospect—and this look is not encouraging. Justice Powell wrote a dissent that was endorsed by Burger, Blackmun, and Rehnquist. Powell's insistence that ten days' absence from school—"less than 5% of the school year"—is not an injury to education can be dismissed as both incorrect and unresponsive to much of White's opinion. More ominous is the impression given that four members of the Court, none of whom was there when *Tinker* was decided, are unwilling to place any limits on the power of school officials: "In prior decisions, this Court has explicitly recognized that school authorities must have broad discretionary authority in the daily operation of public schools. This includes wide latitude with respect to maintaining discipline and good order."[60]

It was Powell who wrote for the Court in *Ingraham* v. *Wright*.[61]

[58] 419 U.S. 565, 580–82.
[59] Ibid., p. 575.
[60] Ibid., pp. 589–90.
[61] 430 U.S. 651 (1977).

Here the Court ruled on corporal punishment in the schools. This practice had been the subject of several federal district court decisions, all of which had sustained it, although one ruling had provided for an exception when parents had notified school authorities in advance that they did not want their children hit.[62] Of course, the fact that parents brought all of these actions indicates that none of them wanted corporal punishment imposed on their children.

Ingraham came to the Court from Dade County, Florida. Its board of education authorized corporal punishment under the following conditions: the teacher must first consult the principal; another adult must be present; no blows were allowed above the waist or below the knees, and none that would produce physical injury [*sic*]. There was no requirement for hearing or parental notice. As late as 1970, the practice was fairly common. The student was usually paddled "one to five 'licks' or 'blows'" on the buttocks with a flat wooden instrument. The rules about notifying the principal and having another adult present were often violated.[63]

The rules about the beating itself were also violated, at least in the two instant cases. When James Ingraham and several other students failed to leave the school auditorium quickly enough to suit their teacher, they were paddled in the principal's office. James got at least twenty blows, and was out of school for several days. Roosevelt Andrews was hit on the arm; he could not use that arm for a week.[64] Both children's parents brought suit.

Neither the Court of Appeals nor the Supreme Court found any constitutional violation. Corporal punishment was not "cruel and unusual" under the Eighth Amendment, nor did the due-process clause require notice and hearing. The Court of Appeals had distinguished this case from *Lopez*: "We believe that there is an important distinction . . . between a suspension, which involves an exclusion from the educational process itself, and a paddling, which involves no deprivation of a property interest or a claim to education and is certainly a much less serious event in the life of a child than is a suspension or an expulsion."[65]

Justice Powell, now writing for the majority, did not stress *Lopez* at all. His argument echoes some long-obsolescent due-process deci-

---

[62]Glaser v. Marietta, 351 F. Supp. 555 (W.D. Pa. 1972). The other cases are Ware v. Estes, 328 F. Supp. 657 (N.D. Tex. 1971); Sims v. Board of Education, 329 F. Supp. 678 (D.N.M. 1971); Gonyaw v. Gray, 361 F. Supp. 366 (D. Vt. 1973); Baker v. Owen, 395 F. Supp. 294 (M.D.N.C. 1975); affirmed without opinion, 423 U.S. 907.

[63]Ingraham v. Wright, 498 F. 2d 248, 254–56 (5th Circ. 1974).

[64]430 U.S. 651, 657.

[65]Ingraham v. Wright, 525 F. 2d 909, 918–19 (5th Circ. 1976).

sions. Powell emphasized the sorts of consideration that had been prominent in such cases as *Twining* v. *New Jersey* and *Wolf* v. *Colorado*.[66] Corporal punishment was sanctioned by common law, has persisted in schools throughout American history, and is still recommended by some authorities.[67] His conclusion that it is not cruel and unusual rests chiefly on this evidence.

A decision that the Dade County regulations were constitutional on their face would not necessarily have settled the controversy. The Court could still have ruled that the regulations had been *applied* (no pun intended) in violation of constitutional rights. But the majority would not even entertain this possibility. Parts of the opinion read like *Irvine* v. *California*.[68] Any abuses, it suggested, might have remedies other than constitutional adjudication: civil suit, perhaps, or state-imposed criminal penalties.[69] Time had proved that notion disastrously wrong with respect to police abuses. But it appears that learning a lesson once is not enough.

How can we explain this obtuseness? Has the Court forgotten how wrong those old decisions proved to be? The problem may be that the Court does not see any similarity between corporal and criminal punishment. The schoolchild, we are told, has "little need" for the protection of the Eighth Amendment.[70] Unlike prison, school is an open institution (except that children have to go there); the child is not physically restrained (except by truancy laws and the need to ask permission to move within or out of the classroom); and at the end of the day the student, unlike the prisoner, returns home.

We are verging here on the fantastic. If the child has little need for protection in school, how did it happen that these two boys were so badly injured there? Their injuries show the need for protection. As Justice White wrote in dissent, ". . . the record reveals beatings so severe that if they were inflicted on a hardened criminal for the commission of a serious crime, they might not pass constitutional muster."[71]

Questions of application aside, the constitutional approval of cor-

[66] 211 U.S. 78 (1908); 338 U.S. 25 (1949).
[67] 430 U.S. 651, 660–63. This mode of argument is not, however, unique to Ingraham; see Gregg v. Georgia, 428 U.S. 153 (1976).
[68] 347 U.S. 128 (1954).
[69] 430 U.S. 651, 674–83.
[70] Ibid., p. 670.
[71] Ibid., pp. 684–85. The Eighth Circuit, with Harry Blackmun writing the opinion, had held in 1968 that beating adult prisoners with a strap was cruel and unusual punishment. It did not rule that all prison corporal punishment was unconstitutional, but the language came very close to doing so (Jackson v. Bishop, 404 F. 2d 571).

poral punishment is unacceptable. Arguments in favor of it apply to parents, not to schools. In these cases, the school officials were upheld over parental objections. Several factors distinguish parental corporal punishment from school corporal punishment. First, whatever the merits of parents' imposing it, no state could effectively legislate against it. Second, doctrines of family privacy could put parental discipline beyond state control. The school, however, is an agent of the state, and is controlled by it. Indeed, a third distinguishing factor is the fact that school corporal punishment is public, no matter where it is performed, or whether other children see it. The very nature and purpose of punishment demands that it become known if it is to have the desired deterrent effect. Being flogged is both painful and humiliating, and it is an intrusion into personal body space, which violates fundamental notions of privacy. For all these reasons, it should be considered cruel and unusual.

But *Ingraham* did not require the Court to say anything of the sort. All it was asked to do was to invalidate severe beatings. And it refused to go even that far, because it could not believe the evidence before it that children need constitutional safeguards; it could not perceive that punishment is punishment, whether for crime or for disobedience; and, above all, it could not quite see children as fully possessing constitutional rights. Adults may not be subjected to arbitrary discipline, but children may; adults may not be beaten, but children may; and children may be abused in a place where they are forced to go. The states have dealt unequally with the young persons under their jurisdiction.

Juvenile Courts and Juvenile Justice

The common law divided infancy into three seven-year periods for the purpose of determining criminal responsibility. Children under seven were never held responsible for criminal acts; from seven to fourteen, there was a rebuttable presumption of irresponsibility; between fourteen and twenty-one, a rebuttable presumption of responsibility. Now the age of full criminal responsibility is fixed by statute. Suspects below this fixed age are labeled "juveniles" and dealt with in juvenile courts, although some states allow courts to prosecute juveniles as adults in certain circumstances.[72] Juvenile courts also deal with abandoned or neglected children and with what are known variously as PINS, JINS, and CHINS (persons, juveniles, or children in need of super-

---

[72] But see Breed v. Jones, 421 U.S. 519 (1975).

vision). Since 1967, the Supreme Court has decided four cases involving juvenile delinquency proceedings. It has ruled that the Constitution grants to juveniles some, but not all, of the protections guaranteed to adults.

That statement implies that before 1967 those courts did not grant these rights. That implication is correct. When the juvenile court movement began early in this century, its advocates were trying to ensure that young people would be helped rather than punished. The goal was "a process designed not as punishment but as salvation."[73] But, as usual, motive did not dictate effect. How far the reality deteriorated from the ideal is shown by the first case, *Re Gault*. This case was not fifteen-year-old Gerald Gault's first brush with the law. He was already under six months' probation for having been in the company of a boy who had stolen a wallet. Gerald's troubles increased when a neighbor accused him of making obscene telephone calls to her. The maximum adult penalty for this offense was a $50 fine and two months' imprisonment, but, after a hearing, the judge committed Gerald to Arizona's Industrial School for six years, until his majority.

The disparity in sentences was bad enough, but it was not the basis for the Supreme Court's reversal. What bothered the Court was that Arizona's juvenile code established proceedings "in which the following basic rights are denied: 1) notice of the charges; 2) right to counsel; 3) right to confrontation and cross-examination; 4) privilege against self-incrimination; 5) right to a transcript of the proceedings; and 6) right to appellate review." For the Court, Justice Abe Fortas acknowledged that traditionally a child had no procedural rights and that the original purposes of the juvenile court system had been benign. Nevertheless, his opinion insisted that, by whatever name, what Gerald Gault had endured was a trial and a punishment. "However euphemistic the title, . . . an 'industrial school' for juveniles is an institution of confinement in which the child is incarcerated for a greater or lesser time." The Court ruled that all listed rights must be granted juveniles. Only Justice Stewart dissented from the entire ruling. Eight justices agreed that notice and hearing must be provided; seven voted for all Sixth Amendment rights; and six on all Fifth Amendment rights.

The ruling did not affect sentencing, standard of proof, or substantive due-process issues. Long sentences for trivial offenses, or even for such nonoffenses as being in bad company, are still possible. And Stewart's dissent showed that the therapeutic model was still alive and

[73] W. v. Family Court, 247 N.E. 2d 253 (N.Y. Ct.App., 1969). See also Re Gault, 387 U.S. 1 (1967).

well: ". . . a juvenile proceeding's whole purpose and mission is the very opposite of the mission and purpose of a prosecution in a criminal court. The object of the one is correction of a condition. The object of the other is conviction and punishment for a criminal act." [74]

In re Winship came to the Supreme Court with a full exposition of this model in the court below. The New York Court of Appeals had ruled that the required standard of proof in juvenile court trials was "preponderance of evidence" rather than "beyond a reasonable doubt." The judge declared:

> The successful juvenile court is concerned primarily with the totality of factors which cause a child to meet difficulty in his life, and only incidentally with the event which brings the child to the court, which may itself play only a small part in that problem.
> . . . A child's best interest is not necessarily, or even probably, promoted if he wins in the particular inquiry which may bring him to the juvenile court.
> . . . If the emphasis is on constitutional rights, something of the essential freedom of method and choice which the sound juvenile court judge ought to have is lost; if range be given to that freedom, rights which the law gives to criminal offenders will not be respected. But the danger is that we may lose the child and his potential for good while giving him his constitutional rights. [75]

In other words, what matters is not whether the child is guilty or innocent, but whether he or she can be "helped." To speak of losing children suggests that we can save them; unfortunately, there is evidence against this proposition. [76] Again, the child has few rights. Not only can children be held to account by parent and school, but they are subjected to "help" and "salvation" by the state. The Supreme Court reversed, but Stewart again dissented. This time Burger joined him in arguing that what the juvenile court system needed was less, rather than more, formality. [77]

A year later, in 1971, *McKeiver* v. *Pennsylvania* held that juvenile court proceedings did not require a jury trial. The Court said that such trials would effectively transform the juvenile court system and "provide an attrition of the juvenile court's assumed ability to function in a unique manner." The Court was unwilling to inflict this transformation on the states. "Perhaps the ultimate disillusionment [i.e., the

[74] 387 U.S. 1, 10, 27, 78–79.
[75] W. v. Family Court, 247 N.E. 2d 253–55, 257.
[76] See, e.g., Edwin M. Schur, *Radical Non-Intervention: Rethinking the Delinquency Problem* (Englewood Cliffs, N.J.: Prentice-Hall, 1973).
[77] 397 U.S. 358, 376.

end of the system] will come some day, but at the moment we are disinclined to give impetus to it." Even Justice Brennan concurred, as long as the proceedings were open to the public. But the dissenters, Black, Douglas, and Marshall, pointed out that every juvenile involved could have been incarcerated for at least five years, and even the plurality opinion admitted that the evidence was weak. "Uniqueness" and "flexibility" sound ominous.[78]

In *Breed* v. *Jones*, a unanimous Court held that for a juvenile to be tried as an adult *after* a juvenile court hearing constituted double jeopardy.[79] There have not been enough cases, or the right kind of cases, to reveal any marked discontinuities between the Warren and Burger Courts. Certainly the juvenile court system still lives, though its flexibilities have been limited in conformity with some basic requirements of due process. But not all requirements: deference to the therapeutic model and to federalism has restrained the Court, and, as so often happens, such deference has allowed abuses to continue. That may not be the Court's problem, but it is the child's.

This discussion cannot end here. These cases involved children who were charged with offenses that, committed by adults, would constitute crimes, but most juvenile court proceedings involve conduct for which adults cannot be punished by law.[80] A New York law is typical of those in many states. It defines a "person in need of supervision" as "a child who is an habitual truant or is incorrigible, ungovernable, or habitually disobedient and beyond the lawful control of his parent, guardian, or legal custodian."[81] For this sort of behavior, a juvenile may be taken into custody, put on probation, or otherwise dealt with by court order.

At least three constitutional problems arise here. First, these are behaviors that could not be made criminal without serious violations of due process. Second, the offenses, as defined, are vague and overbroad. A third problem is one of multiple jeopardy: the child may be subject to punishment by family, state, and possibly school for the same act. Such laws mean that a child is not only fully accountable to her parents, and thirty hours a week to the school, but that the state will step in on request and hold her accountable as well.

---

[78] 403 U.S. 528, 547, 555 (Blackmun), 557–79 (Douglas), 536 (Blackmun) (1971); In re Terry (companion case), 265 A2d 350, 355 (Pa. Sup.Ct. 1970). A decision that juveniles were entitled to jury trials would raise one serious problem: since minors do not serve on juries, how could juveniles get juries of their peers? This factor alone might lead to a rethinking of that particular issue.

[79] 421 U.S. 519 (1975).

[80] See Howard James, *Children in Trouble* (New York: David McKay, 1970).

[81] New York Family Court Act, sec. 732.

Fortas' remark in *Gault* that a child has no rights is an exaggeration, but only a small one. The child has a limited right to freedom of expression—less than an adult's—and a right to some, but not all, procedural guarantees in school and court. But though the child does have a right to "symbolic speech" as long as no one is disturbed by it, she does not have the right to be informed in clear and explicit terms what conduct will get her in trouble. Though the child has a right to a hearing before suspension, she has no procedural rights before being beaten. Though she has the right to other safeguards before being adjudged delinquent in juvenile court, she has none before being committed to an institution by her parents. It sounds very much as though children are saddled with disabilities that make them a "discrete and insular minority."

Legal Agism, or Aged Legalism

The subject of this chapter has not been children's rights alone; it has been age discrimination in general. What, finally, do the old and the young have in common? The cases I have surveyed have generally borne out two of the generalizations we started with: that both older and younger people are presumed to be less competent than that segment of the population between the ages of eighteen and fifty, sixty-five, or seventy; and that often both groups' interests are, explicitly or implicitly, ranked below those of others. The legal status of both groups reflects these two factors. There are, however, two additional factors that affect the treatment of minors. First, others are presumed to act in their best interests. Older citizens are presumed, absent an official determination to the contrary, to act in their own interests. Since many of the disabilities of the young stem from their presumed incompetence, it is no wonder that this chapter has devoted so much more space to children. Junior citizens are restricted in many ways that senior citizens are not.

The second peculiarity of the situation of children is shown by the fact that, while compulsory retirement cases were handled with the standard equal-protection tests, the children's cases were not. Policies affecting the young are not usually thought to raise issues of equality at all. This is true even though, as Chapter 4 suggested, there is no pressing historical argument against their being so considered. Despite such rhetoric as "the condition of being a boy does not justify a kangaroo court" and "neither students nor teachers shed their constitutional rights to freedom of expression at the schoolhouse gate,"[82] the cases do not suggest—indeed, they often reject—any idea that children enjoy any constitutional rights to the same extent that adults do. The cases are not brought as equal-protection cases, and as a result they are not argued with the special terminology of equal protection. Suspect classification does not rear its head, or its two heads, nor do questions of fundamental rights get quite the same weight as they do in cases involving adults. Rights do matter, of course; the two decisions from which I just quoted, *Gault* and *Tinker*, are premised on them. But nowhere are these rights *equal*, so the Court does not compare *Tinker* with *Terminiello*, *Parham* with *Donaldson*, or *Gault* and *McKeiver* with the whole line of due-process cases involving criminal defendants.

What would happen if standard equal-protection doctrine were employed in cases involving children? Certainly, children fall outside the *Frontiero* suspect-classification rule. Youth, like age, does "frequently bear . . . relation to ability to perform or contribute to society." The *Rodriguez* formulation, however, requires us to ask whether children are "saddled with such disabilities, or subjected to such a history of purposeful unequal treatment, . . . as to command extraordinary protection."[83] However much one wants to add, "But . . . ," the conclusion is inescapable: children are so saddled, and so subjected. The question then has to be whether they do in fact get "extraordinary protection" from the social agencies that affect them, the family, the school, and the state. But those are the same agencies that impose the disabilities, so it is rather unlikely. We know by now that protection can become a protection racket.

How can my general theory of constitutional equality be applied to age discrimination? All the laws I have been discussing have, at least in part, been premised on presumptions about competence. When older or younger citizens are denied rights or privileges granted others, or burdened with duties that others escape, the discrimination is usually defended by statements that their abilities are limited or diminished. Chapters 1 through 4, however, argued that constitutional guarantees of equality depend not on the belief that people are equally capable, but on notions of equal humanity and entitlement, most specifically, entitlement to rights. There is no reason to exclude the old or the young from this entitlement.

Chapter 6 suggested a reformulation of this thesis in terms of con-

---

[82] Re Gault, 387 U.S. 1, 28 (1967); Tinker v. Des Moines Community School District, 393 U.S. 503, 506 (1969).
[83] 411 U.S. 677, 686 (1973); 411 U.S. 1, 28 (1973).

stitutional doctrine, adapted from Stone's footnote in *Carolene Products*, Marshall's dissent in *Rodriguez*, and Brennan's opinion in *Bakke*. Here I deal with these opinions in what I think is ascending order of clarity and relevance of import. Brennan's opinion adds to a general understanding of classifications, but it is hard to apply here. He insisted that stigmatizing classifications, those that are premised on ideas of inferiority or reinforce prejudice or separation, are invalid. The question then becomes whether the age-based classifications discussed here do either of these things. The answer has to be that some of them do, but I am not sure how far that gets us.

Some of the decisions—*Bradley*, *Parham*, and *Ingraham* come to mind—do seem to be premised on notions of inferiority, of the absence of a right to equal respect and concern. The real question here, however, is not whether we can find court decisions thus premised, but whether the policies are in themselves grounded in such beliefs. In *Bradley*, the concern for younger Foreign Service officers, suspicious because it excludes those over sixty from equal entitlement, was only one of the justifications for the retirement rule, and one would have to consider the relative weight of it and the other reasons to the rulemakers, not the Court. Because this intent is not always discoverable, it may be impossible to determine whether a given policy stigmatizes in Brennan's sense.

Marshall's contribution to the reformulated doctrine was to emphasize the nature of the classifications involved, the relative importance of the individual claims, and the countervailing force of the state interest. These classifications may or may not stigmatize, but certainly they are troublesome for other reasons. If not immutable, they are involuntary, and they do involve disempowered groups, actually or potentially. The interests involved are all of great importance: a job, in *Murgia* and *Bradley*; mobility, in *Parham*; immunity from arbitrary and even brutal punishment, in *Lopez* and *Ingraham*; self-determination, for Walter Polovchak; and, for Chad Green, Joseph Hofbauer, and Phillip Becker, life itself. *Tinker*, *Yoder*, and the juvenile court cases all centered around claims that even under traditional rules are classified as fundamental rights; so, of course, would most of the cases mentioned if they involved anyone but children.

These considerations weigh heavily in favor of the claimants. But what about Marshall's third test, the state's interests? How should they be weighted? Since the individual claims involved are of crucial importance, and the basis for discrimination is beyond individual control, and some disempowering and branding seems to be involved, the countervailing claims should be more than merely reasonable. They would at least have to satisfy the *Craig* test of substantial relation to an important objective. In *Bradley* that standard is not met, but in *Murgia* it may be—so what conclusions should follow?

In many of the children's cases, there is an intervening claim: the interests of the parents, which in *Hofbauer*, for example, tend to take over in the judges' minds. Newspaper discussions of the Polovchak case show this tendency, too; the conflict becomes state versus parent, not state versus child. Parents do have important rights and duties, and certainly they must have more control over the child than the school or the state does. *Most* of the time they must be presumed to act in the child's interests. But why does this presumption hold in *Parham* and not in *Ingraham*? It is not applied consistently even now, and in such situations as the Polovchak, Hofbauer, and Green cases there is simply too much at stake for it to hold at all. In such cases the children's interests must be considered separately from those of the parents, with the appointment of a separate special counsel for the child, if necessary.[84]

Parham differs from *Hofbauer* in this respect only because the presumed relationship between parental and child interests is not that the parental interest is superior or "fundamental" but that the two are identical. This assumption is maintained in *Parham* even in the face of overwhelming evidence to the contrary. The traditional view of the family that is so loved by Burger and Powell seems to crowd out consideration of the facts.

The school cases usually have the child and the parents united against the state, in the persons of school authorities. Consideration of school interests here have tended to be rather mechanical: uncritical acceptance of "the work and discipline of the school" and a willingness to override the school only when any interference was absent or minimal.[85] Once the strength of the child's claim is recognized, it is hard to uphold the school on the basis of such analysis.

What about the juvenile courts? The decisions, whatever their results, reflect a notion that the purpose of these courts is to help children in trouble, not to punish them. The state's interest here is surely substantial, and not obviously antithetical to the child's. Fair enough, but unfortunately that idea embodies three assumptions: that the state knows when help is needed; that it knows how to help; and that it does help. The cases call all three of these assumptions into question. It was not shown that Gerald Gault needed any rehabilitation; what is evident is that what he got was punishment.

[84] See Farson, "Children's Rights," p. 55.
[85] Tinker v. Des Moines Community School District, 393 U.S. 503, 510.

But does juvenile court treat children more leniently than the criminal courts treat adult offenders? It is not at all clear that it usually does. Juvenile courts deal with some minors who would not be in trouble at all if they were adults, and they often punish children far more severely than adults could be punished for the same behavior. And, more and more, states are providing that children accused of serious crimes will be tried as adults; in other words, they are foreclosing the possibility of greater leniency, which means that the juvenile courts will be used only when they ensure greater stringency. Obviously, it is up to the states whether they maintain separate court systems at all; it would be difficult to mount an argument that juvenile courts are inevitably violative of constitutional rights. Perhaps children would be better off if they were treated as adults; after all, questions of competence can be considered there. We need more knowledge about whether the juvenile court system ever can be truly benign or helpful. Surely there is no good reason for maintaining it *only* to the extent to which it is repressive and punitive.

The children's cases that have actually been decided become easy ones when they are judged by the Stone-Marshall equal-protection rule, for the state interest tends to collapse on analysis. But it may not collapse in all cases involving children, and it did not do so in *Murgia*. I have not argued, nor do I wish to, that *all* legal distinctions based on age are invalid. As I suggested, compulsory schooling seems to me legitimate, though barely. Likewise, the annual physical examinations required of Massachusetts uniformed state police after age forty, or more frequent licensing tests for older drivers, seem to be a sensible way of enhancing public safety without overburdening older citizens. (A law denying a drivers' license to anyone over a certain age would be another matter.) But would the reformulated rule of interpretation allow us to make these distinctions?

For the maximum-age cases, it does work. The interests are important ones, but in each situation they may be fulfilled through a policy that does not infringe on a fundamental interest. Being required to take a test or a physical exam is not nearly so great a deprivation as being forced to stop working or driving. Furthermore, such a policy is enabling, allowing those who do not fit the prevailing stereotypes about competence to maintain their freedom.

But compulsory schooling presents a harder problem. It deprives children of a considerable amount of freedom. It partakes less of education and more of custody than can be desirable, as these cases show. Finally, it applies to all children, even if they have the skills taught in school or can learn them elsewhere. On the other hand, to the extent that schooling achieves its purposes—and only to that extent—it fulfills a vital state interest in having an educated citizenry, and it is valuable for the children themselves. The gap between ideals and reality is so wide, however, that acceptance of compulsory schooling must be reluctant and guarded. There should be room for exceptions; perhaps children might be emancipated from education in the same way that they can now be emancipated from parental control. Some age-based distinctions are acceptable, but perhaps none that has so great an impact should be accepted automatically or universally. The problem here is that even the reformulated doctrine cannot deal adequately with this kind of issue. But the principles behind it can help to guide our thinking.

The question of how to discriminate between acceptable and unacceptable restrictions on children is perplexing. Any argument for "children's rights," even so limited an argument as I have made, is easy to trivialize. As one author asks, what happens if "my son, who gets mad at going to bed at 10:30, goes to court and asks for a later bedtime?"[86] The leading cases do not help us to make these discriminations. But that, I suggest, is precisely the point. The cases are not about bedtimes; they are not even about a boy's right to select a prom date, because the disabilities of minors are so great that they inhibit litigation. Only the most drastic cases get to court at all. And it is very hard to extend the bedtime principle to protect the autonomy of the Beckers, Polovchaks, and Hofbauers.

But if courts begin to uphold children's claims, will such rulings encourage bedtime litigation? Do not families and schools—and courts, too—need to maintain a considerable degree of control over children, and would such rulings not make it harder for them to do so? I am not sure that they would, because they only scratch the surface of children's disabilities. But if they did, I am not sure that would be a bad idea. It is not clear to me why disrespect for a principal, dawdling, or being with a child who steals a wallet should be punishable offenses. The larger point is that it is not clear why the first, most powerful lessons that children—who, after all, will grow up—must learn are obedience and respect for authority. Those are the lessons being taught in these situations. Will those lessons really fit children for life as autonomous adults? Or may they not produce those citizens whom Mark Twain described as having the three precious gifts of "freedom of speech, freedom of religion, and the prudence never to exercise either of them"?

[86] LaMar T. Empey, "Dilemmas in the Search for Utopia," in Empey, ed., *Future of Childhood*, p. 387.

I began this chapter by noting the general public acceptance that age-based discriminations have received. The ensuing discussion has shown that case law has mirrored this acceptance. But the cases have also revealed the prevalence of assumptions that claims to equality must rest on capacity and competence; again and again, laws are defended by generalizations about lack of competence. And while these generalizations may be more accurate than some that have been made about other groups, their application to individuals is limited. They correspond better to the antitheory of equality than to the theory. And they are not compatible with a right to equal respect and concern, or with a commitment to individual rights.

[8]

The Rights of the Disabled

As the 1950s saw the rise of the black civil rights movement and the 1960s the beginnings of the modern feminist movement, the 1970s brought protest movements from the handicapped and homosexuals.[1] So far, the disability rights movement has been the more successful of the two. Within its first decade, it secured passage of several federal spending laws and some fairly strong regulations for their implementation. These laws and regulations were partly the indirect result of federal court victories, but so far the success has been at least as much legislative as judicial. Constitutional arguments have been superseded by statutory ones, and judicial construction of these statutes is still in its early stages. But the Supreme Court cases that have dealt with the merits of this kind of issue could be described without exaggeration as disasters. If similar statutory cases are decided against the plaintiffs, the disabled may return to constitutional litigation.

If they do, they are not likely to get much help from the Supreme Court of the 1980s. But that prediction does not close the issue. It is possible to construct arguments in favor of the disabled which later judges may accept. My reformulation of existing doctrine emphasized an entitlement to treatment as an equal and a linkage between equality and individual rights. Just as this reformulation provided a basis for

[1] I use the words "disabled" and "handicapped" interchangeably. My definition comes from the HEW regulations implementing Section 504 of the Rehabilitation Act of 1973: a "handicapped person" is a person who "(a) has a physical or mental impairment that substantially limits one or more major life activities; or (b) who has a record of such impairment; or (c) is regarded as having such an impairment" (45 C.F.R. 85.31 [1977]).

questioning the law of age discrimination, so, I think, it can allow us to deal in new, creative ways with the rights of the handicapped. Reinterpreting the Fourteenth Amendment can also produce a foundation for the federal laws that the Court has weakened. These laws should be seen as exercises of Congress' enforcement powers under Section 5.

To include the disabled among the subjects of this book implies that it is legitimate to consider them as a disadvantaged group, in the way that blacks or women are. An important study, written for the Carnegie Council on Children, argues that it is more useful to view the handicapped as a minority group subject to oppression than as a clientele group in need of help, as has been the traditional approach.[2] In many cases handicapped people are treated like members of a minority; they are denied employment, sterilized without their consent, even come close to forfeiting their lives. The disabled are indeed subject to the kinds of invidious discrimination with which other groups are familiar.

But the problems go even deeper. The disabled often are not in a position to fight discrimination as other groups have done, for they lack the opportunities to do so. If they are ever to participate fully in society, "equal" will have to mean "more"—more money, more time, more attention.

"Had clumps of handicapped people settled in the colonies, most disabled people believe, America today would be totally accessible to the handicapped."[3] Whether or not that statement is true, America is not accessible now. Public facilities are not designed for the wheelchair-bound, deaf, or blind. Perhaps it need not have been that way, but beyond doubt, changing things will be costly work. If disabled people cannot move around freely, it is hard for them to vote, make demands, organize, or get jobs. So one of their major problems is lack of mobility and access.

But these are not the only necessary preconditions of full citizenship. Another is education, and historically the disabled have been short-changed here. Until the 1970s, most schools could exclude any child whom they judged physically or mentally unfit. As late as 1975, the year the Education of All Handicapped Children Act and the Developmental Disabilities Assistance and Bill of Rights Act were passed, an estimated one million handicapped children in this country got no

---

[2] John Gliedman and William Roth, *The Unexpected Minority: Handicapped Children in America* (New York: Harcourt Brace Jovanovich, 1980).

[3] Sonny Kleinfeld, *The Hidden Minority: America's Handicapped* (Boston: Little, Brown, 1979), p. 22.

schooling at all.[4] Many school systems did make provisions for educating handicapped children. They might get home instruction or attend "special" schools. There are also many private schools adapted to their needs, and some states paid all or part of the tuition. This "special education" provided some schooling for some children, but could hardly prepare them for life among the able-bodied.

Just as handicapped children have often been deprived of education, they have been denied the therapy and training they need to master such basic skills as speech and walking. For the disabled, this help is a necessary part of education. Those who became disabled as adults have fared somewhat better. Vocational rehabilitation (VR) programs have been funded by federal grants to, and sometimes matched by, the states. First established by Congress in 1920, primarily to aid disabled World War I veterans, VR has since been considerably expanded and liberalized. But the program has never met the need. Although VR has gotten thousands of people back to work, no clear statistical evidence of its overall effectiveness exists.[5] The passage of the Rehabilitation Act of 1973 reflected a strong congressional agreement that VR was not enough.

The lack of mobility, education, and rehabilitation—or habilitation—has helped to exclude the disabled from full citizenship. But while improvements in these areas are necessary conditions for change, it is unlikely that even together they would be sufficient. So we come back to the question of direct discrimination. The Carnegie Council study points out that if education does bring the handicapped into full, equal participation in the work force, they will be the first disadvantaged group for which this strategy has worked.[6] Even mobile, trained, and educated handicapped people have suffered discrimination, just as competent blacks and women have. So there are at least three problems here: mobility, education, and discrimination. Federal laws attack all three.

The Rehabilitation Act not only appropriated an unprecedented amount of money, but also addresses the removal of architectural barriers and provides, in its famous Section 504, that "no otherwise qualified handicapped individual . . . shall, solely by reason of his handicap, be excluded from participation, be denied the benefits of, or be

[4] See Gene Maeroff, "Major Bill to Aid Handicapped Pupils Is Nearing Final Passage in Congress," *New York Times*, November 6, 1975, p. 26; Gliedman and Roth, *Unexpected Minority*, chap. 9.

[5] See *Congressional Record*, 118: 32279–316, September 26, 1972 (remarks of Senator Cranston); Gliedman and Roth, *Unexpected Minority*, chap. 13.

[6] Gliedman and Roth, *Unexpected Minority*, chaps. 12 and 13.

subjected to discrimination under any program or activity receiving federal financial assistance."[7] Several amendments to mass transportation bills have required accessibility. The Education of All Handicapped Children Act (usually known by its number, 94–142) does what its title says it does. It establishes for all handicapped children the right to a public education appropriate to their needs, and requires that this education take place in the least segregated setting possible.[8] Thus it encourages what is known as "mainstreaming": integration of disabled children with the able-bodied.

But, as important as these laws are, they came very late in our history; they often go unenforced; and the opposition they have met does not encourage optimism.[9] For example, former president Richard Nixon vetoed the first two versions of the Rehabilitation Act as "too costly," although they had been passed by huge majorities in both houses of Congress. In October 1972, the month of his first veto, he proclaimed National Employment of the Handicapped Week, announcing that "although much has been done, there is more that must be done." If there was any inconsistency here, it escaped the president. When he did sign the bill, in September 1973, the appropriation was roughly half that of the original bill, down to about $1.5 billion. Two years later, President Ford signed 94–142 into law, voicing the same financial worries that had troubled Nixon.[10]

These concerns about cost survived those Republican administrations, as an editorial published by a liberal newspaper while Democrats controlled both presidency and Congress shows. In 1980 the *Washington Post* criticized a district court ruling upholding the power of the secretary of transportation, under Section 504 and several transit laws, to issue regulations making public transportation accessible to the disabled. More precisely, the editorial's concern was with Section 504 itself, which it described as "an unqualified order that should have been tempered to reflect the limits of what is possible." It continued, "Estimates of all this work run anywhere from $3 billion to $7

[7] 29 U.S.C. 701, secs. 792, 794.
[8] 20 U.S.C., sec. 1412 (5).
[9] For example, regulations to implement the Rehabilitation Act were not signed until 1977, after tumultuous national demonstrations and after a court order requiring them. See Cherry v. Mathews, 419 F. Supp. 922 (D.D.C. 1976); *New York Times*, April 1, 1977, p. 12; April 17, p. 29, April 29, p. 1. In 1980, a report prepared by a coalition of children's rights groups charged that the Federal Bureau of Education for the Handicapped had virtually ignored 94–142. See Philip Taubman, "Study Says Schools Ignore the Disabled," *New York Times*, April 17, 1980, p. C3.
[10] *New York Times*, October 6, 1972, p. 39; October 28, 1972, p. 1, 7; March 28, 1973, p. 1; September 15, 1972, p. 58; December 3, 1974, p. 31.

billion and do not take into account the physical disruption involved." [11]

Of course, such concern is legitimate. What is troubling is, first, that what is "possible" appears to be a matter of what society is *willing* to spend, an unspecified amount that is steadily decreasing; second, that the actual regulations require that only some existing facilities be refitted, so that access will still be difficult; and, finally, that there is little recognition of the character of the interests involved. The *Post* put the matter in standard pluralist fashion. "To the handicapped, this is a matter of rights and dignity. . . . But to Congress and all taxpayers, it is a matter of money, technology, and timing." [12] But this is far too subjective a notion of "rights and dignity." Accessibility is related to mobility, and mobility is fundamental to the exercise of individual rights. And if society is truly concerned with the dignity of *all* its members, this statement of countervailing interests is false and dangerous.

Of course, society is not so concerned, and is becoming, if anything, even less concerned. In the 1980s, with a new conservative administration and a Senate controlled by Republicans, the federal budget has shrunk, not expanded—except, of course, for defense spending. But not all the opposition to the laws and rules is merely financial. Some of it implies that the disabled are demanding too much, expecting a place in society that is not rightfully theirs. "But the handicapped *are* different," intoned the last sentence of a *Newsweek* story, "and city officials say that limited public resources should be spent to improve the mobility of the handicapped and not try to satisfy their broader and perhaps impractical claim to equal treatment." [13] The same note has been struck by some handicapped people—who, contrary to the *Post*'s implication, are taxpayers. One letter writer to the *New York Times* wrote, "As disabled people, we must accept the fact that we have limitations." [14]

Equality and Ability

All this, of course, is backlash. By all signs, the disability rights movement is here to stay. At the same time homosexuals came out of

---

[11] "Judge Oberdorfer's Ruling," *Washington Post*, February 9, 1980, p. A12. The case was American Public Transit Association v. Goldschmidt, 485 F. Supp. 811 (D.D.C. 1980). The regulations are codified in 49 C.F.R. 27.81–27.119.

[12] "Judge Oberdorfer's Ruling," p. A12.

[13] "Now, Wheelchair Rights," *Newsweek*, January 15, 1979, p. 36.

[14] Herbert Thatcher, *New York Times*, August 27, 1979, p. 16.

the closet, the disabled emerged from the attic, and there is no reason to expect either group to go back.[15] But identifying opposition as backlash does not render it insignificant. The kinds of backlash that a social movement engenders illuminate the problems that produced the movement.

The current preoccupation with cost is part of the general opinion trend exemplified by California's Proposition 13 of 1978. Many Americans are more concerned with paring expenses than with securing a better life for their fellow citizens. The results of this attitude may be unfortunate, but the feeling is understandable, since tax burdens fall disproportionately on the white- and blue-collar workers who are a majority of the voters. The effects of the "taxpayers' revolt" may be particularly bad for the handicapped, but it is unlikely that the revolt itself has been caused by social attitudes toward disability.

When these arguments are used to oppose new programs for the disabled, however, they display a certain lack of both foresight and perspective. Handicapped people receive, and will continue to receive, federal and state money, such as supplemental security insurance. But many recipients are unable to work not because of inherent personal limitations, but because of barriers and the lack of education and training. The immediate costs of the aid programs is less than that of education, habilitation, and barrier removal, but the long-run costs may be a different story. The aggressive programs seek to get the disabled into the work force, where, as has often been pointed out, they not only will cost the government less in welfare payments but will pay taxes. Some experts estimate that the long-run cost of the new programs will be less than those of current ones.[16] The failure of budget-conscious critics even to try to make these kinds of calculations suggests that both their thrift and their charity are shortsighted.

Another problem with the financial arguments is that they are not applied consistently. Mainstreaming costs less than "warehousing" (i.e., institutionalization); for example, it is cheaper to operate a group home for retarded adults than to keep them in a state hospital. But residents

[15] Florence B. Isbell, "Potomac Fever: How the Handicapped Won Their Rights," *Civil Liberties Review* 4 (November–December 1977): 61–65.

[16] See, e.g., a series of columns by Sylvia Porter, *Washington Star*, December 1976, or Frank Bowe, *Rehabilitating America* (New York: Harper & Row, 1980), pp. 93–94. Bowe, who is director of the American Coalition of Citizens with Disabilities, insists that even if the highest estimated cost of barrier removal, $20 billion over the next decade, is correct, it has to be compared to the cost, in public and private spending and lost wages, of not removing barriers, which he estimates at $1 *trillion*. Recipients of VR aid have, on the average, returned to the federal government in taxes four times the money spent on them (*Congressional Record*, 119:7104, March 8, 1973) (remarks of Rep. Hansen).

of many communities have vehemently opposed such homes. As one case will show, these feelings have influenced legal developments. Something other than financial worry is operating here. Society is far from eager to integrate the handicapped. This feeling is illustrated by the "but they *are* different" arguments we have met.

That disabled people have limitations that they cannot change is true. It is not clear, however, just what it means to say that they must "accept" them; does not acceptance imply choice? But to state the issues only in this manner conceals the fact that some of these differences and limitations result not from disabilities themselves, but from an environment that exaggerates them. For instance, whatever condition puts a person in a wheelchair makes her unable to walk, and probably cannot be changed. It is a limitation she must deal with. But the absence of curb cuts on sidewalks, ramps leading into office buildings, and grab bars on toilets, which may prevent her from working, are conditions that can be changed, and therefore should not be accepted. If we fail to see the difference, we imply that physical limitations entail a kind of limited citizenship. We encourage the disabled to accept a view of themselves as marginal members of society—so marginal, indeed, that it is inappropriate for them to make political demands as most groups do.

Attitudes and Doctrines

I doubt that the attitudes I have been discussing can be blamed on court decisions, but they can be found in some of them. They surface in an opinion I have quoted more than once. Justice Brennan wrote in *Frontiero*, "What differentiates sex from *such nonsuspect statuses as intelligence and physical disability*, and aligns it with the recognized suspect criteria, is that it frequently bears *no relation to ability to perform or contribute to society*." [17] As I suggested, this attitude makes equality dependent on being like most people, on being as competent as the norm. If this ability is lacking—if, in other words, there is a *dis*ability—then by implication, unequal treatment is legitimate. To be "different" is to forfeit the right to equality. This is an idea that pervades many of the decisions examined in this chapter, and one that already has been called into question.

This powerful connection between status and normality has a long history. It is hard to think of the Supreme Court in this connection

---

[17] 411 U.S. 677, 686 (1973). Emphasis supplied.

without thinking of the case of *Buck* v. *Bell*. Here eight justices upheld a Virginia court order authorizing the sterilization of "feeble-minded" Carrie Buck, whose mother and daughter were alleged to be likewise afflicted. The following passage from the opinion for the Court has often been quoted:

> We have seen more than once that the public welfare may call upon the best citizens for their lives. It would be strange if it could not call upon those who already sap the strength of the State for lesser sacrifices, often not felt to be such by those concerned, in order to prevent our being swamped with incompetence. It is better for all the world, if instead of waiting to execute degenerate offspring for crime, or to let them starve for their imbecility, society can prevent those who are manifestly unfit from continuing their kind. The principle that sustains compulsory vaccination is broad enough to cover cutting the fallopian tubes. Three generations of imbeciles are enough.[18]

Few disinterested commentators have had much praise for this reasoning. C. Herman Pritchett put it this way: "Seldom has so much questionable doctrine been compressed into five sentences of a Supreme Court opinion."[19] Walter Berns dealt with the penultimate sentence by remarking: "It is a broad principle indeed that sustains a needle's prick in the arm and an abdominal incision, if only in terms of the equipment used. It becomes something else again in terms of the results obtained: no smallpox in one case and no children in the other."[20]

The facts were as shaky as the law. Berns's article exposed the very dubious, and long since discredited, theories of "eugenics" behind the drive for sterilization of the "unfit" in the 1920s and 1930s. Newspaper reports in early 1980 revealed the results in at least one state of official action on the basis of those theories. They reported that Carrie Buck and her sister, Doris, were among more than 7,500 inmates of Virginia institutions who were sterilized over a forty-eight-year period in a campaign to eliminate "social misfits." And there is considerable doubt whether Carrie or any member of her family was in fact "feeble-minded" or mentally subnormal at all.[21]

What inspired the Court to make such errors? The quoted passage

[18] 274 U.S. 200, 207 (1927).
[19] *The American Constitution*, 3d ed. (New York: McGraw-Hill, 1977), p. 538.
[20] "Buck v. Bell: Due Process of Law?" *Western Political Quarterly* 6 (1953):764.
[21] See, e.g., Sandra G. Boardman and Glenn Frankel, "Over 7500 Sterilized in Virginia," *Washington Post*, February 23, 1980, pp. A1, A20; Robert L. Burgdorf and Marcia Pearce Burgdorf, "The Wicked Witch Is Almost Dead: Buck v. Bell and the Sterilization of Handicapped Persons," *Temple Law Quarterly* 50 (1977):955–1034.

gives some hints, and reveals another, and largely ignored, defect in the opinion. The juxtaposition of the best citizens and the weakest, of the normal and the imbeciles, of society and degenerate offspring, suggests a mentality that consigns "those people" to a marginal position in that society. There is a group of people whose rights do not much matter, because they only sap the state, and anyway, they hardly notice what is being done to them. Society may let them starve, punish them, or sterilize them; there is no notion that they are part of that society or that the best citizens have any duty to them.

This bigotry is comparable to the racism of *Plessy* v. *Ferguson* or the sexism of Justice Bradley's opinion in *Bradwell* v. *Illinois*.[22] It seems, but only seems, anachronistic to us now. It is not clear that anything has changed much. I mentioned Phillip Becker's case in Chapter 7, but because of his handicap, it belongs here, too, even with its happy ending. The boy's doctors testified that surgery could correct his heart defect, a common one for victims of Down's syndrome, and give him "a significant expansion of his life span." Without surgery, Phillip "will suffer a progressive loss of energy and vitality until he is forced to lead a bed-to-chair existence . . . [and] may live at the outset 20 more years."[23]

Phillip's parents refused to permit the surgery. The California courts stressed the fact that surgery did have risks, but the publicity about the case has revealed that the Beckers have other reasons for their decision. They have argued that, if allowed to live, Phillip might "burden" his two brothers, that he would be better off dying than surviving, "neglected," in an institution, and "that his life is inherently not worth living." But Phillip had made good progress in his training program, and would probably be able to work and live in a supervised setting as an adult.[24]

The state appeals court treated this case much as its New York counterpart had dealt with *Hofbauer*.[25] The judge emphasized parental autonomy and cited such "family rights" cases as *Pierce*, *Meyer*, and *Yoder*. "The rule is clear that the power of the appellate court begins and ends with a determination as to whether there is any substantial evidence, contradicted or uncontradicted, which will support the conclusion reached by the trier of fact."[26] Since there was medical testimony that surgery carried the risk of death, this standard was

[22] 163 U.S. 537 (1896); 83 U.S. 130, 140–42 (1872).
[23] In re Phillip B., App., 156 Cal. Rptr. 48, 50 (Ct. App. 1st D. 1979); *New York Times*, August 9, 1981, p. 21.
[24] George F. Will, "The Case of Phillip Becker," *Newsweek*, April 14, 1980, p. 112.
[25] Matter of Hofbauer, 393 N.E. 2d 1009 (N.Y. Ct.App., 1979).
[26] 156 Cal. Rptr. 48, 51.

met. The opinion ignored the evidence that the parents' decision was based on the fact that Phillip is retarded, and that the result of this decision was to suggest that a retarded child does not have the same rights to treatment, and indeed to life, as his normal counterpart. The Supreme Court's refusal to hear the case is silent evidence that it may not have come far enough from *Buck* v. *Bell*. That case reasoned from no smallpox to no children; *Bothman* v. *Warren B.* progresses to no life.

Although a lawyer interviewed on *60 Minutes* described *Bothman* as "an equal-protection case," it was brought and decided as a custody case. What happens, though, if we do consider disability rights issues in a constitutional context? If the handicapped get different treatment, are they being denied their constitutional rights? The answer to that question seems to depend on what they are not getting. If it is education, *Rodriguez* implies a negative answer; as for accessibility, the earliest cases reach a similar conclusion.[27] Neither of these results is beyond challenge, but they do reflect current doctrine.

Is disability a suspect classification? That depends on which version of suspect classification one adopts. Marcia Pearce Burgdorf and Robert Burgdorf have relied on the "discrete and insular minorities" component of *Carolene Products* and the "saddled with such disabilities" text of *Rodriguez* to argue the affirmative, and that argument is tenable.[28] But the *Frontiero* version weighs against it. It is possible to quote it selectively. The Burgdorfs do so in exactly the same way as does a 1976 North Dakota case: "We are confident that the Court would have held that G. H.'s terrible handicaps are just the sort of 'immutable characteristic determined solely by the accident of birth' to which the 'inherently suspect' classification would be applied."[29]

This is law-office history with a vengeance. It cuts *Frontiero* in half. Two scholars, one a lawyer and one a doctor, do try to fit the retarded, at least, into the second half. This classification, they insist, "'frequently bears no relation to the ability to perform or contribute to society' [but] is a stereotyped self-fulfilling prophecy."[30] This argument is not much better, however, for it too easily substitutes the label

[27] Snowden v. Birmingham–Jefferson County Transit Authority, 407 F. Supp. 394 (N.D. Ala. 1975); United Handicapped Federation v. André, 409 F. Supp. 1297 (D. Minn. 1976).

[28] "A History of Unequal Treatment: The Qualifications of Handicapped Persons as a 'Suspect Class' under the Equal Protection Clause," *Santa Clara Lawyer* 15 (1975):906.

[29] In Interest of G. H., 218 N.W. 2d 441, 447 (Sup.Ct. N.D.); Burgdorf and Burgdorf, "History of Unequal Treatment," p. 905.

[30] Bruce G. Mason and Frank J. Merolascino, "The Right to Treatment for Mentally Retarded Citizens: An Evolving Legal and Scientific Interface," *Creighton Law Review* 10 (October 1976):162.

for the condition. And the condition of being retarded is just not comparable to the condition of being a woman. The cases themselves, winding through intricate constitutional and statutory questions, sometimes reach these issues and sometimes evade them.

Education and Treatment

I have suggested that a notion of the handicapped as marginal persons has led society to be stingy about providing them with therapy, habilitation, and education. But *Buck* v. *Bell* reveals another problem, just as serious, which is polar to the first and which is to the fore in the education cases. To say that we regard the handicapped as inferior assumes a real handicap. But such words as "disabled" and "handicapped" do more than refer to conditions. They are also *labels*, which help assign people to social statuses. A major problem with labels is that they can be wrongly applied. This problem is especially severe for children, because they so often run up against government power in the person of school authorities.

Some of the cases that I have to skip over involve the assignment of schoolchildren to "emotionally disturbed" or "educable mentally retarded" classes, often on the basis of IQ tests and over the protests of their parents; most of the children so assigned were black, and there is ground for suspicion that their "handicaps" existed mainly on paper and in their teachers' judgments.[31] One case deals with a school's effort to assign a child to a "special" school because of a less than catastrophic defect.[32] The dangers increase when the label is some fuzzy concept like "minimal brain dysfunction" or "learning disability."[33] Children are vulnerable to "help" and "therapy"—that is, coercion— they do not need. "Mainstreaming" reduces these dangers by making it harder to exclude children from regular classes, but 94–142 does permit flexibility here. Worse, to quote a popular maxim of the child experts, "labeling is disabling"; it can cause or aggravate the very problems we are trying to relieve.

But this concern cannot monopolize our thinking either. Labeling is disabling, yes, but so are blindness, paraplegia, and Down's syndrome. The situation is not perfectly parallel to *Parham* or *Gault*,

[31] See Larry P. v. Riles, 343 F. Supp. 1306 (N.D. Cal. 1972); 502 F. 2d 963 (9th Circ. 1974); Lora v. Board of Education, 456 F. Supp. 1211 (E.D.N.Y., 1978), 623 F. 2d 248 (2d Circ. 1980).

[32] Hairston v. Drosick, 423 F. Supp. 180 (S.D. W.Va. 1976).

[33] See Divoky and Schrag, *Myth of the Hyperactive Child.*

where children were labeled "mentally ill" or "delinquent" without good evidence to support the diagnoses. There are many disabilities that treatment can help, and that are catastrophic without it. The blind or retarded person cannot become self-sufficient without professional help, and, for children, that help may feel very much like coercion. Some labeling is a precondition for receiving this kind of help. However attractive "radical nonintervention" may be as an approach to delinquency, it will not do as an approach to disability.[34]

Both polarities were evident in the next two cases. Decided three months apart in 1972, they were to the disability rights movement what *Brown* was to the fight for racial equality. They were *Pennsylvania Association for Retarded Children (PARC) v. Pennsylvania* and *Mills v. Board of Education*.[35] Both involved suits brought not on behalf of children assigned to special classes or subjected to unwanted "help," but for children excluded from public schools.

Pennsylvania exempted from its compulsory education law, and relieved the state Board of Education of all responsibility for, any child who was classified by a school psychologist as uneducable and untrainable.[36] There were some free public programs for the retarded, and some children attended private schools at state expense, but these programs could not accommodate all children removed from public school. There was evidence of "crass and summary treatment" of the children; in some cases, the parents were not even informed of the decision. During the litigation, however, an interim stipulation provided that any child and parent had a right to hearing, notice, counsel, and cross-examination of witnesses before exclusion.[37]

PARC brought this action on behalf of all retarded children between the ages of six and twenty-one who were excluded from the state's public schools. "Plaintiffs do not challenge the separation of special classes for retarded children from regular classes or the proper assignment of retarded children to special classes. Rather plaintiffs question whether the state, having undertaken to provide public education to some children (perhaps all children) may deny it to plaintiffs entirely." The parties had reached a court-approved consent agreement that obliged the state to educate each child in an appropriate setting.[38]

The District of Columbia gave officials even more power to exclude children than Pennsylvania did. The city's code exempted any child

---

[34] The title of a book by Edwin M. Schur. See Chapter 7, n. 75.
[35] 343 F. Supp. 279 (E.D. Pa. 1972); 348 F. Supp. 866 (D.D.C. 1972).
[36] 24 Purd. Stat. Sec. 13–1330, 13–1375.
[37] 343 F. Supp. 279, 296, 293, 284–85.
[38] Ibid., pp. 297, 285.

who was "mentally or physically unfit."[39] As in Pennsylvania, there was a special education program, but it was inadequate for all eligible children; the school system estimated that more than 12,000 handicapped children got no public education at all. The seven child plaintiffs in *Mills* had been threatened with exclusion because they were allegedly "emotionally disturbed," "behavior problems," "mentally retarded," or "hyperactive."[40] Perhaps unremarkably for Washington, all seven were black. The suit was brought, however, on behalf of all children in the District, of whatever race, excluded from free public education.

Chapter 7 showed that the exclusion of children from school raises grave questions of procedural due process. But there are substantive problems, too, and here they will not go away so easily as they were made to in *Lopez*. Both the Pennsylvania and the District regulations indicate that the potential existed for both problems I have identified, mislabeling and nonhelping. Especially in Washington, the schoolchild was vulnerable to a diagnosis that might or might not be correct. If a school professional labeled her "unfit," she was out (or, rarely, forced into special education classes), whether or not she actually had a disabling condition. This situation is bad enough, but suppose the child was indeed retarded. Unless the parents could afford private schooling, such a child would not get the help she needed.

The three-judge courts were sensitive to both problems. They ruled the laws unconstitutional on both procedural and substantive grounds. Both Judge Thomas Masterson in Philadelphia and Judge Joseph Waddy in Washington emphasized the lack of a hearing (although Pennsylvania had agreed to start holding one). Each opinion forbade special placement without notice, hearing, counsel, or other procedural safeguards, and each went further, into substantive due process and equal protection.[41] The panels ruled that the respective governments had a constitutional duty to provide all children with an adequate education.

Masterson was concerned about "the stigma which our society unfortunately attaches to the label of mental retardation." He cited *Wisconsin* v. *Constantineau*,[42] in which the Supreme Court had invalidated a law that allowed police to forbid the sale of liquor to anyone classified as an excessive drinker and thus established "the necessity

[39] D.C. Code Sec. 31–203, quoted at 348 F. Supp. 866, 874.
[40] 348 F. Supp. 866, 868–70.
[41] Any reader who is puzzled about how equal protection applies to the District is referred to Bolling v. Sharpe, 347 U.S. 497 (1954).
[42] 400 U.S. 433 (1971).

of a due process hearing before the state stigmatizes any citizen." But Masterson went beyond notice and hearing. He attacked the implied identification of "retarded" with "uneducable and untrainable," declaring: "Without exception, expert opinion indicates that all mentally retarded persons are capable of benefitting from a program of education and training." He concluded: "We are satisfied that the evidence raises serious doubts (and hence a colorable claim) as to the existence of a rational basis for such exclusions."[43] Therefore, the law ran afoul of equal-protection guarantees.

Judge Waddy was disturbed less by any lack of rationality than by the denial of what he viewed as a fundamental right. (This was a year before the Supreme Court ruled in *Rodriguez* that education was not to be so ranked.) Waddy cited *Brown* I, as cases on the education of handicapped children often do: "In these days, it is doubtful that any child may reasonably be expected to succeed in life if he is denied the opportunity of an education. *Such an opportunity, where the State has undertaken to provide it, is a right which must be made available to all on equal terms.*" Waddy also relied on *Hobson* v. *Hansen*, where Judge J. Skelly Wright had ruled that the District's ability-grouping system violated the due-process clause.[44] *Mills* ended with seven pages of requirements for publicizing the ruling, notifying the children and parents involved, hearings, and procedures.

The *Mills* and *PARC* decisions suggest comparisons other than *Brown* and *Hobson*. They can be interpreted as doing for, or to, school systems what *Wyatt* v. *Stickney* did for mental hospitals and *James* v. *Wallace* for prisons.[45] Of course, *Mills* and *PARC* could no more enforce themselves than any of those decisions could. But they could and did start events in motion. Indeed, they may turn out to be similar to *Brown* in their ultimate effects. Within a few years, there was important new legislation; ultimately it may have profound and far-reaching effects on social attitudes and behavior.

The Education of All Handicapped Children Act and some state laws have established rights that these two cases grounded in the Constitution, along with some glosses such as "mainstreaming." Therefore, these claims need no longer depend on constitutional arguments. But emphasis on these early rulings is no wasted exercise. Constitutional grounds may ultimately be firmer than laws that can be changed

[43] PARC v. Pennsylvania, 343 F. Supp. 279, 295–97.
[44] Mills v. Board of Education, 348 F. Supp. 866, 875, quoting 347 U.S. 483, 493 (1954) (emphasis supplied by Judge Waddy); 269 F. Supp. 401 (D.D.C. 1967).
[45] 325 F. Supp. 781 (M.D. Ala. 1971); 334 F. Supp. 134 and 387 (1972); 406 F. Supp. 318 (M.D. Ala. 1976).

or appropriations that can be cut. Now that suits under the 1973 and 1975 acts are moving through the courts, judges tend to avoid constitutional questions in favor of statutory ones. But many cases raise both kinds of issues.

Mills and *PARC* avoid certain lines of reasoning that might have been traps. Unlike some writers I quoted earlier, they do not do much with suspect classification. All that is "suspect" in *PARC* is careless labeling, and *Mills* does not get into this aspect of the problem at all. Taken together, the two cases establish, first, that exclusion is invalid when no rational basis for it exists, and second, that education must be provided to all on an equal basis. These are two notions with long pedigrees, especially the first.

Rodriguez, with its ruling that there is no constitutional right to education, may appear to call the second conclusion into question, but the decisions have not been consistent. (Indeed, *Rodriguez* may provide some help here, since it did allow unequal expenditures, and education may be more costly for the handicapped than for normal children.) A 1976 case did rely on *Rodriguez* to justify exclusion of retarded children, and three years later a California court suggested that *Rodriguez* had weakened *PARC* and *Mills*, but had no effect on 94–142.[46] But other decisions have pointed out that *Rodriguez* did not deny that states had a duty to provide all children with an adequate education, nor did it sanction exclusion.[47]

To the extent that *Mills* contradicts *Rodriguez*, I think Judge Waddy has the better argument. The dissenters in *Rodriguez* did an excellent job of arguing that education is fundamental to the exercise of such explicitly granted rights as voting and freedom of expression.[48] But losing the fundamental-right skirmish does not mean losing the case, so these rulings can stand even after *Rodriguez*. For once, traditional due-process and equal-protection analysis work rather well—in those particular cases.

But what happens in subsequent cases? What does an adequate education consist of? If blanket exclusion of the "retarded" is invalid, can a particular child be excluded after an expert determination? Who decides, and how, where to place a child? Is mainstreaming desirable always, sometimes, or never? If ever, when?

---

[46] Cuyahoga County Association for Retarded Children and Adults v. Essex, 411 F. Supp. 46, 50 (N.D. Ohio 1976); Boxall v. Sequoia Union High School District, 464 F. Supp. 1104, 1107–8 (N.D. Cal. 1979).

[47] Fialkowski v. Shapp, 405 F. Supp. 946, 958 (E.D. Pa. 1975); Kruse v. Campbell, 431 F. Supp. 180 (E.D. Va. 1977), vacated and remanded sub. nom. Campbell v. Kruse, 434 U.S. 808 (1977).

[48] 411 U.S. 1, 62–63 (Brennan dissenting), 71–72, 99–102 (Marshall dissenting).

Although the new laws have dealt with these questions, judges—often the same ones—are still tackling these problems. Laws that create rights usually increase rather than reduce the judicial workload, and 94–142 has been no exception. Since some of the cases were begun before the law went into effect, constitutional questions still appear. And since the law is still young, there is not much definitive judicial interpretation.

The cases present a variety of factual situations and legal issues. I have chosen to examine some cases that focus on individual rather than collective applications. The cases do not easily sort themselves into patterns, but I divide them rather loosely into two groups. The first group involves what I have been calling nonhelping: exclusion or inadequate schooling. The second group involves mislabeling: assigning, tracking, even institutionalizing on shaky evidence of the need. One case, arguably, involves both.

Early in 1976, two district court cases reached conclusions that provide a revealing contrast. Eighteen-year-old Diana Taylor, legally blind and multiply handicapped, had entered the Maryland School for the Blind, a residential facility, in 1973. After two years, the school decided to terminate her enrollment, alleging that "despite intense work" she was not benefiting. Some staff members testified that she had actually regressed from a two-year-old level to that of an eighteen-month-old. After a hearing before the school's admissions committee, at which Diana and her parents were represented by counsel, the committee upheld the recommendation. Diana was transferred to a public custodial institution. Her parents sued, but the court upheld the school.

Judge Joseph Young found that "a forced transfer from an educational institution for the handicapped to a custodial one should be governed by the due process clause," but that the hearing satisfied these guarantees. The fact that it was held by the school's own committee did not taint it, since the Taylors had counsel and the right to present and confront witnesses. This case was distinguishable from *Mills* and *PARC* because proper cause for dismissal existed. The judge reviewed the evidence, using the "rational basis" standard. Though there were disagreements, "no matter which standard of review this Court chooses to adopt, it cannot say that the finding of the school that Diana has made no real progress . . . is incorrect."[49]

Taylor suggests that, once procedural rules are observed, substantive barriers to exclusion may fall. In the face of any evidence to support the decision that the child was not educable, the court would

---

[49] Taylor v. Maryland School for the Blind, 409 F. Supp. 148, 151–54 (D. Md. 1976).

uphold the school. This begins to sound like the school cases examined in the last chapter. There, however firm the demands for a hearing, the courts refrained from discussing the offenses the children were being punished *for*. If the judges were troubled that a child was suspended for disrespect or paddled for dawdling, they kept their qualms to themselves.

Generalizing from some of the views honored in those cases, it is plausible to assume that some of the judges were deferring to the supposed superior wisdom of the school officials. Judge Young seems to be doing the same. But it is harder to condemn his deference to pedagogical authority. We might expect judges to have a common-sense understanding of discipline, but—given the fact that they grew up in the days before mainstreaming—is it reasonable to expect them to know much about multiply handicapped children? Why should it occur to Judge Young that from some perspectives two years might seem too soon to give up? The *PARC* consent agreement gathered much general expert knowledge about retardation, but in a specific case it is difficult to argue with experts who know the child.

Taylor is equally disturbing for another reason. It suggests that the educational system has to be taken as a given. Rather than the state having an obligation to design a system from which all children can benefit, the children have to fit into the system as it exists.[50]

It is useful to contrast Taylor with *Hairston v. Drosick. Hairston* touches both poles of mislabeling and nonhelping. It began in September 1975, with a telephone call to the mother of six-year-old Trina Hairston from her prospective first-grade teacher.

Trina had been born with spina bifida. She limped and her bowel control was imperfect, but she was physically and mentally competent to attend regular school. The year before, Gary Grade School in McDowell County, West Virginia, had at first refused to let her into kindergarten, but had admitted her for the second half of the school year. Just before the 1975–76 academic year started, the teacher whose class Trina was to enter telephoned Sheila Hairston to tell her that her daughter was "not wanted" there and would not be admitted.

"Upon going to the school after extensive discussion," Mrs. Hairston was told by school authorities that Trina could attend only if her mother came to class. Finally the school superintendent gave the Hairstons three choices. Trina could attend school with her mother; she could get homebound instruction; or she could go to a school for

---

[50] A similar decision was rendered in Cuyahoga County Association v. Essex, cited in n. 46.

handicapped children. No hearing was held, nor was Trina examined by a school physician. None of these choices was satisfactory to the Hairstons. They charged that the school's actions violated both Section 504 of the 1973 act and the due-process clause of the Fourteenth Amendment.

The district judge agreed. He found Trina's exclusion "without a bona fide educational reason" inconsistent with the statute and the denial of a hearing in violation of due process. He ruled that the Hairstons must have an opportunity to get medical evaluations and other evidence before a hearing was held. In the meantime, the school must admit Trina, who had already lost half a year of first grade.

The opinion found, as matters of fact, that "a great number of spina bifida children," most of them in worse condition than Trina, attended public schools in West Virginia; that Trina would get a grossly inferior education at the special school; and that it was an "educational fact that the maximum benefits to a child are received by placement in as normal environment as possible" and "that handicapped children should be excluded from the regular classroom only as a last resort."[51] The conclusions of law were brief, without rhetoric. Perhaps *Hairston* is a "horrible example," for the attitudes of teachers and officials were extreme. We can welcome the decision, however, for cracking down on this sort of placement—while we must wonder how many children have been ghettoized into special schools, or entirely excluded, on grounds as specious as this. In *Taylor*, it was evident that the schools were dealing with real and serious problems. No one can dispute that educating a blind retarded child is a difficult task. But *Hairston* reads suspiciously as if the problems were of the school's own making. A limp does not interfere with learning to read and write, the main tasks of the first grade, but losing half a school year may. And after all, at that age "accidents" are a common classroom occurrence. *Hairston* may be a horrible example of pedagogical bigotry, but it is a good example of the ways official action can worsen the consequences of a disability. This case fits neatly into Title V of the Rehabilitation Act and the procedural sections of *Mills* and *PARC*. It does leave open one question, however: If a due-process hearing had been held, would a substantive constitutional issue exist?

The question is disturbing, for, as *Taylor* shows, a hearing can be biased in favor of the experts. Equality demands substantive as well as procedural guarantees. Disabled children, like all children, need an education; segregation into "special" schools is no more an equal edu-

[51] 423 F. Supp. 180, 182–84 (S.D. W.Va. 1976).

cation for them than it is for black children. What Chief Justice Warren said in *Brown* is surely true for such children as Trina. Segregation would have generated ineluctable feelings of inferiority and affected her ability to take full part in her community. The new laws are welcome for their efforts to prevent such segregation, but it remains to be seen how effectively they will be enforced.

Rights of Mobility

I have argued that education and training are necessary but not sufficient conditions for full equality for disabled people. An accessible environment is another necessity, and the issues involved here are equally complex and traditional doctrine just as restrictive. The Supreme Court has not dealt yet with this issue. The Court's views may not matter much, however, as barrier removal is not among the priorities of the Reagan administration.[52]

The ramps, curb cuts, and Braille signs that have become familiar sights since the 1970s are testimony to a long history of architectural barriers. Our physical environment has long been inimical to the disabled. Sidewalks, buses, and buildings have been inaccessible to people in wheelchairs, marginally accessible to people using canes and crutches, and ill adapted to the blind and deaf. Perhaps we need not have built curbs, buses with high steps, and multistory buildings with stairs and narrow elevators. But they were built this way, and they have helped to keep the disabled from full participation in American life. This segregation, for such it is, has perpetuated itself, for "the physically handicapped have long been invisible to the majoritarian forces of self-governance."[53] The disabled have thus been in no position to demand the changes that would integrate them.

What forms could such a demand take? How is it possible to speak of a *right* to an accessible environment? Courts have recognized a constitutional right to travel and have struck down direct and indirect limitations on it, but this right has been held not to include rights of accessibility.[54] Several federal laws and regulations, however, do es-

[52] The Architectural and Transportation Barriers Compliance Board's regulations, which mandate that all federal buildings be made accessible, have been a chief target of Vice-President George Bush's Regulatory Review Task Force (Felicity Barringer, "U.S. Board Vote May Spell End to Handicap Regulations," *Albany* [N.Y.] *Times-Union*, July 11, 1981, pp. 1, 5).

[53] Atlantis v. Adams, 453 F. Supp. 825, 829 (D. Colo. 1978).

[54] Crandall v. Nevada, 6 Wall. 35 (1868); Edwards v. California, 314 U.S. 160 (1941); Shapiro v. Thompson, 394 U.S. 618 (1968); cases cited in n. 27.

tablish some limited rights. The first set of regulations implementing Section 504, issued more than three years after the law was passed, stipulated that recipients of federal funds must provide handicapped people with services "as effective as those provided to others," and that, with few exceptions, all new facilities must be fully accessible. The first Supreme Court ruling on 504 threatens this interpretation.[55]

Snowden v. *Birmingham–Jefferson County Transit Authority* and *United Handicapped Federation* v. *André* brought both statutory and constitutional claims against the Birmingham and Minneapolis transit system. Both courts quickly dismissed the constitutional claims. The plaintiffs had asserted that they were denied equal protection, citing *Mills, PARC,* and the right-to-travel cases. *Snowden* was curt: "Plaintiff cannot credibly maintain that access to public transportation facilities is a 'fundamental right' on a parity with the right to an education at public expense which must be made available to all on equal terms. . . . 'The Constitution as a continuously operative charter of government' does not demand the impossible or the impracticable."[56] *André* agreed: "The alleged violations of constitutional rights are not based on allegations that defendants prohibit plaintiffs from riding MTC vehicles, but rather that defendants have failed to specifically equip the buses to transport the wheelchair handicapped. The Court is not convinced that the Constitution, absent a statutory mandate, places an affirmative duty on the defendants to provide special facilities for a special class of people."[57]

This choice of words is striking. What connections might there be between "special class" and "suspect class"? The disabled, as I have argued, do fit one definition of suspect classification, the one that seems better attuned to constitutional intent. And inaccessible transportation saddles handicapped people with disabilities even greater than the ones they already have. The environment militates against schooling, voting, political action, and other rights both fundamental and derivative. Inaccessibility helps to create a disadvantaged group just as powerfully as compulsory retirement does for the elderly.

The difficulty with this argument is that it is not the *law* that makes facilities inaccessible. Such direct discrimination has existed; for example, most airlines once refused to allow the mobility-impaired to travel alone. The *Snowden* and *André* opinions are quite correct in

[55] 45 C.F.R. 84.4(b) (1977), 85.58 (1978); Southeastern Community College v. Davis, 99 S.Ct. 2361 (1979).

[56] 407 F. Supp. 394, 398 (M.D. Ala. 1975). The interior quotation is from Yakus v. United States, 321 U.S. 414, 424 (1943).

[57] 409 F. Supp. 1297, 130 (D. Minn. 1976).

their assertions that no comparable rules exist in these cases. Nor is this situation quite like a facially neutral policy that in fact results in discrimination, such as employment requirements that somehow keep blacks out of all but the lowest-paying jobs,[58] or Anatole France's famous example, the law that keeps both rich and poor from sleeping under bridges. *Snowden* puts it this way: "Such discrimination as may in fact exist results from technological and operational difficulties in designing, producing and operating the kinds of special vehicles needed to allow plaintiffs . . . to utilize BJCTA's bus system with safety and convenience for themselves and others."[59]

But look closely at those difficulties. One that the judge does not mention is that Jane Snowden must use a wheelchair. Medical science cannot get all patients out of wheelchairs and onto their feet. Nor do we know how to build wheelchairs that can climb stairs. All the government can do about either of those limitations is to fund research to find ways of changing them, with no guarantee of eventual success. But the third set of technological difficulties has to do with the bus itself. The technology required to lift wheelchairs into buses has been available for some time; either ramps or lifts are needed. Minneapolis' vans are evidence of this knowledge. Transbus, the result of DOT-funded research, has been a very late effort to use this technology. It will not be available until 1985 at the earliest, and no fully accessible bus now exists, but the transit systems we have now could have been made more accessible than they now are.

As a society, we have chosen not to build buses that way, just as we chose stairs instead of ramps, curbs without cuts, and toilets without grab bars. Designers of public facilities do take human anatomy into account in their work—the anatomy of the able-bodied. Where technology is deficient, as it has been with buses, innovation has not been a high priority. So, in a sense, it is the law—the appropriations not made, the grants not awarded, the limitations not considered—that has made the facilities inaccessible. If the equal-protection guarantees are to be interpreted as I have argued, with an emphasis on empowering and enabling citizens and respecting their dignity, why *not* a constitutional right to accessibility?

On Not Hiring the Handicapped

Hire the Handicapped Week has been an annual event since the late 1940s. Just as predictable but more frequent have been the public-

[58] See Griggs v. Duke Power Co., 401 U.S. 424 (1971).
[59] 407 F. Supp. 394, 398.

service advertisements aired on late-night television, which typically show an exemplary handicapped worker as the adult equivalent of a poster child in a fund-raising campaign. But there is little evidence that either the proclamations or the commercials have encouraged employers to hire handicapped workers.

The earlier sections of this chapter suggest two partial explanations for this failure; first, that many handicapped people have been deprived of the schooling needed to fit them for work; and second, that environmental barriers often immobilize them. But these are not the only reasons. After all, many disabled people have gotten an education, and—whatever contrary impression the last section may have given—most are not in wheelchairs and can cope with their environment. There is a third problem: outright discrimination, often based on prejudice, ignorance, and fear.[60] Here again exclusion has perpetuated itself. Not only has it prevented the handicapped from making claims, but it has prevented the able-bodied from learning about handicapped people. Thus the ignorant remain ignorant.

When the Coalition of Citizens with Disabilities asked to join the Leadership Conference on Civil Rights, a conference official demurred. Although surely he should have known better, he asked, "Can't what you want be accomplished by a little public education?" The coalition official replied, "A permanent injunction against discrimination is about the most effective educational tool I know of."[61] It is arguable, and has been argued, that either the Constitution, Section 504, or both provide the basis for such an order.

The first constitutional case was settled out of court. It was brought by Judith Heumann, who has become a prominent disability rights activist. A polio victim, Heumann has used a wheelchair most of her life. In April 1970 she was twenty-two years old and an honor graduate of Long Island University. She applied to the New York City Board of Education for a teacher's license.

The board turned her down, arguing that she would be unable to protect herself or her students in emergencies. Several blind teachers and persons using canes or crutches, however, had recently been licensed. Heumann filed suit in federal district court. In her ultimately successful struggle, she soon gained an ally in the *New York Times*. An editorial called the board's decision "heartless and thoughtless nonsense." It suggested that handicapped persons, often more admi-

[60] See Frank Bowe, *Handicapping America* (New York: Harper & Row, 1978), chap. 6; Gliedman and Roth, *Unexpected Minority*, chaps. 12 and 13.
[61] Isbell, "Potomac Fever," p. 64.

rable than "acclaimed hero-athletes," could provide "a thought-provoking example" for their students.[62]

That, of course, is the traditional rhetoric of disability. It surfaces mainly in situations such as this; discussions of education and accessibility do not fall back on it. Many disabled people are suspicious of this kind of talk, perhaps because it has long been a staple ingredient of American life, parallel to the long history of bigotry and neglect. It has been easier to praise the disabled than to include them. This sort of editorializing is not a good basis for a decision; perhaps, rather than examples, handicapped teachers would prefer to be regarded simply as human beings. Heumann was suing for employment, not idealization. But for once this rhetoric was joined to a practical recommendation.

The suit was settled when the board reversed itself and awarded Heumann a license. The next year, the state's education law was amended to prohibit discrimination against physically handicapped applicants for teaching positions.[63] The issues were not resolved in court. If they had been, the rational-basis test by itself might have demanded a decision for Heumann, since the evidence showed that others who might be equally unfit in emergencies had been hired.

A judicial determination had to wait until 1976, when Judith Gurmankin sought to become one of the approximately five hundred blind public school teachers in the United States. She had done some student teaching of high school English, and had been interviewed by Philadelphia school authorities, but had not been allowed to take the necessary qualifying examinations. A regulation prohibited anyone with a "chronic or acute physical defect" from taking these tests. Gurmankin alleged that her Fourteenth Amendment rights had been violated. Since no regulations on Section 504 had yet been issued, she could not easily include it.

The evidence on her student teaching was mixed. Her students were enthusiastic about her performance, but her supervisor reported that she needed an extraordinary amount of help from teacher aides. What troubled the district judge, however, was, first, that Gurmankin's interviewers did not give her much opportunity to explain how she would do her job, and second, that the regulation created an "irrebuttable presumption" that the handicapped were incapable of teaching. "I have concluded that Ms. Gurmankin was not evaluated fairly. The grading of the oral examination was based, at least in part, on mis-

---

[62] *New York Times*, April 1, 1970, p. 35; May 27, 1970, p. 33; June 2, 1970, p. 38.
[63] Ibid., June 20, 1970, p. 17; May 6, 1971, p. 55.

conceptions and stereotypes about the blind and on assumptions that the blind simply cannot perform while the facts indicate that blind persons can be successful teachers." [64] The board could take her blindness into consideration, the judge ruled, but Gurmankin would have to be hired to give her a chance to show that she could do the job. [65]

Heumann's and Gurmankin's experiences suggest that if some claims involving the handicapped are assigned to the traditional lower tiers of Fourteenth Amendment adjudication, they may succeed. These two episodes, however, do not dispose of all possible constitutional issues. It is easy to imagine harder cases. Suppose New York City had consistently imposed a requirement that teachers be able to deal with emergencies; or, for that matter, that they be assigned lunchroom or corridor duties. Are these tasks properly part of a teacher's job? They have gotten to be, but does that settle the question? Suppose an applicant could not perform tasks that have come to seem an integral part of teaching, such as writing on the blackboard, or that Judith Gurmankin really did need extra help from aides. Would these be grounds for disqualification? If *a priori* assumptions are abandoned, what constitutes evidence of ability or disability? Must job requirements be accepted as givens, or may they—or must they—be modified to suit the disabled?

The leading Rehabilitation Act case, *Southeastern Community College* v. *Davis*, answered these questions in ways unfavorable to the disabled. [66] But how would constitutional doctrine handle these issues? *Davis* would probably meet the requirements of Guntherian rationality scrutiny. The stereotyped assumptions and irrebuttable presumptions that pervaded *Gurmankin* were replaced by the tested opinions of doctors and administrators.

As for the top tier, there is no better way to reveal the difficulties inherent in both suspect-classification doctrines than to examine discrimination based on disability. The *Frontiero* formulation, taken in its entirety, forecloses inquiry; it depends on lack of connection between characteristic and ability, and here that connection is present by definition. But that formulation is at odds with itself. The opinion also suggests that there is something wrong with penalizing people because of something they cannot help and cannot change. If that concept ap-

---

[64] Gurmankin v. Costanzo, 411 F. Supp. 982, 984–85, 990–91 (E.D. Pa. 1976), citing Vlandis v. Kline, 412 U.S. 441 (1973); Cleveland Board of Education v. LaFleur, 414 U.S. 632 (1974); 411 F. Supp. 982, 987–88.

[65] This decision was affirmed in Gurmankin v. Costanzo, 556 F. 2d 184 (3d Circ. 1977).

[66] 99 S.Ct. 2361 (1979).

plies to gender, which does not limit a person's ability, surely it must apply even more stringently to handicaps, which do. But the opposite is true.[67]

And with good reason. It may be more cruel to burden a blind person than a woman, but it is a fact, for instance, that women make competent truck drivers and blind people do not. Job discrimination against the blind may hurt them, but it is often thoroughly reasonable, even necessary. The application of *Frontiero* thus leads to confusion. Part of that rule refuses the disabled any protection, but another part implies that they deserve it the most. The doctrine leaves a gap here; it does not allow us to distinguish between acceptable and unacceptable types of discrimination.

Although I have a general preference for the "insular minority" formulation of the doctrine, it presents similar problems when applied to disability. It sounds good; who could be weaker, more isolated, more stigmatized than those disabled by an immutable, accidental characteristic? But that formulation would suggest that *any* discrimination against the disabled is unconstitutional, and again, the hypothetical case shows that this cannot be true.

We have been dealing with conceptual problems as well as legal ones. I have applied to the disabled some concepts borrowed from equal-protection litigation. But this practice is not always satisfactory, for it is hard to think about disability rights as we think about the rights of blacks and women. The barriers I have discussed have isolated so many handicapped people, and for so long, that the able-bodied majority is simply not so familiar with the disabled minority as it is with blacks and women. It is hard to know what demands the disabled would make, and in what ways, if they were as visible as other disadvantaged groups.

The legal questions are difficult, too. The deeper one gets into the law of disability, the worse the established categories seem to fit. In some early cases they serve quite well; available precedents allowed attacks on stigmatization by labeling without procedural safeguards, mass exclusion from schools, and employment decisions based on unsupported assumptions. Orthodox due-process and equal-protection analysis led to important gains. But as the official actions have replaced presumptions with determinations, as expertise replaces *a priori* assumptions, and especially as the issue of barriers comes to the fore, the old rules do not work. Scrutiny of classification and rationality alike seem to demand approval of official decisions. The transit cases

---

[67] For a similar criticism, see Ely, *Democracy and Distrust*, p. 150.

do not appear at first glance to require even this much attention, for they seem not to involve legal discrimination at all.

That the standard rules do not permit the desired conclusions is not, of course, sufficient reason for abandoning them if they are sound. But the thrust of this book indicates that the traditional approaches are not good enough, that they distort history and language and rest on philosophical underpinnings diametrically opposed to those accepted by the framers of the equal-protection clause. Viewed in this light, the fact that the doctrines are inadequate for yet another disadvantaged group encourages still more rethinking.

If my reformulation were adopted, how would constitutional doctrine change? First, we would have to decide who was affected by a challenged law, in what ways, and how great the affected interests were. The disabled people affected by the policies examined here are disadvantaged; they are a minority, though, at about 36 million, rather large as minorities go; and they have been stigmatized in the ways discussed in Chapter 6. The fact that the *Rodriguez* majority opinion, one of the bases of this formulation, speaks of groups "saddled with disabilities" makes writing somewhat awkward, but it illustrates some important features of this situation. There is no reason to discard this concern for the disadvantaged when we consider those whose disadvantage stems primarily from physical fact rather than public policy.

The disabilities of the handicapped are imposed by nature rather than law, but these limitations have been aggravated by what may be called second-order disabilities; architectural barriers are a good example. These artificial handicaps have thwarted the exercise of specified constitutional rights. So, however badly the disabled fit into the concept of suspect classification, policies restricting them seem to bear a heavy burden of justification, while policies benefiting them do not. Indeed, equal treatment for the disabled may well require, not just permit, favored treatment: not so much reverse discrimination as extra money, extra schooling, extra attention.

It is the third part of Justice Marshall's constitutional test—the character of the state interest involved—that imposes some limitation on this protection. As I have suggested, there are times when safety demands that people with certain disabilities be excluded from certain tasks. The state interest here is great, but it should be yielded to only after the person is given a chance to demonstrate ability.

The interests that militate against barrier removal and aggressive rehabilitation seem to be primarily budgetary. As I have pointed out, the budgeting has not usually been very sophisticated. But even if the long-run costs of these programs exceed the costs of neglect, I do not think that eventuality would negate my argument. For we will never be able to weigh the costs until we begin to assume them. And once the barriers are removed, the disabled activists who emerge may well make us think about these costs in different ways.

The Constitution recognizes broad, lavish rights of education, habilitation, accessibility, and employment opportunity. Since the 1970s federal laws have explicitly granted some of those rights. Will these laws render obsolete any discussion of the constitutional rights of the disabled? The Supreme Court's construction of three laws does not indicate that obsolescence is at hand. Each of these laws has a wide-open legislative history and invites various conflicting interpretations. Each decision has construed the law narrowly, reversing lower courts to weaken the law. And each case reveals a poor understanding of the scope and sources of congressional power.

The New Judicial Activism

In 1979, *Southeastern Community College* v. *Davis* ended a licensed practical nurse's efforts to get a registered nurse's training. Frances Davis had a severe hearing loss. Although she could lipread, used a hearing aid, and could hear nonverbal sounds, she had a marked difficulty in understanding speech. An LPN since 1967, she had fulfilled all requirements preparatory to clinical work in the associate degree nursing program of Southeastern Community College in North Carolina in 1973 and 1974. But the college rejected her application to the program on the basis of an audiologist's report and the opinion of the director of the state's Board of Nursing that she would threaten the safety of patients in her care.

Davis sued under Section 504. The district court upheld the college, pointing out that in many nursing situations, such as, obviously, the operating room, surgical masks are worn, and therefore lipreading is impossible.[68] By the time the case reached the Court of Appeals, it was 1978 and Joseph Califano, secretary of health, education, and welfare (HEW), had signed the regulations implementing Section 504. The appellate court interpreted these regulations to demand a ruling in Davis' favor. The decision relied on the definition of an "otherwise qualified handicapped individual" as one who "meets the requisite academic and technical standards"; the latter are defined as "all non-academic admissions criteria that are essential to participation in the

---

[68] Davis v. Southeastern Community College, 424 F. Supp. 1341 (E.D.N.C. 1976).

program in question." [69] Although it was true that Davis could not function where she could not lipread, there appeared to be a number of nursing situations in which she could perform adequately. "Thus, we hold the district court erred by considering the nature of the plaintiff's handicap in order to determine whether or not she was 'otherwise qualified' for admittance into the nursing program . . . rather than by focusing upon her academic and technical qualifications as required by the newly promulgated regulations." [70] If she met those standards, the college might have to modify the program to suit her abilities.

The Supreme Court would have none of this. Unanimously, it upheld the college and the district court. In an interpretation exactly contrary to that of the Court of Appeals, Justice Powell wrote:

> Section 504 by its terms does not compel educational institutions to disregard the disabilities of handicapped individuals or to make substantial modifications in their programs to allow disabled persons to participate. Instead, it requires only that an "otherwise qualified handicapped individual" not be excluded from participation in a federally funded program "solely by reason of his handicap," indicating *only that mere possession of a handicap is not a permissible ground for assuming an inability to function in a particular context.* . . .
> The uncontroverted testimony of several members of Southeastern's staff and faculty established that the purpose of its program was to train persons who could serve the nursing profession in all customary ways. This type of purpose, far from reflecting any animus against handicapped individuals, is shared by many if not most of the institutions that train persons to render professional service. It is undisputed that respondent could not participate in Southeastern's nursing program unless the standards were substantially lowered. Section 504 imposes no requirement upon an educational institution to lower or to effect substantial modifications of standards to accommodate a handicapped person.[71]

If that interpretation were true, of course, it would effectively keep blind and deaf applicants out of medical school, and possibly out of other professional or graduate programs as well. After all, texts are not published in Braille, nor are lectures signed; would requiring these modifications exceed the law's mandate? The Court has a point here, however. Either of these two readings of the regulations is supportable. It is just not clear what "all nonacademic criteria" means. The legislative history is not much help either, because the Rehabilitation

[69] 45 C.F.R. 84.3 (1977).
[70] Davis v. Southeastern Community College, 574 F.2d 1158, 1161 (4th Circ. 1978).
[71] 99 S. Ct. 2361, 2366–7, 2370–71. Emphasis supplied.

Act was passed with little opposition or substantive discussion.[72] And a deaf nurse does seem to present problems that a blind lawyer, for example, does not. Even though the safety argument is hard to swallow, since hospitals frequently risk patients' safety at the hands of students, interns, and residents, it is hard to envision the nurse doing her job effectively.

But what about a blind doctor? In 1972 David Hartman became the first blind medical student in recent American history. Though several schools had rejected him, Temple University—which, incidentally, is Gurmankin's alma mater—decided to admit him. The medical school's assistant dean described it as an "experiment" and said that both Hartman and the school would have to compromise. Recording for the Blind taped more than two dozen basic medical texts for Hartman. The experiment worked; he graduated in 1976 and now practices psychiatry.[73]

He did not have to sue to get into medical school, or to stay in. If he had done so—assuming that he waited until the law was passed and the regulations were signed—he almost certainly would have lost, if *Davis* is any guide. But the school was willing both to take a chance on him and to make adaptations as they became necessary. The lesson of this experiment is that no one knew whether a blind person could get through medical school until one was permitted to try. Blind medical students, like women marathon runners, could not prove they could do what there were good reasons for thinking them incapable of doing until the experts let them experiment. Likewise, we will never know whether a deaf person can become a nurse until a similar experiment is made. Theories, expert opinions, and audiologists' reports will not settle the issue.

This is the crucial point. If Section 504 is to have much force, its scope cannot be limited to situations in which handicapped people have already performed the job in question, and therefore animus or ignorance is the only possible explanation for rejection. (And it is far from obvious that generalizations about abilities are uncontaminated by prejudice; the experience of women, blacks, Jews, and numerous other groups suggests otherwise.) Some experimentation, some disregard of expert predictions, will be necessary. The Supreme Court erred in allowing preconceptions to dictate exclusion.

[72] See *Congressional Record*, 119: 5860–5901 (February 28, 1973); 7102–38 (March 8, 1973); 16665–78 (May 28, 1973).
[73] *New York Times*, May 31, 1972, p. 37; September 10, 1972, p. 34; May 28, 1976, I, p. 14. Hartman's efforts to get into medical school were the subject of a fictionalized television film, *Journey from Darkness*, first aired in 1975.

Two years later, *Pennhurst State School and Hospital v. Halderman* did to the Developmental Disabilities Act of 1975 what *Davis* had done to the Rehabilitation Act of 1973.[74] *Pennhurst* involved a confusing mixture of claims, federal and state, constitutional and statutory. The hospital that has been the focus of all this attention is an institution for the retarded in Spring City, Pennsylvania. When the case began, Pennhurst had about 1,200 residents, about half of whom were committed by their families and half by the courts. The residents' average age was thirty-six; the average stay was twenty-one years. Almost three-fourths of the residents were profoundly retarded.

Terri Lee Halderman was admitted in 1966, when she was twelve. In her eleven years at Pennhurst, she lost several teeth and broke her jaw, fingers, and a toe—no one seemed to know how—and her general condition deteriorated. She had a five-word vocabulary when she entered the hospital for training and treatment; by the time her parents removed her, she did not speak at all.

Her experience was typical for residents. The hospital was so badly understaffed that there were not enough personnel to provide therapy, training, or even safety. "The environment at Pennhurst is not only not conducive to learning new skills, but it is so poor that it contributes to losing skills already learned." In theory, adult patients who were not civilly committed were free to leave, but about half the units were locked—and to speak of someone like Terri as being "free" to leave is obvious nonsense.

The Haldermans filed a suit in federal district court which was certified as a class action on behalf of all persons who had been at Pennhurst since 1974 or might be sent there. The federal government was allowed to intervene as a plaintiff. Relying on both the Constitution and Section 504, the plaintiffs alleged that Pennhurst violated its residents' rights to habilitation and treatment.

Judge Raymond Broderick agreed. His findings of fact, which all parties accepted as correct, recounted the dangerous, unhealthy, and repressive conditions of Pennhurst, the neglect of patients, the inadequate training programs, and the physical and mental decline of many residents. He relied on *Wyatt, Donaldson,* and the Eighth and Fourteenth Amendments to conclude, "Once admitted to a state facility, the residents have a constitutional right to be provided with minimally adequate habilitation under the least restrictive conditions consistent with the purpose of the commitment," and "the Equal Protection Clause . . . prohibits the segregation of the retarded in an isolated institution

[74] 101 S.Ct. 1531 (1981).

such as Pennhurst where the habilitation provided the retarded does not meet minimally adequate standards." He also ruled that Section 504 established a statutory right to "non-discriminatory habilitation."

Broderick's order enjoined any further acts of abuse by staff, the use of seclusion, restraint, or medication as punishment or for convenience, and the administering of excessive medication. He ordered Pennhurst to keep all buildings clean, odorless, and insect-free, and to develop an individualized program plan for each resident. All of these requirements were well within the letter and spirit of *Wyatt* and *Donaldson*, but the order went even further. Broderick forbade all further admissions to Pennhurst, and ordered that the hospital eventually be closed. He set no deadline, but he did appoint a "special master" to carry out the order and to arrange for the habilitation of all patients in the least restrictive community setting possible.[75] The Court of Appeals held that the Developmental Disabilities and Bill of Rights Act "grants to the mentally retarded a right to treatment and habilitation," but reversed the part of Judge Broderick's order which required the eventual closing of Pennhurst and prohibited new admissions.[76]

The Supreme Court ruled in favor of the hospital. Writing for the majority, Justice Rehnquist denied that the law created any substantive rights for the developmentally disabled, made federal funding contingent on granting rights, or even necessarily applied to Pennhurst at all. The Court remanded the question of the existence of a private right of action under Section 6010, the respondents' claims under Section 504, and the constitutional questions.

Rehnquist's opinion emphasized the act's legislative history. He first addressed the Haldermans' argument that the law was a valid exercise of Congress' Fourteenth Amendment enforcement powers. Whether or not Congress had this power, Rehnquist argued, the real question was whether it had chosen to exercise it here. "We should not quickly attribute to Congress an unstated intent to act under its authority under the Fourteenth Amendment"—although the Court had not been inhibited from doing so in *Fullilove* v. *Klutznick* the year before. In previous cases where the Court had upheld laws under these enforcement powers, the purpose had been expressly stated. The legislative history of Section 6010 showed no such purpose. Furthermore, "The case for inferring intent is at its weakest where, as here, the rights asserted impose *affirmative* obligations on the States to fund certain

[75] Halderman v. Pennhurst State School and Hospital, 446 F. Supp. 1295, 1302–12, 1319, 1323, 1326–29 (1977).
[76] Halderman v. Pennhurst State School and Hospital, 612 F. 2d 84, 97, 112–16 (3d Circ. 1979).

services, since we may assume that Congress will not implicitly attempt to impose massive financial obligations on the States." [77]

Rehnquist then turned to the spending power, the basis of the federal government's case. He had no difficulty accepting either the notion that this was the power the Ninety-fourth Congress thought it was using or that idea "that Congress may fix the terms on which it will disburse federal money to the States." The question here, however, was "whether Congress . . . imposed an obligation on the States to spend state money to fund certain rights as a condition of receiving federal moneys under the Act or whether it spoke merely in precatory terms." The opinion chose the latter interpretation. The act was not a bill of rights but "a mere federal-state funding statute"; the references to rights were "scattered" and "incidental." [78]

As the Court saw this case, it had little to do with the disabled and much to do with legislative intent and federalism. The majority implicitly conceded that both the spending power and the Fourteenth Amendment give Congress the power to do what the plaintiffs argue the act has done. But the justices balked at concluding that Congress really intended to secure rights for the developmentally disabled or to exert so much control over the states. Every possible presumption is entertained in favor of congressional circumspection and state autonomy.

Board of Education v. *Rowley* continued the trend.[79] The issue was whether 94–142's requirement of a "free appropriate public education" gave ten-year-old Amy Rowley the right to have a sign-language interpreter assigned to her in school. Amy, like her parents, was deaf, but she had some residual hearing. Her parents had trained her in "total communication," a method that includes mouthing words, lip-reading, signing, touching, and hearing aids. When Amy reached school age, her parents had met with school administrators in Westchester County, New York, as the federal law requires, to develop an individual education plan for her.

They decided to place Amy in a regular kindergarten class at Furnace Woods School in Peekskill. She got a hearing aid and, briefly, an interpreter, but he reported that he was not needed. In the first grade, Amy was also given a tutor and speech therapy. The school denied the Rowleys' persistent requests for an interpreter. The parents took their

[77] Pennhurst State School and Hospital v. Halderman, 101 S.Ct. 1531, 1538–45, 1539. Emphasis in the original. The previous cases cited included Katzenbach v. Morgan, 384 U.S. 641 (1966); Oregon v. Mitchell, 400 U.S. 112 (1970). Cf. Slaughter-House Cases, 83, U.S. 36 (1872); Plessy v. Ferguson, 163 U.S. 537 (1896).
[78] 101 S.Ct. 1531, 1539–40.
[79] 50 U.S.L.W. 4925 (1982).

case to a hearing examiner, to the New York State Commissioner for Education, and finally to the federal courts. Meanwhile, Amy stayed with her class at Furnace Woods. Although she understood only about 60 percent of what was said in class, her class performance was above average.[80]

The district court ruled in Amy's favor. The judge's treatment of the case was sensitive and humane. Amy was getting an adequate education, he ruled, but that did not mean that she was learning as much as she would were she not deaf. Perhaps, he surmised, she could do better, both academically and socially, if less of her energy were channeled into compensating for her handicap.

> An "appropriate education" could mean an "adequate education"—that is, an education substantial enough to facilitate a child's progress from one grade to another and to enable him or her to earn a high school diploma. An "appropriate education" could also mean one which enables the handicapped child to achieve his or her full potential. Between these two extremes, however, is a standard which I conclude is more in keeping with the regulations and with the Equal Protection decisions which motivated the passage of the Act, and with common sense. This standard would require that each handicapped child be given an opportunity to achieve his or her full potential commensurate with the opportunity provided to other children.[81]

Again the Supreme Court chose state power over federal, narrow construction over broad. For the majority, Rehnquist wrote, "Noticeably absent from the language of the statute is any substantive standard prescribing the level of education to be accorded handicapped children." Rehnquist found support in the legislative history for a minimal construction of 94–142; he stressed Congress' concern in 1975 for children denied any education. "We conclude that the 'basic floor of opportunity' provided by the Act consists of access to specialized instruction and related services which are individually designed to provide educational benefit to the handicapped child." Amy's success indicated that she had received the required benefits. Justice Blackmun chided the lower courts for their lack of respect for the state officials' judgment.[82]

Rowley, like *Pennhurst*, reflects a view of federal-state relations that

---

[80] Rowley v. Board of Education, 483 F. Supp. 528, 530–32 (S.D.N.Y. 1980); affirmed, 632 F. 2d 947 (2d Circ. 1980).
[81] 483 F. Supp. 528, 534–36.
[82] 50 U.S.L.W. 4925, 4929, 4932, 4934–35. The interior quote is from H.R. no. 94–332, p. 14.

has ominous overtones. With little guidance from statutory language or legislative history, the Court prefers constructions that give wide discretion to the states. This new brand of judicial activism seems to ignore what one had thought was the established principle of federal supremacy.

None of these opinions suggests that Congress *lacks* the power to regulate the states' treatment of the disabled. Rehnquist concedes in *Pennhurst* that the spending power and the Fourteenth Amendment gave Congress all it needed. The spending power also suffices with respect to 94–142 and Section 504 of the Rehabilitation Act. What has troubled the Court is an uncertainty about how much of its power Congress intended to use in enacting these laws, an uncertainty that neither language nor history allays. *Pennhurst* has an incredulous tone reminiscent of *Slaughter-House* and *Plessy*. Surely Congress would let us know if it meant to use its Fourteenth Amendment powers; surely Congress should not be presumed to require the states actually to spend money; surely Congress would say so unambiguously if it meant to enact a bill of rights for the disabled. The Court presumes similar congressional timidity in *Davis* and *Rowley*. But nothing in the Constitution, the laws, or any other authority dictates such timidity.

There is no reason to presume that Congress will always label a law as an exercise of a particular power. Nor is there reason to presume, in general, that Congress will hesitate to direct the states, or, in particular, that Congress will hesitate to use the Fourteenth Amendment to direct the states. Therefore, in construing this kind of law, the Court has no reason to give maximum autonomy to the states and to attribute minimum initiative to Congress. Indeed, since the Constitution explicitly grants broad powers to the national government and leaves to the states what is left over, there is good reason to prefer the opposite kind of interpretation.

In each of these cases, there are good reasons to read the laws as upholding the claims of the disabled parties. In *Davis*, a broad reading of Section 504 was necessary to allow the disabled to compete for jobs; in *Pennhurst*, a broad reading of the Developmental Disabilities Act was necessary to end warehousing; in *Rowley*, a broad reading of 94–142 was necessary to allow a schoolchild to become a full participant in classroom activity. In each case, the Supreme Court needlessly weakened a law that was a legitimate exercise of congressional power.

Indeed, the power to help the disabled goes beyond what Congress has claimed and the Court has conceded. The education and employment laws need not have rested on the spending power, and need not have been limited to programs that receive federal funds. Section 5 of the Fourteenth Amendment grants Congress more power than it has exercised.

Such an interpretation of Section 5 follows from my broad interpretation of Section 1, but would be compatible with narrower readings. One could reasonably conclude that Section 5 gives Congress more power than Section 1 gives the courts. Although Justice Rehnquist has argued that the courts should limit the application of the equal-protection clause to "classifications based on race or on national origin, the first cousin of race," this position does not compel the conclusion that Congress should so limit Section 5.[83] But it would be difficult to justify interpreting Section 5 more *narrowly* than Section 1.

I have argued for a generous interpretation of the Fourteenth Amendment, an interpretation that recognizes many rights for the disabled. Acceptance of Congress' power under Section 5 does not require such an interpretation. But if the Constitution allows the courts to accept the claims to habilitation, accessibility, and employment opportunity, then the Constitution allows Congress to legislate to secure those claims. A broad construction of congressional power follows from a broad construction of individual rights. The Rehabilitation Act of 1973 and the Education Act of 1975 are "appropriate legislation" within the scope of Section 5 of the Fourteenth Amendment.

And these laws do not exhaust that power. The Constitution grants ample legislative and judicial powers to help disabled people become full citizens. If legislative inaction and judicial action instead help keep the disabled in the attic, it will be because government has chosen to do so.

[83] Trimble v. Gordon, 430 U.S. 762, 777 (1977).

[9]

Gay Rights and the Courts

The disability rights movement and the struggle for the rights of homosexuals have more in common than the fact that both emerged in the 1970s.[1] One similarity is revealed by a metaphor used earlier: "Society has isolated the disabled by keeping them in the attic instead of the closet."[2] Both groups have been excluded from community life, and among the factors that keep them isolated are ignorance, fear, and prejudice.

But the limits, and the dangers, of this comparison become clear when we look at some of the uses to which it has been put. The first set of regulations proposed by HEW to implement the 1973 Rehabilitation Act included homosexuality among the handicaps covered by the law.[3] This is the sort of labeling gay activists fight against, and with good reason. To include homosexuals among the handicapped is to say that there is something wrong with them, to imply that homosexuality is like blindness, alcoholism, or drug addiction.

That is what society has traditionally believed about homosexuality. Whether it is called evil or sick, it has been considered wrong. Since colonial times, homosexual activities have been crimes in this country; in some places they still are. For many years, the psychotherapeutic profession viewed homosexuality as a disorder. The American Psychi-

[1] I define "homosexual" as dictionaries typically do: "having erotic desire towards, or sexual relations with, a member of one's own sex." "Lesbian" refers to a female homosexual. I use the words "homosexual" and "gay" interchangeably.

[2] Isbell, "Potomac Fever," p. 64.

[3] See *Federal Register*, 41, p. 20296 (May 17, 1976):29548–49 (July 16, 1976). For the final version, see 45 C.F.R. 85.31 (1977).

atric Association so classified it until 1973; the group's decision to declassify it met strong internal opposition.[4]

Since homosexuality has been labeled criminal, sick, or both, homosexuals have been forced to do something that few minority group members can do: to conceal their difference and thus to hide part of their identities from the rest of society. It is primarily neglect that has kept the disabled in the attic. Social attitudes have helped (and have, of course, contributed to the neglect), but they have not been the major cause. For homosexuals, the situation has been just the opposite. There is no reason to believe that homosexuality itself would ever have kept anyone from full participation in society. The literature and the cases leave the impression that there need never have been a problem, that society created one for itself. Replacing the old labels with a new one, "handicapped," would be not a solution to the problem, but another manifestation of it.

These statements may seem large, but, as I shall argue, they are in fact narrow and cautious. One factor that makes them seem bold and provocative is the backlash to the American gay rights movement. We have been told that homosexuals *are* bad, sick, or defective; that they are a threat to family life; that they will corrupt the young; and that their integration into our society may destroy it. These opinions are held and expressed with such passion that they draw much attention. To claim that we lack reliable evidence that homosexuals endanger society or require its help seems to be an extravagant assertion when in fact it is only a negative one.

The fact is that we know relatively little about homosexuality. Anecdotes, rumors, and theories abound, but knowledge is scant. One reason for this ignorance is that homosexuality has been hidden. While the current gay rights slogan, "We are everywhere," may be an accurate statement, the idea startles most heterosexuals. People whom society stigmatizes are unlikely to be forthcoming with information, especially about the very characteristic for which they are branded.

But that is not the whole story. Another reason we have little reliable information (i.e., knowledge that can be tested rigorously) about homosexuality is that we have little reliable information about sexuality in general. Perhaps this ignorance is inevitable. Not only is sex research a young science—Alfred Kinsey and his associates, working thirty-five years ago, were pioneers—but sex is not a subject that in-

[4]See Boyce Rosenberger, "Psychiatrists Review Stand on Homosexuals," *New York Times*, February 9, 1973, p. 24; "Doctors Urged Not to Call Homosexuality an Illness," ibid., May 19, 1973, p. 20; "The Issue Is Subtle, But the Debate Still On," ibid., December 23, 1973, IV, p. 5.

vites careful, disciplined research and calm, detached thought. Even when scientists do study sexual behavior in this way, their findings rarely meet with the rational, disinterested response that is necessary for further advances in knowledge.

Whatever the sources of this ignorance, its result is that the only kind of statement that can fairly be made about homosexuality is the kind I made earlier: that evidence is lacking. If no one can assert categorically that homosexuality is a disorder, neither can anyone assert the contrary. But it is not clear why that should matter. Proof of mental health or moral rectitude has rarely been a condition of exercising individual rights. Questions about the nature of homosexuality should be separated from questions about law and public policy.

This argument has been made by writers who are far from complete agreement with gay activists. William Safire, for example, wrote in 1974 that although in his view homosexuality is abnormal and should be discouraged, we should not try to coerce or restrict homosexuals in any way: "If society does not like what it sees, society should remove its eye from the keyhole." Similarly, a Roman Catholic theologian criticized those who reason from "the obvious: Homosexuality is a poor substitute for heterosexuality in that it cannot produce offspring" to "the astounding . . . [that] homosexuality is an illness, a sin, a crime." [5] So even these writers do not conclude that the law must be restrictive.

Anyone who tries to write sensibly about this issue confronts conceptual as well as empirical problems. All the talk about whether homosexuality is a sickness, whether it is evil, or whether it harms society uses some imprecise and inexact concepts. The controversy over whether homosexuality should be termed a handicap is a case in point. As early as 1905, Sigmund Freud observed that "inversion is found in people who exhibit no other serious deviations from the normal," [6] and while this is still true, inversion is also found in people who do, and some of Freud's successors have seen what they wanted to see. The HEW regulations on Section 504 define "handicap" as "a condition . . . limiting one or more major life functions." If one defines heterosexual intercourse and/or reproduction among the major life functions, what happens?

This confusion is mild compared to what we confront in discussions

---

[5] Safire, "Don't Slam the Closet Door," ibid., April 18, 1974, p. 41; Michael F. Valente, "On Homosexuality," ibid., January 14, 1975, p. 33.
[6] *Three Essays on the Theory of Sexuality* (1905), trans. James Strachey (New York: Avon Books, 1962), p. 25.

of the effect homosexuality has on society. This excerpt from a law review article is typical:

> The state concern, in our view, should not be minimized. . . . Family life has been a central unifying experience throughout American society. Preserving the strength of this basic, organic unit is a central and legitimate end of the police power. The state ought to be concerned that if allegiance to traditional family arrangements declines, society as a whole may well suffer. . . . The question . . . is a difficult one: should the state be constitutionally required to abandon an ancient sanction, when abandonment might in time lead to increasing, though statistically unpredictable, defections from heterosexual behavior and traditional family life?[7]

This passage recalls the famous law-and-morals controversy that engaged jurists in the years following the publication of the Wolfenden Report, an event whose effects on English jurisprudence were comparable to those of *Brown* v. *Board of Education* in the United States. In 1957 a Committee on Homosexual Offences and Prostitution, chaired by Lord Wolfenden, recommended to the government "that homosexual behavior between consenting adults in private should no longer be a criminal offence." The report's underlying philosophy was diametrically opposed to the passage just cited. The function of the criminal law, it declared,

> is to preserve public order and decency, to protect the citizen from what is offensive or injurious, and to provide sufficient safeguards against exploitation and corruption of others. . . . Unless a deliberate attempt is to be made by society, acting through the agency of law, to equate the sphere of crime with that of sin, there must remain a realm of private morality and immorality which is, in brief and crude terms, not the law's business.[8]

The recommendations did not become law until 1966. Meanwhile, scholars debated the issues. The principal antagonists were Lord Devlin, a former high court judge, who opposed the reforms, and H. L. A. Hart, professor of jurisprudence at Oxford, who supported them. For Devlin,

> what makes a society of any sort is a community of ideas, not only political ideas but also ideas about the ways its members should behave and govern their lives; the latter ideas are its morals. . . . The structure

---

[7] J. Harvie Wilkinson III and G. Edward White, "Constitutional Protection for Personal Lifestyles," *Cornell Law Review* 62 (March 1977):595–96.

[8] *Report of the Committee on Homosexual Offences and Prostitution* (London: H.M.S.O., 1957), para. 61–62.

of every society is made up of both politics and morals. Take, for example, the institution of marriage. Whether a man should be allowed to take more than one wife is something about which every society has to make up its mind one way or another. In England we believe in the Christian idea of marriage and therefore adopt monogamy as a moral principle. Consequently the Christian institution of marriage has become the basis of family life and so part of the structure of our society. It is there not because it is Christian. It has got there because it is Christian, but it remains there because it is built into the house in which we live, and could not be removed without bringing it down.[9]

Devlin presents a general thesis, of which the law review article is a particular version. Devlin asserts that shared morals are crucial to any society; he is not concerned with what those morals are.[10] The article insists that our political community of ideas includes a commitment to family life, and that weakening this commitment would harm our society.

Now, what does all this mean? If these writers are claiming that neither England nor America can survive unless monogamous marriage and family life are the norm, they are guilty of gratuitous speculation. H. L. A. Hart likens this view to the emperor Justinian's belief that homosexuality caused earthquakes. He adds, "There is . . . no evidence to support, and much to refute, the theory that those who deviate from conventional sexual morality are in other ways hostile to society."[11]

But anyone who is familiar with this debate will suspect that that is not the authors' meaning. Whether, and to what extent, society depends on the family is not so much an empirical question as an analytical one. Hart speaks to this point. Lord Devlin, he writes,

appears to move from the acceptable proposition that *some* shared morality is essential to the existence of any society to the unacceptable proposition that a society is identical with its morality as that is at any given moment of its history, so that a change in its morality is tantamount to the destruction of society. The former proposition might be even accepted as a necessary rather than an empirical truth depending on a quite plausible definition of a society as a body of men who hold certain moral views in common. But the latter proposition is absurd. Taken strictly, it would prevent us saying that the morality of a given society had changed, and would compel us instead to say that one society had disappeared and another one taken its place. But it is only on this absurd criterion of

[9] *The Enforcement of Morals* (New York: Oxford University Press, 1959), p. 9.
[10] For criticism of this argument, see Harry M. Clor, *Obscenity and Public Morality* (Chicago: University of Chicago Press, 1969), chap. 5.
[11] *Law, Liberty, and Morality* (New York: Oxford University Press, 1963), p. 51.

what it is for the same society to continue to exist that it could be asserted without evidence that any deviation from a society's shared morality threatens its existence.[12]

The family is viewed as a large part of what society is, and if the
family were to change or be replaced, society would be changed. If
that is true, to say that society depends on the family is tautology. I
think it is true beyond question that a society where homosexuality
was accepted behavior, in which the estimated 10 percent were openly
gay, would be significantly different from the society in which we now
live. Homosexuals would be as visible to the general population as
blacks now are to the white majority. Since that integration occurred
within the lifetimes of most of us, we know how great a change it was.
If the same thing happens with homosexuals, society will have changed,
but it will not necessarily have suffered. That line of argument gives
no justification for prohibiting or discouraging activity that may lead
to social change. Once we clarify just what we are talking about here,
the substance of Devlin's argument turns out to be negligible.

All this debate over law and morals may seem obsolescent now.
Homosexual relations between consenting adults are no longer criminal in England, while in the United States the Supreme Court read the
substance of Lord Wolfenden's theory into the Constitution and then
used it to legalize abortion.[13] On the surface, Wolfenden and Hart
seem to have won, and jurisprudence has gone on to other controversies. For the United States, at least, these impressions are incorrect.
The quoted article was written in 1977, long after Devlin and Hart
had retired from the debate. And homosexual activity is still the law's
business. It has not been included within the "zone of privacy" that
protects heterosexual activity and its consequences. The Supreme Court
has refused even to consider this question. In 1976, in an action that
Gerald Gunther called "irresponsible" and "lawless," the Court let
stand two state laws forbidding private, consensual sodomy.[14] Far from
being a dead issue, legal enforcement of sexual morality is flourishing.

Even where private sexual conduct is not regulated by law, and in
the rather larger number of states where the laws are not enforced,
homosexuals are singled out for other kinds of unequal treatment.

---

[12] Ibid., pp. 51–52. Emphasis in the original.
[13] Griswold v. Connecticut, 381 U.S. 479 (1965); Roe v. Wade, 410 U.S. 113 (1973).
[14] Griswold v. Connecticut, 381 U.S. 479, 485; Doe v. Commonwealth's Attorney for
City of Richmond, 403 F. Supp. 1199 (E.D. Va. 1975), affirmed, 425 U.S. 903 (1976);
Enslin v. North Carolina, 214 S.E. 2d 318 (N.C. Court of Appeals 1975), 425 U.S. 903.
The Gunther quote is from Anthony Lewis, "No Process of Law," *New York Times*,
April 8, 1976, p. 37.

These discriminatory actions are many and varied, but, in addition to laws against homosexual conduct, two such actions raise major constitutional questions: restrictions on rights of association and discrimination in employment.

I have argued that the claims for compensatory discrimination and equal treatment of the young, the aged, and the handicapped fall outside established constitutional categories, and that recognition of these claims requires a fundamental, though legitimate, reinterpretation along the lines I have suggested. With respect to sexual orientation, I doubt that such reinterpretation is needed. The real problem is that the traditional doctrines are being misused. Homosexuals are denied fundamental rights that all other citizens have; they receive unequal treatment on grounds that would be illegitimate for anyone else. The usefulness of the new interpretation is that it would make the abuse easier to recognize and harder to justify.

The right of association has been held to be inseparable from and integral to First Amendment freedoms of expression.[15] Yet whether or not gay activists are allowed to organize on a state university campus depends on the judicial district in which they happen to be. Three cases have established a right of privacy, derived from several provisions of the Bill of Rights, which protects private consensual heterosexual relations from state interference.[16] The courts have refused, on nonexistent grounds, to extend this right to homosexuals. Employment presents a more difficult problem because a job is not considered a fundamental right, but even here discrimination must satisfy equal-protection tests. If sexual orientation were a suspect classification, such laws could not stand.

Are homosexuals an isolated minority, saddled with disabilities? To an extent, they obviously are, but even recognized homosexuals have enjoyed the basic political rights long denied to blacks and women and still denied to children. Individual homosexuals, perhaps many of them, have gained power and influence. We do not know how many or how much because homosexuality has been hidden. The "closet" phenomenon complicates the whole subject. Perhaps this fact itself shows that homosexuals have been stigmatized.[17] At present, homosexuality is a stigma in the sense defined in Chapter 6. If laws affecting homosexuals stigmatize in Brennan's sense of being premised on inferiority or enacting hatred and separation, they are invalid according

[15] The leading case is NAACP v. Alabama, 357 U.S. 449 (1958).
[16] See n. 13 above and Eisenstadt v. Baird, 405 U.S. 438 (1972).
[17] See Gay Law Students v. Pacific Telephone and Telegraph, 595 P. 2d 592, 610 (Cal. Sup.Ct. 1979).

to the test. But that was a minority opinion, and stigmas are not among Justice Powell's traditional indicia of suspectness.

How does the alternative doctrine of suspect classification, that of Brennan in *Frontiero*, apply to homosexuals? There is expert opinion that sexual orientation is indeed an immutable characteristic, whether or not it is determined at birth.[18] But these are the sorts of theories that one contrary case suffices to weaken, if not to refute, and there have always been enough reports of counterexamples to call this opinion into question.[19] There is even reason to doubt that all people are exclusively either homosexual or heterosexual. After all, Plato's *Dialogues* present men who had male lovers and were also husbands and fathers; and at present there are enough lesbians who are mothers to suggest that sexual orientation may be neither constant nor absolute. To make things still more confusing, there is the theory advanced by Sigmund Freud, and widely accepted, that all people go through a homosexual stage as their sexual identity develops.[20] These are questions to which no definite answer is possible.

But, as Chapter 6 showed, even to write in this way raises still thornier problems. I argued there that to say that race is something a person "cannot help," which is what the "immutable characteristics" thesis amounts to, has different connotations for racial minorities than for the white majority. The statement that X cannot help being black does not startle, but the statement that Y cannot help being white does. When either is compared to equivalent statements about other groups, something strikes us as wrong. To say that Z cannot help being disabled makes sense. But is it quite the same thing to make this sort of statement about X's blackness or A's femaleness or B's homosexuality? An undertone of "poor thing" is barely discernible. Do these statements not imply that these are things a person would change if she could? Are we comfortable with that implication?

Chapter 8 has already questioned the relationship between this component of the *Frontiero* test and the second: the lack of relationship between characteristic and ability. That segment of the test would usually provide a strong argument for the rights of homosexuals. With some *apparent* exceptions, which I shall examine, the relationship is not present. But if the first half of the rule is useless, the second cannot help much. It is time now to turn to the cases themselves.

---

[18] See, e.g., Freud, *Three Essays*; Arno Karlen, *Sexuality and Homosexuality* (New York: W. W. Norton, 1957).

[19] See, e.g., Irving Bieber, *Homosexuality: A Psychanalytic Study* (New York: Basic Books, 1962); William H. Masters and Virginia E. Johnson, *Homosexuality in Perspective* (Boston: Little, Brown, 1979).

[20] *Three Essays.*

The Law of Sexual Conduct

By tradition, though not by Constitution, sexual morality has been the concern of the states. As part of their police power, states have often prescribed in minute detail who may not do what, with which, and to whom. Some states forbade any sexual relations except between spouses, and some went so far as to restrict spouses' choices of activity. These laws were rarely enforced, but often the threat of exposure and sanction has been very real. It forced many people into a half-ghettoized existence. Many such laws have been repealed or modified, some have been invalidated by courts, and arrests and prosecutions are even less frequent than they once were, but the state has not ceased to be involved with our intimate lives.

Such interference was a common topic for discussion in the 1960s and 1970s. That discussion often borrowed a phrase from the Wolfenden report to delimit what are conceded to be the legitimate areas of state concern. The phrase "in private between consenting adults" refers to activity considered to be beyond the state's power, but, by exclusion, it also includes. Even the most permissive recognize the government's power to protect the public from unwelcome displays, to prevent coercion, and to safeguard the young and vulnerable. The Wolfenden Report reflected a growing consensus that sexual behavior outside that realm was a matter for individual rather than governmental choice, and since that time ever larger numbers of people have come to agree.

The Supreme Court came close to, but has shied away from, giving these principles constitutional status. In 1965 it ruled that the Constitution established a right of privacy. *Griswold* v. *Connecticut* was far more important for this general principle than for its specific ruling. It overturned a statute prohibiting the use of contraceptives. With the limited exceptions of clinics and vending machines, the law had rarely been enforced. The Court used this issue to recognize a right established by "penumbras, formed by emanations" from the Bill of Rights.

Various guarantees create zones of privacy. The right of association contained in the First Amendment is one. . . . The Third Amendment in its prohibition against the quartering of soldiers . . . is another facet of that privacy. The Fourth Amendment explicitly affirms the "right of the people to be secure in their persons, houses, papers, and effects, against unreasonable searches and seizures." The Fifth Amendment in its Self-Incrimination Clause enables the citizen to create a zone of privacy which the government may not force him to surrender to his detriment. The Ninth Amendment provides: "The enumeration in the Constitution, of

233

certain rights, shall not be construed to deny or disparage others retained by the people."

. . . We have had many controversies over these penumbral rights of privacy and repose. . . . These cases bear witness that the right of privacy which presses for recognition here is a legitimate one.

The present case, then, concerns a relationship lying within the zone of privacy created by several fundamental constitutional guarantees.

. . . We deal with a right of privacy older than the Bill of Rights. . . . Marriage . . . is an association for as noble a purpose as any involved in our prior decisions.[21]

Few were prepared to dispute the Court about the use of contraceptives by married couples. But no one was sure what other interests would fall within that zone. *Eisenstadt* v. *Baird* effectively granted similar freedom to the unmarried. "If the right of privacy means anything, it is the right of the *individual*, whether married or single, to be free from unwarranted governmental intrusion into matters so fundamentally affecting a person as the decision whether to bear or beget a child."[22] Then, in 1973, the Court ruled that this right included a limited right to an elective abortion.

In a line of decisions . . . the Court has recognized that a right of personal privacy, or a guarantee of certain areas or zones of privacy, does exist under the Constitution. . . . These decisions make it clear that only personal rights that can be deemed "fundamental" or "implicit in the concept of ordered liberty" are included in this guarantee of personal privacy. They also make it clear that the right has some extension to activities relating to marriage, procreation, contraception, family relationships, and child rearing and education.

This right of privacy . . . is broad enough to encompass a woman's decision whether or not to terminate her pregnancy. The detriment that the State would impose upon the pregnant woman by denying this choice altogether is apparent.[23]

Roe v. *Wade* provoked an angry controversy that increasingly threatens to dominate American politics. That in itself is no criticism of the decision; after all, the same could have been said of *Brown*. But it is hard to agree that the abortion question is quite so simple as the Court found it. To put it mildly, the opinion could have been better reasoned. So could the *Griswold* opinion, on which it relies.

But an argument that homosexual conduct lies within the zone of privacy does not need to defend legalized abortion. And whether or

[21] 381 U.S. 479, 484.
[22] 405 U.S. 438, 453. Emphasis in the original.
[23] Roe v. Wade, 410 U.S. 113, 152–53.

not the privacy cases were rightly decided, they are binding precedents, and judges must either follow them, distinguish them, or reject
them. In the instant case, a federal district court made a poor effort at
the second of these tasks. The Supreme Court shirked all three of them.

The pseudonymous plaintiff in *Doe v. Commonwealth's Attorney*,
a male homosexual, sought a declaratory judgment against Virginia's
sodomy law, which made it a felony, punishable by one to three years'
imprisonment, to "carnally know, in any matter . . . any brute animal
. . . or any male or female person by the anus or by or with the mouth."
Doe argued that the law was unconstitutional as applied to his private, consensual relationships with other men. His claim was brushed
aside with a masterful display of judicial imperium. Two of the three
judges who heard the case managed to ignore the last ten years of case
law. They stopped at 1965: "In *Griswold* . . . the ruling was put on
the right of marital privacy—held to be one of the specific guarantees
of the Bill of Rights—and was also put on the home and family." After
nearly a page of quotations, they declared:

> With no authoritative judicial bar to the proscription of homosexual-
> ity—since it is obviously no portion of marriage, home, or family life—
> the next question is whether there is any ground for barring Virginia
> from branding it as criminal. If a state determines that punishment there-
> fore, even when committed in the home, is appropriate in the promotion
> of morality and decency it is not for the courts to say that the State is
> not free to do so.

Eisenstadt and *Roe* had made it clear that the right of privacy was
not limited to marital relationships—that, in fact, it belonged to individuals—but the judges dealt with these cases by ignoring them. In
dissent, Judge Robert Merhige argued:

> The Supreme Court has consistently held that the Due Process Clause of
> the Fourteenth Amendment protects the right of individuals to make
> personal choices unfettered by arbitrary and purposeless restraints, in
> the private matters of marriage and procreation. . . . A mature individ-
> ual's choice of a sexual partner, in the privacy of his or her own home,
> would appear to me to be a decision of the utmost private and intimate
> concern. Private consensual sex acts between adults are matters, absent
> evidence that they are harmful, in which the state has no legitimate in-
> terest.[24]

There is another reason that the distinction between marital and
homosexual relationships is unacceptable. The only thing that pre-

[24] 403 F. Supp. 1199–1203.

vents homosexuals from marrying is the law itself. The only fixed, natural difference between heterosexual and homosexual liaisons is that the latter cannot produce children, but children are not a necessary component of marriage. The distinctions of which *Doe* makes so much are artificially created, imposed by the same legal system that now uses them to curtail individual rights.

But suppose the court had been more honest in its use of precedent, and had deemphasized legal distinctions? Is it possible to make a valid argument that heterosexual activity should be protected while homosexual activity should not be? Judge Merhige alludes to the lack of evidence that homosexual acts are harmful, but that is an invitation down a blind alley. The decision that an individual interest is to be ranked as a constitutional right does not depend on its harmlessness. In this context, it depends on whether the interest is personal and intimate. If we rank sexual behavior up there with, say, freedom of expression and religion as a fundamental right, evidence that it can cause harm is not enough by itself to justify abridging the freedom. As *Roe* stated more than once, what is needed is a "compelling state interest" that demands restriction of the right.[25]

Eisenstadt, Roe, and many of the cases cited in *Griswold* refer, again and again, not to marriage and the family but to individual rights. What these decisions protect is the right of human beings to govern the private spheres of their lives. Their choices in marriage and family life are among those activities, but they are not the only ones that belong to the private sphere. Those cases, and the penumbras of the Bill of Rights which give guarantees life and substance, suggest no ground for a distinction based on sexual preference.

Therefore, homosexual relationships, too, are within the zone of privacy. They belong to the upper tier of individual rights, and can be infringed only on a compelling state interest. None of the arguments about the effect of homosexuality on society and on the family even approaches this rigorous standard.

There is no reason to believe that anyone who considered the issue in the light of all the major relevant precedents would ever have thought otherwise. But the Supreme Court was no more ready to do so than the lower court had been. The justices upheld the lower court without opinion in *Doe,* and also in a North Carolina case that had resulted in an actual conviction.[26] Whether this action was due to judicial homophobia, to the efforts of justices with definite opinions to avoid

[25] 410 U.S. 113, 155 (1973).
[26] See n. 14.

the wrong result if their colleagues got hold of this case, or any other factor, it shows a laxity about lower court adjudication which is, to say the least, uncharacteristic.[27] Whatever the reasons, the results are that homosexuals do not have equal rights of privacy. And neither they, the citizens most concerned, nor we, the students of constitutional law, have heard a respectable defense of this ruling.

Homosexuals and the First Amendment

The homosexual rights movement has one important characteristic in common with most contemporary social movements. The college or university campus has often been the locus of activism. Like Students for a Democratic Society, the Young Democrats, or the Young Americans for Freedom, gay student groups have sought to form campus organizations. Most universities have formal procedures that groups must follow in order to use campus facilities, hold meetings and functions, and advertise on campus. These procedures typically include application to some university authority—a committee, a dean, the president, or the trustees—which has the power, sometimes subject to review, to accept or reject the application. Rejections do occur, and they have produced some lawsuits. A 1972 Supreme Court decision established that First Amendment rights of association apply to organizations on state campuses. So far, with one exception, federal courts of appeals have followed this precedent with respect to gay activist groups. But the district courts have not been consistent, and two Supreme Court justices have extended what amounts to an invitation to the circuits to rule against the groups.

The precedent is *Healy* v. *James*.[28] In the fall of 1969, some students had organized an SDS chapter at Central Connecticut State College. They had asked the Student Affairs Committee, consisting of four students, three faculty members, and a dean, for official recognition. The committee approved, but the president rejected the application on the grounds that SDS's "published aims and philosophy, which include disruption and violence, are contrary to the approved policy" of the college.[29] The students brought suit, and three years later—by which

---

[27] See Rhonda R. Rivera, "Our Strait-Laced Judges: The Legal Position of Homosexual Persons in the United States," *Hastings Law Review* 30 (March 1979):799–955; Morton Mintz, "The Supreme Court: Remaining Silent on Homosexuals' Rights," *Washington Post*, December 11, 1979, p. A3.

[28] 408 U.S. 169, 92 S.Ct. 2338 (1972).

[29] 92 S.Ct. 2338, 2343, n. 4.

time at least some of the original plaintiffs had presumably graduated—the Supreme Court voted unanimously to remand the case. It
ruled that the administration bore, and had not met, the burden of
proof that SDS would be likely to produce violence and infringe the
rights of others. In support of the ruling, Justice Powell had some
venerable precedents to cite, including *Tinker*, *Shelton* v. *Tucker*, and
NAACP v. *Alabama*.[30]

One would assume that what applied to SDS would also apply to
homosexual groups. But that turned out to be a chancy proposition
at best. Even when courts have felt bound by *Healy*, university officials have not; and even when universities have followed precedents,
higher officials have caused problems.

The first case was *Wood* v. *Davison*, just six months after *Healy*.
The University of Georgia had forbidden a Committee on Gay Education to hold a conference and dance. In the absence of any evidence
that illegal or disruptive activity would result, the judge ruled that
Healy was controlling.[31] The next decision, *Gay Students' Organization* v. *Bonner*, got wide publicity, at least in New Hampshire, whose
state university had given the GSO official recognition in May 1973.
In November the group sponsored a dance on campus, an event that
attracted media coverage. Governor Meldrim Thompson, Jr., publicly
criticized the university for allowing this dance.

The Board of Trustees responded to Thompson's statement by forbidding GSO to hold a party scheduled for December, but it was allowed to present a play on the same evening. Two "extremist homosexual publications" were distributed at the play; the GSO claimed it
had nothing to do with them, but some witnesses disputed this statement. A week later, Thompson wrote an "open letter" to the trustees,
stating that "indecency and moral filth will no longer be allowed on
our campuses. . . . Either you take firm, fair, and positive action to rid
your campuses of socially abhorrent activities or I, as governor, will
stand solidly against the expenditure of one more cent of taxpayers'
money for your institutions." UNH's president, Thomas Bonner, then
issued a statement condemning the distribution of the literature, ordering an investigation, and tightening restrictions on GSO activities.
The group sued in federal district court, alleging violations of its First
and Fourteenth Amendment rights.

Within a month, Judge Hugh Bownes sustained the group's claims.
Relying on *Healy* and *Wood*, Bownes ruled that the ban on social

[30] 393 U.S. 503 (1969); 364 U.S. 479 (1960); 357 U.S. 449 (1958).
[31] 351 F. Supp. 543 (N.D. Ga. 1972).

functions alone, even apart from the ban on "more traditional First Amendment rights" to distribute literature, infringed these rights. "Support for this position lies in the pervasive importance of social functions in the university setting." Turning to the Fourteenth Amendment claim, the judge remarked, "Although the students' rights cases have developed along First Amendment lines, many have involved, almost *sub silentio*, Equal Protection underpinnings." The denial to homosexuals of rights enjoyed by other groups constituted "differential treatment [that] must rationally further some legitimate interest." That is rather mild, but in fact, no such interest was involved here. There was no evidence of any violations of law or other disruptive activity. In December the Court of Appeals unanimously upheld Judge Bownes. The state did not persist.[32]

Thompson made himself an easy target. Such an extreme reaction has been the exception. On many campuses, homosexual organizations have been granted the rights enjoyed by other groups without opposition or incident. The denials that have occurred have rested, as we shall see, on fears of illegal or harmful activity. The Fourth, Fifth, and Eighth Circuits all upheld the student groups, although the Fifth Circuit did rule against students in one case because the rejection came from the student-controlled campus newspaper rather than from the administration.[33] The most interesting of these cases, which has reached all three levels of the federal judiciary, resulted from the conflict between a group known as Gay Lib and the University of Missouri.

This group's struggle for official status began in February 1971, when it applied to the Missouri Student Association. It was successful there, and with the joint faculty-student review committee, but the dean of student affairs vetoed the recommendation a year later. Gay Lib appealed the veto. After the controversy had made its way up through the university hierarchy, the Board of Curators scheduled a hearing. The hearing was held, be it noted, in August 1973, when few students were on campus, and resulted in a 290-page transcript. The hearing examiner recommended against recognition, and the board adopted his conclusions verbatim.

At every level of review, the reasons for denial were similar, and twofold. First, it was alleged that official recognition of a gay organi-

---

[32] 367 F. Supp. 1088, 1092, 1095, 1096, 1098 (D.N.H. 1974); Gay Students Organization v. Bonner, 509 F. 2d 652 (1st Circ. 1974).

[33] Respectively, Gay Alliance of Students v. Mathews, 544 F. 2d 162 (1976); Gay Student Services v. Texas A & M University, 612 F. 2d 160 (1980); Gay Lib v. University of Missouri, 558 F. 2d 848 (1977), cert. den. 434 U.S. 1080 (1978); Mississippi Gay Alliance v. Goudelock, 536 F. 2d 1073 (1976), cert. den. 430 U.S. 982 (1977).

zation would encourage and increase violations of Missouri's antisodomy law. Second, several participants believed that homosexuality was a mental disorder and that such a group would spread it, especially among "those students who, during this period of their growth and development, may, from time to time, be concerned about their sexual identity." Although the American Psychiatric Association was soon to vote otherwise, two well-known psychiatrists, Harold Voth and Charles Socarides, testified at the hearing in support of the "disorder" theory.

The district court ruled for the university, accepting both of these claims. Judge Elmo Hunter distinguished *Healy* by asserting that "the members of Gay Lib are free to express within the law their beliefs and views of homosexuality and of the Missouri Criminal Statutes on that subject. But it is a far different thing to show a right under the First Amendment than to receive official school recognition of Gay Lib with all of the associational conditions that are likely to result therefrom." And he found Voth and Socarides more persuasive than the one physician who testified for the students.[34]

If the sodomy laws are, as I have argued, unconstitutional, the possibility of their violation is no grounds for restricting rights of association. But there is no need to go that far in order to reject the court's argument. If the possibility that lawbreaking may be encouraged is a ground for restricting group activities, that ground could apply to other campus functions; administrations could ban beer parties because they may lead to drunken driving or football games because they encourage disorderly conduct and destruction of property. Why apply the principle only to homosexuals?

There is, however, a subtler point to be made. Is it not dubious to limit freedom of expression because it *may* encourage crime at some indefinite point in the future? The old Smith Act cases seem to have worked to a decisive rejection of that notion.[35]

The appellate court reversed. On a page with more footnote than text, the majority declared that "the many Supreme Court cases dealing with prior restraints and other First Amendment issues make clear that the restriction of First Amendment rights in the present context may be justified only by a far greater showing of a likelihood of imminent lawless action than that presented here." The treatment of the psychiatric testimony was equally curt. The court found that "defend-

---

[34] Gay Lib v. University of Missouri, 416 F. Supp. 1350, 1355, 1370 (W.D. Mo. 1976), quoting from Dean Edwin Hutchins' letter to the Committee on Student Organizations, February 1, 1972.

[35] See Dennis v. United States, 341 U.S. 494 (1951); Yates v. United States, 355 U.S. 66 (1957).

ants' evidence turns solely on Dr. Voth's conclusory 'inference' and Dr. Socarides' 'belief,' for which no historical or empirical basis is disclosed," and that "as demonstrated by the substantial body of professional medical opinion conflicting with defendants' case, it must be acknowledged that there is no scientific certitude to the opinions offered."

The dissenting judge, however, was convinced by the expert testimony "that homosexual behavior is compulsive and that homosexuality is an illness and clearly abnormal." The university, perhaps interpreting this statement as a cue, petitioned for a rehearing en banc. The petition was denied by an equally divided court, but two dissenters recorded agreement with Voth, Socarides, and Judge Hunter.[36]

The university asked the Supreme Court for review. By now the case had a new name, in honor of the university's president, C. Brice Ratchford.[37] The petition for certiorari was denied, but in far from typical fashion. There were three recorded dissenting votes, which of course meant that the university had fallen only one vote short of review. Even more unusual, one dissenter wrote a revealing opinion.

Justice Rehnquist, joined by Justice Blackmun, thought the case fell within the Rule 19 guidelines for granting of certiorari, that it should be decided by the Court, and that it had been decided in conflict with applicable decisions. Ignoring the fact that the circuits were in agreement, he wrote, "The sharp split amongst the judges who considered this case below demonstrates that our past precedents do not conclusively address the issues central to this dispute." *Healy* "was decided in what may fairly be described as a factual vacuum"; Connecticut had made no attempt to show that lawbreaking would result from formation of an SDS chapter. "Here, such a demonstration was undertaken, and the District Court sitting as a finder of fact concluded that petitioners had made out their case." So *Healy* might not be controlling. Furthermore,

> the University's view of respondents' activities and respondents' own view of them are diametrically opposed. From the point of view of the latter, the question is little different from whether university recognition of a college Democratic club in fairness also requires recognition of a college Republican club. From the point of view of the University, however, the question is more akin to whether those suffering from measles have a constitutional right, in violation of quarantine regulations, to associate together and with others who do not presently have measles, in order to urge repeal of state law providing that measles sufferers be quarantined.

[36] Gay Lib v. University of Missouri, 558 F. 2d 848, 854–55, 858–61 (8th Circ. 1977).
[37] Ratchford v. Gay Lib, cert. den. 434 U.S. 1080 (1978).

The very act of assemblage under these circumstances undercuts a significant interest of the State which a plea for the repeal of the law would nowise do. Where between these two polar characterizations of the issue the truth lies is not as important as whether a federal appellate court is free to reject the University's characterization, particularly when it is supported by the findings of the District Court.[38]

Presumably, one writer remarks, "Justice Rehnquist believes that homosexuality is contagious."[39] That is not quite fair, of course; Rehnquist did not say he believed that. He said that the truth lay somewhere between the two poles of Republicans and germ spreaders—an analogy that is problematical enough.

But this singular metaphor cannot be dismissed as either irrelevant or a joke, however great the temptation to treat it humorously. Like the "crime" argument, the "disease" argument is not applied consistently to all relevant activities. One useful exercise is to think not about measles, but about alcoholism. That disease is spread on campus, and with full legal sanction. But even worse, Rehnquist's "on the one hand, on the other hand" approach invites lower courts to base their rulings on some very questionable medical opinion that is no longer representative, if it ever was, of the psychotherapeutic profession, and that, to the negligible extent that it is backed by reliable data, is still subject to disproof, and is opposed by some contrary evidence.[40]

Rehnquist's treatment of the crime issue is, if possible, even less persuasive. Every other group in the country—the Communist party, the Ku Klux Klan, Animal House, or whatever—is allowed to organize, meet, hand out literature, hold parties and rallies, and discuss illegal activity to the heart's and mind's content. No one can predict when rebellion, cross burning, or drunken mayhem will result, but no restrictions are premised on those possibilities. But here, just as in *Doe*, one group of people—homosexuals—is singled out for special restrictions, and rights granted all other citizens are jeopardized for them. The courts have nearly created a special outlaw class.

Homosexuals and Employment

Unlike privacy and association, employment is not ranked as a constitutional right. Perhaps it should be; to individuals, it is an interest

---

[38] Ibid., pp. 1082, 1085, 1084.

[39] Rivera, "Our Strait-Laced Judges," p. 930, n. 829.

[40] See the authorities cited in n. 4 above and Robert E. Gould, "What We Don't Know about Homosexuality," *New York Times*, February 24, 1974, VI, pp. 13ff.

of the greatest importance. Losing one's job, or not getting one, has been and continues to be a common consequence of known or suspected homosexuality. This is not true for all jobs, but it is true often enough to help explain why the closet door has remained closed. The stigma attached to homosexuality has provided a rationale for employers' behavior. After all, are not such employees vulnerable to blackmail or extortion? This argument was particularly effective in security-sensitive government positions. As the ignominy attached to homosexuality has diminished, this rationale has lost force. And once a worker has disclosed his or her preference, the threat of exposure is empty.

The openly gay employee, however, has often fallen victim to another rationale for dismissal: that the notoriety resulting from disclosure would harm the employer, customers, or clients. These rationales put the worker in a classic no-win situation. Either overt or covert homosexuality becomes grounds for discrimination. And, as we shall see, this double bind does not exhaust the rationales.

The cases I discuss here are fairly recent, most having been decided since 1970. The Supreme Court's only participation has been in denial of review. The lower courts have been left without guidance to develop their own doctrines. With few exceptions, the decisions have been unfavorable to the homosexual plaintiffs. Some of the cases turn out, on analysis, to involve provisions of the Bill of Rights, most notably the First Amendment. The pattern of the last two groups of cases recurs: general precedents from which courts depart in this particular setting.

Most of the cases involve public employment: the military, as in the famous *Matlovich* case;[41] the U.S. Civil Service; the state campus; or the public school. In the 1960s the District of Columbia Court of Appeals dealt with a few civil service cases.[42] After a shaky start, this court, often over the dissent of Warren Burger, arrived at the position that unsubstantiated charges were insufficient grounds for rejection or dismissal.[43] *Matlovich* and similar rulings established that the military could not dismiss homosexuals unless it had a set of self-limiting rules to guide decisions.[44] In the states, a California case, *Morrison v. Board of Education*, reinstated a high school teacher who had been fired

[41] Matlovich v. Secretary of the Air Force, 414 F. Supp. 690 (D.D.C. 1976), 591 F. 852 (D.C. Circ. 1978).

[42] See Dew v. Halaby, 317 F. 2d 582 (1963).

[43] Scott v. Macy, 349 F. 2d 182 (1965), 402 F. 2d 644 (1968); Norton v. Macy, 417 F. 2d 1161 (1969).

[44] See n. 41 above; Berg v. Claytor, 436 F. Supp. 76 (D.D.C. 1977), 591 F. 2d 849 (D.C. Circ. 1978); Saal v. Middendorf, 427 F. Supp. 192 (N.D. Cal. 1977).

after admitting a past homosexual episode.[45] But neither military nor civilian federal authorities are forbidden to dismiss homosexuals at all,[46] and the states retain even more leeway.

McConnell v. *Anderson* was the indirect result of a famous skirmish in the struggle for gay rights. James Michael McConnell had been offered a job as a librarian at the University of Minnesota, to begin in September 1970. Before the Board of Regents formally approved the appointment, McConnell and his lover, Jack Baker, applied for a marriage license, which was to be repeatedly denied them. This action was noted in the press, and as a result the board rejected McConnell's appointment, stating that his "personal conduct, as represented in the public and University news media, is not consistent with the best interest of the University."[47]

In September the district court ruled that McConnell had been denied due process. Citing both the civil service cases and the loyalty-security rulings of the 1950s and 1960s,[48] the judge stressed the lack of any demonstrated relationship between homosexuality and competence.[49] But he was reversed; a year later, the Court of Appeals ruled in favor of the Regents. The opinion insisted that more than homosexuality was at issue. This was "a case in which the prospective employee demands . . . the right to pursue an activist role in *implementing* his unconventional ideas concerning the social status to be accorded homosexuals and, thereby, to foist tacit approval of this socially repugnant concept upon his employer. . . . We know of no constitutional fiat or binding principle of decisional law which requires an employer to accede to such extravagant doctrine."[50]

Well, none if we leave out the First Amendment. Presumably we have traveled some distance from Holmes's famous pronouncement that a person has a constitutional right to freedom of speech, but no right to be a policeman.[51] When compared to the loyalty-security cases, *McConnell* seems plain wrong. But it is still good law. Not only did the Supreme Court refuse to hear the case, but the appellate court's reasoning has been duplicated in other rulings.[52]

---

[45] 461 P. 2d 375 (Cal. Sup.Ct. 1969).

[46] See Singer v. U.S. Civil Service Commission, 530 F. 2d 247 (9th Circ. 1976), vacated and remanded, 429 U.S. 1034 (1976), no final disposition as of 1981.

[47] 316 F. Supp. 809, 811 (D. Minn. 1970).

[48] See n. 43 above; Wieman v. Updegraff, 344 U.S. 183 (1952); Slochower v. Board of Higher Education, 350 U.S. 551 (1976); Schware v. Board of Bar Examiners, 353 U.S. 232 (1957); Keyishian v. Board of Regents, 385 U.S. 589 (1967).

[49] 316 F. Supp. 809, 811ff.

[50] McConnell v. Anderson, 451 F. 2d 193, 196. Emphasis in the original.

[51] McAuliffe v. Mayor of New Bedford, 29 N.E. 517 (Mass. Sup. Jud. Ct. 1892).

[52] 405 U.S. 1046 (1972).

Activism proved equally dangerous to Joseph Acanfora, a junior high school teacher in Rockville, Maryland, a suburb of Washington. His five television appearances, including one on *60 Minutes*, during the 1972–73 school year led to a forced transfer to a nonteaching position. The Board of Education made the familiar argument that a gay teacher may serve, intentionally or not, as a role model for students, but this was not the grounds for decision. District Judge Joseph Young cited, of all cases, *Schenck* v. *United States*:[53]

> Despite the apparent lack of connection, it is perhaps noteworthy that the "panic" of the crowded theater in the illustration has some similarity to the reaction of parts of the school community in this case. The instruction of children carries with it special responsibilities, whether a teacher be heterosexual or homosexual. The conduct of private life necessarily reflects on the life in public. There exists then not only a right of privacy, so strongly urged by the plaintiff, but also a duty of privacy.

To liken the effects of a teacher's publicizing his homosexuality to those of falsely shouting "Fire!" in a crowded theater is sheer nonsense. To write about correlative rights and duties in a First Amendment case is to reduce the provision to the Mark Twain caricature quoted in Chapter 7. Judge Young has also come very close to stating that public school teachers do not have the same rights as do other citizens, and he removed any doubt about his position: "The point is that to some extent every teacher has to go out of his way to hide his private life, and that a homosexual teacher is not at liberty to ignore or hold in contempt the sensitivity of the subject to the school community."[54]

The Court of Appeals affirmed, but it did reject some of this reasoning. It cited a case Judge Young ignored, *Pickering* v. *Board of Education*, which might be called the *Healy* v. *James* of the public school. In *Pickering*, the Supreme Court unanimously ruled in favor of a teacher who was fired for making public statements critical of the board.[55] Acanfora's statements, then, were protected by the First Amendment. But he was not entitled to relief because on his job application he had omitted Homophiles of Penn State from his list of college extracurricular activities. "Acanfora purposely misled the school officials so he could circumvent, not challenge, what he considers to be their unconstitutional employment practices. He cannot now invoke the process of the court to obtain a ruling on an issue that he practiced deception

[53] 249 U.S. 47 (1919).
[54] Acanfora v. Board of Education, 359 F. Supp. 843, 855–57 (D. Md. 1973).
[55] 391 U.S. 563 (1968).

to avoid." This was the loophole left by the loyalty-security cases; one could not be fired for one's memberships or for refusing to give information about them, but one could be fired for withholding information. So Acanfora was punished first for revealing and then for concealing. Again, the Supreme Court denied certiorari.[56]

It is useful to compare this discussion to parts of Chapter 7. The message sent to public school teachers is something like this: "You work long hours at a low-paying, low-status job. Your employers are free to ask all sorts of questions about your activities. You must carefully limit your participation in community life, making sure that you do nothing that could disturb your employers, your students, or their parents. But you may go to the head of the cafeteria line, you may punish the students for lack of respect for you, and you're pretty much free to hit them." Somehow, it all sticks together.

Teaching has been a precarious occupation for homosexuals. These cases repeat a pervasive fear that homosexual teachers will somehow influence their students to emulate them, whether by seduction, verbal encouragement, or serving as a role model. These are separate concerns, and need to be carefully distinguished. Seduction of schoolchildren is sexual abuse, and must be prevented. But this is true whether homosexuals or heterosexuals do the abusing, and there is no evidence that the former are more likely to abuse children than the latter.[57] The "role model" issue is more subtle, though not much more. If it is true, as some experts think, that sexual orientation is fixed by the age of five, the age at which public school education usually begins, teachers cannot have much influence. But this expert opinion is not unanimous, and, as I have suggested, there is some knowledge that tends to refute it.[58] Russell Baker, however, has responded perfectly to this argument. In a column published in 1977, during Anita Bryant's crusade in Dade County (the site of *Ingraham v. Wright*), Baker wrote that the controversy "prompted me to ponder teachers I haven't seen, and scarcely thought about, in decades, and for the first time I reflected on how their sex lives had affected my own. My first thought was that it was curious, perhaps perverse, that I have not turned out to be a spin-

---

[56] Acanfora v. Board of Education, 491 F. 2d 498, 504 (4th Circ. 1974); 419 U.S. 836 (1975).

[57] See, e.g., Editorial, "Should Homosexuals Be Teachers?" *New York Times*, May 24, 1977, p. 34.

[58] See, e.g., testimony of John Money, cited in Acanfora v. Board of Education, 359 F. Supp. 843, 847–50; Bieber, *Homosexuality*; Masters and Johnson, *Homosexuality in Perspective*.

ster."[59] The point is obvious, and the intensity of the feelings on the other side does not make the arguments any stronger.

However solid the arguments, the opinions were intense enough to lead to the dismissal of John Gish in Paramus, New Jersey, and James Gaylord in Tacoma, Washington. Though Gish held office in gay organizations, he was not so prominent as Acanfora. And Gaylord, far from being an activist, had not revealed his homosexuality even to his family. It made no difference.

In July 1972, a month after Gish became president of the New Jersey Gay Activists Alliance, the Paramus Board of Education ordered him to undergo a psychiatric examination, as state law allowed. When he refused, he was suspended without pay. Without having met Gish, the board's consulting psychiatrist stated that his "overt and public behavior . . . indicated a strong possibility of psychological harm to students of the school district as a result of their continued association with him."[60]

"Protection of school children from teachers who have shown evidence of harmful, significant deviation from normal mental health," the Superior Court ruled, "is without question not only a valid legislative concern but one classifiable as a compelling state interest. This being so, the fact that the statute may intrude upon a teacher's right of association, expression and privacy does not render it unconstitutional." The appellate division was more generous about Gish's rights, but endorsed the school board's interest in student mental health and noted that a psychiatric examination was not, after all, a dismissal.[61]

James Gaylord had taught at Wilson High School in Tacoma for twelve years, earning tenure and consistently excellent evaluations. His troubles began about the same time John Gish's did. In October 1972 a former student told the school's vice-principal that he thought Gaylord was homosexual. It is not clear how, or even whether, the student knew; there was no allegation of sexual relationships with students. When confronted, Gaylord admitted his preference. He was fired after a hearing two months later. The dismissal rested on the allegation that he was an unfit teacher.

The Washington Supreme Court heard the case twice, en banc. The

---

[59] "Role Models," *New York Times*, June 26, 1977, VI, p. 10.
[60] Gish v. Board of Education, 366 A. 2d 1337, 1339–40 (N.J. Super.Ct., Appellate Division, 1976).
[61] Kochman v. Keansburg Board of Education (same case), 305 A. 2d 807, 812 (N.J. Super.Ct., Chancery Division, 1973); Gish v. Board of Education, 366 A. 2d 1337, 1341–42.

first time, two and a half years after Gaylord's discharge, it remanded the case to the trial court, on the grounds that the school district had met its burden of proof by the administrators' testimony that students' and parents' complaints would affect Gaylord's fitness.[62] But when the court got the case again, in January 1977, it was satisfied. What apparently convinced the judges was the negative testimony of three fellow teachers, a student, and the opinions of moral and medical authorities, including the *New Catholic Encyclopedia.* Judge Charles Horowitz wrote:

> After Gaylord's homosexual status became publicly known, it would and did impair his teaching efficiency. A teacher's efficiency is determined by his relationship with his students, their parents, the school administration and fellow teachers. If Gaylord had not been discharged after he became known as a homosexual, the result would be fear, suspicion, parental concern and pressure on the administration.[63]

So people become unfit when others accuse them, a sectarian reference work is an authoritative source, and an informer can get a teacher fired. This opinion must stand as its own best refutation. But five years after the cases had begun, the Supreme Court denied review in both *Gaylord* and *Gish.*[64]

McConnell, Acanfora, Gish, and *Gaylord* present a grim picture of what Gunther has called irresponsible and lawless court actions. But there are some glimmers of responsibility and lawfulness. Perry Aumiller, a theater manager at the University of Delaware, fared better. Aumiller's immediate superiors knew he was gay, but the university's president did not. He found out when Aumiller was mentioned in articles in the student newspaper on gay activists on campus, and he was not pleased. He refused to renew Aumiller's contract.

The district court ruled in Aumiller's favor. Judge Murray Schwartz cited *Pickering,* and did not find Aumiller's activities notorious enough to be controlled by *McConnell.* He did not mention *Acanfora,* even though it was binding precedent in the same circuit, but perhaps he thought that decisions about secondary school teachers did not apply to university employees. "The fundamental purpose of the First Amendment," he wrote, "is to protect from State abridgement the free expression of controversial and unpopular ideas. . . . The decision not to renew Aumiller's contract because of his public statements contra-

---

[62] Gaylord v. Tacoma School District No. 10, 535 P. 2d 804 (1975).
[63] Gaylord v. Tacoma School District No. 10, 559 P. 2d 1340, 1342 (1977).
[64] 434 U.S. 879 (1977).

venes these most basic teachings of the First Amendment and cannot be tolerated."[65]

Gay Law Students v. *Pacific Telephone* is an exciting case. In 1979 the California Supreme Court ruled that the company's policy of not hiring homosexuals violated the equal-protection clause of the state constitution and the California Public Utilities Code. This decision is binding only in California, but it is important because the state's equal-protection guarantee is identical to that of the Fourteenth Amendment and because the court called such discrimination "arbitrary exclusion of qualified individuals from employment opportunities."[66] Between them, *Aumiller* and *Pacific Telephone* could transfer the double bind from the homosexuals who seek employment to the employers who wish to reject them. If homosexuality is known, rejection violates the First Amendment; if homosexuality is unknown, discrimination is arbitrary. This argument makes far more sense than the unproved theories about notoriety and harm. But so far, the weight of precedent is on the restrictive side, however ill grounded that precedent is.

Conclusion

In the Old West, the outlaw was a person whom the laws of the region did not protect. He might be captured, punished, or even murdered without those procedural safeguards that generally prevailed. The contemporary homosexual is not in quite so dire a situation. To describe homosexuals as outlaws would be an exaggeration. But it is not an exaggeration to say that homosexuals are denied several of the constitutional rights of adult American citizens, and that among these rights are privacy, freedom of association, and freedom from arbitrary discrimination. Again and again, judges depart from the classic precedents of constitutional law to produce new, special dogma applicable only to homosexuals:

Sometimes, as in *Doe*, the judges have ignored relevant precedents. Or as in *Acanfora*, they have delegated the case to the only remaining loophole. But perhaps the most disquieting cases are those, such as the district court *Acanfora* ruling and the second *Gaylord* case—and, of course, Rehnquist's dissent in *Ratchford*—in which the judges try to defend this special treatment. In *Acanfora* we learn that a gay teacher can cause a danger similar to the panic produced by falsely shouting

---

[65] Aumiller v. University of Delaware, 434 F. Supp. 1273, 1301 (D. Del. 1977).
[66] 595 P. 2d 592, 598–99 (1979).

"Fire!" We might ask how: will the students rise up and stone him to death, or will they trample one another in their rush to safety? The situation would seem to be nearer to *Tinker*, or the discomfiture allegedly caused by a pregnant teacher hinted at in *Cleveland Board of Education* v. *LaFleur*,[67] than to *Schenck* (although, of course, the "panic" analogy was not very good there, either).

The "impaired teaching efficiency" that cost James Gaylord his job came about because a student made a report about him, an administrator took that report seriously, and some fellow teachers made a self-fulfilling prophecy. If Gaylord was rendered unfit, his unfitness was at least as much the result of others' reactions to reports about him as of his own conduct. The record suggests that the way to get people fired is to start rumors about them. Justice Rehnquist's comparison of homosexuality to measles is startling, but what is most objectionable about that statement is that he finds those acceptable words to put in university officials' mouths, and thus tacitly approves of such notions as a basis for decisions.

What the cases share is less an opinion on homosexuality, though that does surface on occasion, than a judicial conception of what public opinions about homosexuality are legitimate bases for abridgment of constitutional rights. The cases reveal, though the opinions do not always endorse, the deep hostility, distrust, and fear—"hatred" is not too strong a word—that many Americans feel toward homosexuals. All sorts of vague fears about influence, encouragement, the effects on youth, and the "spread" of homosexuality abound. The fears may be formless, but they are not mild; the passion with which opinions are held is striking. And many of the judges seem to think that when these intense feelings are expressed in public policy, it is their official duty to honor them. The Supreme Court, in its repeated refusals to hear these cases, has made no effort to instruct those judges otherwise.

And there might be such a duty, were it not for the fact that the claims on the other side involve what have been recognized as constitutional rights. Where freedom of association is involved, the state may not penalize a person simply because citizens or officials feel that he or she *might* present a danger or be an unfit employee, however intense that feeling is. When no relationship between sexual orientation and performance exists, dismissal is arbitrary and capricious, no matter how strongly people believe otherwise. There appears to be no need for any reformulations of constitutional doctrine. What is in-

[67] 414 U.S. 632, 641, n. 9 (1974).

volved here is irresponsible, unfounded departure from established doctrine.

Why, then, should cases dealing with the rights of homosexuals concern us here? I discuss them for two reasons. First, as I have indicated, considering homosexuals in the light of some traditional categories, such as suspect classification, reveals some—still more—inherent defects in that concept. Second, I am convinced that, while my reformulation may not be *necessary* in this area, it is *useful*. For Judge Bownes, in the first *Bonner* case, was right. These claims do have equal-protection underpinnings. One of the failings of these decisions is that these features are either ignored or put in the old categories and dismissed, as in *Acanfora*, when Judge Young rejected the *Frontiero* version of suspect classification as "inconclusive" in its application.[68] Adjudication is marked by a kind of Balkanization of the Constitution, from which Douglas' opinion in *Griswold* was a bold departure, whereby judges focus either on the constitutional claim or on a series of claims separately and in succession. They may start with the First Amendment and, having disposed of that issue, move on to the equal-protection clause, but, except for Judge Bownes, they do not consider these two provisions *together* and ask what they might do *in combination*.

This structural interpretation finds support in the legislative history of the Fourteenth Amendment. Both the House and Senate floor leaders, it will be recalled, argued that the amendment included provisions of the Bill of Rights. Whether or not Justice Black's "incorporation" thesis is correct, it is clear that the framers of the amendment saw a strong relationship between its limitations on the states and rights already secured against the federal government.

If we assume such a relationship—adopting a formulation similar to that of Justice Marshall's *Rodriguez* dissent—we get a new idea of what is happening in these cases. People are being deprived of either a constitutional right or an interest of paramount concern—sometimes both. That much, of course, most of the decisions recognize. But those decisions weigh the individual claim against the state interest; they do not view the individual plaintiff as part of a group. The equal-protection approach lets us do so.

What now becomes clear is that a group of people is being singled out for deprivations not imposed on others. Homosexuals are treated differently from everyone else; they lose rights and vital interests that others have. This, certainly, is legal stigmatization. Indeed, once it is

[68] 359 F. Supp. 843, 852.

recognized that what is involved is classification, is it not clear that, to paraphrase Brennan in *Bakke*, these are "classifications that are drawn on the premise that homosexuals are inferior to others" and that "put the weight of the government behind hatred and separatism"?[69]

We then have to ask why this stigmatization is happening. What differentiates homosexuals from Communists, atheists, women who want abortions, and all the other people who espouse a variety of causes? Apparently the crucial difference lies in the attitudes people have about homosexuality, and these attitudes arise from ignorance and prejudice.

Fitting this situation into Marshall's scheme clarifies the point. First, the threatened interests are paramount. Second, the trait that is the basis for classification—sexual preference—may or may not be immutable, may or may not be involuntary. But surely it is of a deeply personal nature, something that pertains to a most private aspect of an individual's life. The classification may or may not be suspect, or even semisuspect, but the privacy cases make it one that is outside of state concern, in much the same way that religion is. Finally, when we consider the third part of Marshall's test, the government interest in restriction, we find none of any substance.

The lesson of the gay rights cases is how easy it is for courts to ignore settled constitutional law when a group is newly active and feeling against it is strong. The decisions are wrong, even as the law now stands. They are so bad that consideration of the complex issues surrounding homosexuality is not even necessary. But one reason these decisions have been possible is that traditional ways of thinking about constitutional cases have hidden the real import of such rulings. A new formulation, one that is closer to the meaning of constitutional equality, could go a long way toward granting this semioutlaw class the true citizenship it deserves.

[69] 438 U.S. 265, 357–58 (1978).

[10]

Toward a Theory of Constitutional Equality

We have been engaged in a search for the meaning of equality under the Constitution. Its center has, inevitably, been the Fourteenth Amendment, which contains the only specific guarantee of equality; but from that center the search has spread outward to the entire body of Reconstruction legislation and the rest of the Constitution, backward to the origins of the idea of equality, and forward to the definitions and interpretations that the provision has been given. They could have come from Congress, but in fact they have come mostly from the courts. And the courts' rulings, I have argued, have crabbed and confined a bill of rights that was lavish and expansive in its design.

Part of my argument has been that the concept embodied in the equal-protection clause was derived from the Declaration of Independence, which in turn was derived from ideas as old as the New Testament and as new as the Levellers. In Chapter 2 I examined the roots of this concept to rediscover what in fact we have always known: that the American idea of equality was not a notion about capacities or abilities, but a notion of *entitlement*. "All men are created equal" meant that all deserved what Dworkin has called equal respect and concern. For the author of the Declaration, this notion of equality was compatible with his belief in the inherent inferiority of one racial group. Jefferson was in no hurry to ensure that blacks received, here on earth, the equality to which their Creator had entitled them. But he did not except them from his broad principles.

Equality, then, did not mean that all were endowed with identical or equivalent abilities. It meant entitlement; but entitlement to what? The Declaration goes on to answer this question. All men "are endowed by their Creator with *certain inalienable rights.*" What rights? "*Among* these"—the language, note, is open, not closed—are three. First, "life"; as long as we stick to the eighteenth century and leave out one of the most vexing controversies of the twentieth, this term has a clear and limited meaning. But then comes "liberty," and finally "the pursuit of happiness." That last is a substitute for Locke's "property"; together, the two rights could hardly be broader or more sweeping. So equality is quickly linked to a catalogue of rights that does not contain its own limitations.

The Declaration contains grand rhetorical statements, and the easiest possible criticism to make of its author, its editors, and its signers is that they were a long way from practicing what they preached. Slavery is, of course, the best example of this disjunction. But the striking fact is that the men who adopted the Declaration and those who enacted the Constitution recognized this inconsistency. At the constitutional convention in 1787, one delegate stated baldly that slavery was inconsistent with the principles of the Declaration. No one argued with him; the reactions he provoked amounted to a suggestion that he was out of order.[1] No one tried to resolve the terrible contradiction, but the framers showed no united commitment to ending it.

The next century brought its end, though at a grievous price. In the years between the founding and the Civil War, activists committed to the abolition of slavery hammered home the contradiction between principle and reality, and rooted those principles not only in the Declaration but in the Constitution itself. Such men as Theodore Weld, James G. Birney, and John Bingham drew liberally from the Declaration, from political philosophy, and sometimes even from religion to insist that slavery violated principles that were somehow implied by, or contained in, or inseparable from, the Constitution. The fact that several provisions in the actual document implicitly supported slavery did not deter them from this kind of theorizing.

As the movement for abolition grew in size and strength, a proslavery reaction developed and became increasingly vocal in its challenge. No one ever argued successfully that slavery was compatible with the principles of entitlement and endowment, but John C. Calhoun did attempt to justify the institution by providing what I have called an antitheory of equality, a thesis that attacked the Declaration itself.[2] Calhoun rejected the idea that people were entitled to equal respect and inalienable rights regardless of their individual worth or merit.

[1] See Chapter 2, p. 55.
[2] *Disquisition on Government.* See Chapter 3, pp. 66–67.

He insisted that equality had to be earned, by some level of intelligence or virtue. Because slaves did not possess these qualities, they were not entitled to equality and liberty.

The opponents of slavery rarely tried to refute these conclusions about the abilities of the slaves. Indeed, many of them did believe, or assume, that blacks *were* an inferior race. But for abolitionists that did not matter. Inferiority did not justify slavery, or any other system of government that denied equality of rights. The abolitionists were no more specific about what these rights were than Jefferson had been; the lists grew ever longer.

The Civil War ended slavery, but it did not end the debate. The Radical Republicans now had an opportunity to rewrite the Constitution, and that is what they did, producing three constitutional amendments and a series of laws to enforce them. The amendments, read together, provide guarantees of equality that are as significant for what they do not say as what they do. The Thirteenth Amendment abolishes slavery and involuntary servitude, except as punishment for crime. It does not distinguish among black, white, red, and yellow, citizen and alien, man and woman, adult and child: only between those convicted of crimes and all others. The Fourteenth Amendment contains three extraordinary provisions, all of which mention individual rights. First are "the privileges and immunities of citizens of the United States" which no state may deny;[3] this wording revises Article IV, Section 2, of the original Constitution, which grants to citizens of any state the privileges and immunities of citizens of the several states. Second, the language of one clause of the Fifth Amendment is applied to the states: "nor shall any state deprive any person of life, liberty, or property without due process of law." Section 1 ends with the only explicit mention of equality: "nor deny to any person within its jurisdiction the equal protection of the laws."

Section 2 is narrower. It provides that representation in the House shall be proportionately reduced for any state that denies the vote to any of its adult male citizens. The states may deny the vote to women, to aliens, and to anyone under twenty-one years old. The section specifies exactly who is to be included, exactly what basis for discrimination is forbidden.

The Fifteenth Amendment does directly what Section 2 attempted to do indirectly: "The right to vote . . . shall not be denied or abridged by any State on account of race, color, or previous condition of ser-

---

[3] John Hart Ely has pointed out that it is not clear whether these privileges and immunities are even limited to citizens. See *Democracy and Distrust*, pp. 24–25.

vitude." Again, it is clear just who is included, and who—namely, women, children, and aliens—is not covered. The scope of the right is specifically limited.

So the Civil War amendments contain two kinds of guarantees. To take them up in reverse order, there are those that prohibit discrimination on the basis of certain characteristics, but leave to the states the power to discriminate because of other characteristics. The provisions in the Fourteenth and Fifteenth Amendments related to voting are of this kind. But the provisions of the Thirteenth Amendment and of Section 1 of the Fourteenth Amendment are of a different nature entirely. They refer to rights and immunities for all citizens or all people. The Thirteenth Amendment makes one exception; the Fourteenth Amendment makes none. The Thirteenth Amendment grants one immunity: from slavery or involuntary servitude. The Fourteenth Amendment recognizes a whole series of undefined, unspecified rights and privileges, couched in the broadest possible terms. No one may be denied due process or equal protection, nor may any state restrict the privileges and immunities of citizens. There is no limit expressed or implied with respect to characteristics that can be a basis for discrimination, no indication that the amendment is concerned with race but not with sex, age, or anything else. Indeed, the specifications of Section 2 and the Fifteenth Amendment suggest, if they suggest anything, that no such limitations were intended.

But what was *included* in Section 1? The text does not provide much guidance on that point. Because the text itself limits neither the bases for discrimination that are precluded nor the rights that are secured, Chapter 4 turned to an examination of the congressional debates.

This task, like that of tracing the intellectual history of equality, has been done before. My justification for doing it again is that no historical investigation can ever be perfected: as new issues arise, it is necessary to refer to first principles, to ask what the provisions meant to those who enacted them, and how their meaning can be applied to our own time. The scholarship that was stimulated by *Brown* v. *Board of Education* was excellent, and reached conclusions that my investigation has reaffirmed: that the framers of the Civil War amendments and the Reconstruction laws intended to enact into the Constitution the principles of the Declaration. The scholars who developed this thesis were concerned with one specific conclusion that could be drawn from it: that racial classifications that were neutral on their face were in fact invidious, and violated the equal-protection guarantee. Agreeing completely with both thesis and conclusion, I have argued that they can lead much further, to protect the rights of groups never even discussed by the Reconstruction Congress.

The debates themselves were conducted, as Alfred Kelly wrote, in terms of grand symbolism. They rarely got down to specifics, either about groups or about rights. When they did, they permit only two specific conclusions that are important for my purposes here. First, there was general agreement that the Fourteenth Amendment extended to racial minorities other than blacks; in the context of the 1860s, this meant Orientals. Second, the rights protected included those listed in the Civil Rights Bill and the Freedman's Bureau Bill of 1866, which were limited to protections from racial discrimination.

Beyond that, there is ambiguity and confusion. The House and Senate floor leaders argued that Section 1 made the first eight amendments of the Bill of Rights binding on the states. Their word has to be given great weight, but it became clear both that other members did not go so far and that leaders went even further. Several members of Congress argued that Section 1 did not extend to women or children. The problems here are, first, that no one was able to give an argument for excluding women that made much sense or was compatible with other arguments about the amendment's scope; and second, that other provisions made it absolutely clear when women and children were excluded. Since Section 1 does not do so, there is no reason to read in any such limitations.

A rereading of the debates suggests that equal-protection cases have tended to ask the wrong questions. They have been concerned with whether or not the characteristic that provides the basis for discrimination is a permissible basis and have focused on whether that characteristic is similar or dissimilar to race. But Congress was not often concerned with distinguishing between legitimate and illegitimate classifications. Its focus was not nearly so much on *who* was protected as on *what* sort of official conduct was forbidden. Slavery was odious not because it was imposed according to race, but because it relegated people to a permanent, inferior status; worse, to the status of something less than a person. It was wrong because it branded and stigmatized; because it deprived people of fundamental rights; because it was oppression sanctioned by law. As slavery was wrong for these reasons, so were any southern attempts to restore it under other names.

The reason these practices were wrong was not that they were imposed on people who were equal in wisdom, virtue, or merit to the dominant white race. Few members of the Reconstruction Congress, even the Radical Republicans, were prepared to offer that argument.

I have quoted Raoul Berger's statement that the North was shot through with Negrophobia; the debates tend more to support this statement than to refute it. But that was beside the point. The Reconstruction amendments chose the abolitionist theory of equality, not Calhoun's antitheory. Equality did not have to be earned. It belonged to human beings because they were human beings. And that principle was enacted, finally, into the Constitution.

But how can one go about interpreting, and limiting, so broad and general a guarantee? Ronald Dworkin writes of rules in general:

> Suppose I tell my children simply that I expect them not to treat others unfairly. I no doubt have in mind examples of the conduct I mean to discourage, but I would not accept that my "meaning" was limited to these examples, for two reasons. First, I would expect my children to apply my instructions to situations I had not and could not have thought about. Second, I stand ready to admit that some particular act I had thought was fair when I spoke was in fact unfair, or vice versa, if one of my children was able to convince me of that later; in that case I should want to say that my instructions covered the case he cited, not that I had changed my instructions. I might say that I meant the family to be guided by the *concept* of fairness, not by any specific *conception* of fairness I had in mind.[4]

This example is a good analogy to the Fourteenth Amendment. It is an instruction to respect individuals' rights, to give them due process, to treat them equally. This book has confronted each of the two situations Dworkin discusses. Reverse discrimination, disability rights, and the cases involving homosexuals demand that we apply those instructions to problems that did not concern the authors of the amendment. Segregation, antimiscegenation laws, and sexist laws are problems of the second type: these laws involve situations the Reconstruction Congress did know about, and policies that it thought were consistent with the principles it was enacting. But they were not consistent, and we can demonstrate as much with reference to the legislative history itself.

There is a third possible situation, however, which Dworkin does not mention. His children might try to convince him that some act he thought fair was unfair, or vice versa, and fail. Is there a constitutional analogy here? Yes, with *Lochner* v. *New York* and the other early substantive due-process cases. The legislative debates indicate that Holmes was right: the Fourteenth Amendment did not enact Herbert Spencer's *Social Statics*. How can we know that it did not? Because,

---

[4] *Taking Rights Seriously*, p. 134.

again and again, debates and reports drew attention to the existence of a weak, powerless group of people who were being oppressed, voiced grave concern with this problem, and argued for the use of the law to protect this group. That was not the theory of *Lochner*, which presumed an equality of condition that did not exist; nor was it social Darwinism, which would have let people stand or fall on their own. The principle on which *Lochner* depends simply is not there in the legislative history. That is also true of *McLaughlin* and *Loving*. The legislative history did contain a principle that made those laws unconstitutional, but, as Chapter 5 showed, those decisions rested on another principle, which was not part of that history. *Lochner* was plain wrong; *McLaughlin* and *Loving* were right, but for the wrong reasons.

The guarantees are broad, but they do contain their own limitations. The last paragraph suggested two: they do not mandate survival of the fittest, and they do not invalidate all forms of racial discrimination. The provisions can bear, and have borne, those interpretations, but they should not have and they need not have. They have not borne other interpretations, however, which they could have supported.

Chapter 5 examines what the courts have made of these guarantees. It has been nothing even close to what Dworkin suggests, and what the legislative history invites. The real transformation of the Fourteenth Amendment[5] has been exactly the opposite of what Raoul Berger, Lino Graglia, and a now popular line of scholarship argues. The Court has not overextended the amendment; it has shackled it.

This process began with the *Slaughter-House Cases*, the first decision. A tone of incredulity pervades the opinions, as I suggested; Congress and the ratifying states surely could not have intended such fundamental change in the relationships among the national government, the states, and the individual. The decision effectively killed the privileges-and-immunities clause. Since then the due-process clause has been made to do much of what that provision might have been read to do, but only at the cost of manufacturing the concept of substantive due process, which, as one scholar has argued, makes about as much sense as "green pastel redness."[6] The equal-protection clause was read to apply only to "discrimination directed against [Negroes] as a class."[7] Those conclusions were dicta in that case, but a similar idea appears in later cases.

Yick Wo v. *Hopkins* did extend the reach of the amendment to pro-

---

[5] The subtitle of Raoul Berger's book *Government by Judiciary*.
[6] Ely, *Democracy and Distrust*, p. 18.
[7] Slaughter-House Cases, 16 Wall. 36, 81 (1873).

tection of Orientals. But *Plessy* v. *Ferguson* restricted it to laws directed against one racial group; it rejected the notion that neutral discrimination might also be forbidden. This argument could have found some support in the legislative history, but the trouble was that the neutral discrimination did in fact do what the amendment in principle forbade: it was premised on, and reinforced, the inferior status of blacks. Justice Brown's opinion for the Court missed this point and Justice Harlan's dissent only touched on it. *Brown* rectified the error in the decision, but not in the reasoning; *Brown* has been interpreted to enact Harlan's dissent, to establish that the Constitution is color-blind and that any racial discrimination, neutral, invidious, or benign, is unconstitutional.

A sweeping guarantee of protection from stigmatization and oppression was thus narrowed into a protection against a certain kind of discrimination and classification. Although the Court abandoned the "separate but equal" doctrine, it did so in a way that has made it harder to return to the principles of the amendment for guidance. *Brown* found the legislative history "inconclusive." In the context of that case, that argument was acceptable, but it has tended to produce two kinds of results. In the intermarriage cases of the 1960s, the Court used it to read into the legislative history a principle that does not belong there. It insisted that Congress had intended to reject any racial discriminations. The problem was that several members of Congress insisted, more than once, that they intended no such thing, and said so particularly with respect to intermarriage. They did, however, establish principles that would in fact forbid these laws.

The second result is that history is often simply ignored. That is what has happened in the sex discrimination cases. A superficial glance at the debates suggests that this inattention is fortunate, because there are statements there that seem to exclude women from the guarantees. But in fact the same disjunction between principle and application exists here as with intermarriage, and more thorough research could have discovered this inconsistency.

The judicial transformation seems even stranger, and stingier, when we turn to cases that determine how far, and where, the scope of the guarantees can be extended beyond race. Again, the guarantees are narrowed into restrictions on classification and discrimination. The doctrine that emerges is one whose primary purpose seems to be to classify classifications. There appear to be two kinds, innocuous and suspect. Innocuous classifications go onto the lower tier of laws; they are presumed to be legitimate, and usually survive. Suspect classifications are those that in some way are like race. Laws based on them are treated like laws that restrict fundamental rights. They are assigned to the upper tier; demand strict or rigid scrutiny; and can survive only if there is compelling justification for them. (But they can survive.) And here we run into confusion, for there exist two versions of what suspect classifications are, of what factors make a classification like race and unlike ordinary classifications.

One version was articulated (though since modified) by Justice Brennan, in his plurality opinion in *Frontiero* v. *Richardson*. For a classification to be suspect, two things have to be true about it. First, it must be immutable, involuntary, an accident of birth—like race. But "no one has bothered to build a logical bridge, to tell us exactly *why* we should be suspicious of legislatures that classify on the basis of immutable characteristics."[8] Some of the cases suggest that such classifications violate what are grandly called "American traditions," but that depends on which traditions we emphasize. Other cases imply that we should not restrict people because of traits they cannot help and cannot change, but that principle is never consistently applied; people use it to challenge racial classifications but not those based on age, for example. Brennan went on to add a second criterion, which eliminates many involuntary, immutable traits, such as disabilities. To be suspect, a classification must be largely unrelated to individual abilities. "At that point there's not much left of the immutability theory, is there?"[9] This criterion is not applied consistently, either. The Court has ruled that laws cannot discriminate against men or women on the basis of generalizations imperfectly related to individual traits, but it may use equally imperfect generalizations this way with respect to age. No one has built a logical justification for that practice, either.

Chapter 8 showed that there is a real discontinuity between the two halves of this rule. It leaves out the people who are most disadvantaged by conditions they can do nothing about. Chapter 9 revealed still another difficulty. The cases show no reason why something the individual can change, such as sexual behavior (whether or not we can change sexual orientation, we certainly have control over whom we seek out as sexual partners), is a more legitimate basis for restrictions than a characteristic one cannot change.

The *Frontiero* rule is a tenuous balance between theory and antitheory. Its second half could have come from Calhoun's *Disquisition on Government*. It implies that equality has to be earned by some degree of merit or ability. In the particular context, it implies that

[8] Ely, *Democracy and Distrust*, p. 150. Emphasis in the original.
[9] Ibid.

women have a right to equal respect and concern because, by and large, they have as much ability to contribute to society as men do, just as blacks deserve equality because they can contribute as much as whites can. That idea may sound reasonable, but it is not the notion that was the basis for the Fourteenth Amendment. Instead, it was such ideas that necessitated it.

The other version of suspect classification originated in Chief Justice Stone's *Carolene Products* footnote. Stone hinted—no more than that, really—that "prejudice against discrete and insular minorities may be a special condition" calling for relaxation of the usual presumption of constitutionality.[10] This formulation led to the exclusion from the suspect category of children living in low-income school districts and people over fifty, and, briefly and somewhat mystifyingly, to the inclusion of aliens.[11] It has undergone some refinement; since the school financing case, the typical formulation is "groups . . . saddled with such disabilities, or subjected to such a history of purposeful unequal treatment, or relegated to such a position of political powerlessness as to command extraordinary protection from the majoritarian political process."[12]

That formulation is an improvement on the footnote, for it does correct the curious pluralist notion that only majorities can oppress and only minorities can be oppressed. And it does seem to get closer than *Frontiero* does to what the authors of the Fourteenth Amendment were concerned with. But the formulation is not perfect. First, it ignores the fact that laws can have a dynamic effect in turning groups into disadvantaged minorities as well as a static effect of reinforcing the disabilities with which some groups are already saddled. Second, it abandons any control over the kinds of justifications that can be used for laws that affect groups not put on the upper tier; thus, in *Vance* v. *Bradley*, it allowed the claims of the forced retirees to be ignored in favor of the presumed interests of others. This rather blatant denial of equality is left undisturbed.

No one seemed to notice that there were two not entirely compatible versions of suspect classification in use until 1978, when the *Bakke* case forced a choice. If suspect classifications were those that were immutable and involuntary, Allan Bakke would win, as race was

---

[10] 304 U.S. 144, 152–53, n. 4 (1938).
[11] San Antonio v. Rodriguez, 411 U.S. 1 (1973); Massachusetts Board of Retirement v. Murgia, 427 U.S. 307 (1976); Graham v. Richardson, 403 U.S. 365 (1971). But see Foley v. Conellie, 435 U.S. 291 (1978); Ambach v. Norwick, 441 U.S. 68 (1979); and Plyler v. Doe, 50 U.S.L.W. 4650 (1982).
[12] San Antonio v. Rodriguez, 411 U.S. 1, 28.

such a characteristic as much for him as for a minority medical school applicant. If suspect classifications were those directed against disadvantaged, disabled groups, he might lose, as whites are not such a group. In fact, the Court dealt with the problem by confusing the doctrine even more. Race, declared Justice Powell, was a suspect classification, regardless of what race was helped or harmed by a particular law; furthermore, it was suspect because it just was, not because it fitted either or both parts of the definition. Gender, on the other hand, was not a suspect classification, whether a law discriminated against men or women. In the context of *Bakke*, this distinction permitted the inference that a medical school could legally reserve some of its places for women but not for minorities; at a time when nearly half of the people enrolling in medical school were women, this seemed rather silly. Beyond race and sex, it was not clear just which classifications were suspect and which were not, or why.

Thus prevailing equal-protection doctrine was confused; moreover, neither version of suspect classification was satisfactory. Both definitions worked best for race and sex, but, apparently for political reasons, the Court shied away from drawing that conclusion with respect to sex-based classifications. Almost any other characteristic one could think of might or might not be suspect, depending on which definition was used. Such cases as *Bakke*, where the Court, or at least some members of the Court, try to use the concept, show just how incomprehensible it has become; the opinions contain more than one instance of complete misstatements of what earlier decisions had done.

The doctrine, or doctrines, had at least three more difficulties. First, it left a loophole. No restriction, however oppressive, was forbidden; as the Japanese relocation cases showed, any classification would survive if a good enough reason was found for it. Second, it was, as Justice Marshall insisted, too rigid; it encouraged what I have called a Balkanization of the Constitution, whereby the individual interest involved and the appropriate ranking to be given it were considered in isolation from the classification involved and the group affected. In such cases as *Rodriguez* and *Murgia*, this approach obscured what was at their core: that people were being denied, or were getting much less of, a benefit of paramount concern to them, and that this inequality was justified by some very dubious distinctions. Balkanization had even worse results in cases that fell so far outside the framework that the classifications involved were never seriously questioned, such as those involving children and homosexuals. The model encouraged courts to miss entirely the fact that the cases had strong equal-protection overtones, that people were being denied near-fundamental rights, and in some cases specified rights, which others enjoyed, for no good reasons at all. Third, it had very little to do with the constitutional provisions it was supposed to interpret.

With the two ancestor cases, *Carolene Products* and *Korematsu*, that result might seem defensible, for the relevant segment of the former was dictum and neither was a Fourteenth Amendment case. But certainly the legislative history of that amendment would have been a legitimate source for Justice Black to turn to in *Korematsu*. What kinds of conclusions would that history have permitted about what had been done to the Japanese? But whether or not Stone or Black looked to that history, at some point those who grafted their doctrines onto the Fourteenth Amendment might have done so. Several features of current doctrine of suspect classification, the two-tier-and-a-mezzanine theory, are unsatisfactory. It is not clear; it is not rooted in history; it does not fit the constitutional language; and it permits inconsistent and troubling results. It is necessary, then, to try to fashion a better theory of equality under the Constitution.

Process-Bound Adjudication

In 1980 a book appeared which presented a fresh approach to judicial review. The author was John Hart Ely, a professor at Harvard Law School; the book was *Democracy and Distrust*, based on several lectures Ely had given in the past. Ely's thoughts have some features in common with mine, but his doctrine is, I think, ultimately unsatisfactory. He, too, rejects "clause-bound interpretivisms" in favor of permitting courts to look for "norms that cannot be discovered within the four corners of the document." The Fourteenth Amendment, in particular, is among several clauses that contain "provisions that are difficult to read responsibly as anything other than quite broad invitations to import into the constitutional decision process considerations that will not be found in the language of the amendment or the debates that led up to it." [13]

So far, so good, although that last may depend on how extensively one examines the debates. Ely's reformulation of judicial review, however, is troublesome. He would "limit courts to the correction of failures of representation and wouldn't let them second-guess the substantive merits" of legislation.[14] Laws disadvantaging racial minorities

[13] *Democracy and Distrust*, pp. 1, 14.
[14] Ibid., p. 181.

would thus have rough going, because these minorities usually are not adequately represented in decision making and are the victims of prejudice that helps to exclude them. But laws disadvantaging the white majority, such as most schemes of reverse discrimination, would pass muster.[15] This argument does lead to some conclusions harmonious with mine. Laws directed against homosexuals would be suspect because of what Ely rather awkwardly calls "a combination of the factors of prejudice and hideability."[16] I think Ely would also agree that classifications that disadvantage the handicapped are vulnerable, because of the barriers that keep them from full participation.

But his model does not work with women, the young, or the old. Gender-based classifications might or might not be suspect, depending on when they were enacted, the purposes they serve, and the extent to which women are denied access to decision making. They were once excluded, Ely admits, but they are not now; if new discriminatory laws get passed, some women must endorse them. It is true—sadly, from my viewpoint—that "many women do seem to prefer the old stereotype to the new liberation," but can this fact really decide the issue?[17] Should the extent to which people are granted equality depend on their success in getting others like them to agree with them? The rejection of substantive review could lead to this result, and that is giving up too much.

A second problem with Ely's thesis transcends the issue of sex discrimination. The notion that any ruling group must permit token representation of out-groups in order to maintain its power is a commonplace of elite theory.[18] Outsiders get into the elite, but the ruling group remains the ruling group. Thus members of disadvantaged groups can get access to decision making without any significant changes resulting. We cannot assume that representation entails equality.

Ely does not commit himself on the issue of age discrimination, but he does seem to be moving toward a conclusion that these classifications are acceptable. "It is at least arguable," he writes, "that the facts that all of us were young, and most expect one day to be fairly old, should neutralize whatever suspicion we might otherwise entertain respecting the multitude of laws (enacted by predominantly middle-aged legislatures) that comparatively advantage those between, say, 21 and

---

[15] See also Ely's article "The Constitutionality of Reverse Racial Discrimination," *University of Chicago Law Review* 41 (Summer 1974):723–41.

[16] *Democracy and Distrust*, p. 163.

[17] Ibid., p. 167.

[18] See Peter Bachrach, *The Theory of Democratic Elitism* (Boston: Little, Brown, 1966), chap. 2.

65 vis-a-vis those who are younger or older." [19] Before I reject this suggestion, I do want to examine it, because it is valuable if for no other reason than that it helps us see some important cases in a new light. *Murgia*, it will be recalled, insisted that old age "marks out a stage of life that each of us will reach if we live out our normal life span." [20] The case did not involve old age, of course; the line was drawn at fifty. Is it completely beside the point that the classification marked a stage of life that all members of the Court had already reached? Might they not have been wary of striking down a law whose primary target was people like themselves?

But should we conclude that legislation against the middle-aged by the middle-aged is acceptable? (The temptation is irresistible to retort that there have been rather few compulsory retirement laws affecting legislators.) The same difficulty arises here as with women. When we consider laws affecting the young as well, an additional difficulty emerges. To assume empathy is to reason rather as Burger and Powell do in such cases as *Parham*, to ignore facts recited plainly before us. The defects of Ely's theory become manifest if one reads the passage I just quoted and then immediately reads or rereads *Ingraham* v. *Wright*. The American experience with poor people who later became rich does not suggest that human beings necessarily feel empathy for those in their own former condition.

Ely's remarks about age are discordant with his discussion of gender-based laws. Ely finds it important that women now participate in the policy process, and that the middle-aged not only participate but may well dominate. When he gets to the young, however, Ely nowhere mentions the fact of their exclusion from power.

Democracy and Distrust is welcome for the creativity of its theory. But it permits too many abuses and denials of rights to be accepted on its own. Still, it remains to be seen if a new model can incorporate some of the virtues of this approach.

Adjudication without Tiers? [21]

How, finally, can one construct new doctrine that will preserve the right of all people to treatment as equals? I have devoted much attention to analyzing what is wrong with the models developed by judges

---

[19] *Democracy and Distrust*, p. 160.
[20] 427 U.S. 307, 314 (1976).
[21] I apologize. The temptation was irresistible.

and law professors. I now propose to entertain the notion that they have been doing something right, and that it would be worthwhile to look for features of the old theories that deserve to be saved. That search is fruitful, for the years of judicial dialogue and academic debate have produced insights that provide direction for my efforts.

I have argued that the old model contains dichotomies that are too rigid, and that such decisions as *Rodriguez* and *Murgia* illustrate the trouble with this model. But at least it does make some necessary distinctions. It is vital to recognize that some claims are more important than others, and that some ways of classifying people are worse than others. That distinction could get lost in a reformulation, and it should not get lost. It has been a long time since anyone suggested that constitutional rights could be abridged whenever government had reasonable grounds for doing so, and no one wants that rule to make a reappearance.[22] The freedom to buy beer is nowhere near as important as freedom of speech; likewise, restricting jury service to people over eighteen has nothing like the impact of restricting it to whites or to males. The ways in which the old model ranks the distinctions are dubious, but the differences of degree and kind which it recognized are essential.

A second theme that runs through many Supreme Court opinions and through Ely's book has already received much discussion and I think has to be incorporated into any new doctrine. This is the theme first timidly articulated in the *Carolene Products* footnote, then refined through Powell's majority opinion in *Rodriguez* and Brennan's separate opinion in *Bakke*: that there is something wrong with laws that burden people who are already disadvantaged, weak, disempowered, stigmatized, despised—those who, somehow, are treated as inferiors. This theme is articulated again and again in the Reconstruction debates, as Chapter 4 showed. It is not enough, as I have argued. *Rodriguez*, *Murgia*, and *Bradley* show that law can effectively be used to transform neutral collections of people into weak, disadvantaged groups, and that is no more justifiable than reinforcing this status once it exists.

The old model, in effect, demanded that we begin to make decisions by asking two questions. First (though the order does not matter much), how is the interest involved to be ranked: as a right or as a nonright? Second, what sort of class is affected here: innocuous, suspect, or somewhere in between? This is what Powell does in *Rodriguez*, and no case better shows why this is a bad approach. The Court got so involved in those complex questions that it lost sight of what the school

---

[22] See Gitlow v. New York, 268 U.S. 652 (1925).

financing scheme actually did, and even Justice Marshall got confused, although he was on the right track. The two-tier model obscured the central fact: minority children were getting an inferior education.

I suggest that a better approach would be one that begins with the simplest possible questions. First, *what* does the law do; what deprivation does it impose? Second, *whom* does the law deprive? The third question is not always answerable, but the situations in which it can be answered tend to be crucial: *why?*

These questions are simple, of course, only in form; each leads to a series of other questions, each demands that we rank and classify at some point, and each leads inexorably into the other two. The first question demands that we rank individual interests, a task that raises complex problems. I have implied that we can distinguish interests that must rank as fundamental constitutional rights from interests that are less important. Not everyone would agree that such distinctions are valid. Ely devotes a chapter of his book to what he views as the futility and inherent duplicity of "discovering fundamental values."[23] The problems with this concept are similar to those attending its relative, "natural law." Too many values have been ranked, by someone or other, at some time or other in our history, as "fundamental," and many are mutually contradictory. After all, slavery and segregation were once defended as fundamental values and natural law principles. A jurist who tries to choose values from this fertile ground will discover either propositions so general as to be meaningless or rationalizations of what are, in fact, personal preferences. Worse, these preferences may reflect the biases of the professional class:

> People understandably think that what is important to them is important, and people like us are no exception. Thus the list of values the Court and the commentators have tended to enshrine as fundamental is a list with which the readers of this book will have little trouble identifying: expression, association, education, academic freedom, . . . personal autonomy. . . . But watch most fundamental-rights theorists start edging toward the door when someone mentions jobs, food, or housing; these are important, sure, but they aren't *fundamental*.[24]

A valid point, and one calculated to kick the liberal jurist right in the guilt—although it is curious that Ely's professionals have only class biases, not race or sex biases. The criticism is not, however, as devastating as Ely finds it. Distinctions and discriminations among rights are possible. I have argued that the Fourteenth Amendment's legisla-

[23] *Democracy and Distrust*, chap. 3.
[24] Ibid., p. 59. Emphasis in the original.

tive history contains principles associated with Ronald Dworkin, for example, but not principles associated with Herbert Spencer. The constitutional text also permits distinctions. Some of the rights Ely mentions are, after all, specified there; others, such as education, are derivable from such rights. But perhaps the crucial difference between, say, the right to an education and the right to a job is that the latter has rarely been presented in what one might call a "clean" case. The rights of workers have tended to get confused, as in *Lochner*, with those of employers. Recognition of employment rights partook of class bias even more than recognition of First Amendment rights. Furthermore, Ely, like the Court, makes the problem worse than it needs to be by implying a sharp distinction between fundamental and nonfundamental rights. Evading that trap allows us to grant the importance of jobs, food, and housing.

Suppose, then, we take up the "what" question in several situations found in cases throughout the book. The restrictions on homosexuals' freedom of association deprive them of what is, beyond question, a fundamental constitutional right. The laws that forbid private homosexual activity between consenting adults deprive them of the right to privacy, which is not specified in the Constitution but which has been ruled, I think rightly, to belong there. I postpone for now the question of just how any of these laws are to be judged, but, at the very least, a heavy presumption of unconstitutionality has to attach to those I just mentioned. The policies that deprive disabled people of mobility are indirect but effective deprivations of constitutional rights; they limit the ability of the disabled to participate in the political process, to travel, to express themselves, to make demands.

In Chapter 8 I argued for recognition of a constitutional right to education. But even if we accepted the Court's conclusion that there is no such right, education has to rank very close to that status. The courts have not ruled that compulsory retirement laws violate constitutional rights, either, but, like the education laws, they infringe interests that, in importance to the individuals involved, rank about that high; so does denying a job to a handicapped person or a homosexual.

I have implied that there are hierarchies of rights and interests, and that some deprivations are more severe than others. One can think of several ways to push this argument further. A permanent deprivation is ordinarily more severe than a temporary deprivation. At one end of the age discrimination scale, deprivation is outgrown. At the other end, however, it is not; a law establishing a maximum age for driving, for instance, would be constitutionally dubious. The generalizations about age and ability are probably no worse, and no less broad, than those about youth and ability, but the deprivation would continue for the rest of the person's life. This is another reason, of course, to challenge compulsory retirement laws.

But there is a temptation to take this argument too far. We would not be justified in concluding from the fact that minimum-age deprivations are temporary that all age-based policies restricting young people are legitimate. In *Hofbauer*, *Green*, and *Becker*, the deprivation was just too severe; it was of life itself, and to suggest that those children could make their own medical decisions as adults would be ludicrous if it were not so callous. This was also true for such children as J. R. from Georgia, whose parents put him in a state institution, or James Ingraham, who was badly beaten in school, or the children in the juvenile court cases. These situations all involve denials of constitutional rights or at least quasi-rights, and there is no justification for concluding that children have less of such rights than anyone else.

There are, certainly, interests that do not rank anywhere near this high. No one has a right to go to law school or to medical school. But the reverse discrimination decisions deal with issues that lead us right into my second question. *Bakke* ruled, more or less, that race could not be grounds for restricting a person's ability to compete for a place in medical school, but, by implication, many other factors might be. I disagreed with that ruling, concluding that quotas could not be imposed to limit the opportunities of members of certain racial and ethnic groups, blacks prominently among them, whereas they could restrict the opportunities of white applicants. So, although no one has a right to graduate or professional education, one has a right not to have one's opportunities to get it limited because one is black.

Why? Not because blackness is unrelated to ability or competence, or because it is immutable; that is equally true of whiteness, and there is no correlative right for white applicants. The reason is the one Brennan articulated so well in *Bakke*. To discriminate against blacks here is to stigmatize: to presume that they are inferior, or ("and" is better here) to use governmental power to reinforce hatred and oppression.

How do we know that? We know it because of what Richard Wasserstrom, Charles Black, and other writers have told us, because our society has and has always had many ways, both blatant and subtle, of indicating that blacks are inferior to whites, and because blacks still have far less than a proportionate share of power, money, education, and all the other important resources in society. That last factor builds the bridge between stigmatization and another notion prominent in the opinions, that of special concern for groups saddled with disadvantages and disabilities.

We have the same kind of knowledge about Hispanics and Orien-

tals, though for other ethnic groups the question would be more problematical; we also have it about women. Therefore, any law that burdens these groups stigmatizes them. Any superficially neutral law based
on race or sex does the same; as Black, Wasserstrom, and the *Hernandez* decision showed, it is not hard to find indications of this fact. And
that is just as true of *de jure* single-sex education as single-race education; the decisions make clear that the presumptions behind these
policies were of female inferiority, however rhetorically masked.[25] They
also reinforce that inferiority, by excluding females from a valuable
network of acquaintance. Laws that give special benefits to the disadvantaged groups do not stigmatize, do not presume inferiority or
award what Dworkin calls public insult to the advantaged. Therefore,
they should not be presumed invalid. What about children; do laws
directed against them stigmatize, too? I suggested in Chapter 7 that
we can find some indicators that, by analogy with Charles Black and
Helen Hacker, might be seen as stigmas. And certainly children are so
saddled with disabilities as to be without power. The problem here is
the "why," and I am not sure that this question is answerable. I suggest
one partial solution in my discussion of the "what" question. But more
can and later will be said.

Consideration of the remaining two groups, homosexuals and the
handicapped, suggests similar complicated conclusions. We have found
that some policies directed against them infringe or impede fundamental rights. Both groups can be and have been described as stigmatized
groups. Homosexuality and handicap are indeed stigmas. But we face
here the question raised in Chapter 6: Does the fact that the groups
are stigmatized mean that the laws stigmatize? Some do; it is hard to
view the decisions on homosexuals' employment in any other way
than as the application of labels to discredit individuals. The decisions
on disability rights vary. The Heumann and Gurmankin cases are
troublesome not only because the denials rested, as they did, on
stereotyped characterizations. They also revealed assumptions that the
handicapped were inferior, and evinced prejudices against them very
similar to traditional racist and sexist biases. But what about *Davis*?
The nursing school's determination did not involve presumptions;
Frances Davis was interviewed and tested. Nor is there evidence of
stigmatizing thinking. But that decision was a disturbing one, nevertheless.

Laws that stigmatize should be struck down. The problem in each
of these areas, however, is that there are troubling consequences of

[25] See, e.g., Williams v. McNair, 316 F. Supp. 134 (D.S.C. 1970); Vorchheimer v.
School District of Philadelphia (3d Circ. 1976).

accepting the inference that any law that does not stigmatize is valid. In Chapter 6 I contrasted *Bakke* with *McDonald*, where white workers were fired for misconduct for which blacks went unpunished. That discrimination does not stigmatize, but it is illegitimate. Punishment, by its very nature, has to be related to individual responsibility, and in that case it was imposed differentially because of a factor beyond individual control. Punishment is one of a limited number of situations in which it is illegitimate to penalize a person because of a factor unrelated to personal responsibility.

With race or sex discrimination, there is yet another possible situation. I indicated that the right to buy beer is less than a fundamental right, and I will stand by that statement. One of the important cases, *Craig* v. *Boren*, did involve this interest, and the Court invalidated a restriction against males, who are not a stigmatized or disadvantaged group. I would defend that decision, but on what are basically lower-tier grounds, as Justices Stewart and Stevens did. The fit between the state's purpose, preserving traffic safety, and its means, forbidding young men (but not young women) to buy (though they could drink) 3.2 percent beer (though both men and women had to wait until twenty-one to buy other alcoholic beverages) was too tenuous and capricious. The only evidence to support it was data that young men were more often arrested for drunken driving than young women, and that is just not enough to justify so banal a discrimination. This same principle would, I think, apply to sexual distinctions like the one involved in *Kahn* v. *Shevin*. They are just too silly, too trivial, and too capricious to withstand any scrutiny.

When we turn to the other groups we find further complexities. Children are without power; not only that, but they are accountable— fully accountable—to three authorities: family, school, and state. Any restriction imposed on children has to meet a heavy burden of justification, because it controls those who are already controlled within an inch of their lives. But some of the restrictions imposed on them do serve to mitigate the power that other authorities have over them. Compulsory schooling, for example, does give children an opportunity of which their parents may not deprive them. Conversely, parental authority can be used, as in *Tinker*, to limit the control of the school. Similar arguments cannot be made either about the corporal punishment cases or about Walter Polovchak's case. In these situations, questions have to be asked about what, in fact, the restriction does.

There is another reason why laws that apply to children and to the aged as well cannot be uncritically accepted. This reason relates directly to the usual justification for these policies: namely, that children and older people really do lack certain kinds of competence. That is true of at least some children and at least some abilities, and may well be true of at least some older people. But the problem with these laws is that they sweep too broadly. As Chapter 7 shows, presumptions about juvenile incompetence cover a much wider age range and many more abilities than the facts justify. A concept from due-process litigation is useful here: laws make irrebuttable presumptions.[26] Courts have never ruled that such presumptions are invalid, but some judges have viewed them with strong disfavor. A chance for rebuttal could be built into many of the laws affecting children. I referred to emancipation of minors or individual immunities from school attendance in Chapter 7, and this still seems like a good idea, perhaps as a subject for congressional action under Section 5.

We could remove the defects of the Massachusetts law upheld in *Murgia* by changing the presumption from an irrebuttable one to a rebuttable one, by requiring an annual physical examination for police officers over fifty rather than making them all retire. That solution would not work with *Bradley*, because here in fact the classification does stigmatize; it is drawn on the presumption that people over sixty in the Foreign Service do not get respect and concern equal to their younger colleagues.

The Heumann and Gurmankin cases, too, rested on such presumptions. The Davis case, as I have admitted, did not. But the decision was still wrong. Frances Davis was not given a chance to show what she could do in actual nursing situations, where she might have been able to perform; she was rejected on the basis of untestable generalizations from tests and interviews to that situation. The only way to judge whether she could do a job that, as far as was known, a deaf person had not done before was to let her try. Any other decision, in so far as it depended on her handicap rather than some other qualification, is too broad-based a denial of an important interest. This country has known a long history of denying people opportunities on the basis of generalizations about their capacities which, first, were often proved wrong on the basis of actual experience, and second, have often masked prejudice. People once believed, after all, that Jews could not teach English literature or that women could not do college work without ruining their health.[27]

---

[26] See Cleveland Board of Education v. LaFleur, 414 U.S. 632 (1974).

[27] Several readers of this chapter have doubted that people ever held either of these beliefs. I can document both. With respect to Jews, see Norman Podhoretz, *Breaking Ranks* (New York: Harper & Row, 1979), p. 11; on women, see William L. O'Neill, *Everyone Was Brave: The Rise and Fall of Modern Feminism* (Chicago: Quadrangle Books, 1969), p. 80, citing Edward H. Clarke, *Sex in Education* (1873).

Here, then, are four situations where the "who" is crucial. Presumptively, at least, law cannot be used to stigmatize or to reinforce stigmatization; it cannot rely on characteristics unrelated to personal responsibility in a certain limited class of judgments that must depend on that responsibility; its discriminations have to make some sense; and it cannot use irrebuttable presumptions based on stereotyped notions. The foregoing discussion has skipped back and forth between the "who" and the "what," but that, I think, was unavoidable; some kinds of laws directed at the same group of people are acceptable when some are not, and some individual interests may be abridged on the basis of some characteristics and not of others. The discussion has also touched on the third question, "why?" That question can be asked in two different ways. The first is a question about motive, and that is a tricky question, for several reasons. First, it is not always possible to discover what the official motive was. Second, motives can be mixed; my first book argued that exactly this was true about special labor laws for women.[28] Third, motives do not dictate effects. In some situations, however, we know enough about motives to dictate a conclusion about the law. Jim Crow laws were one example. Another was Executive Order 9066. It is true that the United States was at war, that the Japanese were our enemies, and that there was genuine fear. But it is also true—and no one with any memory or knowledge of that episode can dispute it—that there was race hatred. The motives were mixed, but racism was among them, and that is enough to render those regulations invalid. Justice Murphy was right; they dragged the country into "the ugly abyss of racism."[29] When motives are this clear and this odious, there is no reason for judicial timidity.

But what of the ordinary situation, where motives are harder to ascertain? Here the "why" questions are manageable chiefly as questions about state interests: what purposes does the law serve? At this point, my approach becomes quite similar to Justice Marshall's in *Rodriguez*, and so far it suffers from the same defects: it does not set up rules for weighing these interests.[30] But I am going to try to develop some rules, and to suggest that far more than two, or two and a half,

---

[28] *The Chains of Protection* (Westport, Conn.: Greenwood Press, 1978), chap. 1.

[29] 323 U.S. 214, 233 (1944).

[30] 411 U.S. 1, 98–107 (1973). At this point an unpleasant issue arises, one that leaves me a choice between appearing naive and appearing cynical. I have read the account in Bob Woodward and Scott Armstrong, *The Brethren* (Simon & Schuster, 1979), pp. 258–59, which alleges that Marshall neither wrote the dissent in *Rodriguez* nor read it; that the author was an unnamed law clerk. I have no way of either verifying or disproving this account. Therefore, I simply assume that the named author was the real one, and label the dissent as Justice Marshall's.

or three, are needed. And I will end by suggesting that often the "why" question, the question of countervailing state interest, is irrelevant; and that even when it is relevant, it is less important than other questions.

There is one possibility that none of the tests allows for, and that I think has to be included in any scheme. This is the possibility that some laws are never justified, under any circumstances, for whatever purposes. My last paragraph implies that Executive Order 9066 was one instance; that statement, I think, is one with which most of my readers will now agree. But I am going to argue that this is true for *two* reasons, not just one. The first is the racist motive. The order stigmatized; it put the government's weight behind racism, and in Justice Black's words, it curtailed the civil rights of a single racial group. Therefore, it is not suspect, but invalid. It would have been invalid even if some Japanese-Americans had engaged in treason or armed rebellion. To punish an entire racial group because of the actions of a few members is no more justifiable than to punish the group because of fear and rumor. Our recent experiences in the Iranian crisis indicate that advancing this argument is not flogging a dead horse, much as I wish it were.

But it is not the racial factor alone that made those restrictions unconstitutional. Would we want to argue that singling out some people charged with no crime, imposing a curfew on them, ordering them to a specified place, and confiscating most of their property is constitutional as long as the criterion for selecting the people is not racial? To frame this question is to answer it. What such action would be doing is depriving them of liberty and property without due process of law. In such cases the "why" is irrelevant. The purpose that justifies them is no purpose; the need is no need compelling, substantial, or reasonable.

So laws that stigmatize and laws that deny due process or procedural rights are invalid. Can we think of any contemporary examples? I can think of three, all of which involve children. One is the law upheld in *Parham*, which permitted the incarceration of children without a due-process hearing. The second is the juvenile court system, about which enough was said in Chapter 7. The third was a response to a widely publicized series of crimes. In 1980 and 1981, several black children were murdered in Atlanta. For a time, while the killer was loose, the city imposed a curfew on all children. Presumably the intent was protective. But would we be happy with a law that tried to stop rape by imposing a curfew on women? Is it likely, ever, for any reason, that adult males would be subjected to a curfew when women were not? The regulation deprived children of liberty, without process, and therefore this scheme would render it unconstitutional. The purpose, however noble, cannot justify the restriction.

We do, of course, deprive people of these freedoms under certain circumstances. Incarceration is not always a denial of rights. But when? We commit someone to an institution by force when a proceeding has determined that he or she has engaged in dangerous conduct; we imprison people when they have been convicted of, or have pleaded guilty to, specific crimes. We do these things, in other words, *with* due process of law; there is a proceeding on the individual case. To do so at random, or because of race or age, is a denial of both due process and equal protection, and can never be permitted.

A discussion of procedural rights leads easily into consideration of substantive rights. Two such rights that got much attention in Chapter 9 were freedom of expression and the right to privacy. Several cases, *Roe* v. *Wade* prominent among them, have established the rule that the appropriate question here is whether the government has a compelling interest in curtailing the right involved. First Amendment cases have been dealt with by the now barely alive "clear and present danger" test, which can be classed as a subspecies of "compelling justification."[31]

These rules reflect our common agreement that substantive rights are not absolute. Only Justice Black argued consistently that they were.[32] Forceful as he could be, few of us have ever been comfortable with some implications of his thesis: for example, that it would be permissible to publish troop movements in wartime. But Black was not simply wrong. The merit of his argument can be seen in the fact that most of us have never been very comfortable with such rules as "clear and present danger" or any other rule devised for deciding these cases; the rules have seemed, nearly always, to yield too much to the government. And they do. Witness *Schenck* v. *United States*, whence emerged that particular test; it sent people to prison for doing no more than many of us did in the 1960s, with nothing like the dire results suggested by Justice Holmes's analogy to causing a panic in a theater. The *Dennis* case, just over thirty years later, revealed another defect in the test: it had the expansive properties of an accordion.[33]

"Compelling state interest" is even more vague, and thus more flex-

[31] Schenck v. United States, 249 U.S. 47 (1919).

[32] He made this argument for about the last ten years of his career. See "The Bill of Rights," *New York University Law Review* 35 (April 1960):865–81; *A Constitutional Faith* (New York: Alfred A. Knopf, 1969).

[33] Dennis v. U.S., 341 U.S. 494 (1951).

ible. In the context of *Roe* v. *Wade,* however, it leads to at least one inescapable conclusion: we do not want women "aborting" live babies. *That* is a compelling interest, although we can think of many interests that might be so labeled which are less powerful. And a comparison is to be drawn here with the troop movements case which is not ludicrous. Each involves an imminent threat to human life, which is itself a right protected by the Constitution. The consequences of allowing people to exercise their constitutional rights are so disastrous, in each situation, that the right has to be curtailed.

The best approach was, I think, advanced by Charles Black, in a 1961 article on Justice Hugo Black's absolutism.[34] Charles Black argued there that the justice was in fact advocating not a literal reading of the Bill of Rights, but an attitude: that we should think of those rights as absolutes, so that only in the most extreme circumstances will abridgment be permitted. Justice Black lived long enough to make clear that that was not what he had meant, but, with respect, I suggest that that is what he should have meant. Laws that curtail substantive rights should be presumed unconstitutional, with *no* qualifying "unless" rule built in. Thus any argument for abridgment would have to start *de novo,* with no stock phrases to rely on.

The results, in the concrete cases that have concerned us, would be to increase individual freedom and curtail the oppressive power of government. A law such as the one upheld in *Doe* v. *Commonwealth's Attorney* could not stand, nor could restrictions on homosexuals' freedom of association or firings that in effect abridge their First Amendment rights. Those freedoms are so fundamental that they cannot be curtailed on the basis of who a person is, and here the "equality" component comes in; the presumption of unconstitutionality gives no basis whatsoever for arguing what the cases have ruled, that homosexuals have fewer rights and less protection than others.

What about such rights as employment, education, and mobility? The last two are so necessary to the exercise of the listed rights that they must be ranked as fundamental, and curtailing them must, I think, also be presumed unconstitutional. But how equally must they be granted? Chapter 8 discussed many cases where "equal" had to mean "more"; for some of the disabled children to get an equal education, more money and more resources had to be spent on them than on able-bodied children. But here the discrepancy rests on the right of all children, able and disabled, to treatment as equals. The discrepancies

[34] "Mr. Justice Black, the Supreme Court, and the Bill of Rights," *Harper's,* February 1961, pp. 63–72.

in *Rodriguez* cannot be reconciled with this right, and therefore cannot be sustained under this test.[35]

Employment is a more difficult problem. It has not been ranked as fundamental since the days of economic due process. But it is not clear that employees' rights were fundamental even then. What *Lochner* and its successors actually enshrined was not the worker's right of contract with respect to hours and conditions of labor, but the employer's right to exploit the employee without state interference. In retrospect, that whole controversy has a false ring. Employment should not be ranked so high again unless we can be very sure that professional class bias is absent from the ranking.

However, I do not see how employment can be classified on the traditional lower tier of interests, either. The best way to approach this problem, which I think is capable of solution, is indirectly. I conceded, in my analysis of both the retirement and the disabled applicants' cases, that there were some, perhaps many, circumstances in which rejection or dismissal of a disabled person or someone over a certain age would be justified.

What are these circumstances? Certainly the state has a substantial interest in ensuring that work is done competently and safely. I have argued, however, that this interest does not justify the dismissal of all workers over a certain age, or the refusal to hire handicapped workers, any more than, in *LaFleur*, it allowed schools to dismiss teachers in the fifth month of pregnancy. Massachusetts would, however, as I have admitted, been justified in requiring all uniformed state police officers over a certain age to have a regular physical examination—and justified in carrying this requirement to its logical conclusion by retiring a worker who was found unfit.

Similarly, Southeastern could legitimately have barred Frances Davis from its nursing program if it had shown that she could not cope safely in any or most nursing situations. There is a still harder case, which I mentioned in Chapter 8: what about the blind applicant for a driver's job? It is tempting to dismiss this hypothetical case by suggesting that we are unlikely to encounter such an applicant. But, to make things interesting, suppose a blind person insisted that, by using laser devices or whatever, she could drive safely. I think she has to be given a chance—as long as the vehicle is equipped with dual controls, as the typical driving-school car is. At our present state of technology, she would almost certainly fail the test. But who knows what will happen in the next ten, twenty, or fifty years? Someone may invent a

---

[35] For a similar argument, see Dworkin, *Taking Rights Seriously*, chap. 9.

device that will enable blind people to drive safely. And if we refuse to test such people, the question has to arise about what our real reasons are.

What justifies the infringements I have described? Not the magnitude of the state interest involved, but, first, that the right involved does not quite rank as a constitutional guarantee, and second, that the degree of infringement is limited to what is necessary to determine what limitations the state interest requires. The irrebuttable presumptions and stereotyped characteristics are unacceptable whatever the nature of the governmental purpose.

The keen-eyed reader may suspect at this point that there is a gaping hole in this argument. If the state may restrict older and handicapped workers in this way, may it also do so with respect to, say, black, female, or (as in *Gish*) homosexual workers? And if it may not, does that conclusion not lead right back into the connection between equality and ability which I have been trying to break? It does, but only to a limited extent; that link goes where it belongs, on what used to be the lower tier of innocuous deprivations and classifications. Imposing special tests on workers because of race, sex, or sexual preference would not be justified, not because there is something special about those characteristics (except perhaps in the limited case of indirect infringement on a homosexual's right to privacy) but because such action would be as irrational as a state law forbidding young men to buy 3.2 percent beer. We could reject this sort of policy without bringing out the big guns of constitutional adjudication.

The crux of my argument so far has been that the crucial questions to be asked about challenged laws do not have to do with the nature of the classification imposed or the countervailing state interest. Four questions must be prior to those, though they need be asked in no particular order: What is the nature of the *interest* infringed (the "what" question)? How severe is the infringement? What group of people is affected by the infringement (the "who" question)? And finally, what *judgments* has the state made about the people it is restricting (the limited version of the "why" question).

This approach has isolated two types of deprivations that are categorically unconstitutional: those that stigmatize and those that deny or abridge procedural rights. It has also discovered actions that are presumed unconstitutional: those that deny or abridge fundamental substantive rights, or rights on which those rights depend; and those that rest on irrebuttable presumptions or stereotyped characterizations, at least with respect to age or disability. A policy such as that challenged in *McDonald* would, I think, have to rank among the actions presumed to be unconstitutional. Like irrebuttable presumptions, it ignores the factor of individual responsibility, and does so where that factor is crucial.

But what about laws affecting children, laws that do not infringe recognized fundamental rights? These questions have provoked the most vehement responses from people with whom I discussed them. The notion that homosexuals are entitled to the rights enjoyed by everyone else, or that handicapped children have a right to an education, get a fair hearing and often receive some, if grudging or indulgent, acceptance. But arguing in favor of Joey Hofbauer or Walter Polovchak, or that minors have a right to read dirty books, too, or that worrying about advertising directed at people without income is rather silly, can put a stop to rational discussion.

How can we deal fairly and dispassionately with issues involving children? I have argued that equal rights do not depend on competence or ability, but on a prior entitlement common to all human beings. "All" means children, too, and implies that their assumed, and often real, incompetence cannot be the basis for denying them a right to equal respect and concern. But what, precisely, does that equality demand? I have suggested that in some situations, but not in others, temporary deprivations are less odious than permanent ones, and that consideration can be built into a hierarchy of rights. Here irrebuttable presumptions of incompetency and stereotyped assumptions about ability can be made, although perhaps it would be wiser policy if they were not made so frequently. But when they are made, as they are made with respect to school attendance, for instance, it seems to me that we have to build into the new doctrine a heightened concern for the individual's rights, not the weakened one shown in such cases as *Tinker* and *Ingraham*. Perhaps because laws affecting children are the only examples of temporary rather than permanent restrictions, the cases do not fit well into any model; and that may be why children have gotten such curt treatment in court decisions. But I think Chapter 7 contained enough documentation of the catastrophic results of this inferior treatment to indicate that we need to build these cases in.

What situations remain to be dealt with? What used to be the lower tier has been stripped of some of its furniture, but much remains: all of those less-than-substantial interests, all of those unremarkable classifications, which can survive as long as they are reasonably related to some legitimate governmental purpose. All, or nearly all, of the laws regulating business and commerce, the traffic and motor vehicle laws, the tax laws, the zoning laws, and so many of those other policies that have been presumed valid and can continue to be. An immense area of legislation is left untouched by my approach, an area where things can go on as usual.

This new constitutional doctrine of equality would mean, for instance, that although the race-is-a-suspect-classification rule has been abandoned, relatively few racial classifications would survive. They would fall, however, for different reasons: some because they stigmatize, some because they deny fundamental rights, some because they are arbitrary. The same would be true of sex discrimination; and, for the first time, for age discrimination. The claims involved are too various, and the reasons behind the governmental actions too diffuse, to permit neater classification.

And that is what appears to be the defect of my approach. It does not permit the systematic categorization of the old two-tier, or whatever, model. It demands that we approach decisions by asking not two questions, but several; and it does not provide slots into which we can automatically fit cases once we have decided what is involved, slots that provide a test by which to weigh the countervailing state interest.

Unfortunately, I do not think this apparent defect can be remedied. Justice Marshall was right. A rigidified, tiered model gives away too much; too many rights and too many denials cannot fit it. Neither the claims nor the classifications can be fitted into a prelimited number of categories. All three questions—the "what," the "who," and the "why"—must be asked of each case, and each question must be asked in conjunction with the two others, not in isolation from them. This approach is not simple, but it does allow us to deal with more issues of equality than the old model did. And though the last several pages have roamed far from the Reconstruction debates, I think the new doctrine allows decisions that are better in tune with the legislative history. Complex and difficult as it is, I think this approach gets closer to the meaning of equality under the Constitution.

A final, and old, problem remains. Does my doctrine give too much power to the courts, thus encouraging the government by judiciary which would be incompatible with self-government? The position I have taken demands an activist view of the judicial role, but the necessary question is "Activist compared to what?" The usual contrast is between judicial activism and judicial restraint, but Ronald Dworkin has done a good job of showing that what passes for judicial restraint is in fact judicial deference to other branches of government.[36] My views are more activist and less deferential than those of Felix Frankfurter and John Marshall Harlan II, but those justices have been gone

[36] Ibid., chap. 5.

for a long time.[37] Some justices now sitting make a show of judicial deference; Chief Justice Burger's dissent from a ruling giving equal educational opportunity to alien children is an example.[38] But the show is just that; this deference is not consistently in evidence.

When my arguments are compared to Burger Court decisions, my interpretation of the Fourteenth Amendment is no more activist and no less deferential than the Court's construction of federal laws.[39] If my views are too activist, so are those of Burger, Powell, Rehnquist, and O'Connor. The differences between my views and theirs cannot be described in terms of activism, restraint, or deference; the differences are political and ideological. But two wrongs do not make a right. The question remains: Does my liberal activism encourage judicial usurpation?

The guarantee I have been most concerned with was broad, and was written to be interpreted broadly; as Charles Black argued years ago, if powers are to be given broad reading, there is every reason why rights should be, too.[40] In the context of the Fourteenth Amendment, this is particularly important. That amendment gave implicit powers of interpretation to the courts, and explicit enforcement powers to Congress. The latter have rarely been used, so there has been wide scope for the former. This is a special illustration of a general truth about individual rights. In this country they have never gotten very far without appeals to the Court, and in the relatively rare situations where Congress has been vigorous in protecting them, there has been a history of previous judicial involvement. After two centuries the United States has learned some lessons about government, and one is that individual rights do not get protected by majorities or by elected representatives. For them to have any meaning at all, a separate branch, neither accountable nor responsible in a direct manner, is needed. The judiciary, with neither purse nor sword, is still as Alexander Hamilton described it, the weakest and least dangerous branch; it is always instructive to make a list of things the Court cannot do which the other branches can. What it does do is to deal with cases, to mediate between the state and the individual when asked to do so. If we took away that power, or constricted it by insisting on deferential doctrines, there would be little hope for rights or for equality.

[37] For Frankfurter, see Minersville School District v. Gobitis, 310 U.S. 586, 591–600 (1940); West Virginia State Board of Education v. Barnette, 319 U.S. 624, 646–71 (1943) (dissent). For Harlan, see Reynolds v. Sims, 377 U.S. 533, 615–25 (1964) (dissent).

[38] Plyler v. Doe, 50 U.S.L.W. 4650, 4661–64 (1982).

[39] In addition to the cases discussed in Chapter 8, see General Electric v. Gilbert, 429 U.S. 125 (1976); National League of Cities v. Usery, 426 U.S. 833 (1976).

[40] *The People and the Court* (Englewood Cliffs, N.J.: Prentice-Hall, 1960), chap. 4.

Conclusion

The 1980s are bad times for equality. The Equal Rights Amendment has been defeated; a new administration has drastically reduced funding for implementation of the two major disability rights laws; a self-styled Moral Majority attacks all lifestyles but the conventional family; and budget cuts particularly threaten those who have been stigmatized and powerless. The Supreme Court, reconstructed by Richard Nixon and Ronald Reagan and redirected by Warren Burger, will not be much help, even in those situations amenable to litigation. I have written this book with increasing pessimism about the likelihood of its having any influence in the near future.

Those considerations, of course, should never dictate and rarely influence a scholar's conclusions. If anything, they mean that liberal activists will have to work and argue even harder. This study is offered in the spirit that has motivated many a Supreme Court dissent, as an appeal to the brooding spirit of a later day. It appeals to the future, and tries to link us with part of our past. The authors of the Reconstruction amendments, with which I have been so much concerned, were a group of men committed to equality and human rights as few have ever been. They have long been subjected to ridicule, after their deaths as in their lifetimes, and have been accused of failings ranging from fanaticism to intellectual sloppiness. If they were fanatics, it is hard to think of a better cause to be fanatic in; and I have argued that their thought was not muddled but appropriate and on target.

They enacted provisions that were lavish grants of equality and of rights. Over the years, those guarantees have shrunk, as Congress has rarely enforced them and the courts have timidly construed them. When the Supreme Court, in particular, has departed from its usual narrow reading of these rights, it has been accused of judicial usurpation. But in fact the real misuse of judicial power has been the refusal to protect that which was recognized. The Fourteenth Amendment was designed to protect, and should be read to protect, far more than has ever been alleged.

I have applied my historical conclusions to four issues that seem to me to raise some of the most crucial questions about equality which now confront us as a people. Thirty years ago, many scholars did the same with respect to the largest issue of their day, the question of *de jure* racial segregation. Their answers were not perfect, but they were good enough to serve for that issue and that time. Now, as new issues have arisen, issues unlike any we have faced before, it is necessary to return again to the historical record. And I suspect that, years from now, as still different problems arise to perplex us, we will have to return to that record yet again.

We need to reconstruct the current constitutional doctrine of equality, and we can do so in a way that is more compatible with the meaning of the guarantee. Equality is no impossible dream. It is a part of our history and collective conscience, if not of our past. If we are faithful to that conscience, we can reclaim that history. If we do not yield to greed or stinginess, or hamper ourselves by false deference, our people may realize equality under the Constitution.

Bibliography

BOOKS

Adair, Nancy, and Casey Adair. *Word Is Out: Stories of Some of Our Lives.* New York: Delacorte, 1978.

Adams, Alice Dana. *The Neglected Period of Anti-Slavery in America, 1808–1831.* Gloucester, Mass.: Peter Smith, 1964.

Allport, Gordon. *The Nature of Prejudice.* Rev. ed. Garden City, N.Y.: Doubleday Anchor Books, 1958.

Aristotle. *The Politics.* Trans. Ernest Barker. New York: Oxford University Press, 1958.

Avins, Alfred, ed. *The Reconstruction Amendments' Debates.* Richmond: Virginia Commission on Constitutional Government, 1967.

Baer, Judith A. *The Chains of Protection.* Westport, Conn.: Greenwood Press, 1978.

Barnes, Gilbert Hobbs. *The Anti-slavery Impulse, 1830–1844.* New York: Harcourt, Brace & World, 1933.

——— and Dwight L. Dumond, eds. *Letters of Theodore Dwight Weld, Angelina Grimké Weld, and Sarah Grimké, 1822–1844,* vols. 1 and 2. New York: Da Capo Press, 1970.

Becker, Carl. *The Declaration of Independence.* New York: Harcourt, Brace, 1922.

Berger, Raoul. *Government by Judiciary: The Transformation of the Fourteenth Amendment.* Cambridge: Harvard University Press, 1977.

Bickel, Alexander M. *The Least Dangerous Branch.* Indianapolis: Bobbs-Merrill, 1962.

———. *The Morality of Consent.* New Haven: Yale University Press, 1975.

———. *The Supreme Court and the Idea of Progress.* New York: Harper & Row, 1970.

Bieber, Irving. *Homosexuality: A Psychoanalytic Study.* New York: Basic Books, 1962.

Black, Charles L. *The People and the Court.* Englewood Cliffs, N.J.: Prentice-Hall, 1960.

———. *Structure and Relationship in Constitutional Law.* Baton Rouge: Louisiana State University Press, 1969.

Boorstin, Daniel J. *The Lost World of Thomas Jefferson.* New York: Henry Holt, 1948.

Bowe, Frank. *Handicapping America: Barriers to Disabled People.* New York: Harper & Row, 1978.

———. *Rehabilitating America: Toward Independence for Disabled and Elderly People.* New York: Harper & Row, 1980.

Boyd, Julian P. *The Declaration of Independence: The Evolution of the Text.* Princeton: Princeton University Press, 1945.

Brodie, Fawn M. *Thaddeus Stevens: Scourge of the South.* New York: W. W. Norton, 1959.

Bruns, Roger, ed. *Am I Not a Man and a Brother?: The Anti-slavery Crusade of Revolutionary America, 1688–1788.* New York: Chelsea House, 1977.

Cahn, Edmond. *The Sense of Injustice.* Bloomington: Indiana University Press, 1949.

Calhoun, John C. *A Disquisition on Government.* Vol. 1 of *The Works of John C. Calhoun,* ed. Richard K. Crallé. Columbia, S.C.: A. S. Johnston, 1851.

Cover, Robert M. *Justice Accused: Antislavery and the Judicial Process.* New Haven: Yale University Press, 1975.

Craven, Avery. *The Coming of the Civil War.* New York: Scribner's, 1942.

Crosskey, William W. *Politics and the Constitution.* 2 vols. Chicago: University of Chicago Press, 1951.

Davis, David Brion. *The Problem of Slavery in the Age of Revolution, 1770–1823.* Ithaca: Cornell University Press, 1975.

———. *The Problem of Slavery in Western Culture.* Ithaca: Cornell University Press, 1966.

Devlin, Patrick. *The Enforcement of Morals.* New York: Oxford University Press, 1959.

Divoky, Diane, and Peter Schrag. *The Myth of the Hyperactive Child.* New York: Pantheon, 1975.

Donald, David. *Charles Sumner and the Coming of the Civil War.* New York: Alfred A. Knopf, 1960.

———. *Charles Sumner and the Rights of Man.* New York: Alfred A. Knopf, 1970.

———. *The Politics of Reconstruction, 1863–1867.* Baton Rouge: Louisiana State University Press, 1965.

Dreyfuss, Joel, and Charles Lawrence III. *The Bakke Case: The Politics of Inequality.* New York: Harcourt Brace Jovanovich, 1979.

Duberman, Martin. *The Uncompleted Past.* New York: Random House, 1969.

———, ed. *The Antislavery Vanguard: New Essays on the Abolitionists.* Princeton: Princeton University Press, 1965.

Dumond, Dwight L. *Anti-slavery Origins of the Civil War in the United States.* Ann Arbor: University of Michigan Press, 1959.

———, ed. *Letters of James Gillespie Birney, 1831–1857,* vol. 1. Gloucester, Mass: Peter Smith, 1966 (AHA, 1938).

Dworkin, Ronald. *Taking Rights Seriously*. Cambridge: Harvard University Press, 1977.

Eaton, Clement. *Freedom of Thought in the Old South*. New York: Peter Smith, 1951.

Ely, John Hart. *Democracy and Distrust*. Cambridge: Harvard University Press, 1980.

Empey, La Mar T., ed. *The Future of Childhood and Juvenile Justice*. Charlottesville: University Press of Virginia, 1979.

Farson, Richard. *Birthrights*. New York: Macmillan, 1974.

Fehrenbacher, Don E. *The Dred Scott Case*. New York: Oxford University Press, 1979.

Feinberg, Joel. *Doing and Deserving: Essays in the Theory of Responsibility*. Princeton: Princeton University Press, 1970.

Fitler, Louis, ed. *Wendell Phillips on Civil Rights and Freedom*. New York: Hill & Wang, 1965.

Fitzgerald, Frances. *America Revised*. Boston: Little, Brown, 1979.

Flack, Horace E. *The Adoption of the Fourteenth Amendment*. Baltimore: Johns Hopkins Press, 1908.

Flexner, Eleanor. *Century of Struggle*. Rev. ed. Cambridge: Belknap Press of Harvard University Press, 1975.

Freud, Sigmund. *Three Essays on the Theory of Sexuality*. Trans. and ed. James Strachey. New York: Avon Books, 1962.

Friedenberg, Edgar Z. *Coming of Age in America*. New York: Random House, 1965.

———. *The Dignity of Youth and Other Atavisms*. Boston: Beacon Press, 1965.

———. *The Vanishing Adolescent*. Boston: Beacon Press, 1959.

Friedman, Leon, ed. *Argument: The Oral Argument before the Supreme Court in Brown v. Board of Education of Topeka, 1952–55*. New York: Chelsea House, 1969.

Gans, Herbert J. *More Equality*. New York: Pantheon, 1973.

Ginger, Ann Fagan, ed. *De Funis v. Odegaard and the University of Washington: The University Admissions Case*. Dobbs Ferry, N.Y.: Oceana, 1974.

Glazer, Nathan. *Affirmative Discrimination: Ethnic Inequality and Public Policy*. New York: Basic Books, 1975.

Gliedman, John, and William Roth (for the Carnegie Council on Children). *The Unexpected Minority: Handicapped Children in America*. New York: Harcourt Brace Jovanovich, 1980.

Goldstein, Joseph, Anna Freud, and Albert J. Solnit. *Beyond the Best Interests of the Child*. New York: Free Press, 1973.

Goodell, William. *Slavery and Anti-slavery*. New York, 1853.

Graglia, Lino A. *Disaster by Decree: The Supreme Court Decisions on Race and the Schools*. Ithaca: Cornell University Press, 1976.

Graham, Howard Jay. *Everyman's Constitution*. Madison: State Historical Society of Wisconsin, 1968.

Hand, Learned. *The Bill of Rights*. New York: Atheneum, 1974.

Harmon, M. Judd, ed. *Essays on the Constitution of the United States*. Port Washington, N.Y.: Kennikat Press, 1978.

Harris, Robert J. *The Quest for Equality*. Baton Rouge: Louisiana State University Press, 1960.

Bibliography

Harrison, Barbara Grizzutti. *Unlearning the Lie: Sexism in School.* New York: Liveright, 1973.

Hart, H. L. A. *Law, Liberty, and Morality.* Stanford: Stanford University Press, 1963.

Hobbes, Thomas. *Leviathan.* New York: E. P. Dutton, 1950.

Holt, John. *Escape from Childhood.* New York: Ballantine Books, 1975.

———. *Freedom and Beyond.* New York: Dell, 1972.

———. *The Underachieving School.* New York: Pittman, 1969.

Houlgate, Lawrence D. *The Child and the State: A Normative Theory of Juvenile Rights.* Baltimore: Johns Hopkins University Press, 1980.

Illich, Ivan. *Deschooling Society.* New York: Harper & Row, 1971.

Jaffa, Harry V. *Equality and Liberty: Theory and Practice in American Politics.* New York: Oxford University Press, 1965.

James, Howard. *Children in Trouble.* New York: David McKay, 1970.

James, Joseph B. *The Framing of the Fourteenth Amendment.* Urbana: University of Illinois Press, 1956.

Jay, Karla, and Allen Young, eds. *Out of the Closets: Voices of Gay Liberation.* New York: Douglas, Links, 1972.

Jenkins, William Sumner. *Pro-Slavery Thought in the Old South.* Chapel Hill: University of North Carolina Press, 1935.

Jordan, Winthrop D. *White over Black: American Attitudes toward the Negro, 1550–1812.* Chapel Hill: University of North Carolina Press, 1968.

Karlen, Arno. *Sexuality and Homosexuality.* New York: W. W. Norton, 1971.

Kendrick, Benjamin B. *The Journal of the Joint Committee of Fifteen on Reconstruction.* New York: Negro University Press, 1969. (Ph.D. dissertation, Columbia University, 1914.)

Keniston, Kenneth, and the Carnegie Council on Education. *All Our Children: The American Family under Pressure.* New York: Harcourt Brace Jovanovich, 1977.

Kleinfield, Sonny. *The Hidden Minority: America's Handicapped.* Boston: Little, Brown, 1979.

Kluger, Richard. *Simple Justice: The History of Brown v. Board of Education and Black America's Struggle for Equality.* New York: Alfred A. Knopf, 1975.

Koch, Adrienne, and William Peden, eds. *The Life and Selected Writings of Thomas Jefferson.* New York: Modern Library, 1944.

Kraditor, Aileen S. *Means and Ends in American Abolitionism: Garrison and His Critics on Strategy and Tactics, 1834–1850.* New York: Pantheon, 1969.

Kurland, Philip B., and Gerhard Casper, eds. *Brown v. Board of Education.* Vols. 49 and 49A of *Landmark Briefs and Arguments of the Supreme Court of the United States: Constitutional Law.* Arlington, Va.: University Publications of America, 1975.

Lakoff, Sanford A. *Equality in Political Philosophy.* Cambridge: Harvard University Press, 1964.

Lash, Joseph P. *Helen and Teacher.* New York: Delacorte, 1980.

Levine, Erwin L., and Elizabeth M. Wexler. *P. L. 94–142: An Act of Congress.* New York: Macmillan, 1981.

Levy, Leonard W. *Judgments: Essays on American Constitutional History.* Chicago: Quadrangle, 1972.

Locke, John. *Second Treatise on Civil Government.* Ed. Russell Kirk. Chicago: Henry Regnery, 1955.

Locke, Mary Staughton. *Anti-slavery in America, 1619–1808.* Gloucester, Mass.: Peter Smith, 1965. (Radcliffe College Mimeograph no. 1901.)

Long, Kate. *Johnny's Such a Bright Boy, What a Shame He's Retarded.* Boston: Houghton Mifflin, 1977.

Lusky, Louis. *By What Right?: A Commentary on the Supreme Court's Power to Revise the Constitution.* Charlottesville, Va.: Michie, 1975.

McKitrick, Eric L., ed. *Slavery Defended: The Views of the Old South.* Englewood Cliffs, N.J.: Prentice-Hall, 1963.

Marotta, Toby. *The Politics of Homosexuality.* Boston: Houghton Mifflin, 1981.

Mason, Alpheus Thomas. *The Supreme Court from Taft to Burger.* Baton Rouge: Louisiana State University Press, 1979.

Mellen, George W. F. *An Argument on the Unconstitutionality of Slavery* (embracing an abstract of the proceedings of the national and state conventions on this subject). Boston: Saxton & Pierce, 1841.

Nozick, Robert. *Anarchy, State, and Utopia.* New York: Basic Books, 1974.

Nye, Russell B. *Fettered Freedom: Civil Liberties and the Slavery Controversy, 1830–1860.* East Lansing: Michigan State College Press, 1949.

O'Neill, William L. *Everyone Was Brave: A History of Feminism in America.* New York: Quadrangle, 1971.

Paludan, Philip S. *A Convenant with Death: The Constitution, Law, and Equality in the Civil War Era.* Urbana: University of Illinois Press, 1975.

Pennock, J. Roland, and John W. Chapman, eds. *Nomos IX: Equality.* New York: Atherton, 1967.

Phillips, Wendell. *Review of Lysander Spooner's Essay on the Unconstitutionality of Slavery (1847).* New York: Arno Press and New York Times, 1969.

Pogrebin, Letty Cottin. *Growing Up Free: Raising Your Child in the 80s.* New York: McGraw-Hill, 1980.

Postman, Neil. *Teaching as a Conserving Activity.* New York: Delacorte, 1979.

——— and Charles Weingartner. *Teaching as a Subversive Activity.* New York: Delta, 1969.

President's Committee on Mental Retardation, ed. *The Mentally Retarded Citizen and the Law.* New York: Free Press, 1976.

Rawls, John. *A Theory of Justice.* Cambridge: Belknap Press of Harvard University Press, 1971.

Rice, David, Rev. *Slavery Inconsistent with Justice and Good Policy.* New York: Arno Press, 1969.

Rosenheim, Margaret K., ed. *Pursuing Justice for the Child.* Chicago: University of Chicago Press, 1976.

Rossi, Alice S., ed. *The Feminist Papers.* New York: Columbia University Press, 1973.

Rossum, Ralph A. *Reverse Discrimination: The Constitutional Debate.* New York: Marcel Dekker, 1980.

Ryan, William. *Equality.* New York: Pantheon, 1981.

Sabrosky, Judith A. *From Rationality to Liberation: The Evolution of Feminist Ideology.* Westport, Conn.: Greenwood Press, 1979.

Schur, Edwin M. *Radical Non-Intervention: Rethinking the Delinquency Problem.* Englewood Cliffs, N.J.: Prentice-Hall, 1973.

Shapiro, Martin. *Freedom of Speech*. Englewood Cliffs, N.J.: Prentice-Hall, 1966.

Silberman, Charles E. *Crisis in the Classroom: The Making of American Education*. New York: Vintage Books, 1970.

Slocum, Alfred A., ed. *Allan Bakke v. Regents of the University of California*. 6 vols. Dobbs Ferry, N.Y.: Oceana, 1978.

Sowell, Thomas. *Affirmative Action Reconsidered: Was It Necessary in Academia?* Washington, D.C.: American Enterprise Institute for Policy Research, 1975.

Spooner, Lysander. *The Unconstitutionality of Slavery*. Boston: Bela Marsh, 1853.

Stacey, Judith, Susan Bereaud, and Joan Daniels, eds. *And Jill Came Tumbling After: Sexism in American Education*. New York: Dell, 1979.

Ten Broek, Jacobus. *Equal under Law*. Rev. ed. London: Collier, 1965.

—— and Floyd W. Matson. *Hope Deferred: Public Welfare and the Blind*. Berkeley: University of California Press, 1959.

Thomas, John L., ed. *Slavery Attacked: The Abolitionist Crusade*. Englewood Cliffs, N.J.: Prentice-Hall, 1965.

Tiffany, Joel. *A Treatise on the Unconstitutionality of American Slavery, 1859*. Miami: Mnemosyne, 1969.

Warsoff, Louis A. *Equality and the Law*. New York: Liveright, 1938.

Weld, Theodore Dwight. *American Slavery as It Is* (1839). New York: Arno Press and New York Times, 1969.

Wills, Garry. *Inventing America: Jefferson's Declaration of Independence*. New York: Vintage Books, 1978.

Wolff, Robert Paul. *Understanding Rawls*. Princeton: Princeton University Press, 1977.

Woodhouse, A. S. P., ed. *Puritanism and Liberty*. London: J. M. Dent, 1938.

Woodward, C. Vann. *The Burden of Southern History*. Baton Rouge: Louisiana State University Press, 1960.

——. *The Strange Career of Jim Crow*. 2d rev. ed. New York: Oxford University Press, 1966.

ARTICLES

Agresto, John. "The Limits of Judicial Supremacy: A Proposal for Checked Activism." *Georgia Law Review* 14 (Spring 1980):471–95.

Ake, Christopher. "Justice as Equality." *Philosophy and Public Affairs* 5 (Fall 1975):68–69.

Areen, Judith, and Leonard Ross. "The Rodriguez Case: Judicial Oversight of School Finance," *Supreme Court Review*, 1973, pp. 33–55.

Avins, Alfred. "The Equal 'Protection' of the Laws: The Original Understanding," *NYU Law Forum* 12 (Fall 1966):385–429.

——. "Social Equality and the Fourteenth Amendment: The Original Understanding," *Houston Law Review* 4 (Spring 1967):640–56.

Baer, Judith A. "Sexual Equality and the Burger Court." *Western Political Quarterly* 31 (December 1978):470–91.

——. "Reverse Discrimination: The Dangers of Hardened Categories." *Law and Policy Quarterly* 4 (January 1982):71–94.

———. "The Burger Court and the Rights of the Handicapped: The Case for Starting All Over Again." *Western Political Quarterly* 35 (September 1982):339–58.

Berlin, Isaiah. "Equality." *Proceedings of the Aristotelian Society* 56 (1955–56):301–26.

Berns, Walter. "*Buck* v. *Bell*: Due Process of Law?" *Western Political Quarterly* 6 (1953):762–65.

Bickel, Alexander M. "The Original Understanding and the Segregation Decision," *Harvard Law Review* 69 (November 1955):1–65.

Black, Charles L., Jr. "The Lawfulness of the Segregation Decisions." *Yale Law Journal* 69 (January 1960):421–30.

———. "Mr. Justice Black, the Supreme Court, and the Bill of Rights." *Harper's*, February 1961, pp. 63–72.

Blackstone, William T. "Reverse Discrimination and Compensatory Justice." *Social Theory and Practice* 3 (Spring 1975):253–88.

Blakely, Susan Smith. "Judicial and Legislative Attitudes toward the Right to an Equal Education for the Handicapped." *Ohio State Law Journal* 3 (1979):603–33.

Brest, Paul. "Accommodation of Majoritarianism and Rights of Human Dignity." *Southern California Law Review* 53 (January 1980):761–64.

———. "In Defense of the Anti-discrimination Principle." *Harvard Law Review* 90 (November 1976):1–54.

Burgdorf, Marcia Pearce, and Robert Burgdorf, Jr. "A History of Unequal Treatment: The Qualifications of Handicapped Persons as a 'Suspect Class' under the Equal Protection Clause." *Santa Clara Lawyer* 15 (1975):855–910.

Burgdorf, Robert L., Jr., and Marcia Pearce Burgdorf. "The Wicked Witch Is Almost Dead: *Buck v. Bell* and the Sterilization of Handicapped Persons." *Temple Law Quarterly* 50 (1977):995–1034.

Burt, Robert A. "The Constitution of the Family." *Supreme Court Review*, 1979, pp. 329–95.

———. "Developing Constitutional Rights of, in, and for Children." *Law and Contemporary Problems* 39 (Summer 1975):122–32.

"Children and the Law." *Law and Contemporary Problems* 39 (Summer 1975). Special issue.

Crosskey, William Winslow. "Charles Fairman, 'Legislative History,' and the Constitutional Limitations on State Authority." *University of Chicago Law Review* 22 (Autumn 1954):1–143.

Curtis, Charles P. "A Better Theory of Legal Interpretation." *Vanderbilt Law Review* 3 (April 1950):407–37.

Davis, David Brion. Review of Garry Wills, *Inventing America*. *New York Times Book Review*, July 2, 1978, pp. 1, 17.

Dimond, Paul R. "The Constitutional Right to Education: The Quiet Revolution." *Hastings Law Journal* 24 (May 1973):1087–1127.

Dressler, Joshua. "Gay Teachers, a Disesteemed Minority in an Overly Esteemed Profession." *Rutgers-Camden Law Journal* 9 (Spring 1978):399–445.

Dworkin, Ronald. "The Bakke Decision: Did It Decide Anything?" *New York Review of Books*, August 17, 1978, pp. 20–25.

———. "How to Read the Civil Rights Act." *New York Review of Books,* December 20, 1979, pp. 37–43.

———. "Social Rules and Legal Theory." *Yale Law Journal* 81 (April 1972):855–90.

———. "Why Bakke Has No Case." *New York Review of Books,* November 10, 1977, pp. 11–15.

Ely, John Hart. "Constitutional Interpretivism: Its Allure and Impossibility." *Indiana Law Journal* 53 (Spring 1978):399–448.

———. "The Constitutionality of Reverse Discrimination." *University of Chicago Law Review* 41 (Summer 1974):723–41.

Ezorsky, Gertrude. "It's Mine." *Philosophy and Public Affairs* 3 (Spring 1974):321–30.

Fairman, Charles. "The Attack on the Segregation Cases." Foreword, "The Supreme Court, 1955 Term." *Harvard Law Review* 70 (November 1956):83–94.

———. "Does the Fourteenth Amendment Incorporate the Bill of Rights?: The Original Understanding." *Stanford Law Review* 2 (December 1949):5–139.

———. "A Reply to Professor Crosskey." *University of Chicago Law Review* 22 (Autumn 1954):143–56.

———. "The Supreme Court and the Constitutional Limitations on State Governmental Authority." *University of Chicago Law Review* 21 (Autumn 1953):40–78.

Feinberg, Joel. "Justice: Fairness and Rationality." *Yale Law Journal* 81 (April 1972):1004–31.

Fellman, David. "Principles Other than Human Dignity in Constitutional Analysis." *Southern California Law Review* 53 (January 1980):765–71.

Fiss, Owen M. "Groups and the Equal Protection Clause." *Philosophy and Public Affairs* 5 (Winter 1976):107–77.

Frank, John P., and Robert F. Munro. "The Original Understanding of Equal Protection of the Laws." *Columbia Law Review* 50 (February 1950):131–69.

Friedman, Joel W. "Constitutional and Statutory Challenges to Discrimination in Employment Based on Sexual Orientation." *Iowa Law Review* 64 (March 1979):527–72.

Gleicher, Jules. "The Straying of the Constitution: Raoul Berger and the Problem of Legal Continuity." *Continuity* 1 (1981):99–123.

Goldman, Alan H. "Affirmative Action." *Philosophy and Public Affairs* 5 (Winter 1976):178–95.

Goldstein, Stephen R. "Interdistrict Inequalities in School Financing: A Critical Analysis of *Serrano* v. *Priest* and Its Progeny." *University of Pennsylvania Law Review* 120 (January 1972):504–44.

Graham, Howard Jay. "The 'Conspiracy Theory' of the Fourteenth Amendment." Pt. 1. *Yale Law Journal* 47 (January 1938):371–403.

———. "The Early Anti-slavery Background of the Fourteenth Amendment." Pt. 1. *Wisconsin Law Review* (April 1950):479–507.

Graves, Jon D. "Mass Transportation: Separate but Equal." *Washburn Law Journal* 18 (Spring 1979):673–81.

Greenawalt, Kent. "Judicial Scrutiny of Benign Racial Preference in Law School Admissions." *Columbia Law Review* 75 (April 1975):559–602.

Grey, Thomas C. "Do We Have an Unwritten Constitution?" *Stanford Law Review* 27 (February 1975):703–18.

———. "Origins of the Unwritten Constitution: Fundamental Law in American Political Thought." *Stanford Law Review* 30 (May 1978):843–93.

Griswold, Erwin H. "Some Observations on the De Funis Case." *Columbia Law Review* 75 (April 1975):512–19.

Gunther, Gerald. "In Search of Evolving Doctrine on a Changing Court: A Model for a Newer Equal Protection." *Harvard Law Review* 86 (November 1972):1–48.

Haggerty, Dennis E., and Edward S. Sacks. "Education of the Handicapped: Towards a Definition of an Appropriate Education." *Temple Law Quarterly* 50 (1977):961–94.

"The Handicapped: HEW Moving on Civil Rights in Higher Education." *Science* 1974 (December 24, 1976):1399–1402.

Harris, William F., II. "Bonding Word and Polity: The Logic of American Constitutionalism." *American Political Science Review* 76 (March 1982):34–45.

Hart, H. L. A. "Are There Any Natural Rights?" *Philosophical Review* 64 (1955):175–91.

Henkin, Louis. "De Funis: An Introduction." *Columbia Law Review* 75 (April 1975):483–94.

Heyman, Ira Michael. "The Chief Justice, Racial Segregation, and the Friendly Critics." *California Law Review* 49 (March 1961):104–25.

"Historical Overview: From Charity to Rights." *Temple Law Quarterly* 50 (1977):953–60.

Hull, Kent. "The Specter of Equality: Reflections on the Civil Rights of Physically Handicapped Persons." *Temple Law Quarterly* 50 (1977):944–52.

Isbell, Florence B. "Potomac Fever: How the Handicapped Won Their Rights." *Civil Liberties Review* 4 (November–December 1977):61–65.

"Justice: A Spectrum of Reponse to John Rawls' Theory." *American Political Science Review* 69 (June 1975):588–674.

Karst, Kenneth L., and Harold W. Horowitz. "Affirmative Action and Equal Protection." *Virginia Law Review* 60 (October 1974):955–74.

Kelly, Alfred H. "Clio and the Court: An Illicit Love Affair." *Supreme Court Review,* 1965, pp. 119–58.

———. "The Fourteenth Amendment Reconsidered: The Segregation Question." *Michigan Law Review* 54 (June 1956):1049–86.

Kitch, Edmund W. "The Return of Color-Consciousness to the Constitution: *Weber, Dayton,* and *Columbus.*" *Supreme Court Review,* 1979, pp. 1–15.

Krass, Marc S. "The Right to Public Education for Handicapped Children: A Primer for the New Advocate." *University of Illinois Law Forum* 4 (1976):1016–79.

Lavinsky, Larry M. "*De Funis* v. *Odegaard*: The 'Non-Decision' with a Message." *Columbia Law Review* 75 (April 1975):520–33.

McCracken, Samuel. "Are Homosexuals Gay?" *Commentary* 67 (January 1979):19–29.

Mason, Bruce G., and Frank J. Merolascino. "The Right to Treatment for Mentally Retarded Citizens: An Evolving Legal and Scientific Interface." *Creighton Law Review* 10 (October 1976):124–69.

Miller, Darwin L., and Marilee A. Miller. "The Education for All Handicapped Children Act: How Well Does It Accomplish Its Goal of Promoting the Least Restrictive Environment for Education?" *De Paul Law Review* 28 (Winter 1978):321–50.

——— and ———. "The Handicapped Child's Civil Right as It Relates to the 'Least Restrictive Environment' and Appropriate Mainstreaming." *Indiana Law Journal* 54 (Fall 1978):1–28.

Morrison, Stanley. "Does the Fourteenth Amendment Incorporate the Bill of Rights?: The Judicial interpretation." *Stanford Law Review* 2 (December 1949):140–73.

Murphy, Walter F. "Civil Liberties and the Japanese American Cases: A Study in the Uses of *Stare Decisis.*" *Western Political Quarterly* 11 (March 1958):3–13.

———. "Constitutional Interpretation: The Art of the Historian, Magician, or Statesman?" *Yale Law Journal* 87 (July 1978):1752–71.

———. "An Ordering of Constitutional Values." *Stanford Law Review* 53 (January 1980):703–60.

Nagel, Thomas. "Equal Treatment and Compensatory Discrimination." *Philosophy and Public Affairs* 2 (Summer 1973):348–63.

Nickel, James W. "Preferential Policies in Hiring and Admissions: A Jurisprudential Approach." *Columbia Law Review* 75 (April 1975):534–58.

Note, "Abroad in the Land: Legal Strategies to Effectuate the Rights of the Physically Disabled." *Georgetown Law Review* 61 (July 1973):1501–24.

Note, "In re Hofbauer: May Parents Choose Unorthodox Medical Care for Their Child?" *Albany Law Review* 44 (July 1980):818–48.

Note, "The Right of Handicapped Children to an Education: The Phoenix of *Rodriguez.*" *Cornell Law Review* 59 (March 1974):519–45.

Note, "A Statistical Analysis of the School Finance Decisions: On Winning Battles and Losing Wars." *Yale Law Journal* 81 (June 1972):1303–41.

"Now, Wheelchair Rights." *Newsweek,* January 15, 1979, p. 36.

O'Fallon, James M. "Adjudication and Contested Concepts: The Case of Equal Protection." *New York University Law Review* 54 (April 1979):19–82.

Oppenheim, Felix. "The Concept of Equality." In *International Encyclopedia of the Social Sciences* (New York: Crowell Collier and Macmillan, 1968), 5:102–7.

Perry, Michael J. "Modern Equal Protection: A Conceptualization and Appraisal." *Columbia Law Review* 79 (October 1979):1023–84.

Pollak, Louis H. "De Funis Non Est Disputandum." *Columbia Law Review* 75 (April 1975):495–511.

———. "Racial Discrimination and Judicial Integrity: A Reply to Professor Wechsler." *University of Pennsylvania Law Review* 108 (November 1959):1–34.

Raz, Joseph. "Legal Principles and the Limits of Law." *Yale Law Journal* 81 (April 1972):823–54.

Remz, Sanford F. "Legal Remedies for the Misclassification or Wrongful Placement of Educationally Handicapped Children." *Columbia Journal of Law and Social Problems* 14 (1979):389–452.

Richards, David A. J. "Taking *Taking Rights Seriously* Seriously." *New York University Law Review* 52 (December 1977):1265–1340.

Rodham, Hilary. "Children under the Law." *Harvard Education Review* 43 (November 1973):487–514.

Rothman, David J. "Documents in Search of a Historian: Toward a History of Child and Youth in America." *Journal of Interdisciplinary History* 2 (Autumn 1971):367–77.

Simon, Robert. "Preferential Hiring." *Philosophy and Public Affairs* 3 (Spring 1974):312–20.

Siniscalco, Gary R. "Homosexual Discrimination in Employment." *Santa Clara Law Review* 16 (Summer 1976):495–512.

Sorkin, Nathaniel. "Equal Access to Equal Justice: A Civil Right for the Physically Handicapped." *Case and Comment* 78 (March–April 1973):41–42.

Stevens, Ronna J. "Public Transportation and the Handicapped." *Wayne Law Review* 25 (November 1978):135–46.

Storing, Herbert J. "Slavery and the Moral Foundations of the American Republic." In Robert H. Horwitz, ed., *The Moral Foundations of the American Republic*, pp. 214–33. Charlottesville: University Press of Virginia, 1979.

"The Supreme Court, 1978 Term." *Harvard Law Review* 93 (November 1979):60–274.

Tate, Wayne R. "The Education of All Handicapped Children Act of 1975: In Need of an Advocate." *Washburn Law Journal* 19 (Winter 1980):312–29.

Ten Broek, Jacobus. "Admissability and Use by the United States Supreme Court of Extrinsic Aids in Constitutional Construction." *California Law Review* 26 (March 1938):287–308.

———. "The Right to Live in the World: The Disabled in the Law of Torts." *California Law Review* 54 (May 1966):841–919.

Thomson, Judith Jarvis. "Preferential Hiring." *Philosophy and Public Affairs* 2 (Summer 1973):364–84.

Tribe, Laurence H. "Perspectives on *Bakke*: Equal Protection, Procedural Fairness, or Structural Justice?" *Harvard Law Review* 92 (February 1979):864–77.

Wald, Michael S. "Children's Rights: A Framework for Analysis." *University of California, Davis, Law Review* 12 (Summer 1979):255–82.

Wasserstrom, Richard A. "Racism, Sexism, and Preferential Treatment: An Approach to the Topics." *UCLA Law Review* 24 (February 1977):581–622.

Weinstein, Jack. "Education of Exceptional Children." *Creighton Law Review* 12 (Summer 1979):987–1039.

Weintraub, Frederick J., and Alan R. Abeson. "Appropriate Education for All Handicapped Children: A Growing Issue." *Syracuse Law Review* 23 (1972):1037–58.

Wilkinson, J. Harvie, III, and G. Edward White. "Constitutional Protection for Personal Lifestyles." *Cornell Law Review* 62 (March 1977):563–625.

Will, George F. "The Case of Phillip Becker." *Newsweek*, April 14, 1980, p. 112.

Williams, Bernard. "The Idea of Equality." In Peter Laslett and W. G. Runciman, eds., *Philosophy, Politics and Society*. 2d ser. London: Basil Blackwell, 1962.

Wollheim, Richard. "Equality." *Proceedings of the Aristotelian Society* 56 (1955–56):281–300.

General Index

Court cases listed in the cross-references can be found in the Index of Cases.

Index of Cases

Library of Congress Cataloging in Publication Data

Baer, Judith A.
  Equality under the constitution.

  Bibliography: p.
  Includes indexes.
  1. Equality before the law—United States.
  2. Civil rights—United States. I. Title.
  KF4764.B33 1983   342.73'085   83–6220
ISBN 0–8014–1555–1   347.30285
ISBN 0–8014–9880–0 (pbk.)

Call Tom - Steno